# Drupal's Building Blocks

# Drupal's Building Blocks

## Quickly Building Web Sites with CCK, Views, and Panels

Earl Miles
Lynette Miles
with Emma Jane Hogbin and Karen Stevenson

♦♦Addison-Wesley

Upper Saddle River, NJ • Boston • Indianapolis • San Francisco
New York • Toronto • Montreal • London • Munich • Paris • Madrid
Capetown • Sydney • Tokyo • Singapore • Mexico City

*Library of Congress Cataloging-in-Publication Data*

Drupal's building blocks : quickly building web sites with cck, views, and panels / Earl Miles ... [et al.].
    p.   cm.
  Includes bibliographical references and index.
  ISBN 978-0-321-59131-9 (pbk. : alk. paper)
 1. Drupal (Computer file) 2. Web sites—Authoring programs. 3. Web site development. I. Miles, Earl.
  TK5105.8885.D78D77 2010
  006.7'8—dc22

                                        2010043527

ISBN-13:  978-0-321-59131-9
ISBN-10:      0-321-59131-3
Text printed in the United States on recycled paper at RR Donnelley in Crawfordsville, Indiana.
First printing, December 2010

**Associate Publisher**
Mark L. Taub

**Executive Editor**
Debra Williams Cauley

**Development Editor**
Michael Thurston

**Managing Editor**
John Fuller

**Full-Service Production Manager**
Julie B. Nahil

**Project Management**
LaurelTech

**Copy Editor**
Jill E. Hobbs

**Indexer**
Jack Lewis

**Proofreader**
Charles Roumeliotis

**Technical Reviewers**
Jen Lindner
Andy Wilson
Chris Hanson
Clay Robeson

**Publishing Coordinator**
Kim Boedigheimer

**Interior and Cover Designer**
Gary Adair

**Compositor**
LaurelTech

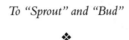

*To "Sprout" and "Bud"*

# Contents at a Glance

## IV: Appendices

# Contents

# Foreword

There was a time, in the 1950s, when to be a computer programmer you had to be something of an electrical engineer. You had to be handy with wire cutters and strippers and be willing to get your hands dirty—literally. That all changed over the decades, and programming a computer became a simple feat by contrast. Still, it remained the domain of only a few people with the proper education and technological sense. It was the advent of microcomputers and the Internet that made the world of technology more accessible, or at least began the process of attracting more people.

It was that time and those elements—that first major wave of public inclusion—that called for easier methods and for better tools for programming, for making use of computers, and for communicating information throughout the world.

It seems that each decade—perhaps not exactly in 10-year increments—brings with it a new wave of technology that makes the use and manipulation of technology accessible to more people. Each period begins with only people of certain technology prowess being able to participate fully. But in time the demand becomes so great, and the desires of the greater community so intense, that new innovations are achieved and new ways are determined in which more people can be part of the creation process and not just be on the receiving end.

It was just 15 years ago or so that Web design required an in-depth understanding of HTML, skills in network configuration, and the ability to program using less-than-intuitive programming languages to be able to do more than create a few flat Web pages. To be able to create forms, allow users to enter information themselves on a site, and provide many of the features that are commonplace today required the advanced and diverse programming skills of a Web developer—not to mention a sense of design, an understanding of marketing, and good writing abilities. So, many sites were either poorly constructed or else were the result of a heavily orchestrated organization that employed many people from diverse backgrounds. Web design was simply inaccessible for most people and organizations.

That has all changed as well and is continuing to change. We're in the middle of a new period of accessible technology, it seems. Drupal is changing the way Web sites are built. While Drupal can be used as a Web programming framework, it doesn't have to be. Unlike many other Web design tools, you don't have to be a programmer to build a Web site with Drupal.

In the Drupal world, many people build Web sites very easily. You just decide what you want on your Web site—text, photographs, a blog, places for visitors to comment, a feed from your Twitter account, and many, many other things—and then download the modules you need based on your wish list (you can have all that you wish for now), install each module, do a bit of configuring through your Web browser (mostly pointing and clicking, with the occasional typing of content), and you're done. Zero programming is required. It's that easy.

The Drupal community has created thousands of modules, all freely available from the drupal.org Web site. It's a credit to the collective efforts of thousands of smart people working together for years, not only for their own interests, but even more so for the benefit of others. Each module alters and extends Drupal's core capabilities and adds new functionality to a Drupal site. Owing to the vast amount of modules available from the Drupal community, the number of distinctly different sites that can be built using Drupal is unlimited, and the number that have already been built using Drupal is extensive. The speed at which sites can be assembled using Drupal and Drupal modules is surprising and unmatched. Not a single proprietary content management system has the depth and breadth of Drupal—not to mention that it's free.

Nevertheless, two contributed modules stand out from the rest: Content Construction Kit (CCK) and Views. Not only are they the most popular modules, but they are also two of the most flexible modules. I have repeatedly been surprised by how Web developers use Drupal, and what they build using CCK and Views. More than once, I've been shown "new tricks" of what can be done with CCK and Views without a single line of programming. The world of CCK and Views is an interesting one. The true depth and richness of these two modules have been mastered by only a few people, because ultimately the limits of what you can do with these modules has more to do with the data provided to them than it has to do with the capabilities of the site builder. The Panels module, while not standing out quite as strongly as Views and CCK, allows site builders the opportunity to tune their sites more carefully to look and feel the way they want. It gives them large amounts of control and organization, again without needing to write a single line of code. It, too, has allowed surprising systems with only a few tricks.

Behind the code that makes these modules work is a strong community of committed volunteers. One of these people is Earl Miles, a coauthor of this book. As an active member of the Drupal community for many years now, he has contributed a great deal to the direction of Drupal. More specifically to the topic of this book, he is a key contributor to CCK and the principal author of Views and Panels. I cannot think of a better person to write about these particular modules. Coauthor Lynette Miles, in contrast, is not a developer at all, and yet these modules have allowed her to contribute to the Drupal project by providing support for the usage of these modules both on drupal.org and in IRC. Her knowledge of the questions people ask when learning to use these modules is instrumental in understanding how to explain these sometimes difficult concepts to users.

Even if you're already a seasoned user of CCK, Views, or Panels, I have no doubt that this book will provide you with several new techniques and methods for getting the most out of these extremely essential modules. It certainly has for me.

*Dries Buytaert*
*Founder and project lead of Drupal,*
*CTO of Acquia*
*October 2010*

# Preface

Drupal is an open source software package that is offered for free to download, modify, and use. It has been implemented by thousands of people around the world and is used by millions of people daily as the basis for discussion Web sites, community portals, corporate intranets, e-commerce Web sites, vanity Web sites, resource directories, image galleries, podcasts, and more. By choosing to use Drupal, you are accessing not only an award-winning Web platform, but also its vibrant community.

Often referred to as "The Big Three," the Content Construction Kit (CCK), Views, and Panels modules have fundamentally changed the way developers, site builders, and designers create Drupal Web sites—and yet they are all contributed modules. In this book, the core contributors to these three suites of modules teach you how to build better Web sites. The modules described are widely considered essential modules that will be installed on almost every site. They allow for a level of customization that is unparalleled in the market, and are a key reason that Drupal is being chosen over its competition.

The book assumes you are familiar with how to install Drupal and enable modules. Web developers and administrators of Drupal Web sites are the target audience, although the book is written so that devoted Drupal enthusiasts can fully customize their sites using the information provided here.

# Part I—Content Construction Kit

Content Construction Kit is a module that allows you to define the data that makes up your site's content types. It lets you add new fields chosen from a variety of field types, such as text, numbers, dates, and even references to other content. It handles input forms and provides a variety of output styles for each field. Throughout the first part of this book, you will learn how to use CCK to customize your data objects to conform to your needs, rather than making your needs conform to the core content types.

## Chapter 1

In Chapter 1, we explain the basic concepts needed to understand the powerful but complicated creature known as CCK, including how it came to be, how the basic Drupal structure is defined, and why the level of flexibility and customization offered by the node system is important.

## Chapter 2

Expanding on the general usage of content types and fields, Chapter 2 delves into how CCK works its magic, both from an administrative user interface (UI) point of view and within the Drupal database itself. To do so, we explore two potential Web sites: a homebrewer's journal and a T-shirt sales site.

## Chapter 3

There are an extensive number of ways you can use content fields to create your Web site. Understanding and using fields and helpers for those fields creates possibilities for any kind of data. In Chapter 3, we dig more into field types and consider why you might want to use one type of field over another in your content type. We also look at some field types that you might want to add, but that are not part of the core CCK package.

## Chapter 4

Now that your content is created, it's time to make it look professional and easy to read. CCK does a great job of allowing you to add plenty of customized content. What it doesn't do as well is display the data in a fashion that is clean and nicely readable for users. In Chapter 4, we take a look at the theme system and how CCK interacts with it.

## Chapter 5

CCK includes methods that PHP developers can use to create fields outside of the user interface. This creates even more flexibility, but requires a definite knowledge of the PHP language as well as familiarity with Drupal's development style. In this chapter, we delve into integrating CCK with other modules.

# Part II—Views

The Views module is a powerful query builder designed to simplify the task of building custom query displays. It accomplishes this feat by providing lists of all table and field information that it knows of and letting the user assemble items from these lists together. After a complete rewrite for Drupal 6, Views has a new interface with more options than ever before. With the addition of a live preview and query display, site builders can nail down their displays in a way that was previously impossible to do without making changes that can affect all users.

## Chapter 6

Drupal relies on an SQL database to store information, and it currently supports MySQL and PostgreSQL. Properly using Views requires an understanding of how the database stores data, how it is related across various tables, and how Drupal works with the database to retrieve data. This chapter is directed toward newer users and programmers.

## Chapter 7

In Chapter 7, we focus on the Views UI, including how each function works. We look at how each piece creates part of a query, and how the results of those queries fit into pages and blocks. We also discuss the most important filters you may need as well as how to create relationships between node content that does not otherwise share information.

RSS, styles and fields, and the Views Bonus Pack are other important topics when determining what you want out of your view; they are also covered in this chapter.

## Chapter 8

Supplying arguments to Views is one of the ways the Views module becomes even more powerful and flexible. Relationships bring data together in new ways, and expand the information available to the rest of Views. Chapter 8 describes how to customize your views even more through the power of relationships, arguments, and filters.

## Chapter 9

Views can be themed just like anything else in Drupal. The Views module provides an entirely new level of classes, theming templates, and strategies over its predecessor. In Chapter 9, we discuss the template files and their contents, change some CSS, and look at how we can approach rendering data by multiple methods.

## Chapter 10

One of the biggest questions facing the developers of any software installation of any kind is, "How much time will each part of this application take?" Entire software packages exist to measure this kind of information. For some people, optimization is the key to a well-run and well-maintained site. For others, this issue represents a giant hassle. In Chapter 10, we provide a few suggestions as to when and why it might be appropriate to do some customization to your Views-generated queries.

## Chapter 11

In Chapter 11, we explore the nuts and bolts of how Views is put together—at the code level. You will learn about the data architecture of Views, the life cycle of a view, and its database schema. We also introduce the plugins and handlers needed to control custom queries and formatted output.

# Part III—Panels

Now it's time to really customize how you want your site to look. The Panels module supplies a group of standard layout templates. In this part of the book, you learn how to create panels that override default page layouts, explore how to theme these layouts, and get an introduction to the Panels API.

## Chapter 12

The core functionality of the Panels module is layout; designing the layout is when things start to look polished. With an understanding of Panels, administrators can create a style that is easily applied to every page of a site, or a different style for every page. Chapter 12 provides an introduction to how Panels works.

## Chapter 13

In Chapter 13, we investigate the Panels UI, including how each part fits together to create a wide range of panels. You learn how to create your very first panel, add content to a range of panel types, and override the core display pages for each of your site's content types.

## Chapter 14

Panels incorporates a few major features that can take you from the basics of Web site development to real complexity. Using arguments, relationships, and contexts, you can build connections between pieces of content in your panel layouts.

## Chapter 15

We've come to the final steps of designing a Web site with Panels—theming. This development phase puts the last touches on a Web site and brings everything together. Chapter 15 covers styling that can be done from within the Panels UI. You also learn how to apply custom CSS selectors that you can hook into from your own CSS files. Prepare yourself to be amazed at the level of control Panels gives you for theming your site.

## Chapter 16

Once a site is built, it must be deployed and made available for use. In Chapter 16, we touch on some of the challenges and changes that come with moving a site from testing to production. Views, Panels, and CCK all have the ability to export their structures, giving you the most leverage over site control; in this chapter, you find out how.

# Part IV—Appendices

The appendices cover a range of topics you'll need to truly succeed with this suite of modules. Appendix A covers other, relevant modules you'll want to check out when building a site with CCK, Views, and Panels. Appendix B teaches you the "best practices" for reporting an issue. Appendix C gives you an overview of the plugin classes that are available to programmers in the Views API.

# Acknowledgments

Earl and Lynette would like to thank more people than they can possibly remember for their help and support during the writing and production of this book. First, our editor, Debra Williams Cauley, had much more patience than we could have asked for or deserved. Emma Jane Hogbin was instrumental in the final push to complete this book—not to mention being generally sympathetic and otherwise all-around awesome. Karen Stevenson also deserves mention for her significant contribution of the Content Construction Kit API chapter. Our friends as well as cohorts in the Drupal community—Clay, Chris, Andy, and Yves—provided lots of valuable feedback about where things were good, bad, and "What in the world were you trying to say here?" We would also like to thank the technical and copy editors at Pearson who made sure we were up to standard and cleaned up after us; any errors are most definitely ours, not theirs. Finally, we would like to thank our family and friends, with a special "thank you" to famous writer C. E. Murphy, for being encouraging and offering lots of helpful advice on how to keep making progress.

# About the Authors

**Earl Miles** is a permanent member and founder of the Drupal Association. In 2005, Earl found Drupal and thought it was exactly what he needed to build a Web site in his spare time. When he found that Drupal lacked some key features, Earl ignored work for three weeks and created the Views module, which has been instrumental in Drupal's continued growth. Earl has been active in the community, providing support, as well as posting tips and tricks when the mood strikes him.

Happily married, Earl's first child was born May 2007. He is an amateur writer (sci-fi fantasy) and a gamer. A lifelong programmer, he is currently employed by iO1, a company that actively participates in the development and consumption of open source software.

Earl's Drupal blog is Angry Donuts (www.angrydonuts.com).

**Lynette Miles** has worked for 15 years in professional software technical support, mainly for Alcatel-Lucent. During that time, she has done everything from respond to customer issues via phone, email, and ticketing systems to writing and editing documentation for corporate software. She has also spent entirely too much time building and maintaining technical support knowledge bases for customers and support team members.

She became involved with Drupal after attending DrupalCon Brussels and DrupalCon Barcelona with her husband and becoming tired of listening to him talk about how active his issue queue was. Since then, she has spent most of her contributing time working with the Drupal Documentation Team and triaging the Views and Panels queues. She actively maintains that she is not a coder, stating, "I have people for that."

Lynette is a gamer, a spinner, and a knitter. She has cheerfully created her own Drupal hats based on Emma Jane Hogbin's pattern, complete with glow-in-the-dark faces. Most of her time is spent ensuring that she and Earl's daughter (also a DrupalCon fixture) learn the proper way to work with Drupal, "Don't hack core!"

# Content Construction Kit

Content Construction Kit, commonly known as CCK, is a module that allows you to define the data that makes up your site's content types. It lets you add new fields chosen from a variety of field types, such as text, numbers, dates, and even references to other content. It handles input forms and provides a variety of output styles for each field. With CCK, you can customize your data objects to conform to your needs, rather than changing your needs so that they conform to the content types available.

# 1

# Introducing CCK
# and Nodes

*The atom is the fundamental building block of all matter in the universe; the node is the fundamental building block of all Drupal sites on the Internet.*

In this chapter, we explain the basic concepts needed to understand the powerful but complicated creature known as Content Construction Kit, including how it came to be, how the basic Drupal structure is defined, and why the level of flexibility and customization offered by the node system is important. We start off with an explanation of how Drupal's core node system works and then look at how CCK provides new, enhanced functionality to your Web site.

## The Node System

Simply put, a *node* is a piece of user-created information that is stored within a Drupal Web site's database, with a goal of having a consistent API for access, expansion, storage, and output. Okay, perhaps that wasn't quite so simple. More simply put, a node is a post. It can be a blog post, a forum post, or a news article. Of course, it can also be much more than that. It could be a recipe in a searchable database. Or perhaps it might represent a track on a CD, even containing the audio file that lets the user play that track.

Likewise, a node can also be the CD that the track appears on, as well as the artist who recorded that track. Depending on the needs of the Web site, the label that distributed the CD might be a node. Press releases related to that CD might also be stored as a node. Fans might post their reviews of the CD—also as nodes—and the artist might upload photographs of a recent concert tour promoting the CD.

Long story made short, nodes are the main unit of information available for display in a Drupal Web site. Deciding what will be a node depends on which information you think may deserve a page of its own, and which logical item makes the most sense to display or make lists of for your users to view or search on.

## Why Nodes Are Important

One of the reasons nodes are important is that they have a flexible API that allows modules to act upon them, and that enables a designer to use a theme to control how they are presented. Many of these tools are available right in the core Drupal installation. For example, the Upload module can add file attachments to a node. The Path module, which supports general URL aliasing, provides a specific method of creating paths to nodes. The Menu module lets you put your nodes right into the navigation system.

External modules can do even more. Various voting modules, such as Fivestar, can be used to allow your users to place a rating on any kind of node. The Inline module creates an easy method for attaching images and displaying them within the body text of a module. This list goes on and on, but the important point is that this common API means that even simple node types can have very powerful features when you enable the right module.

Drupal comes with a basic set of content types already enabled. Other modules create more exotic content types. If you are just starting out with Drupal and trying to figure out exactly what you want to or can do with your site, exploring the content types in the Drupal administration pages is a good starting place.

It is valuable to know what the base content types are, as well as their internal and external fields, to decide whether you should use an existing type as is, modify a current type, or create a new one altogether.

## Default Content Types

Navigate to Administer >> Content management >> Content types to see which content types are currently available for your installation. If you have not added many modules, you will have only a few content types to start with, but many of the modules available might well have added more types. You'll have to check your module's documentation to see what these types are or do.

The default Drupal content types are Page and Story:

- **Page:** The page is one of the content types created for you during the installation process. It exists primarily for historical reasons. Back in the days when Drupal couldn't easily have arbitrary content types, the page node type was used to create static pages as a way to provide basic structure for the site. The most common example of a page node might be the classic "About this site" page, which doesn't change very often.
- **Story:** Story is the other content type that is automatically created as part of the installation process. It's meant to be an example to guide new users into Drupal, but it's actually an exercise in confusion because new users have no idea what the Story content type is for. The simple answer is that the Story content type is for whatever you want it to be. In the classic sense, a Web site posts "stories," which are often thought of as articles that are placed on the front page to be read as news. Story could easily be called News or Article, but it could also be called Post

and be just as meaningful. The important point is that the story node type can be used for whatever you want—or, if you prefer, nothing at all.

The following content types are also available in Drupal core but are not turned on by default:

- **Blog entry:** One of the most common forms of Web communication, a blog entry allows you to write a journal or diary type of page for your own purposes. This type is provided by the Blog module. Interestingly enough, the Blog module is actually meant for a single site with multiple bloggers. If you are creating a site with just one blogger, you are (counterintuitively) best off not enabling the Blog module and instead creating your own blog content type.

- **Book page:** Book pages are intended to be used as part of a group of nodes. In Drupal-ese, a book is a series of posts that are arranged in a hierarchical structure to provide a consistent experience for reading. Manuals and presentations are excellent examples of a book. This content type is provided by the Book module.

- **Forum topic:** Forums are the classic Web-based message board. They create containers for posts, and those posts can have comments. As of Drupal 6, forums can have more than just forum topics posted in them. This content type is provided by the Forum module.

- **Poll:** A poll is a question with multiple possible answers where users can choose a response and see how many other users have chosen each topic. As an example, you might create a breakfast poll with choices such as scrambled eggs, pancakes, peanut butter on toast, or nothing. This content type is provided by the Poll module.

When the administrator creates a new content type, it starts off looking very much like the Story type. There are no special fields, no new screens, and no places to enter data that are different than you would expect. Node types are often created by other modules, and will come with a full form to fill out for each new piece of content.

## Parts of a Node

As mentioned previously, a node is, generically, "a piece of content." Let's explore what exactly makes up that piece of content. To start with, every node has a number called the node ID or *nid*, which is used to uniquely identify it. The nid is assigned automatically when the node is created.

One important thing nodes have is a path or a URL. After all, Drupal is about building for the Web, and if your node can't be found on the Web, it's not very interesting. Given its nid, a node can always be found at the URL "node/nid." For example, http://www.drupal.org/node/162242 is the "Getting Started" page for CCK. Using the node/node ID structure should always take you to the page, even if an *alias* for that page is in place. An alias allows you to use other methods to refer to a given node.

There are two primary ways that a node can be viewed, plus a few other ways that we'll talk more about in the Views section. The first way is the full node view, which is normally only seen when visiting the URL for that node—node/node ID in our previous example. In this view, you normally see the node's title, the node's body, and any other data that has been added to the node, such as file attachments and voting widgets. The full node view also shows the node's *links*, which will include such commands as those for adding new content plus whatever other actions modules add. Some examples of these actions might be to bookmark the node, set the node's published or sticky flag, and share the node with a social networking site such as Digg. In addition, the node will have *local tasks* (more commonly known as *tabs*) that provide commands to edit the node, view the node's revisions, and perform many other actions (usually administrator specific).

The other way a node can be viewed is within a list. Drupal's front page is a prime example of a list of content, as well as the blog page and the taxonomy list pages. These pages are referred to as *river of news* listings, because they tend to always place the newest content on the top, and the node view is called the *teaser view*. The teaser view typically consists of the node title, a shortened version of the body, and links to get to the full node body and/or comment on the node. This view is designed to provide just enough of the content to let the user decide if he or she wants to read the content, but does not necessarily show all the content. With proper theming (see Chapter 4), you can actually create multiple teaser views, which can be used situationally. Some may be more compact because they reside in smaller areas, such as on complicated front pages with a lot of different content; others may be much larger because they are used in a river of news.

The list below contains the attributes that Drupal automatically assigns to nodes, although only Title and Body will be listed in the "Manage field" section when you go to manage the content. Title and Body are input; in general, the rest of the attributes are handled by yes/no flags or by the database, as discussed in greater detail in Chapter 2.

Following are the required parts of a node:

- Author: The user who created or owns the content.
- Post date: The date when the node was first created.
- Updated date: The last time this information was updated.
- Title: The title of the content. It is surprising that this information is required, but to administer content, nodes are most easily identified by the title. There are ways to deal with this requirement, however.
- Published: Is this content published? Published content is available to all visitors who have permission to access content; unpublished content is available only to users who can administer nodes.
- Promoted to front page: Content that is promoted to the front page will appear in Drupal's default front page. If you change the default front page, you get to use this flag for whatever you like!
- Sticky: Sticky content should appear at the top of most lists containing such content and will be styled differently from the rest of the list.

Nodes have other data that is not required but is nonetheless important and useful:

- Teaser: This is a short version of the full information in the node. In a news story, it could be the first paragraph(s) of an article.

- Body: The body is the entire (long) version of the node content.

- Input format: This controls how the teaser and the body are interpreted. It provides restrictions to HTML help provide security for the Web site, as well as options to make the text look cleaner. Those options include the line break filter and other optional filters such as bbcode and markdown.

Together, `node` and `node_revisions` are the tables upon which all Drupal content is built. Consider your content: you may not need to have revisions on at all. Most user content won't need it. Revisions are a type of source control. If you have the revisions feature turned on, it will keep track of which changes were made, and which user made them. This promotes accountability and provides a relatively quick and painless way to reverse a mistake or deletion of information. It is especially useful for documentation: revisions can be added to and updated as new information becomes available, while keeping a record of previous versions.

## Why Add Fields to Nodes?

For some users, the starting list of fields will satisfy their needs perfectly. This is true of users whose needs consist mainly of free-form text areas in which they can enter whatever content they like without consideration for calculating values, showing images, or any other operation that needs specific data. Other users—likely the majority—will have a need to enter exact, discrete data using a standard format.

The body field of a node is an example of an unstructured or free-form text area. You can enter any text you want here, and it will be stored and returned when the node is displayed. This capability can be useful for taking notes, writing recipes, or any number of other tasks. The body can be broken into two parts within the field itself, so as to create the teaser. It has the bonus of being clear and very easy to use. The downside is that the body field is not easily styled, can easily become cluttered, and is not structured. Users who are adding new nodes using just the body can put data wherever they want, and none of the parts can be called out specifically for special attention.

Using CCK to add fields eliminates the downsides of using an unstructured text area by creating input areas that meet the exact needs of your site. By enforcing rules for each text area on allowable input, this module helps create a consistent look and feel for the site, as well as consistent data. Using a structured field like the ones CCK creates will ensure that your prices, dates, and products all look and behave in the desired fashion. Along with promoting data integrity, CCK fields can be themed separately from each other and from the rest of the node. That enables you to change the look of every piece of information on your site with relative ease.

# Quest for the Grail: How CCK Was Born

Ever since the early days of Drupal, flexible, administrator-controlled content design management has been one of the many Holy Grails of the Drupal community. But what does this mean, exactly? Content management is the ability to control (sort, moderate, categorize, delete, or otherwise do whatever you like) existing, dynamic content in the system. Content design management, then, is the ability to control *the form this content takes within your system.*

For example, a blog post basically consists of a title, the post, perhaps a category, and a few tags, as well as a few other administrative fields. This data is no big deal; Drupal already has all of it. A recipe, by comparison, is a title, a description, a collection of ingredients, and maybe some other interesting callouts, such as the preparation time, a rating, the nutritional value, and any number of other items. These items may even be specific to the site that is storing the recipe—a site specializing in healthy foods might want a breakdown of calories, fats, carbohydrates, or maybe even some clever calculation to assign some sort of health or point value to the recipe. As these two examples suggest, there is a real need for a better way to store both types of content—some way that would suit most uses and allow for standard ways to maintain and update the data.

When Drupal was first developed, the problem was, of course, that none of these decisions could be controlled by the administrator. They could be controlled only by the developer. Every new type of content required a new module, and each module had to create the database tables, work out the database schema, provide the input form for the node, handle all of the reading and writing to the database, and tell the Drupal core about the plan. For a developer, doing all this isn't difficult work, but it is tedious, especially if you have a lot of content. Also, custom code requires extra maintenance, especially because of the way Drupal system upgrades work. Unfortunately, the upgrade process is not exactly one of Drupal's greatest strengths. Administrators want a standard way of handling things like recipes, and they want to know that for every item that is created, all of the standard Drupal hooks and menu items and image storage capabilities will be there. A consistent application programming interface (API) was sorely needed.

In Drupal 4.4, along came a module named Flexinode. Flexinode gave Drupal Web site builders who were not code writers the promise of newfound freedom: freedom to create new content types and add fields to them. And this newcomer was pluggable! New types of content could be added to the system, leading to a vast—indeed, bewildering—array of individual types of content that could be bolted onto a node and turned into whatever you might desire.

However, there were some major limitations in the Flexinode module. First, new fields were specific to their content type and could not be used for more than one set of data. As a consequence, you could not easily query for all of the results that matched between two content types. For example, if you had a field for phone numbers, a content type for employees, and a content type for customers, you couldn't query for phone number and get both employees and customers in the same query. While both types have a phone number, as far as the database is concerned these fields are no more equivalent to each other than the title is to the author.

Another problem was the method of database storage. Due to the manner in which Flexinode stored information, very large queries with multiple joins would have to be created to retrieve all of the information for a particular node. While this requirement didn't appear to be a problem with smaller node types with only a few thousand nodes in the system, sites with dozens of fields per node could quickly bog down badly on the server side. The reality of database mechanics caused this method to fail to scale for very large content types—something no company that relies on its Web site for revenue generation could afford.

These real problems were fundamental to the design of Flexinode. Through several versions of Drupal, the module continued to suffer from these problems created early on in its development. These flaws could not be fixed, at least not without a significant amount of recoding. Ultimately, these limitations spelled the death of Flexinode, despite the efforts of some within the community to save it, and Flexinode work finally stopped with the advent of Drupal 4.7.

Well before Drupal 4.7 was released, however, Jonathan Chaffer (known as JonBob on drupal.org) reached out to the community. At the very first DrupalCon, a group of 30 or so devoted Drupal developers got together in Antwerp, Belgium, to hash out the design and milestones to create a replacement for Flexinode.

### CCK Historical Context

You can find a forum post that was used by JonBob to keep the community apprised of the status of CCK at http://drupal.org/cck-status

This replacement was called Content Construction Kit. And while Flexinode was largely just the work of Chaffer, the scope of CCK was significantly larger than that of Flexinode. To handle this burden, Chaffer organized a community effort. He did the core work needed to create the system, while others in the community helped out.

CCK finally became a reality—albeit a rather immature reality—in Drupal 4.7. While the base was workable, there was still a good deal of functionality that needed to be added.

CCK has many advantages over Flexinode, not the least of which is the redesign and streamlining of the code, but most of these differences aren't apparent to a Web site's visitors. The most important difference is to the person who is creating or administering content types: CCK provides greater control over the storage mechanism, which creates a consistent database schema that is more easily used by other modules (such as the more recent Views module), thereby allowing for a richer integration. This approach also allows CCK to utilize more caching and other performance enhancements so that it can scale to large content types with large amounts of data. Although CCK still has flaws, many of these problems are related to the design of Drupal itself, and each successive release of Drupal is addressing them.

**Drupal and Version Numbers**

Drupal went quickly from version 1 to version 4, but the major version remained at 4 for several years, leading to some confusion about Drupal version numbers. Right around Drupal 4.3, which was quite close to Drupal 4.0, the developers started creating point releases to fix bugs, calling them 4.3.1, 4.3.2, and so on, but continuing to do major feature and API rewrites inside the 4.x line. By the time Drupal 4.7 (the last of the 4.x line) was released in 2007, the codebase barely resembled what was found in version 4.0.

A lengthy discussion ensued—within a community that barely resembled the community that had existed for Drupal 4.0 in 2002—and it was realized that Drupal had been misusing the so-called minor version releases. It was decided the next version would be Drupal 5, to be followed by Drupal 6, and that point releases would not include new features or API upgrades.

The real problem, of course, was user confusion. When people installing Drupal modules and maintaining Drupal Web sites saw Drupal 4.6 and 4.7, they assumed that the two versions were relatively close together in terms of features and, more importantly, module compatibility. Unfortunately, this was not the case. Over time, the community did recognize the problem created by the numbering scheme and it was corrected. If for some reason you come across an older site that needs to be upgraded, you may want to keep this point in mind.

For example, Drupal 5 added the ability to create arbitrary content types right in the core system, whereas previous versions of Drupal required modules to do this. As a result, CCK was able to completely remove that part of its codebase, let core Drupal do the work, and became a field manager instead of a node manager.

# Getting Started with CCK

If you haven't got an installation of Drupal running, now is the time to do so. You'll need a base install with the CCK, Views, and Panels modules. There are many options for Drupal out there. You need PHP, a supported database, Drupal, a Web server, and the modules discussed in this book: Views, Panels, and CCK.

One of the most popular ways to get Drupal up and running quickly is to use one of the various XAMPP stacks; these include WAMP, LAMP, MAMP, and so on. These stacks include PHP, Apache, and the MySQL database, installable on Microsoft Windows, Linux, and Macintosh, respectively. With this base, installing Drupal is almost a piece of cake! One of the best places to find information on how to install Drupal is the Drupal install guide, located at http://drupal.org/getting-started/install.

The primary modules we'll be using through the book are located at these pages:

- Content Construction Kit: http://drupal.org/project/cck
- Views: http://drupal.org/project/views
- Chaos Tool Suite: http://drupal.org/project/ctools
- Panels: http://drupal.org/project/panels

You will need to download these modules. Pick the most recent recommended version, which will be in green and say "recommended for 6.x" on its project page. Once the download is complete, you will need to unzip the `.tar.gz` files in a fashion appropriate for your particular installation. The Drupal.org installation page in the Getting Started handbook has several recommendations to help you with this task.

Modules should be installed into `drupal_directory/sites/all/modules`; this directory holds modules that are not part of Drupal core. Best practices for Drupal indicate that you never install or modify anything inside the core, including the core directories. Placing these new directories under `sites/all/modules` keeps your additional modules and themes in one place. This consideration becomes critically important when you are upgrading; upgrades involve removing the entire core directory. If your add-on modules are there, it's much, much harder to back them up before performing an upgrade.

Once the modules are installed, log into your site through a Web browser, navigate to Administer >> Site building >> Modules, and enable the appropriate modules. For now, you need to enable only the CCK modules. Enable them all; we'll talk about them and use most of them in various examples.

If you're not completely comfortable with the process of installing all the modules yourself, you might consider something like the Acquia Drupal stack available at http://acquia.com/downloads. It will install everything you need to run Drupal, as well as some of the most popular modules (such as CCK and Views). You'll still have to get Panels and CTools on your own, though.

## Creating a New Content Type

CCK is a small group of modules that assist in the creation of new fields for content types. Drupal core allows you to create a content type, and CCK adds the fields you want to have in that content type to make it suit your needs. This allows for the ultimate in flexibility and customization.

Figure 1-1 shows the list of available content types for your Web site. To reach it, navigate to Administer >> Content management >> Content types.

| Content types | List | Add content type | Fields | Export | Import | | | |
|---|---|---|---|---|---|---|---|---|
| Below is a list of all the content types on your site. All posts that exist on your site are instances of one of these content types. | | | | | | | | |
| **Name** | **Type** | **Description** | | | | **Operations** | | |
| Page | page | A *page*, similar in form to a *story*, is a simple method for creating and displaying information that rarely changes, such as an "About us" section of a website. By default, a *page* entry does not allow visitor comments and is not featured on the site's initial home page. | | | | edit | manage fields | delete |
| Story | story | A *story*, similar in form to a *page*, is ideal for creating and displaying content that informs or engages website visitors. Press releases, site announcements, and informal blog-like entries may all be created with a *story* entry. By default, a *story* entry is automatically featured on the site's initial home page, and provides the ability to post comments. | | | | edit | manage fields | delete |
| » Add a new content type | | | | | | | | |

Figure 1-1     The Content types page

The Content types page employs a group of links for the creation, editing, and deletion of your content types. When you create your own content types later in this chapter, they will appear on this page. To create your own content type, you need to think about exactly which kind of data you need to provide for your Web site visitors. For example, suppose I want to create a Web site about homebrewing. I have friends who are interested in alcohol as well, so I want to share my knowledge and recipes with them. At the very least, I'll need a Blog or Story content type and a Recipe content type. Drupal already comes with Blog and Story, but does not provide a Recipe type by default (more about the base node types later). I'll have to make one myself. I brew beer and mead—but what if I want to try making wine someday, or cider? Do I want to have a generic "ingredients" label or do I want to make specific groups of types of ingredients? All of these beverages use yeast. What else might they share? Do I even need to worry about that issue yet?

As another example, suppose that I have a client who wants to sell shirts. He'll eventually want to be able to show the shirts, the sizes that are available, and the different styles. He might want to have specials on a given shirt. Which content types does he need?

Let's take a look at the first step of creating your own fully customized data by creating a content type. Figure 1-2 and the following exercise show you the Content type

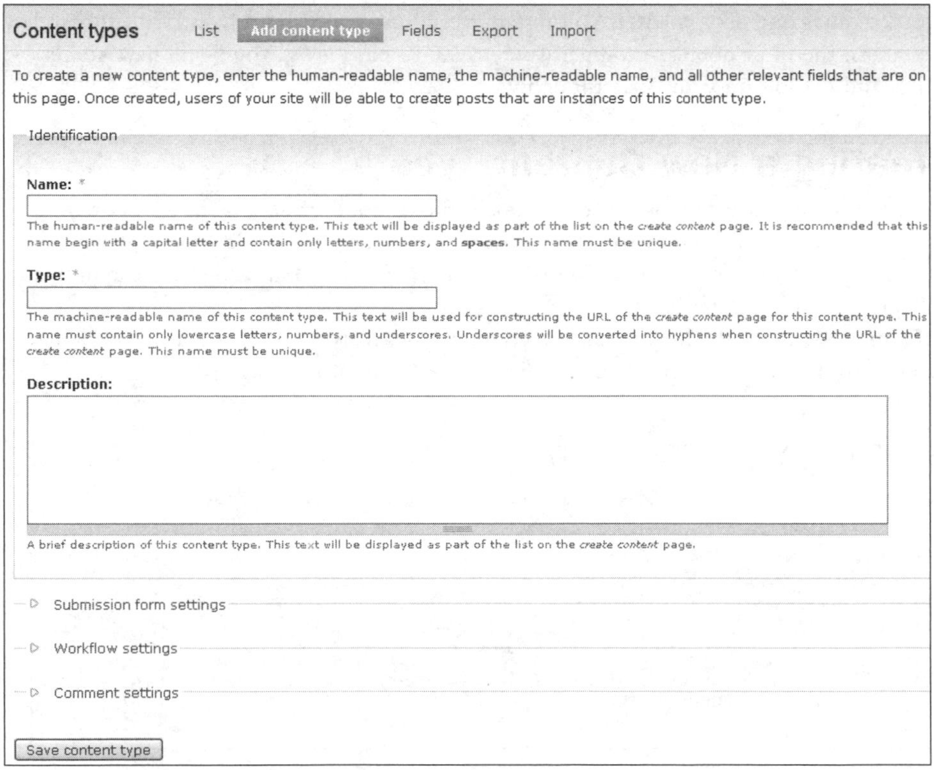

Figure 1-2  Creating a new content type

page and walk you through the steps needed to complete it. In later chapters, we'll take this content type and discuss the technical implication of each field.

---

## Exercise 1-1

### Creating a New Content Type: Beer Recipe

You've got a Web site where you'd like to keep track of your homebrew recipes. You need to create a content type to contain recipe information.

1. Click the Add content type link.

2. Give the new content type a Name, Type, and Description.

| Field | Value |
|---|---|
| Name | Beer recipe |
| Type | beer_recipe |
| Description | Homebrew recipes—relax, don't worry! |

3. Save the content type.

4. Open the submission guidelines fieldset and enter "About this recipe" in the submission guidelines.

5. Open the Workflow settings fieldset and check the boxes labeled "Published" and "Promoted to front page" as well as the radio button under the heading "Attachments" labeled "Enabled."

6. Save the content type.

When you go back to the Content Type List page, your new content type will be added to the listing of available nodes to create. Clicking the Edit links will take you back to the content type creation page with the values you entered previously. You can also add a new homebrew recipe for your Web site from this page.

---

CCK's purpose is to help you do one real task: add fields to your content types. It does so primarily by adding an engine and user interface (UI) that assists you by asking for some information and using that data to create and update tables with spaces for new fields. Fields are primarily defined by the type of data they will contain—numeric, text, image, and so on. With CCK and the addition of some helper modules, you can create a storage place for nearly any kind of data you want.

CCK is a project that contains several modules, which are listed later in this section. These are not the only modules available for CCK, of course; they're just the ones that are installed when you download CCK and add it to your Drupal installation. Two general types of modules exist: field modules and helpers. Field modules help you create new fields, and helper modules perform data or display manipulation.

Here are all of the CCK modules and their purposes:

- Content: The basic required module.

### Helpers

- Content Copy: Used for importing and exporting fields. It is useful for migrating field definitions between multiple installations.
- Content Permissions: Allows the administrator to add and update permissions on a per-field basis.
- Fieldgroup: Creates groups for fields. It allows fields to be grouped together visually on input forms and content display. A fieldgroup might be used for a mailing address, for example, to group each street address, ZIP code, and state into a single area on the Web page.

### Fields

- Nodereference: Adds a field that allows the administrator to create relationships between nodes. It is especially useful when a node contains another node. An author node may contain a "published works" node that holds images from a book, for example.
- Text: Adds field types to enter short (single-line input boxes) or long (text area) amounts of text.
- Userreference: Allows the administrator to establish a relationship between a node and a user.

Many modules can be added to CCK to accomplish a variety of tasks. These add-ons have been contributed to the community for everyone's use. We recommend visiting the project's modules page (http://drupal.org/project/Modules/category/88) to see the full list of available add-on modules. Be warned: There are many, many add-ons and the list can be overwhelming! The majority of these modules are classified as either field or helper modules.

Some examples of CCK field modules are Number and Date, both of which were created to meet very common user needs. For example, Date helps you to customize how your system stores and displays dates so that you can personalize the system based on the needs of your audience, wherever they might be located. Add-on helper modules include CCK Blocks, CCK Formatters, and Range, all of which modify how data from CCK-based fields is displayed.

CCK is only as powerful as the designer using it. When creating a Web site, as with any development work, thinking ahead about design is at the very least a good strategic move, if not a crucial one for facilitating later work. Take some time to plan out what content you will need. From product descriptions to images to prices, there is a hefty amount of potential content. If you take the time to do some planning, you'll know what information you have, which content types that information is in, and what has been intentionally shared from the beginning. This will go a long way toward helping you understand where your data is when you try to create a list for display.

CCK may give you the nails, but without a plan in place, you're going to hammer those nails into the wrong boards and your construction will fall apart. Knowing how nodes are put together gives you the basic structure to start putting new information into your site.

## Summary

CCK enables a user to easily draw down a node creation form, placing all of the node's fields in one clear and easily accessible place. Each form contains clearly marked slots to hold easily identifiable information. Users can be given as much or as little help as necessary with the use of additional text to ease the creation of nodes. The downside is that the administrators need to set that form up in a fashion that is easy to use and makes sense to the user.

The power of CCK strengthens the core of Drupal Web sites, allowing site creators to take the next step by adding fields and bringing the site to life. And once you've used CCK to set up your fields, your users' experience is both enriched and significantly easier.

# 2

# Field Concepts

Fields are the protons, neutrons, and electrons of the Drupal atom. You can't build a node without fields, and every content type is made up of fields.

This chapter expands on the general usage of content types and fields. We'll talk about how they're created and about what happens in the database. To do that, we'll explore two potential Web sites: a homebrewer's journal and a T-shirt sales site.

## What You Should Know Before Creating Fields and Content Types

Basic field and content type creation is one of the more common tasks to accomplish once you've made a plan for what you wish to create. The real work begins when you try to figure out how to actually create what you want.

Drupal has a number of overlapping names for different functions and concepts. One overlap that we should cover before going on is the difference between fields, field types, and field instance settings. *Fields* are any area on the page where you can add information—an identified slot of information that is often referred to as a form field. A *field type* is the type of data that the field can store, such as a date, a number, or text. *Field instance settings* are options that can be set for a particular field in a node type. We'll talk in more depth about specifics later. For now, just recognize that fields are what make up a content type, and their structure depends on the choices you make in creating them.

## The Content Type Pages

Creating multiple new content types requires a fuller understanding of the content types pages. We created one content type in Chapter 1, so the landing page is not completely unfamiliar. In addition to the List page that lists your types there is also an Add Content Type page where you can add new types.

On the content types List page, you'll find a list of all of the currently available content types for your site. The name, the type, the description of the content type, and the operations you may perform on that content type are all detailed on this page. The edit, delete, and manage field operations are available as well. When CCK is not installed, this page looks a little different, and the manage field operation is not available.

The following operations are available on the List page when CCK is installed:

- Edit: Allows you to change the basic settings for a content type.

- Delete: Removes a content type entirely.

- Manage fields: Goes directly to the Manage fields tab inside that content type. This page may also be reached by choosing the "edit" option next to a content type, and then selecting the Manage fields tab.

The second tab is Add Content Type. This page is a little more complex, but it's useful to understand what everything here does. This tab is where you define the foundation of new content. You could create a recipe, a weekly specials node type for a storefront, or any number of other things. This page is divided into four sections you need to understand before you can create a new content type: Identification, Submission form settings, Workflow settings, and Comment settings.

To explain how this process works, we'll create a new recipe content type. Because I'm a brewer and I want to keep track of my recipes, I'll create a new Beer recipe content type.

## Identification

Identification is broken up into three form fields, two of which are mandatory. First is the Name field, which is the user-friendly name that will show up on the user interface (UI) when the content creator wants to add new information to the site. When creating a new content type, you'll want to choose something simple and reasonably obvious as the name. For our example, we'll use two words: Beer recipe.

The Type field gives the base of the actual name of the database table you are going to create. The Type also will become part of the URL construction when you edit the content type later. It's a very good idea to make this machine name short and descriptive and probably similar to the Name. Because I want to keep my Type consistent with the Name and be descriptive, I'll use `beer_recipe`.

Last is the Description field, which is optional. Description is where you can add some text explaining to your users what the purpose of this content type is. This information will appear on the content type List page, so it should be short but explicit. For our example, I'll explain to my users that these recipes are for tasty homebrewed beer—relax, don't worry.

Figure 2-1 shows what this section of the page looks like.

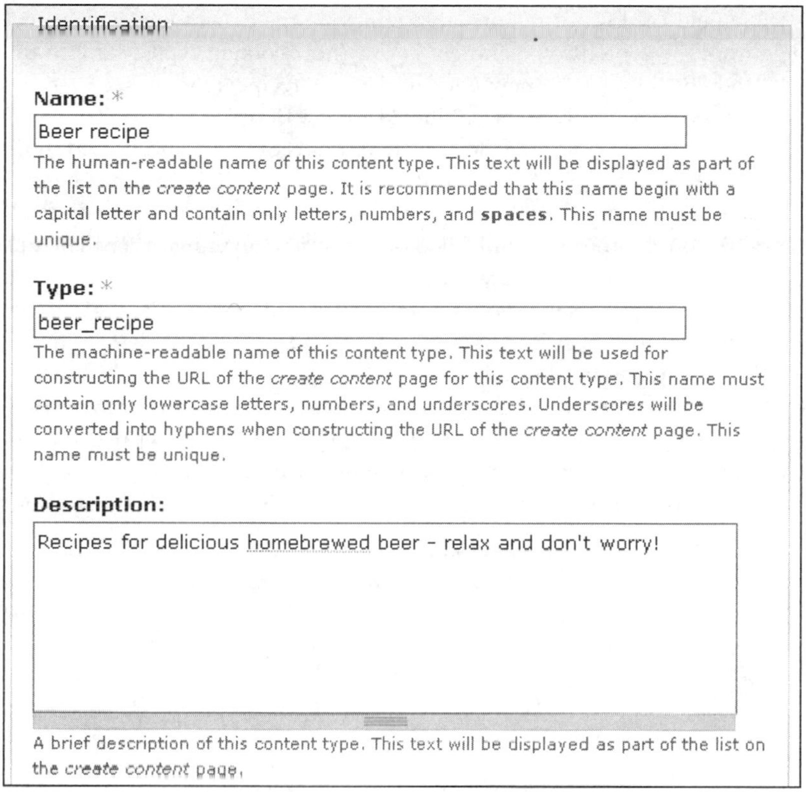

Figure 2-1    Content type identification

**Special Characters**

The Name and Type fields are limited in the characters that can be used to define them. The Name should include only alphanumeric characters and spaces. The Type should include only lowercase letters, numbers, and underscores (any Unicode character of type a–z, 0–9, or _).

The Name and Type field names must both be unique, and are required.

## Submission Form Settings

Submission form settings specifies the defaults and requirements for the new node to be submitted. The Title field label is a required field; the information provided here will appear as the title of the submitted content. In many cases, the Title field should be left untouched. For our recipe example, I'll leave the Title field alone; I almost certainly am going to want to have a different name for each recipe, and the title should be an obvious marker. At best, I could change the label to "Recipe name" to make it more in character with the actual working of the node.

The Body field label is not required, but removing the default text will remove the Body field from the content type entirely. For my new content type, I have to think about the Body field label. The new content type is a recipe: Does it need a Body? A question often asked by CCK users is, "Should I use a Body field or a CCK field?" On the one hand, it's easiest to use the Body field. It is already there and is used in the same fashion in many other content types. On the other hand, a CCK field can be defined to do many things and is very flexible. For now, I'll stick with the default body field; I don't have a good reason not to do so, and I don't need to use anything other than a plain text box for my description—and that's what Body already provides.

For our example, each recipe should have a description of what it is, so that other brewers know what to expect if they try this recipe themselves. I'll change the label to "About this beer:" to clarify this point.

The Minimum number of words field adds a requirement for the amount of text that must be provided before the new content can be added to the site. Explanation or sub-missions guidelines is a text box where the administrator can place help text that will guide node authors later when they are adding content. Right now, I don't want to

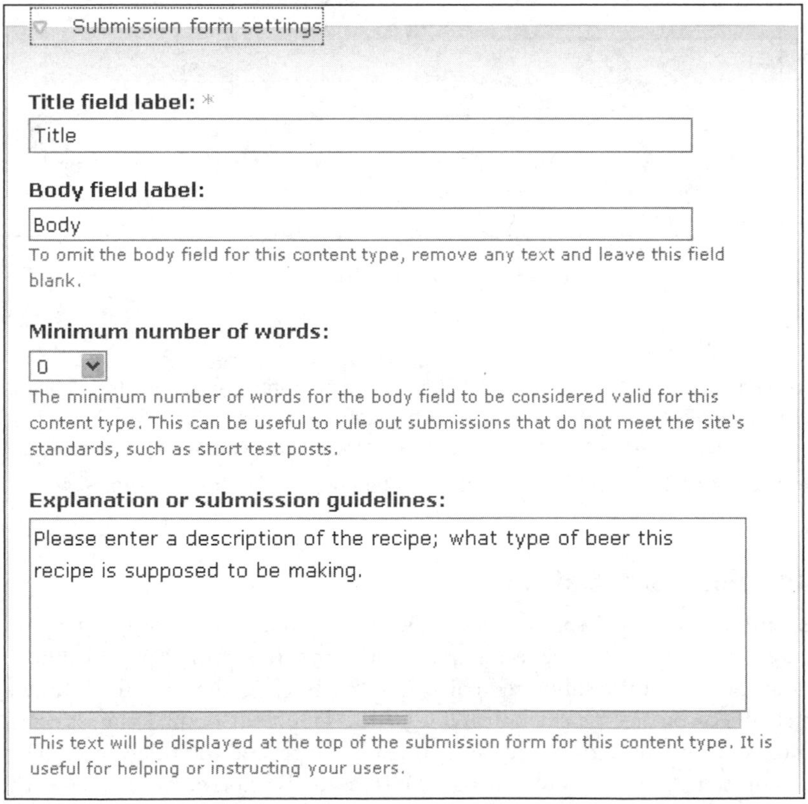

*IS A NODE*

*CCS EDITABLE ?*

**Submission form settings**

**Title field label:** *

Title

**Body field label:**

Body

To omit the body field for this content type, remove any text and leave this field blank.

**Minimum number of words:**

0

The minimum number of words for the body field to be considered valid for this content type. This can be useful to rule out submissions that do not meet the site's standards, such as short test posts.

**Explanation or submission guidelines:**

Please enter a description of the recipe; what type of beer this recipe is supposed to be making.

This text will be displayed at the top of the submission form for this content type. It is useful for helping or instructing your users.

Figure 2-2   Submission form settings

specify a minimum number of words to submit the new content, so I'll leave the drop-down menu at 0 and make a note in the Explanation guidelines indicating that this field should tell other brewers what the recipe is intended to create.

Figure 2-2 shows what the section looks like when filled out as indicated.

## Workflow Settings

The Workflow settings section, shown in Figure 2-3, specifies two things for new content: default options and attachments. These can be set up by node type. Default options include "Published," "Promoted to front page," "Sticky at top of lists," and "Create new revision."

For example, the Story type is published and promoted to the front page by default. For my recipe example, I plan to leave "Published" and "Promoted to front page" checked. Chances are that when I'm submitting a new recipe, it's because I've just brewed a novel beverage and I want people to see what I've done most recently.

The "Sticky at top of lists" option sets the sticky bit in the database and forces content with this flag set to remain at the top of its content area. For my recipe, setting the sticky bit probably isn't too useful. If I were writing an example recipe for other users to follow, however, setting the sticky bit would make it very easy for a new user to find it.

The "Create new revision" option turns on revision controls for this content type. This allows you to save a record of each change that is made to that specific node. For example, I typically want to duplicate a beer recipe as it is written. But what happens if I have a recipe that I want to reuse, but I can't get one of the ingredients I used before? I'll have to revise the recipe. I'll go ahead and check the "Create new revision" box so

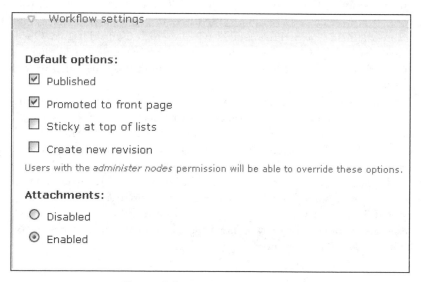

Figure 2-3    Workflow settings

that I can easily make a revision while preserving a copy of the original recipe. It is appropriate to leave "Create new revision" turned off for most content types; however, if you know you'll want to refer back to older versions of nodes on your Web site, you should enable this option.

## Comment Settings

The Comment settings section, shown in Figure 2-4, covers the myriad options available for commenting on nodes. The default comment setting is the basis for the rest of the choices. If comments are disabled, none of the other settings is necessary. The rest of the options determine how comments on a node are displayed, in what order, and so on. Comments are part of a node, and you may occasionally see them listed with node types, but they are not nodes in and of themselves. Comments are not critical to the creation of a node, and CCK is not concerned with comments as a rule. That leaves comments out of the general scope of our discussion here. They might be useful for the recipe, but I'll leave comments alone, and call it done.

Once these fields are completed, click the Save content type button at the bottom of the screen. Drupal will swing into action to create tables and fields that point to the new content type in the database.

## Fields, Export, and Import

Three additional tabs are found on the content type page: Fields, Export, and Import (the module Content Copy must be enabled).

The Fields tab lists all of the fields that have been created for content types. It does not lead directly to the creation of new fields—something that is not immediately obvious in the user interface. When Drupal and CCK are first installed, this page is empty. Only after CCK has been put to use does this page's purpose show. It lists the field name, the field type, and the content type in which the field is used. Once you have some field types created, you can go directly to the edit page for a field type to find a specific content type for that field. We'll talk more about this issue when we begin creating fields.

The Export tab allows you to take some or all of your data definitions from a particular content type and make them available to other installs or applications. First, you must choose a content type. From there, you are taken to a check box form on which you choose the fields to be exported. Once you click the Export button, the resulting page shows a text box with code that can be copied and pasted into another Drupal site. This code will create a new copy of the content type and its associated fields. The Import tab is where you can paste in code that was previously exported. You can choose the content type to add fields to, or you can create a new data type entirely.

We've talked about adding new content types and what content types are. Now let's talk about fields and field creation.

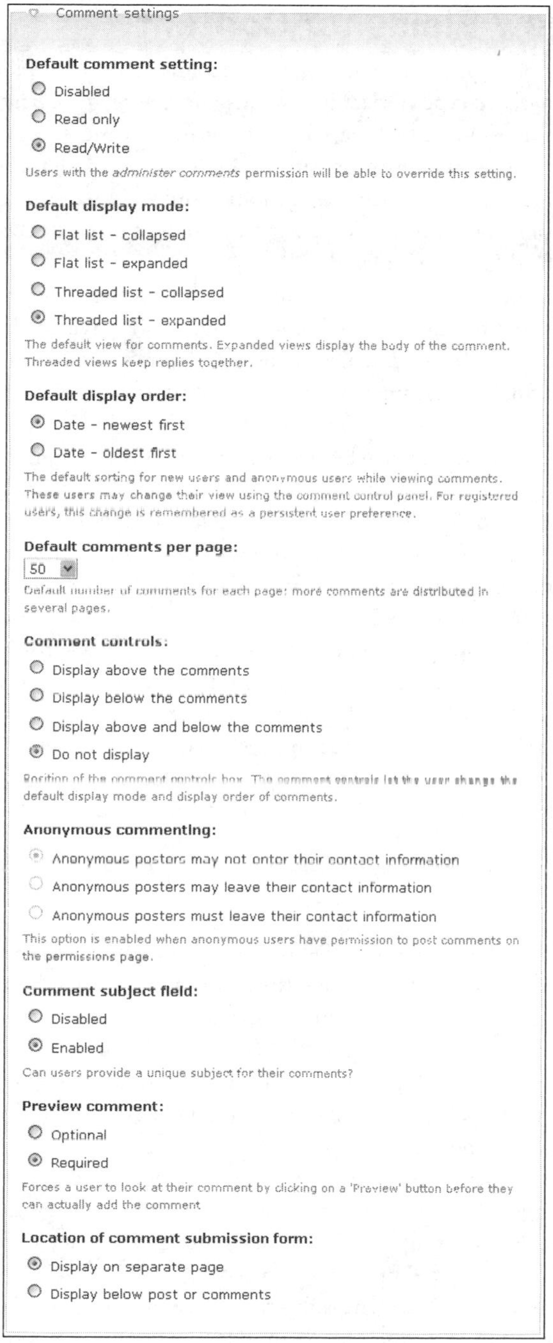

**Default comment setting:**

○ Disabled

○ Read only

◉ Read/Write

Users with the *administer comments* permission will be able to override this setting.

**Default display mode:**

○ Flat list - collapsed

○ Flat list - expanded

○ Threaded list - collapsed

◉ Threaded list - expanded

The default view for comments. Expanded views display the body of the comment. Threaded views keep replies together.

**Default display order:**

◉ Date - newest first

○ Date - oldest first

The default sorting for new users and anonymous users while viewing comments. These users may change their view using the comment control panel. For registered users, this change is remembered as a persistent user preference.

**Default comments per page:**

[ 50 ▾ ]

Default number of comments for each page; more comments are distributed in several pages.

**Comment controls:**

○ Display above the comments

○ Display below the comments

○ Display above and below the comments

◉ Do not display

Position of the comment controls box. The comment controls let the user change the default display mode and display order of comments.

**Anonymous commenting:**

◉ Anonymous posters may not enter their contact information

○ Anonymous posters may leave their contact information

○ Anonymous posters must leave their contact information

This option is enabled when anonymous users have permission to post comments on the permissions page.

**Comment subject field:**

○ Disabled

◉ Enabled

Can users provide a unique subject for their comments?

**Preview comment:**

○ Optional

◉ Required

Forces a user to look at their comment by clicking on a 'Preview' button before they can actually add the comment.

**Location of comment submission form:**

◉ Display on separate page

○ Display below post or comments

Figure 2-4     Comment settings

# Creating New Fields for Content

A field is a piece of discrete information with a specific identifier or identifiers. It is defined by two things: the type of data it contains and the *machine name*. The machine name is the name you assigned to Type when you created your new content type. It is the name that the database will use to create a table or field. Underscores may be used as separators in machine names consisting of a multi-word field name, such as `my_title_field` or `first_name`. Neither the machine name nor the data type can be changed once the field has been created.

Fields have other properties that define how much data they can hold, how the data can be chosen, and how the user can remember what field is which. These data properties include the Label; the Widget, which helps determine how a field accepts data; and the Required flag, which determines whether a field must be present before submission is accepted. Other properties in this category include the help text, the default value (if one is needed), and an indicator of whether the field will use a single or multiple values.

Finally, fields have a set of secondary properties that are tied to both the field type and the widget that is selected. Some settings for the field are tied into the content type; global settings affect the field in whatever content type it is in. These secondary properties have several functions, but as a rule they fall into three categories: settings that limit the range of values that can be used, settings that affect the widget, and settings that change how the field is displayed. Some might consider the last settings to represent a formatter; certainly, the current maintainers of CCK have considered this possibility. A number of modules add changes for display in this area. In a future version of CCK, this section of the UI may be reworked once more to place these settings with the rest of the formatters.

Now that we have an overview of what the parts of a field are, we can get specific about how these parts are created.

## Adding Fields

Let's look at the screens for adding new fields to your content types. Choose a content type from the content types List page, using the Manage fields tab. This choice takes you to a new page that handles all field operations for managing the internal workings of the content type. From this page, you can use the Display fields tab or the Add, Configure, and Remove fields. You may also add new groups (enable the module Fieldgroup). The user interface for CCK in Drupal 6 brings all of the basic field creation and management functionality together in one place.

Upon initial install, there won't be any fields to manage or display until we create them, so let's talk about that task first. At the bottom of the Manage fields tab is a form for creating new fields and groups, as shown in Figure 2-5. After you have created a field, a section to edit the existing field becomes available.

The New field section of the form is the row of elements in the Add fieldset. In essence, it is the first page of a multistep form. Each page contains a group of fields and widgets that must be completed to make a new field available for use.

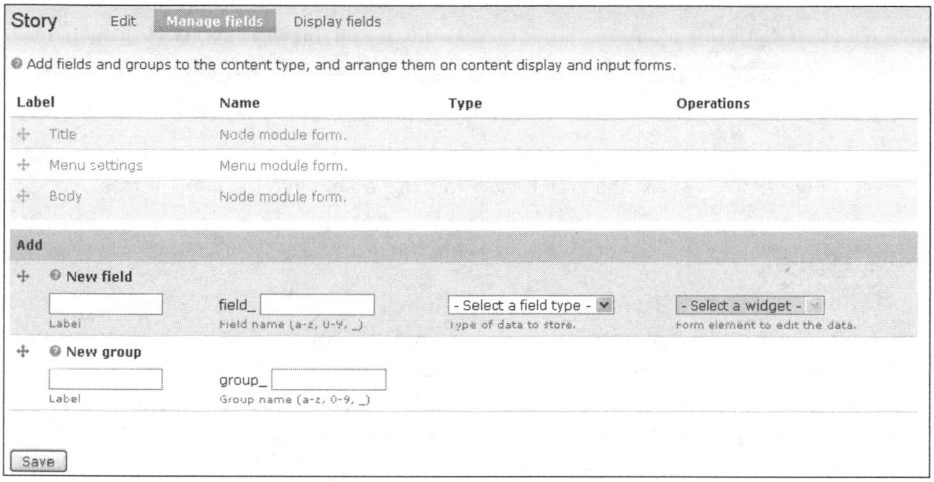

Figure 2-5    The field management form

The first form page specifies information related to the label, the field name, the field type, and the widget. Like the Type field used in content type creation, the field name cannot be changed once it has been created. The Label field is the user-facing name. The Type field determines the data type for the field, and the widget is tied to that type.

Type is a drop-down menu that determines the kind of data that will be allowed as input into the node form field. These data types are described in more detail in the next section.

The content of the second group of fields at the bottom will vary depending on whether any fields have been created. If fields have been created, you'll be able to change them here. If not, then the second group will be identified as a "New group." The "New group" data form allows you to create a fieldgroup by entering a label for the group and a machine-readable group name. Fieldgroups are, unsurprisingly, a way to group fields together. Their purpose is to improve formatting by allowing for the gathering of fields that belong together into a single fieldset. When creating a recipe, for example, you might create an "ingredients" fieldgroup that contains all of the components for the recipe and a "directions" fieldgroup that contains instructions on cooking.

One important thing to note here: "New field" and "New group" have grab handles to their left. You can move these field forms out of the Add section, and up into the area of the page where you want them to go—including placing the "New field" under "New group" (see Figure 2-6). When the field or group creation is finished, that field or group will automatically be placed in the section of the content type where you placed it before creation.

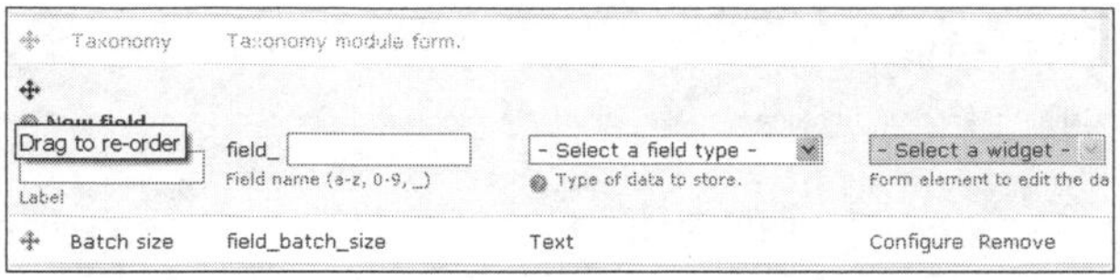

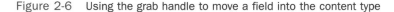

Figure 2-6    Using the grab handle to move a field into the content type

## Data Types

Once you have chosen a data type and created the field, you cannot change the data type. CCK starts off with six data types already available, most of which are commonly used and understandable. The six basic field types are Decimal, Float, Integer, Node Reference, Text, and User Reference. Decimal, Float, and Integer are all available for entering various types of numbers. The Text type allows you to enter general text information. Node Reference and User Reference are a little different from the rest of the data types, but they are similar to each other in behavior.

- Decimal: A numeric value allowing for a decimal placement. Useful for things like prices and salaries.
- Float: A numeric value that allows for specific and significant figure entry. Useful for scientific notation.
- Integer: A basic numeric value that does not use decimals. Useful for salaries or prices or other numbers not requiring significant figures.
- Node Reference: A field that allows a reference to another node. Useful for linking things like artists, album names, and CD tracks.
- Text: A generic text field. Can store any piece of information.
- User Reference: A field that allows the node to link to a user. Could be used to link an artist to multiple pieces of art.

For example, you could enter a salary—an annual salary could use an integer field with a value of 50000, or an hourly wage might use a decimal or a float such as 14.50. Either of those values could also be entered in a basic text field, though it would prevent further computations from being performed on that field. Using a field type is the first step in validation; it ensures that only a specific kind of data can be entered. Types provide a behind-the-scenes guide for users.

As an example, let's look at one of the default content types: Story. Perhaps you decide you would like to add a field called "Originally written on" because you want to preserve the original date you wrote a story, not just the day you published it on your site. For the moment, we'll pretend that we've never heard of the Date module and that you just want enter a date manually in this field.

> **Note**
>
> The Date module would be very useful here, because it would allow us to create a field that is already preformatted to look like the dates we're all familiar with. Date offers several options for entering data and integrates very well with Views. We'll talk about the Date module in Chapter 3.

If you choose to edit the content type (in this case, the Story type), you'll be taken to a new page that defines the parameters of the Story content type and the basics of how it will be displayed to your site's users who want to create a new Story. From here, we click the Manage fields tab and scroll to the bottom of the page to fill out the form for creating a new field. Let's create a field name of `written_date`, label it as "Originally written on," and choose a plain Text type. For the last box, we probably just want a plain text field.

Next, we move to the configuration page for this specific field, where we decide which options we want for the "Originally written on" field that we're creating; that's located at Manage fields >> Configure if you want to come back and edit this information again later. Right now, let's leave the Story settings alone, but change the Global settings. We want to make sure every story has a date, so we'll check the Required box and give it one value. We'll leave the Text processing to Plain text choice, and save our changes. This returns us to the Manage field summary page for our content type. We are now ready to create a new Story with an updated content type.

# Exercise 2-1

## Creating a Field for an Existing Content Type

Here are the steps for creating the "Originally written on" field discussed in the previous paragraphs.

1. Navigate to Administer >> Content Management >> Content types >> Story >> Manage fields.

2. Scroll to the end of the page. Under Add >> New Field, enter these values in the field data boxes:

   | Field | Value |
   | --- | --- |
   | Label | Originally written on |
   | Field name | written_date |
   | Type of data to store | Text |
   | Widget | Text field |

3. Save the field.

4. The settings page opens. Check the Required box, and set the value to 1.

5. Save the field.

The Story type now has a field for holding a date. Realistically, any plain text could be entered into this field because we aren't validating the data.

To modify the settings for any field, simply navigate to the summary page for that content type and click the link labeled "edit" next to the field you want to modify.

Two types of settings are defined by the field creation page: settings that affect the field across the content-specific type and global settings that affect the field across every instance of that field, regardless of the content type in which it appears. In other words, global settings affect the entire installation, so changing them leads to a global change for the field (see Figure 2-7). This can be very confusing if you are sharing a field across multiple content types. In short, global settings determine how field data is stored in the database; changing a global setting affects all instances of that field that use the same database storage.

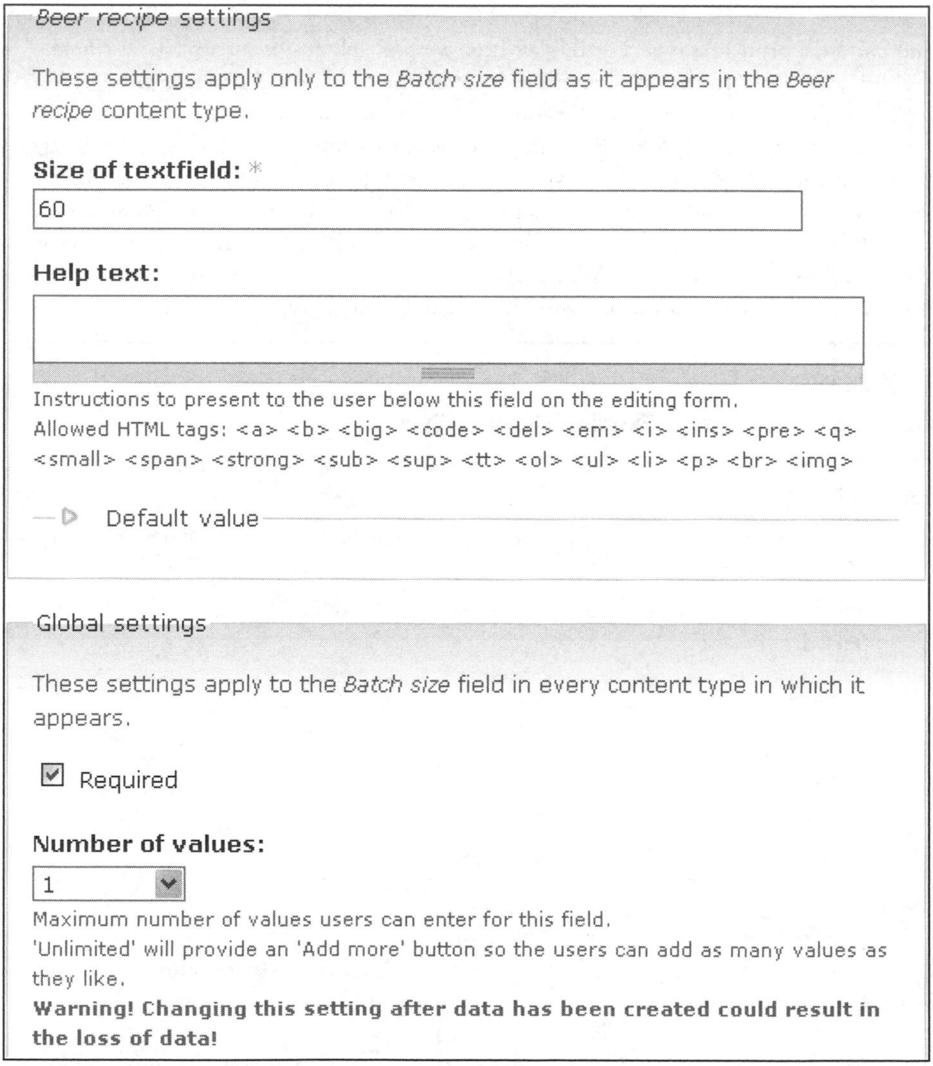

*Beer recipe* settings

These settings apply only to the *Batch size* field as it appears in the *Beer recipe* content type.

**Size of textfield:** *

```
60
```

**Help text:**

Instructions to present to the user below this field on the editing form.
Allowed HTML tags: <a> <b> <big> <code> <del> <em> <i> <ins> <pre> <q>
<small> <span> <strong> <sub> <sup> <tt> <ol> <ul> <li> <p> <br> <img>

   ▷   Default value

Global settings

These settings apply to the *Batch size* field in every content type in which it appears.

☑ Required

**Number of values:**

```
1        ▼
```
Maximum number of values users can enter for this field.
'Unlimited' will provide an 'Add more' button so the users can add as many values as they like.
**Warning! Changing this setting after data has been created could result in the loss of data!**

Figure 2-7    Part of the settings groups on the field creation/Manage field tab

Settings for the specific content type vary somewhat depending on the type of field you are creating and the way you choose to create it. For the most part, they boil down to simple matters: how much data (in number of characters) can be entered into the field, and which text you want to provide to help your users enter data properly.

When looking at the global settings, all field types share three settings: "Required," "Number of values," and "Allowed values." Selecting the "Required" check box forces a user who is creating content to enter a value for that field; this choice is useful if you absolutely want a field to contain data. In our example, we're using this setting to force the user to enter something that we hope is a date. The "Number of values" setting forces the content creator to input a specific number of values, which you might use in a "pick two of four options" situation. In addition, text and number types share the setting "Allowed values." This setting gives the site administrator the ability to create a list of fields a content creator can choose from. You might use allowed values in a store when adding sizes to the content type.

Remember that phone number example in Chapter 1 that we used when talking about Flexinode's limitations? With CCK, you can have a single phone number field, which is then shared by the customer type, the employee type, and the vendor type. Then, when performing a query against a phone number, you can retrieve any of those content types.

### Note

When you share fields between content types, the database structure changes for the shared fields. This point can have major implications for performance, Views queries, and other uses of the data. We'll talk about this issue more later.

More issues must be addressed as you go further into field creation. Each field type's general settings may change based on the widget type. It may seem that there is some circular logic in the page structure for this section of CCK. You need to know what you want your data to look like so that you will choose the correct data type, but you have to choose the data type long before you can decide in Drupal what the format actually does look like. Again, this is where planning is absolutely crucial. To plan correctly, it will be useful to know exactly which options are available for each data type and widget and how they interact.

### Warning!

Changing the global settings for a field under one content type can have unexpected repercussions for another content type.

It is critical to keep track of shared fields if you plan to change any global settings.

## Widgets

By using widgets, you can create lists of options for your users to choose from when adding data. A widget is a special piece of field data that is dependent on the field type. Widgets can be a select list, an autocomplete field, check boxes or radio buttons, a single on/off check box, or a simple text field. Other modules can add more widgets, too. Once a widget is chosen, submitting the form will create the field in the database, making it impossible for you to change the field type without data loss.

# Putting the Parts Together

We've seen how easy it is to create just one field with very simple settings. Suppose we are creating a Web site that sells shirts. Shirts need sizes, descriptions of their styling and materials, prices, pictures, a way to sell them, and possibly a number of other things. A base content type comes with a Body field, which can be used for a description, but we'll need to create most of the other fields in this case. Let's take a look at a new field with some more complex settings.

One thing you might notice when working in this part of the interface is that the breadcrumbs at the top of your screen don't exactly match where you're working. In particular, the label "Content types" will be missing from the breadcrumbs trail. This makes it more difficult to get back to the list of content types. You have to navigate back to Administer >> Content Management >> Content types to get to the list, and that can be confusing. This is a side effect of the menu system within Drupal, for which no change is currently planned. Our hope is that knowing the breadcrumb works this way will help to eliminate confusion.

---

# Exercise 2-2

## Creating a Field for Shirt Sizes

You've been asked by Joe's Clothes to create content with sizes for the company's T-shirt line. What is the best field type to use for shirt sizes? Look through the various data types—the only one that really works is Text.

1. Click the link labeled "Add content type."
2. Give the new content type a name, a type, and a description.

| Field | Value |
| --- | --- |
| Name | Joe's Shirts |
| Type | t_shirts |
| Description | Joe's T-Shirts for sale |

3. Save the content type.
4. Open the content type.
5. Scroll down to the Add >> New field section.
6. Create a new field. All boxes are required.

| Field Option | Field Value |
| --- | --- |
| Label | T-shirt size |
| Field name | shirt_size |
| Field type | Text |
| Widget | Select list |

We know Joe has some sizes, and he might add more at a later date, so a select list is a good option. Using a select list with a text field type lets us enter any type of size we want.

7.  Save the changes.

Once you have created a field, you may go back and edit its Widget type. Figure 2-8 shows the button labeled "Change basic information" that must be clicked before you can edit the label and Widget type. The machine name cannot be changed.

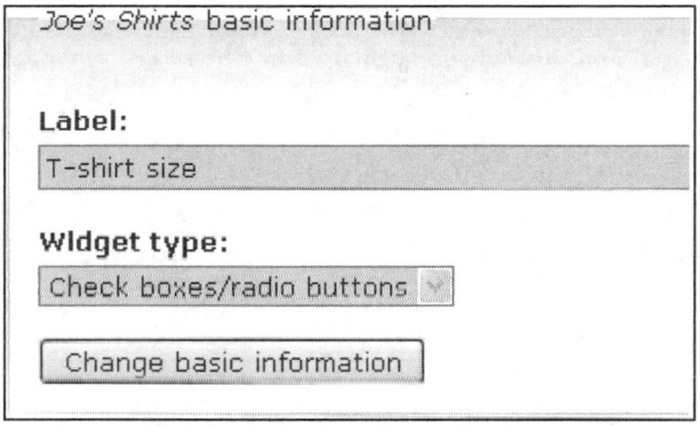

*Joe's Shirts* basic information

**Label:**

T-shirt size

**Widget type:**

Check boxes/radio buttons

Change basic information

Figure 2-8    Creating the shirt size field

8.  Now we're down to the specific details for this field. First we need to update the settings for this field that are particular to the Joe's Shirts content type. There are no values for the field yet, so we can't set a default. Joe doesn't have his clothes grouped in any particular way yet, so we have no groups. Create some help text to let Joe's employees know which data they should enter in this field.

9.  Now look at the global settings (Figure 2-9). Set this field up as follows to so it can be used later for other content types.

| Field Option | Field Value |
| --- | --- |
| Required | Checked |
| Number of values | Unlimited |
| Text processing | Plain text |
| Maximum length | Leave blank |
| Allowed values | XS\|X-Small |
|  | S\|Small |
|  | M\|Medium |
|  | L\|Large |
|  | XL\|X-Large |
|  | 2XL\|XX Large |
|  | 3XL\|XXX-Large |
| PHP code | Blank |

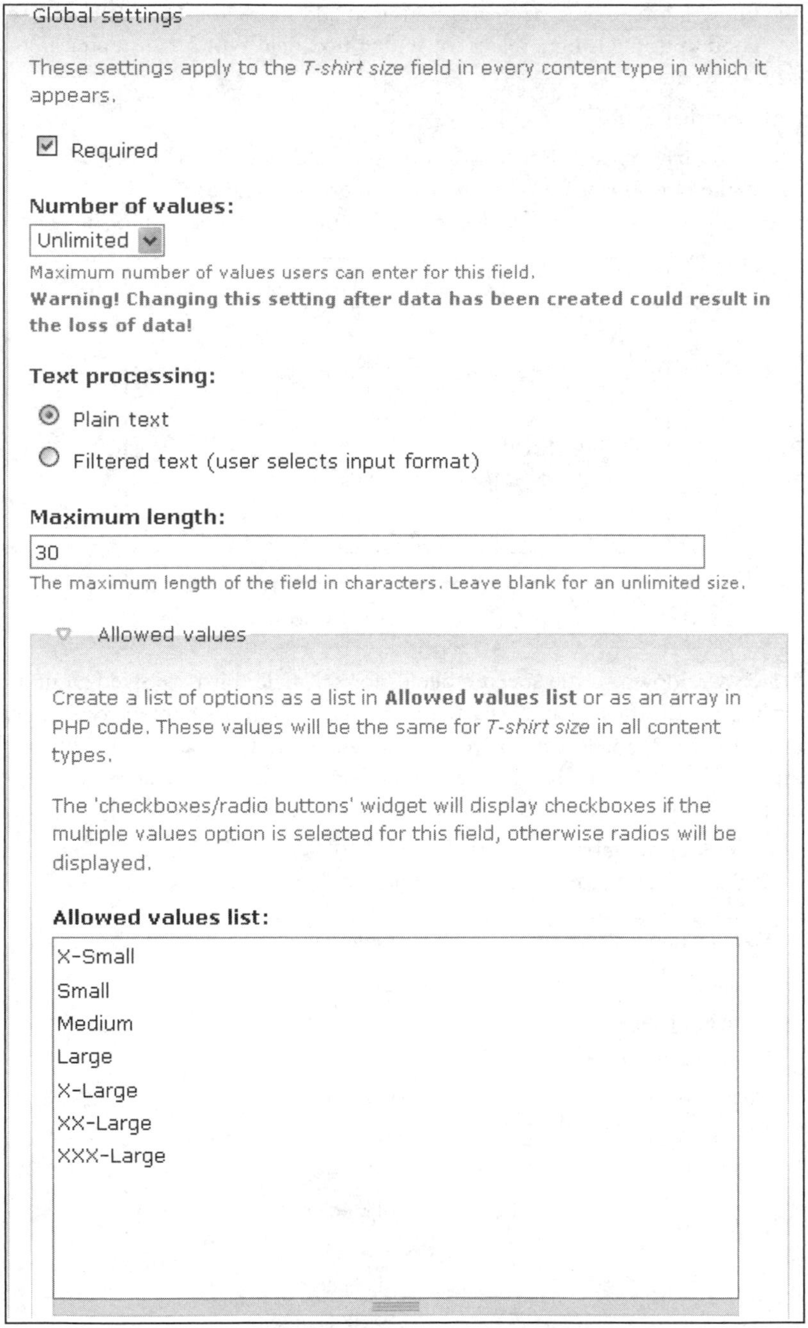

**Global settings**

These settings apply to the *T-shirt size* field in every content type in which it appears.

☑ Required

**Number of values:**

Unlimited ▾

Maximum number of values users can enter for this field.
**Warning! Changing this setting after data has been created could result in the loss of data!**

**Text processing:**

◉ Plain text

◯ Filtered text (user selects input format)

**Maximum length:**

| 30 |

The maximum length of the field in characters. Leave blank for an unlimited size.

▽    Allowed values

Create a list of options as a list in **Allowed values list** or as an array in PHP code. These values will be the same for *T-shirt size* in all content types.

The 'checkboxes/radio buttons' widget will display checkboxes if the multiple values option is selected for this field, otherwise radios will be displayed.

**Allowed values list:**

X-Small
Small
Medium
Large
X-Large
XX-Large
XXX-Large

Figure 2-9    Global settings for shirt size

10. Save the field.

Now you can view the new field for Joe's Shirts. If Joe decides to carry children's sizes later and needs to add that information, it's a simple change to add those sizes to the Allowed values field by coming back to this page. In the Allowed values field, we're also using an alias; as a result, X-Small is displayed on the page, but only XS is stored in the database.

## Changing the Field Display

Take a moment to look at the content type creation page for the Joe's Shirts content type (Create content >> Joe's Shirts). Currently there is a multi-select box for shirt sizes. Consider the types of people who are likely to be entering content for this site. Our current choice might actually not be the best possible field display for choosing sizes. It's prone to errors in clicks, especially when someone is selecting multiple values.

The Manage fields tab, shown in Figure 2-10, is the primary page that deals with the display of fields. Fields required by the content type, such as Title and Body, will be grayed out and cannot be modified from this page. Once you have created new fields, those new fields will be visible in regular text. The first three columns come directly from the first two pages of the wizard used to add a new field: Label, Name, and Type. The last column lets you go back and edit some of the details of the field later if you decide to change any of the field's specific or global settings. Alternatively, you can remove the field entirely if you decide it is not useful or needs to be recreated in another format.

The Manage fields tab provides a level of control for the placement of fields on your form. By clicking on the grab handle and then dragging the fields up and down, you can use the grab handle to move the new field up or down in the page order. Looking again at the "Originally written on" field we created, we might think the date should appear early, so we could use the grab handle to move it up right after the title. (Don't forget to save the change!) Now, when we navigate to Create Content >> Story, the new field appears directly under the title. When you create a story and publish it, the "Originally written on" field is also displayed right below the title and your name.

Notice on the Manage fields page that a list of fields available for editing appears under the main tabs, and the field being edited is displayed in the upper-left corner of the main screen. This allows you to move quickly between fields without having to go back to the main Manage fields screen.

At the bottom of the field management page is the option to add a group fieldset. If the Fieldgroup module is enabled, you will be able to create groups and place fields into them. In the Story module, you might want to group "Originally written on" and some other fields so that they are part of the same group, as a permanent header to every story.

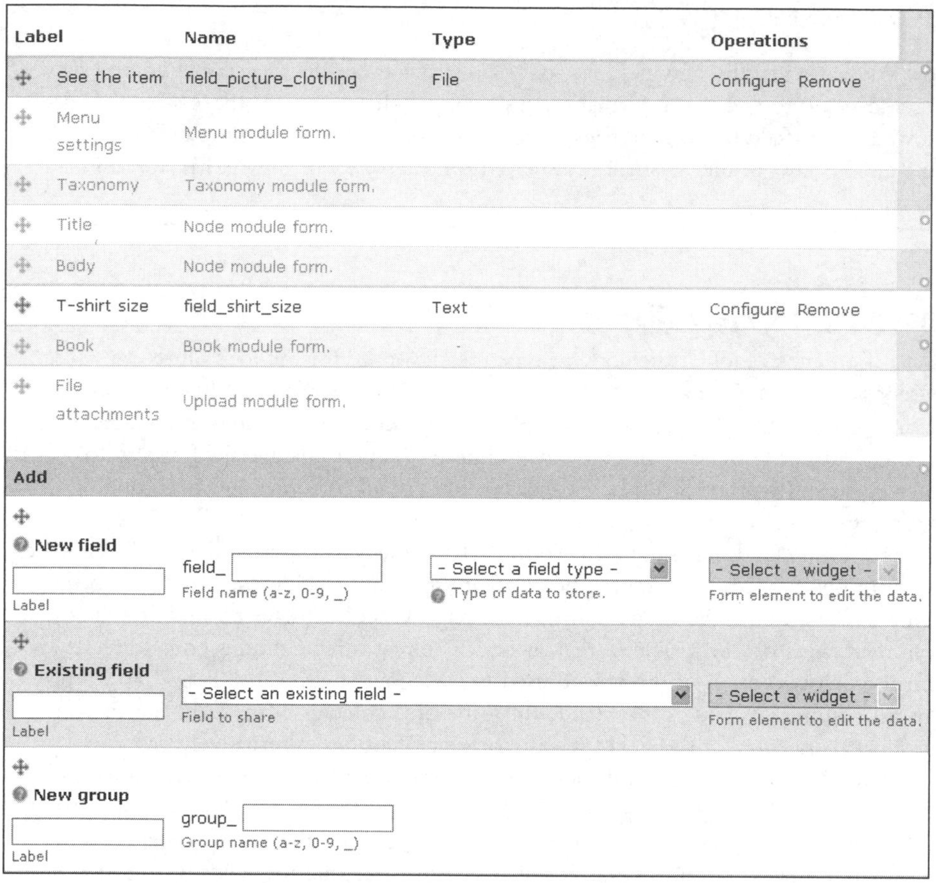

| Label | Name | Type | Operations |
|---|---|---|---|
| ✛  See the item | field_picture_clothing | File | Configure  Remove |
| ✛  Menu settings | Menu module form. | | |
| ✛  Taxonomy | Taxonomy module form. | | |
| ✛  Title | Node module form. | | |
| ✛  Body | Node module form. | | |
| ✛  T-shirt size | field_shirt_size | Text | Configure  Remove |
| ✛  Book | Book module form. | | |
| ✛  File attachments | Upload module form. | | |

**Add**

✛
⊘ **New field**

[_____]    field_ [_____]    - Select a field type -  ⌄    - Select a widget -  ⌄
Label             Field name (a-z, 0-9, _)   ⊘ Type of data to store.   Form element to edit the data.

✛
⊘ **Existing field**

[_____]    - Select an existing field -  ⌄    - Select a widget -  ⌄
Label             Field to share                      Form element to edit the data.

✛
⊘ **New group**

[_____]    group_ [_____]
Label             Group name (a-z, 0-9, _)

Figure 2-10    The Manage fields page

You can then easily move the entire group of fields around in your content type and keep them together. This capability makes the construction of the content type page quicker and cleaner. Note that only fields created by CCK can be added to field groups. Fields that are part of the default node structure, such as Title and Body. cannot be included in groups. They can, however, be moved up and down in the node display by using the grab handles.

You can also adjust the display with the Display Fields page. Two subpages are available on this page by default: Basic and RSS. By enabling additional modules, you can refine the display settings even further. When the core module Search is available, a corresponding Search Display Field setting becomes available; when the contributed module Print (http://drupal.org/project/print), or the core module Book, is enabled, a corresponding Print Display Field setting becomes available. In the Display Fields page, you can configure how each field is displayed for each type of display. A drop-down

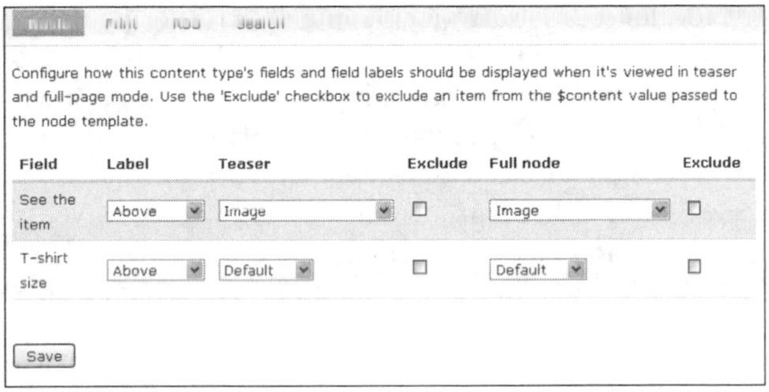

Figure 2-11    Display fields, Basic page

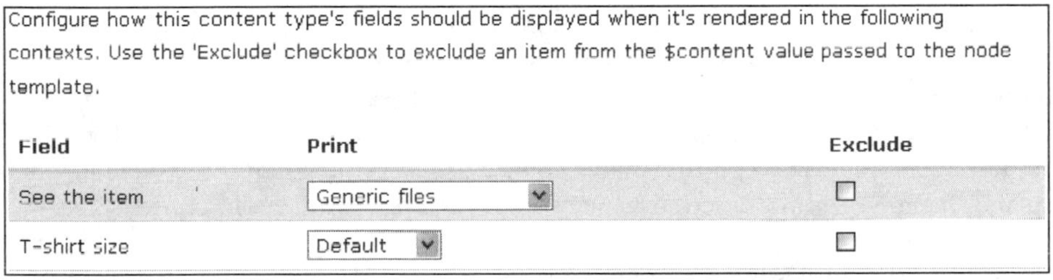

Figure 2-12    Display fields, Print page

menu offers variations for displaying the field. In the Basic settings, you may set the field's label above the field value, place it inline with the field value, or hide it altogether (Figure 2-11). In the Print, RSS, and Search settings, you may adjust only one of the display settings for the main content (Figure 2-12), but not the label as well.

The Teaser and Full node drop-down menus change depending on which type of field is being edited. Text fields allow only plain text or trimmed text. Node Reference fields (Figure 2-13) give you the option to display the title of another node with or without a link to that node; alternatively, you can show a teaser or a copy of that node. A decimal value will give a group of options for how to display that decimal number, governing comma placement, decimal number placement, and so forth.

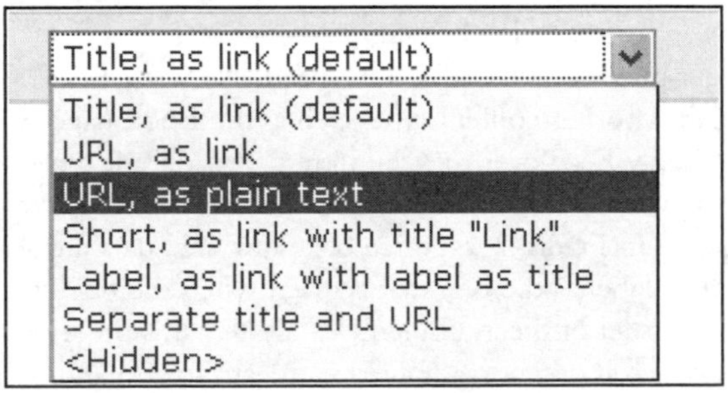

Figure 2-13    Display fields, Node Reference field

The Print page provides some more quick options for rendering the field when it gets passed to the node template. Don't worry; we'll talk about the node template later. This page just says exactly what gets printed, and how text can be printed by the default manner or trimmed; images can print the image file, a path to that image, or other options. Each CCK type is associated with its own set of options.

The RSS and Search tabs have drop-down menus that will allow you to customize how fields are submitted to RSS feeds or searches. They also allow for fields to be hidden from these feeds. That's handy in a case where you have posted a picture, but don't want to post it to the feed—just the picture title that you have captured in a teaser.

## Sharing Fields

CCK allows you to share fields between content types. This ability is extremely useful in many situations. For instance, if you are creating a Web site to sell products, you are probably going to use many of the same fields across the different types of products. However, some items may have a distinct difference that sets them apart from other products. Suppose you are selling soap and shampoo. You might sell soap by the bar, but shampoo might come in 8- and 16-ounce containers. Everything else is the same for the soap and shampoo—name, description, ingredients, and price. You could create a Soap content type and a Shampoo content type, and have a different "unit" size for each, but share the rest of the fields between the two types.

There are some caveats that Drupal Web site creators need to keep in mind when sharing fields between content types. First, you need to know that the database structure changes drastically when you start sharing fields. When you create a field within a content type, the field is included in the main content type table. Once you share the field with another content type, that field moves out of the original content type table and into its own table. The original field is removed entirely—something that catches many Views users off guard when they attempt to create a view to show information from one table, expecting that the field will be there. Sharing fields also makes some changes to the user interface. Navigating to Content types >> Fields, for example, will show multiple entries in the "Used in" column for each content type that a field is a part of.

Another issue here is performance. Every shared field adds a JOIN statement to queries built to retrieve and display the table data. On a small site, this additional overhead may not be an issue. On a larger site with many custom fields, however, it could have a significant impact on page load times.

Consider one of our previous examples: the "Originally written on" field. It might make sense to use this field for another content type, such as the Book page. If you want to share this field, you would simply head over to Administer >> Content types >> Book page >> Manage fields. You'll now want to use the second set of field form boxes under Add >> Existing Field. As you see in Figure 2-14, three boxes for field data are available here. The first is the label, the same label as the one that is given when the field is created. Next is a drop-down menu that lists all of the available fields created; it is the only thing you need to worry about right now. Scroll down to the field you want to add and select it. When you select the field, everything else will be filled in automatically; the field just needs to be saved.

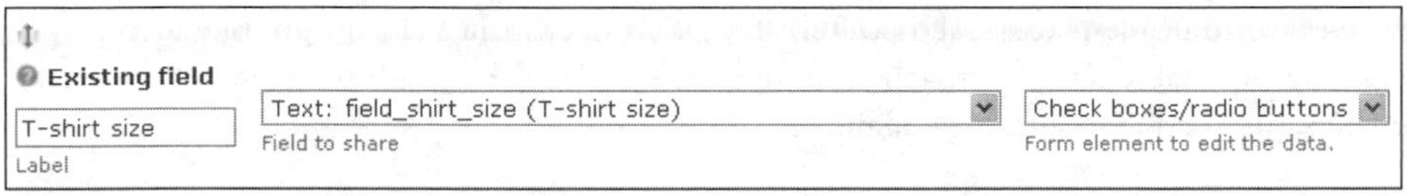

Figure 2-14　Using the T-shirt size field in a different content type

Fields can be used only once in any given content type. When you are attempting to share a field, only fields that are not currently in the content type you are trying to modify will be available. When the field is saved after being added to a second content type, this process creates what is called a new *field instance*. When a field is shared, most of the properties are also shared for each instance; the properties are stored only once in the database, so all of the instances of that field are accessing the same information to build the form that the field is being used in.

Once the save operation kicks off, it starts the database changes that remove the field from its original table (if that field had never been shared before) and move it to a new table. In the database, these tables are easily spotted by looking for the naming pattern `content_field_<fieldname>`. However, these tables are not always for shared fields. They also can hold field types that are set to have multiple values allowed.

---

# Exercise 2-3

## Sharing a Field

There are many instances where you might want to share a field that you've created. Suppose Joe wants an original date on his shirts. We can use the "Originally written on" field for that.

1. Navigate to Administer >> Content management >> Content types >> Joe's Shirts.
2. Click the Manage fields tab.
3. Scroll down to "Existing field."
4. In the "Field to share" box, you should find a selection with this text: "Text: field_written_date (Originally written on)." When you select that choice, the "Label" and "Form element" boxes will automatically be filled in.
5. Save the changes.

You've just shared a field between content types.

---

Going back to our example, we've shared the "Originally written on" field, which had a machine name of `written_date`. When you look at the database structure, you will find a table named `content_field_written_date`. The new table gets its own node and version IDs (`nid` and `vid`, respectively), plus the field that is actually being shared. Creating a separate table for a shared field type makes it significantly easier to use the field type in multiple places; each content type that needs the field simply needs to access the new table. This approach is quite a bit simpler for the administrator than creating the same field over and over again.

### Field Instances

Help text, default values, and PHP settings are applicable only to the instance of the field they are added to.

Shared fields do not necessarily keep the same default values and settings—they keep the data type and widgets.

## Summary

By themselves, CCK's basic features greatly increase the flexibility of Drupal's standard node structure. The ability to add fields to content types along with the ability to create complete new types in the Drupal core ensures that your Web site will do the things that you need it to do and allows you to employ a level of uniqueness and creativity in developing that site. Starting with a well-thought-out plan for your content will enable you to make the most efficient use of content types and corresponding fields.

3

# Deeper into Fields

In this chapter, we'll dig more into fields and all the detailed information for each one. We'll discuss field types in greater depth and explore why you might prefer one type of field over another in your content type. We'll also look at some field types that you might want to add that are not part of the core Content Construction Kit (CCK) package. And we can't forget about dates, or special uses of fields where you want to derive a value from other information.

## Choosing Field Types

In Chapter 2, we went through the processes of creating a new content type and adding a field to an existing content type. To this point, we've looked at the various data types. Most of them are straightforward, but others aren't as obvious to a new user. This section provides more information about these types, as well as field settings that come after basic field creation.

A key question when working with fields is, "How do I choose one field type over another?" User and Node Reference fields are specialized enough that their use is clearly preferable in certain situations. In many situations, the choice is obvious. For example, you wouldn't use a Text field where an image is needed, but you might not be sure where to use a Float type versus a Decimal. These are the absolute basic field types you need to create specialized content for your nodes, and it is imperative that you have a full understanding of the options for each one before getting started with Web site development using the CCK module.

When field modules other than CCK are installed, each adds a new data type, widget, and configuration page specific to the needs of that module—just like CCK. They all have the same style, but the options for each one will differ. Most of the global settings for the computed field are specific to each data type.

In the following sections, we'll cover use cases for the different types of fields and see what each field is best at.

## Using Text

In our previous examples, we saw how a Text field can be used for nearly anything you want. Text fields are the easiest to create and use. Every Web site user knows what a Text field is and what is generally expected to be entered in those fields. Almost any alphanumeric data and many special characters can be put into a Text field.

Plain Text fields are simple to use, and easy for users to understand. They are an excellent choice to store descriptions, names, addresses, and the like. Plain Text fields can also be used to store numbers. If you decide to do so, however, you must carefully consider both the present and the future of the site. Text fields should not be used for storing numbers. If there is any chance that the field will ever be used to do a computation, such as determining sales tax on a purchase, then you should not use a Text field.

Other considerations must be taken into account as well. Views will give you options for filtering data. Text fields are filtered differently than numeric fields; the Text type uses alphabetical order for sorting purposes. Using a Text field to store numbers also does not ensure that only numbers will be stored there. Perhaps your intent is to have numeric input, but your users might enter text accidentally (or on purpose!). A Text field does not provide validation or error checking for numeric values.

## Using Numeric Types

CCK has three different field types that are best used for storing numbers: Decimal, Float, and Integer. Using one of these field types helps to future-proof your site for changes. All of these types are similar in function, which can cause confusion when you're trying to choose one for a particular functionality.

A Decimal field is ideal for storing monetary values such as prices and salaries. It allows values to have a maximum of two places to the right of the decimal marker, which limits this type's use for scientific notation purposes. Decimal fields allow further mathematical calculations to be performed, so they can be manipulated and can create information for other fields much more easily than a Text field can. This field type also has settings to change which marker/fractional symbol is used as the decimal placeholder, which makes this field type more easily used internationally, as different countries use the fractional symbol in different fashions.

Float fields are the best option when you want to store either very small or very large numbers. This type does not limit the number of digits before or after the decimal marker, which makes it perfect for use in mathematical calculations.

Integer fields hold whole numbers. This field type is very useful for quantities in store inventories or supply lists.

When you're looking at using Views filters, numeric fields give you better options for filtering on numbers that are greater or less than a given value. Numbers also take up less database space, and validation can easily be implemented to ensure that only numeric data is entered into the field.

## Using Node Reference

A Node Reference field is a highly useful method of relating a node to one or more other nodes. This option can be used much like an index or for a series of news stories. For example, on a clothing sales site, it could be used to link a shirt offered for sale to user-submitted pictures of that shirt being worn. Node Reference fields help to create a direct link between different nodes. You can also create a view that uses those references to query for specific nodes.

Consider some other uses for node references. Suppose a musician's Web site has a list of CDs, and each CD has a group of tracks. A Node Reference field can easily handle the relationship between artist and CD, artist and track, and CD and track. This allows someone visiting the artist's Web site to easily navigate back and forth, and permits the Web site developer to create a discography quite easily. To achieve that, you would use a content type for artist, CD, and song, and each of those types would use a Node Reference field that refers to the other two content types. For complete navigation, the artist would link to the CD and song, the CD would link to the artist and song, and the song would link to the CD and artist.

When linking nodes with Node Reference, each of the referring fields would need to be created separately; Node Reference is unidirectional. When a Node Reference field is created, node A refers to node B, but a link from node B back to node A must then be created if you want the navigation to be both ways. For instance, linking artist to CD is one direction; linking CD back to artist would require another Node Reference field.

---

# Exercise 3-1

## Creating a Node Reference Field

Returning to our previous homebrewing example, recall that we have created the content type for recipes. We also need a separate content type to keep track of the different times we've brewed that recipe.

1. Create a new content type for the product (a batch of beer), using these values:

| Field | Value |
| --- | --- |
| Name | Batch brewed |
| Type | batch_brewed |
| Description | Information on a batch of beer, wine, and so forth |

2. Add a field to the content type.

| Field | Value |
| --- | --- |
| Field name | recipe_used |
| Label | Recipe |
| Field type | Node Reference |
| Widget type | Autocomplete Text field |

3.  On the next page, go down to the global settings. We want to place some restrictions on the field.

| Field | Value |
| --- | --- |
| Required | Checked |
| Number of values | 1 |
| Content types that can be referenced | Beer recipe |

Now, when you create a batch, you can type the name of a recipe into the Recipe field, and it will search the database for a name that matches what you have entered into the field.

Node Reference is a very powerful tool when used appropriately. Think about which paths your users might want to follow when they are looking at content on your site that might not follow the traditional breadcrumb method.

## Using User Reference

The User Reference type creates a relationship between a node and a user outside of the node author; a user's information is also a node, but this is a relationship outside of that. User Reference is very useful for creating teams and adding players. It could be used to add a sales contact to a product, for example, or to add staff to a scheduled event.

If you need to create a group that people belong to, User Reference can be used as a very basic way to do so. Drupal contains other modules specifically intended to create groups (such as Organic Groups: http://drupal.org/project/og). Those modules are reasonably large and rich in functionality specific to creating and maintaining groups.

Figure 3-1    A node with a Node Reference field in use

The User Reference type also contains one invaluable function: It has the ability to create reverse links (see Figure 3-2). Using this functionality, you can establish a two-way link between a user and a node. If you were to use this feature to add a user to an event, you would also add that event to the user's profile page. A flag for the field is set based on the content type; it is visible as a check box in the content type settings when you are creating or managing the field. User Reference can refer to a default value, so a new piece of content may always have a link to a specific user.

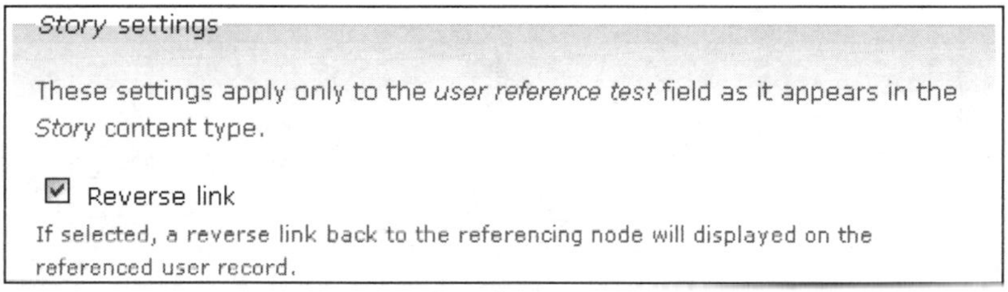

Figure 3-2    Creating a reverse link with User Reference

User Reference works much like Node Reference, but uses certain types of global user permissions rather than node types to limit the things that can be linked to. Drupal site administrators may create *roles* for the site's users, giving or denying permission to perform actions such as creating or editing content. The basic user role is authenticated user. A User Reference field that works with an authenticated user will allow every available user with login access to be chosen as a valid value.

You can also use the final flag on the User Reference type to do a more general limit on users. Drupal users are either active or blocked (i.e., banned from access). User Reference normally would create a list from all valid accounts in a role, but if the Active flag is checked, only active user accounts will be included in the select list or autocomplete search. If your site has a large number of users, this can narrow down your search time considerably. And, much like with the Node Reference field type, users can be defined by Views.

As noted earlier, User Reference helps you to link nodes to other users, and the available widgets create limits specifying what users can be linked to. The user roles limitation with User Reference is much like the content type references under Node Reference. Your site may have a few roles or many, and you can choose to allow a field to reference only users with particular permissions. You will need to define those roles for your site; only the administrative role is available initially. You can also decide to allow only active users to be referenced. By default, the only available settings for user status are Active and Blocked.

# Constraining Data with Widgets

As described in Chapter 2, each created field has two types of settings: settings for that field specific to that content type (Figure 3-3) and global settings that are used for the

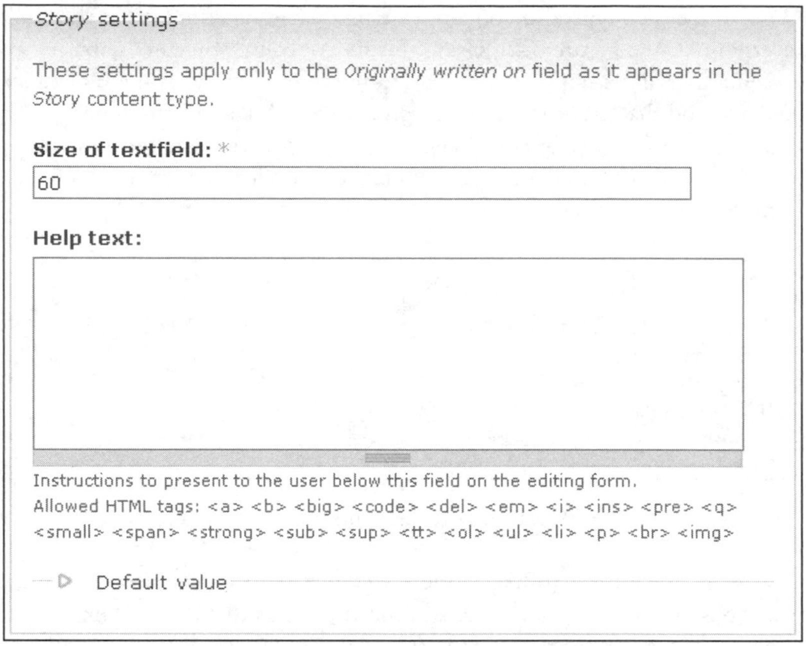

Figure 3-3    Settings for a field per node type

field in that content type as well as every other content type it appears in (Figure 3-4). Widgets are also known as form elements.

Figure 3-3 shows an example of settings that can be enacted on a field within one content type. In this case, we are looking at a Text field, and we can limit its size and give some help text to assist the user in filling in the field properly.

The global settings (Figure 3-4) affect the field, regardless of what content type it is in. Thus, if you use the field in more than one place, these settings will continue to apply.

Once you are sure which field type is the right one for your Web site, you have many other options available to help you get input and determine the basic display properties. Each field type uses a *widget* to restrict and define the allowable values (not the Allowed values—that's another setting!).

Widgets are similar to very specific formatters. They don't determine how the field is displayed, but rather regulate how the content of the field itself is chosen or input. Each field type comes with its own set of available widgets, and each widget has deeper settings to control how it works. For example, if you want to use a number, there are multiple options to consider depending on the situation. In theory, widgets are interchangeable: the purpose for which they are needed determines which widget is

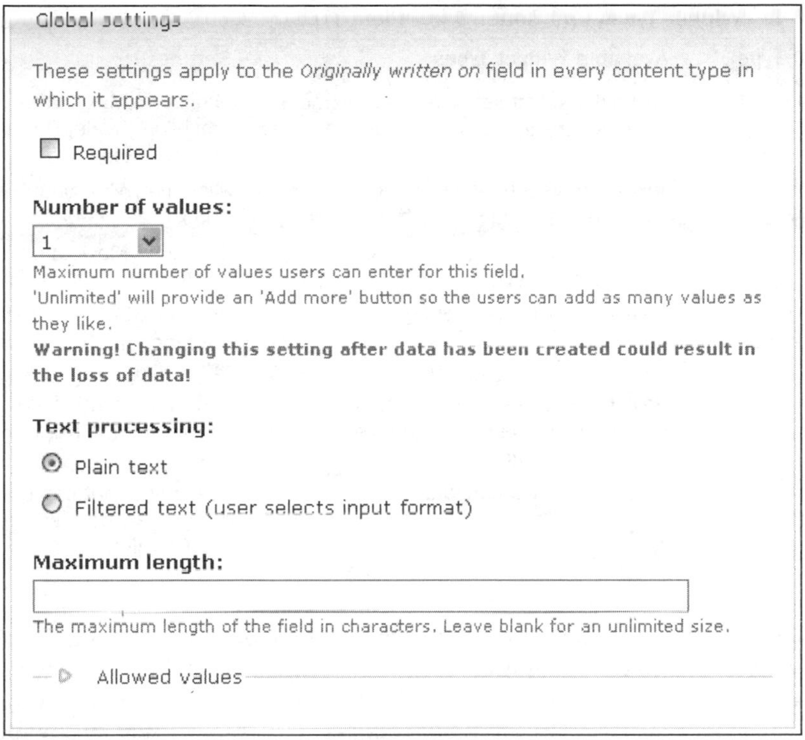

Figure 3-4    Global settings for a field across all node types

appropriate in a given situation. Following is a list of the widgets that are available with CCK at install:

- Text field: Stores any basic string of text.
- Select list: Gives a choice of a prepopulated list of user-defined options.
- Check boxes/radio buttons: Allow for the definition of a multiple-choice checklist or a single-choice radio button.
- Single on/off check box: Allows one check box.
- Autocomplete: Allows a user to type in part of a node name, with Drupal then attempting to fill in the rest of the field by searching through the database to find matches.
- Multi-row text area: Creates a larger than one-line text box.

Certain widgets are available only for particular data types. Unlike with the field's data type, however, you can change the widget for the field later if your needs change or if you find that your original widget choice is not well suited to what the field really needs to do. Each widget has a group of settings as well, to further refine its usage (Table 3-1).

Table 3-1    **Widget Types and Settings per Field Type**

| Field Type | Available Widget Types | Settings |
|---|---|---|
| Decimal | Text field, select list, check boxes/radio buttons, single on/off check box | Minimum, Maximum, Precision, Scale, Decimal marker, Prefix, Suffix |
| Float | Text field, select list, check boxes/radio buttons, single on/off check box | Minimum, Maximum, Prefix, Suffix |
| Integer | Text field, select list, check boxes/radio buttons, single on/off check box | Minimum, Maximum, Prefix, Suffix |
| Node Reference | Select list, autocomplete | Content types that can be referenced, Node/views to be referenced |
| Text | Select list, check boxes/radio buttons, single on/off check box, Text field, multi-row text area | Text processing (plain or filtered text), Maximum length |
| User Reference | Select list, autocomplete | User roles that can be referenced, User status that can be referenced |

Decimal, Float, and Integer share most of their attributes; given that they all deal with numbers, this makes a great deal of sense. The Minimum and Maximum settings allow the administrator to set a limit on the highest and lowest values, respectively, that can be entered for the field. The Precision setting designates how many total numbers for this field will be stored in the database on both sides of the decimal. Scale limits the number of the digits to the right of the decimal. Decimal marker determines what delimiter is used in a number and has three options: decimal point, comma, or space. The Prefix and Suffix settings determine what goes before or after the field, respectively; these are places where you might put monetary symbols (prefix) or units of velocity (suffix).

Node Reference is very specialized, and its use depends on what you have defined on your site. One of the Node Reference widgets limits the links to specific content types. The Views module helps you to create lists and content displays, giving you a non-content type–specific group of nodes that can be referenced. We'll talk much more about this operation in Part II of this book.

Text is the most general field type, and has the fewest options for widgets. Plain text is run through an internal filter that does not allow any code of any type or special characters (non-alphanumeric characters). This limit helps to ensure that your content remains safe from hacking. Filtered text allows the user to select a particular filter that will be processed when the node is displayed. The available filters are Basic or Full HTML, which allows the field to contain HTML code. The Body field on the default Story module with its input format selector below the text area is an example of filtered text. The Maximum setting gives a cutoff for how many characters can be included in the Text field. You might use it in a description or a customized teaser for a longer article.

## Exercise 3-2

### Changing the Widget Type

It turns out that the Text field multi-select list widget wasn't quite what Joe's Shirts needed. Check boxes might make it easier for a user to see all of the shirt sizes available. Let's make widget a check box and observe the changes.

1. Navigate to Administer >> Content management >> Content types >> Joe's Shirts >> Manage fields >> T-shirt size >> Configure.

2. Click the button labeled "Change basic information." It will return you to the screen where you chose your widget type.

3. Change the widget type to check boxes/radio buttons and continue.

4. No further changes are needed, so save the field settings.

When you try to create a new shirt (Create content >> Joe's Shirts), observe the change (see Figure 3-5). The multi-select text box has been replaced with check boxes. This format will make it easier for Joe's employees to see all of the available sizes and will help them avoid making multi-click mistakes. It also will let them uncheck particular sizes easily if they run out of a size. If you haven't created any shirts, take some time to do so and see how the added field works.

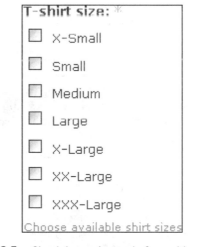
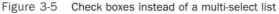

Figure 3-5     Check boxes instead of a multi-select list

# Date Module

The Date module is one of the single most useful add-ons to the core of CCK. Date is a Drupal module that is designed to use CCK's structure, forms, and user interface (UI) to add dates to content types. While not in the core feature set of CCK, the Date module is one of the most useful additions you can make to your toolset.

Date brings an entire set of new features to the party, enabling you to set up specially formatted fields for different date functions. Drupal provides a timestamp within its core; this module takes dates and modifies them to fill your own needs.

## Install the Date Module

At this time, we're going to look at what Date does with CCK, namely how it adds new field types and what options it makes available to you.

Date can be downloaded from http://drupal.org/projects/date. Take a few minutes to download, install, and enable the module.

Date creates three new field types: Date, Datestamp, and Datetime. Datestamp is the UNIX timestamp, which is very useful for programming, database work, and some levels of sorting, but is not very user friendly. Realistically, users should not see the raw internal values of the database. Datestamp also has the disadvantage of only allowing for dates back to January 1, 1970. The Date field type is a basic string, stored as text. This is very user readable, but it cannot be used for anything except display. The Datetime field type provides a database-native timestamp that can be used for most dates needed by users. It can be sorted, easily queried for, and used in calculations. This type provides all the same benefits as Datestamp, but has greater flexibility in actual calendar date usage. We recommend using Datetime over the other date field types for its increased flexibility as well as its better performance for indexing.

Date also introduces some new widget types: a Text field with custom input format, a Text field with jQuery pop-up calendar, and the familiar select list. The jQuery calendar provides a simple clickable interface that makes it very easy to pick a date, while the custom input format is a drop-down menu in the field settings that gives you over a dozen ways to set the date display.

Settings for the particular data type start with a default value, which is amenable to further customization depending on the option you choose. You can leave the field blank, default to the time when you're creating the content, or choose a relative date. If you choose a relative date, you must open and use the Customize Default Value collapsed fieldset, shown in Figure 3-6. To make the best use of the relative date, you'll need to have an understanding of PHP. The fieldset contains a link to the appropriate PHP reference page. A relative time value uses the PHP strtotime function. Check the PHP documentation for a full explanation of its usage.

You can create a custom input format for your date display. The regular drop-down menu for input format lets you choose which way the year, month, day, and exact time

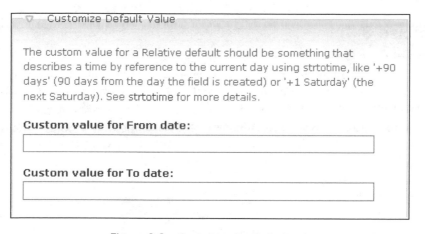

Figure 3-6    Customize the default value

should be displayed under normal circumstances. If a custom format is provided, it will override the default date display for that field in that content type.

One of the things Date can do is provide choices for how far forward or back your year selection list should go, if you use the select list widget. It defaults to three years in either direction. Time increments can be adjusted for the minute and second fields if they are visible.

One of the most noticeable differences between the Date and CCK settings for the original field types is the field label formatter. "Customize date parts" shows the options for placement of the labels of year, month, day, and so forth. We'll be able to change the look of it when we talk about themes later in this book. However, like the base CCK fields, it still contains the same text box to provide user-facing help text.

The Date module has its own complete group of global settings that are specific to its use, as well as the basic "Required" and "Number of values" settings that all CCK-based fields have. Global settings start off with a "To date," which may be optional, required, or never used at all. It is useful for things such as news articles about events that run for a certain length of time. Next is "Granularity"; these check boxes break down the time in year, month, day, hour, minute, and second increments. Unchecked boxes are not displayed on the content creation page.

Finally, the "Date display" shows the format in which your users will see the date on your content pages. It also can accommodate a custom format, which uses PHP's date format string. The collapsible fieldset for "Additional Display Settings" gives further options for showing dates, such as long, medium, and short—all of which have the option to show a custom format.

The last field is "Time zone handling." It determines which time zone the user viewing content will see. You may want to standardize your site to your local time zone, UTC, or always show the user his or her own time zone.

## Exercise 3-3

### Using the Date Field

To keep track of our batches for our homebrewing example, we will use a date for each batch brewed. We'll want to have an easy reference back to the original recipe used, even if we made modifications for a particular batch.

1. Go to the content type page (Administer >> Content management >> Content types), and select "Manage fields" next to the Batch brewed content type.

2. Add a new field using these values:

| Field | Value |
|-------|-------|
| Label | Brewing date |
| Name | brewing_date |
| Field type | Datetime |
| Form element | Select list |

3. Save the new field.

4. Change the default value to "Now" for this content type. No customization is necessary right now—we'll assume the batch information is being entered on the day it is made. Input format is fine the way it is, and we don't have a need to change the "Years back and forward" or the "Time increment."

   If you're doing something like converting a handwritten notebook of recipes into a database, you might change the "Years back and forward" selection. If you have 15 years worth of entries with dates, changing the "Years back" adds 15 years into the calendar drop-down menu.

5. Customize the date parts. Having the labels above the date seems reasonable for now.

6. Skip down to the global settings and enter the following values:

| Field | Value |
|-------|-------|
| Required | Checked |
| Number of values | 1 |
| To date | Never |
| Granularity | Year, Month, Day |
| Default display | Medium |
| Time zone handling | No time zone conversion |

7. Save field settings.

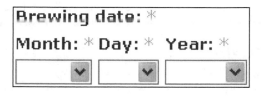

Figure 3-7    The Brewing date field on the Batch brewed creation page

## Computed Fields

Computed Field (http://drupal.org/project/computed_field) is another add-on module with a basis in CCK. Unlike many CCK modules, however, it requires some knowledge of PHP to be useful. This module can create a value from other values and return that value to you. You can choose to store this value in the database, decide whether to display it, and do some level of formatting. Because the computed value is calculated by PHP, this field is able to access anything that Drupal itself can access.

The new data type and widget for this field are easily spotted, as both of them also have the name Computed. Computed data fields allow use of only the computed widget, so there is no room for confusion in what to choose.

The most critical field form data is the Computed Code field. This Text field contains PHP that will calculate a value based on other values. A limited number of variables are available for use: $node, $field, and $node_field. This is definitely an area where an understanding of PHP and Drupal internals becomes useful. If you don't have either type of knowledge, that's still okay! Just follow along: Our hope is that the discussion here will give you an idea of how the Computed Field module works and a base for where you'll take your own data.

The next pair of settings deals with the field display. Selection of a check box determines whether the computed field will appear in the node when it is displayed to the end user. In addition, a Text field uses PHP to determine how the field will be displayed. It uses the PHP $display variable, which needs to have a value assigned to it.

The remaining fields are a group that determine whether and how your data will enter the database. If you decide to save the data, it is calculated and stored when the node is saved. Selection of a check box determines whether the data will be stored. If the box is checked, then you must choose which SQL format the data will be stored in: int, float, varchar, text, or longtext. This is a group of radio buttons, so you must choose one. Data length is a field that is also required for storage purposes; you may set a default value for this field. The "Not NULL" check box flags the field for display only if it has a value, and the final check box flags the field for sorting.

## Exercise 3-4

### Creating a Computed Value

One thing all brewers want to know is how strong a batch is. The strength of beer, which is known as alcohol by weight (ABW), varies depending on many factors during the brewing process. A formula is used to determine that strength based on the original and final specific gravities of the fluid: alcohol by weight = 76.08(original gravity − final gravity)/(1.775 − original gravity). We want to keep these together, so let's use a field-group. Let's add this formula to our homebrewing example.

1. Open the Batch brewed content type (Administer >> Content management >> Content types >> Batch brewed).

2. Create a new group using "Add group" and these values:

| Field | Value |
| --- | --- |
| Label | Alcohol level |
| Group name | alcohol_level |

3. Save the group. You do not need to make any changes on the configuration screen.

4. Create a new field for original gravity with these values:

| Field | Value |
| --- | --- |
| Label | Original Gravity |
| Field name | original_gravity |
| Field type | Float |
| Widget | Text field |

5. Create a second field for final gravity with the same settings used for original gravity.

6. Create a third field for the computed value with the following settings:

| Field | Value |
| --- | --- |
| Label | ABW |
| Name | alcohol_by_weight |
| Field type | Computed |
| Widget | Computed |

7. In the global settings for the Computed Code field, include the following snippet of code:

```
$og = $node->field_original_gravity[0]['value'];
$fg = $node->field_final_gravity[0]['value'];
$node_field[0]['value'] = 76.08 * ($og - $fg) / (1.775 - $og);
```

This code sets a pair of new variables ($og and $fg), sets their values to the value a user inputs on the form, and uses a third variable ($node_field) to calculate a final value that will be returned.

8. Make sure "Display this field" is checked; it should be by default.

9. For the database storage settings, use the Float data type, with a data length of 5. This is a longer value than will ever be needed.

Now we have a place to enter original and final gravity values for our batch. When a batch is entered and saved, the computed field will calculate the percentage and display it on the page.

If you wanted to take matters a step further, this field could be used to calculate alcohol by volume (ABV). ABW is generally used for beer, while ABV is used for wines. To do that, you would need another field.

1. Create a new field for Batch brewed using these values:

| Field | Value |
| --- | --- |
| Name | alcohol_by_volume |
| Label | ABV |
| Field type | Computed |
| Widget | Computed |

2. Use the following for the computed code:

```
$abw = $node->field_alcohol_by_weight[0]['value'];
$fg = $node->field_final_gravity[0]['value'];
$node_field[0]['value'] = $abw * ($fg / 0.794);
```

3. Use the same settings for the other fields as you used in the ABW field, and save the changes.

ABV will appear as another value in your batch. When you created the fields, none of them were marked as required. You won't know the final gravity until the batch is done, and it's always best to enter batch information while it's fresh. Another thing to be aware of: Because ABV is using ABW for its calculation, ABW must be calculated first. If your fields are out of order, your values will be incorrect. Order matters!

4. Look at the list of fields. Use the cross (grab handle) to move all of the fields we just created into the "Alcohol Level" group.

5. Save the changes.

| ✛ Alcohol level | group_alcohol_level | Standard group |
|---|---|---|
| ✛   Original gravity | field_original_gravity | Float |
| ✛   Final gravity | field_final_gravity | Float |
| ✛   Alcohol by weight | field_alcohol_by_weight | Computed |

Figure 3-8    The Alcohol level fieldgroup

Now all of the fields are grouped together and can be positioned with one grab of the handle next to the fieldgroup name, as shown in Figure 3-8. Notice how the fields within the group are indented, making it easy to tell which fields belong to that group.

The Computed Field module can cause a great deal of frustration for those without PHP development experience. However, even a little knowledge can turn this field into one that your site simply cannot function without.

## Link and Email Fields

Link and Email are two additional contributed modules that add new fields to your CCK user interface. Link is found at http://drupal.org/project/link; Email is available at http://drupal.org/project/email. The fields added by these modules have similar functions, but slightly different uses. Both modules provide a field that allows the node to have a specific place to add HTTP or email links. In some cases, you may provide these links in the body of the node. Using the field types has several advantages, however. The field type will be easily usable by Views; like other fields, it can be themed separately so it is more obvious to the page viewer; and it can have its own label.

The Link module has a number of potential uses. For example, you might create a node that contains a blog roll or a wish list. You could use it for news articles to create links back to the original photo or other source material. The Link module also provides the nofollow option, which helps prevent some search engines from following the provided link. Link has a somewhat unusual feature in its global settings in that it has the ability to add the link to CSS classes, feeding it automatically to some styles.

Email fields are among the simplest fields in functionality and configuration terms. The Email module creates only one new field type and uses only one widget, a plain Text field. When used, this CCK add-on allows an address to be input that creates a `mailto:` link in the node. It will check to ensure that the email address has a valid format. With the Invisimail module, it can also have the email address encrypted, thereby preventing spam bots from harvesting addresses from your site.

# Highly Visual Media

One of the major uses of content in Web site development today is to provide highly visual media. Pictures, streaming audio, and video are big business and vitally important to many corporate Web sites. For example, clothing stores want pictures of their items to be available to potential customers, musicians want tour photographs and album covers to be visible, and so on. Again, add-ons to CCK add to the power of Drupal and enable designers to meet these challenges.

The various Image modules (e.g., ImageField, ImageCache, ImageAPI) provide the first step toward meeting these needs. Unlike the field types previously discussed, the Image modules are a group, and they require another field add-on module: FileField. As a group, these modules provide a way to feed images to a specific content type, or to feed to other modules via the API.

## FileField

FileField (http://drupal.org/project/filefield) performs a function that some users may question: its purpose is to upload files. An optional module is included with the Drupal core called Upload, whose purpose is to upload and attach files. So why is FileField needed?

First, file fields as CCK fields are more flexible than the core's functionality. Core upload is limited by the size of the file that can be uploaded, and only a certain group of file types can be uploaded at all. Files uploaded using core upload are listed as file attachments. That terminology is not very clear when you have a specific need for a particular type of file, or if you want to provide text to help users decide what they should be uploading.

The FileField module is very similar to the other CCK extensions. It creates a File field type and adds new widgets for its own use: File Upload, Extensible File, and Image. This module allows you to attach a file that can be text, an image, or some other type of file and to make this file available to others viewing a particular node. In theory, you could simply use FileField to upload images, but the Image modules give you significantly more control over the files and the ability to manipulate pictures to some degree as they are being uploaded to your site.

FileField has a few content type-specific settings that are specialized for its use as well as global settings that restrict viewing of uploaded files. For each content type, you may specify the file extensions (e.g., `.jpg`, `.txt`, `.doc`) that are valid for uploading to a node. You may also limit the upload size for each file as well as the total upload size for all of the files. For example, you might specify a 5-megabyte limit per node, which means that a user could upload five 1-megabyte files or one 5-megabyte file. If you use this functionality to upload an image using the Image widget, you also have the option to limit the resolution of the file being uploaded.

Globally, the field type requires to two values to be set: "Default list value" and "How should the list be handled." The default list value option determines whether the files are hidden from view when they are attached. The list handling question determines if the user attaching the file can change the visible or hidden setting versus the default being strictly enforced by the module so that users cannot change it.

## ImageField

ImageField (http://drupal.org/project/imagefield) starts with the same base as FileField. This again begs the question of why you would use ImageField instead of image. The difference is, again, the advantages of CCK fields for creating data within a node versus using a separate module to create an entire node.

When you create the field, the field type Image is available, with Image as the single available widget. The settings page, however, looks exactly like the Image widget for FileField, with the same settings and instructions. ImageField's permitted extensions for upload are prepopulated with image-based extensions (e.g., .jpg, .jpeg, .png, .gif) rather than the default .txt extension provided by FileField, but otherwise they are the same. It is recommended that the ImageField module and widget be used over FileField's module and widget, however. ImageField is set up specifically to deal with images, and does not have to make allowances for other types of files.

Once you have created a field, you can go to the content type. There, a field with a browse button will be available when you create a new node. When an image is uploaded, it appears in a list format on the node. This means the picture is not embedded into the page, but rather a link with the image's filename is provided.

## ImageAPI, ImageCache, and ImageCache UI

ImageAPI, ImageCache, and ImageCache UI form a set of helper modules. CCK obtains a link from ImageCache to provide formatters for ImageField, if ImageField is present.

ImageAPI is a module that is not visible to the general user. It performs basic image manipulation for other modules such as ImageCache such as resizing, rotation, and cropping so that images can fit into the required space provided by the content type administrator. Note that this module does not actually save images—that task is left to other modules.

ImageCache works in conjunction with the ImageAPI to create a namespace in which the image is stored. Using this module, you can set up a group of default actions (presets) to be performed on an image, which in turn can be used by other modules to always perform those presets when an image is uploaded. ImageCache also defines a theme function so that your template file can easily add a modified image to any node of that particular type. The module includes a UI to make tasks easily visible in the administrator's interface.

# Summary

There are many ways you can use a field to create the site you're seeking. Understanding and using fields and helper modules for those fields creates possibilities for including any kind of data on a Web site. Knowing the core of CCK's provided data types and widgets lets you examine how well those functionalities can fit the needs of what you need to create. With the addition of the various modules that contribute to the extension of CCK, you can go farther, faster.

# Themes and CCK

Now that your content is created, it's time to make it look professional and easy to read. CCK does a great job of allowing you to add plenty of customized content. What it doesn't do as well is display the data in a fashion that is clean and nicely readable for users. In this chapter we take a look at the theme system and the way in which Content Construction Kit interacts with it. We also examine the Contemplate module, which can help you along. Drupal's theme and templating system in version 6 goes a long way toward making theming your site easier. Finally, we consider additional help modules that will make theming Drupal even easier.

## Theme Basics

Themes have two basic parts: the functions and the theme template. Drupal and its modules hand information off to the theme layer for display—if you're working on files outside of the theme's template files, you're doing it wrong. Template files end with the extension `.tpl.php`. The template file can live in a number of places in your installation. The base files are in the themes directory, but each module may also have a themes directory containing more specific information for each part of a module. As a reminder, Garland and its subtheme Minelli are used for install and upgrade; modifying them is not good practice.

In looking at the various directories, you will see a number of files that have the same name. These are defaults that Drupal will use if you make no changes of your own. Drupal uses a theme (such as Garland) to style content. Many modules, such as CCK, Views, and many others, provide plugins to extend the theming capability of Drupal. Figure 4-1 shows some of the template files that are used by Drupal's default theme, Garland. Figure 4-2 shows CCK's theme directory, which contains the files to override the base theme's styling.

If you want to modify one of the base themes, there are some steps you should take to preserve the theme and your sanity.

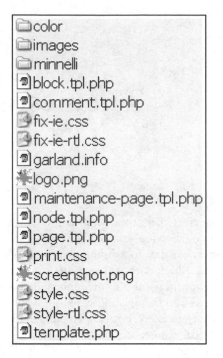

Figure 4-1    The /themes/garland directory

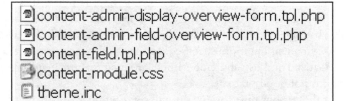

Figure 4-2    The /cck/theme directory

## Exercise 4-1

### Preserving the Base Theme

Preservation of the base theme is not technically a part of theming CCK, but it is important to know the safest way to modify a base theme. If you tangle with the administrative theme, you run the risk of accidentally hiding your content, rendering it too small or too large to read, or doing any number of horrible things that are hard to track down in the stylesheet.

1. Navigate to the `/sites/all/themes` directory. The `sites/all` directory should already exist. If `/sites/all/themes` does not exist, create it.

2. Create a new directory for your new theming files—these files will override information in the base theme. My base theme is Garland, so to keep things simple, my directory name is `garland_extend`. Thus the complete path name is `/sites/all/themes/garland_extend`.

3. Create a `.info` file for your theme extension. This step is important! Without it, your theme won't know where to look for the base theme. Your `.info` file name must match the name of the theme's directory. For this exercise, use the name `garland_extend.info`.

4. Add information to your `.info` file that will enable your theme to find its base theme, and be usable by your own site. For example:

```
name - garland_extend
description = Tableless, recolorable, multi-column, fixed width theme.
version = VERSION
core = 6.x
base theme = garland
stylesheets[all][] = garland_extend.css
```

5. Create the CSS file that the theme will use for modifications. From the previous step, you can see that my file will be `garland_extend.css`. If you want to create the file now, go ahead. It will be an empty file until we decide to change things.

## Stylesheets in Themes

It is good practice to add a stylesheet name to your `.info` file, even if the CSS file itself is empty. If you do not supply a stylesheet, the theme will use style.css as the default.

The potential problem here is that many themes use style.css as their standard stylesheet, and your new, empty stylesheet will override it. That behavior is fine if you want to completely remove the old sheet, but it presents a problem if your new sheet has no CSS information in it.

Your new theme folder contains only two files: `garland_extend.css` and `garland_extend.info`.

6. Now you can enable the "new" theme on your site and changes to that theme will have an effect. In addition, you'll be able to use the original Garland theme when it's time to upgrade!

7. Go to Administer >> Site building >> Themes. Select the check box next to your new theme (`garland_extend`), and choose the radio button next to it for the default. This enables your theme.

# CCK Specific Theming

CCK output can be broken into three levels for theme creation: formatters, field templates, and node templates. Each of these levels can be broken down again into pieces that affect particular characteristics of the page or pages you are displaying. Remember that the theme engine renders formatting information in order from the most specific template to the least specific one. Specific theming overrides more generic templates. Theming for one particular field (such as the username) has a higher precedence than the general theming information for all fields. Files that can override the default theme files are called *suggestions*—suggestions are more specific files for themes.

## Formatters

We looked at the formatters for fields in particular content types back in Chapter 2. Reviewing the key points quickly, the formatters based in the user interface do simple field placement, and are found by the following navigation path: Home >> Administer >> Content management >> (choose a content type) >> Display fields.

Formatters use the default Drupal theme layer, which enables you to use all of Drupal's overrides, templates, and other theming functionality for CCK fields. Many of the supplied formatters use theme functions. The general function of a formatter is to take the data for one field and wrap it in the appropriate HTML for output.

## Field Templates

One of the most powerful aspects of theming for CCK (and Views!) is the ability to create and use a theme for every single field on every single display. This is possibly considerably more control than you will ever want or use. Field templates are not tied specifically to CCK (or Views), but knowing about them enables you to determine where you need to break down your theme much more quickly.

Field templates and formatters perform similar functions to a certain degree because they're dealing with the same type of data. However, field templates focus much more on the question "How does this field look?" rather than "Where is the label, and should it even show up?" A formatter enables you to put the label "Price" on the page; the template and CSS enable you to make the actual price "$19.99" be in bold font and green color.

We've already mentioned that template files use the extension .tpl.php and shown some examples of the template names. CCK field types allow for the use of extremely specific field names for theming each field, and the naming structure follows a convention that can help you to identify what it does.

> **Warning!**
>
> You should never modify the default theme files in the module directory for any module (such as /sites/all/modules/cck/theme). Doing so scatters your theme across the installation and can cause serious confusion when you need to make changes later.
>
> Always copy the default file to the directory of the theme you are working in (/sites/all/modules/theme_name), and modify it there.

**Template Files and Filenames**

The general template file for a field is `content-field.tpl.php`. If you have no theming templates that are more explicit, this is the file that will be used for layout of content for your fields. The Devel module can help you figure out how to get more explicit with your theming files. The default `content-field.tpl.php` file can be found at `/cck/theme/content-field.tpl.php`.

The next step in drilling down to uniqueness in the theme is to change the field itself, across all content types. Note that if you are not sharing fields across multiple content types, this action does not actually affect much. In contrast, if you are sharing fields across content types, it's a good way to change the layout of the field across the entire site. Unfortunately, it's also a good way to lose track of why a field for content type A changed when you create a template file for a field in content type B. The `.tpl` filename convention looks like this: `content-field-<FIELD_NAME>-<CONTENT_TYPE_NAME>.tpl.php`. In the case of our Joe's Shirts content type, `content-field-field_shirt_size.tpl.php` is the template for the T-shirt size field.

Drilling down again allows you to specify the display of all fields for a particular node type. This step prevents themers from accidentally overriding shared field types, but keeps that display from being shared. If a shared field is shown one way for one content type, it can be shown a different way for another. In our example, this file becomes `content-field-t_shirts.tpl.php` for Joe's T-shirts: `content-field-<CONTENT_TYPE_NAME>.tpl.php`.

At the lowest level, you can create theme information for one specific field for one content type. The naming format for this type of file is `content-field-<FIELD_NAME>.tpl.php`.

To summarize, CCK always adds "field" to the beginning of each field name, even though the template files are already using "field" in the name. CCK theming looks for these files in the following order of precedence:

---

```
content-field-<FIELD_NAME>-<CONTENT_TYPE_NAME>.tpl.php
content-field-<CONTENT_TYPE_NAME>.tpl.php
content-field-<FIELD_NAME>.tpl.php
content-field.tpl.php
```

---

If none of these files are present in your theme folder (or your base theme's folder), CCK will use its default theme template.

**Variables Available in the Field Template**

The variables available to the field template should not be surprising to anyone who is familiar with the structure of a Drupal node or who has done any theming work. This list is taken directly from `content-field.tpl.php`, with some expansion on some of the descriptions.

- `$node` The entire node object.
- `$field` A field array that contains all of the fields available to the node.
- `$items` An array that contains the values of all items in the field array. Each value in this array contains the fully formatted and filtered value.

- `$teaser` Determines if this content field is displayed within the teaser.

- `$page` Determines if this content field is displayed as a full page. A field can be in either the teaser or the page, in both, or in neither.

- `$field_name` The name of a particular single field.

- `$field_type` The type of data the field contains.

- `$field_name_css` The name that CSS will use when referring to this field. This field and `$field_type_css` are the same as `$field_name` and `$field_type`, respectively, except that the values of the _css version of the field replace underscores (_) with dashes (-) when a page is output for viewing. This means that when using `field_shirt_size` in CCK, the CSS class will be `field-shirt-size`.

- `$field_type_css` The data type CSS will use when referring to the field. This field acts in the same manner as `$field_name_css` with regard to underscores and dashes.

- `$label` The label that the item has been given, such as "T-shirt size."

- `$label_display` The position of the label display as determined by the formatter: inline, above, or hidden.

- `$field_empty` A TRUE or FALSE value. It is set to TRUE if the field has no data to display.

## Exercise 4-2

### Changing Part of a Theme: Field Color

Joe's Clothes wants to make the available shirt sizes for each shirt type very obvious to its customers. The company would like to have the sizes appear in red.

1. Determine the correct template file to use. For now, let's assume that if Joe expands his store, he'll want to use the same look for all his size fields. In this case, `content-field-<FIELD_NAME>.tpl.php` is the best candidate for the job.

2. Copy the `content-field.tpl.php` file to your `/sites/all/modules/theme/garland_extend` directory, and rename it to `content-field-field_shirt_size.tpl.php`.

3. Now we need to change the CSS file to set up the new color for the size. We have a `garland_extend.css` file for our stylesheet, which will be called by the theme. Open the CSS file, and enter the following style information:
```
div.field-field-shirt-size div.field-items {
color: #FF0033;
}
```

4. Save the file.

When you reload any T-shirt page that had size information available, those sizes will be shown in red. You may have to force a full refresh, as many browsers will cache stylesheets.

Perhaps you are wondering where the name for the div came from to pick out the color change. The template file for the field tells us all we need to know. Here's a snippet of the `content-field-field_shirt_size.tpl.php` file:

```
<div class="field field-type-<?php print $field_type_css ?> field-<?php
print $field_name_css ?>">
  <?php if ($label_display == 'above') : ?>
    <div class="field-label"><?php print t($label) ?>: </div>
  <?php endif;?>
  <div class="field-items">
```

The last line is the one we're most interested in. It says `field-items`, meaning the values within the field itself. We need to isolate the text color change so that it uses just those values, so we need to be exact. The selector `div.field-field-shirt-size` isolates the style to only the shirt size field, and the `div.field-items` selector refines this restriction further to change only the values, instead of both the values and the label. If you wanted to change the label, you could use the following CSS selector to specify just the label in the shirt-size field:

```
div.field-field-shirt-size div.field-label
```

## Node Templates

Node templates are big wrappers for entire pieces of content. They're very much part of the core theming system. The node template encapsulates data and placement and is one of the easier pieces of theming to create if you don't need multiple colors for text, or have special requirements for images or other data.

Most themes will include a default node template: `node.tpl.php`. Drupal's core theming system allows you to modify this choice to narrow the scope of the theme. The default of `node.tpl.php` covers the look of all nodes. If you want something a little different for one content type, you can simply copy the default file to a new one, and modify the name to `node-<CONTENT_TYPE>.tpl.php`. To change the theme for all story nodes, your node template would be called `node-story.tpl.php`. Once you have created this template, you can modify the look of all your stories without affecting the rest of the system!

CCK provides several variables to the node template that handle most use cases for theming a node.

`$<FIELD_NAME>_rendered`

This variable provides the fully rendered output of the selected field, complete with HTML. It is the ultimate output of the field template. The rendered output supplies all of the field's values as well as all of the settings that were created by the formatters.

`$<GROUP_NAME>_rendered`

Like the `$<FIELD_NAME>_rendered` variable, this variable produces fully rendered output; in this case, it is for an entire fieldgroup if one is being used. In our Batch brewed content type, we're using a fieldgroup for "Alcohol level." This variable could be used within the node template to change all of the fields in the group at once, using $alcohol_level_rendered. In essence, $<GROUP_NAME>_rendered is a superset of $<FIELD_NAME>_rendered.

$FIELD_NAME

This variable contains two groups of data. One comprises only raw data, without any of the formatter information provided to the previously described variables. This data is provided in the same array formation that CCK uses internally. Each time this array is used, the contents can be different based on the type of field being themed.

$FIELD_NAME contains a second set of data, held in a "view" element. This element does not actually relate to the Views module, so don't let the name confuse you. Instead, it holds the same information you would see in the $<FIELD_NAME>_rendered variable, so you have the clean data available for display as well as the raw data available for manipulation.

> **Note**
>
> The raw data provided by $FIELD_NAME is not sanitized for output! It may be useful to the themer or the developer, but should not be used directly for output.
>
> For display purposes, use the values contained in the "view" element, or use the content_format() function to ensure the data being passed to the display is clean.

## Exercise 4-3

### Theming a Fieldgroup

Sometimes you may have a group of fields that you want to call out or deemphasize in your content type. CCK gives group names as part of the output that is ultimately printed to the browser. In our example, we have "Alcohol level" as a fieldgroup in the Batch brewed content type.

1. Determine the group name that has been passed as a class name. Any node with that content present will have the group name available where we can readily find it.

2. View the source code for that page.

3. Search the source code for "fieldgroup". You might find a line that looks something like this:

   ```
   <fieldset class="fieldgroup group-alcohol-level">
   ```

   This class lets us theme either all fieldgroups or just group-alcohol-level.

4. Open the garland_extend.css file, and add this code:

   ```
   fieldset.group-alcohol-level {
     font-size: x-small;
   }
   ```

5. Save the CSS file, and refresh the browser page.

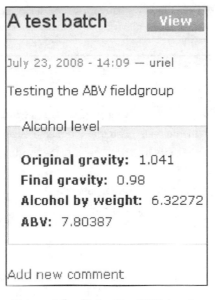

Figure 4-3    Before the CSS change

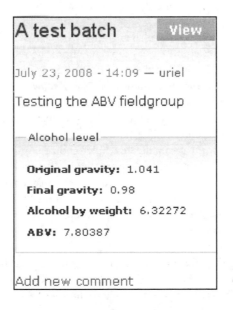

Figure 4-4    After the fieldgroup is changed

Using the fieldgroup as the class lets us change just one set of fields, instead of affecting the entire node. It also lets us change all of those fields at once, instead of theming each field individually.

---

### Adding Files to Themes

Drupal caches the list of files available to a given theme. If you create a new template file, you must rebuild the theme registry so that the theme engine finds the new files.

You can rebuild the theme registry by doing one of these two things:

- Navigate to Administer >> Site configuration >> Performance. Scroll to the bottom of the page and click the button labeled "Clear cached data."
- Using the Devel module's "Clear cache" link.

## Excluding Fields

When any piece of content in its entirety is displayed on a Drupal site, it is fed primarily by the $content variable. This variable contains the entire rendered HTML that goes in the main part of the page. In most cases, this is fine. You often want your site to be themed consistently, so having all of the add-ons and widgets printed as part of the single variable is a good thing. Those elements includes thing like attached images and voting widgets, for example.

On some occasions, however, this behavior is not what you want. For example, you might want some parts of your content to display separately from the rest of the content. You can prevent fields from being contained in the $content variable by checking the "Exclude" box on the Display fields tab for the content type. Navigate to Administer >> Content management >> Content types >> (Pick a content type) >> Display fields. On this tab, you can exclude things from the teaser or the full node. Note that there's a difference between the "Hidden" and "Exclude" choices. The "Hidden" choice includes the data but doesn't display it on the page. By comparison, the "Exclude" choice prevents the data from being added to the variable at all. Go back and take another look at Figure 2-11 to see where an Exclude button is available. If you pick a field from the Display fields tab, the drop-down menus for "Teaser" and "Full node" both allow you to choose "Hidden" to hide the field.

At this point, you can customize your template file by using $<GROUP NAME>_rendered or the $<FIELD_NAME>_rendered variables in a PHP print statement to place them wherever you want within your page.

Be aware that using the "Exclude" check boxes excludes that field data from all of your themes. However, each theme may have different information in $content, so the actual fields printed may vary from one theme to another.

## Node Reference

The Node Reference type has some special variables and other issues that go with it that can produce even more changes in your theme. Node Reference fields use all of the previously discussed theme functionality, but also include some special templates that can be used when Node Reference fields are being used to display nodes when using the teaser or full node formatters. These templates check the type of node being referred to and theme them accordingly. These suggestions take precedence over the others.

`node-nodereference-<REFERRING_FIELD_NAME>-<CONTENT_TYPE_NAME>.tpl.php`

This is the most specific suggestion template. It looks at the referring field as well as the type of the node being referred to. In previous exercises, we created a Node Reference field for the Batch brewed content type. Its purpose was to refer back to the recipe used to create that particular batch. Technically, we didn't force the user to specify a recipe in that field, so it could refer to any other field. If you wanted to use it to refer to a recipe, you would use a template name like this:

`node-nodereference-field_recipe_used-beer_recipe.tpl.php`

If this referencing field was used to refer to a story, the template name would change to `-story.tpl.php` instead of `-beer_recipe.tpl.php`.

`node-nodereference-<CONTENT_TYPE_NAME>.tpl.php`

This template would theme all Node Reference fields where the field being referred to is the specified content type. If the template was named `node-nodereference-t_shirts.tpl.php`, for example, it could be used to theme any `t_shirts` node when a Node Reference field is referring to it.

`node-nodereference-<REFERRING_FIELD_NAME>.tpl.php`

The referring field, whenever it is being used, causes this template to be used to theme the node being referred to.

`node-nodereference.tpl.php`

This template themes any node that is referred to by a Node Reference field.

Using these templates, you could create a "fall lineup" for Joe's shirts, and use the Node Reference field to refer to each shirt node. Users looking at the full catalog could then easily see which products are new in the fall lineup if you chose to theme the referred-to nodes a little differently than the standard.

Finally, CCK presents two more variables for use in the template files when you are using node references:

`$referring_field`

This variable picks out the field that is referencing the current node. It could potentially be used to trace the theme back to its origin.

`$referring_node`

This variable stores the node that contains the field that is referring to the current node.

# Helper Modules

You don't need to figure everything out on your own when you are working with Drupal themes. A variety of helper modules are available that make theming Drupal a lot easier. A few of our favorites are described in this section.

## Theme Developer

Theme Developer (http://drupal.org/project/devel_themer) is not strictly a module used to create themes. It is, however, one of the most invaluable tools available to help you determine which templates are affecting any given part of your content. To install this module, you will also need the Devel module (http://drupal.org/project/devel)—a module that comes with a lot of useful functionality, too.

When this module is installed and enabled, Theme Developer provides a check box in the lower-left corner of your browser window labeled "Themer info." When active, this check box disables the ability to follow any links in that particular page. If you click on a given section of the page, a window will pop up that lists exactly which .tpl files affect that piece of page content. An entire path of prioritized templates is provided, ordered from most to least specific. This list includes all candidate template files that could affect the content, even if those files do not exist on the system. Use this information when you need to decide if you should change the overall theme, or if you want to override the theme down to as specific a point as one field for one content type. When you are armed with this knowledge, it's much easier to determine which template file you should alter.

The list of template files is clickable, which makes it significantly easier to open a template file. Instead of hunting through your system to find a file, it is made readily available in a tidy list. This consideration is especially important when template files have the same name. For example, there is a default content-field.tpl.php file, but CCK also includes a template with the same name that will be used by default. The "Themer info" check box explicitly identifies which file is being used to theme each piece of content.

# Exercise 4-4

### Viewing Theme Information with the Themer Module

This exercise shows you how powerful and helpful even a little bit of Themer assistance can be, by helping you figure out what your template files may be.

1. Install the Themer and Devel modules.

2. Navigate to Administer >> Site building >> Modules and enable both the Devel and Theme Developer modules.

3. Open your site's home page.

4. Click the "Themer info" check box in the lower-left corner of the screen.

5. Click on any component of the page.

If you created a T-shirt during the earlier exercise, click the "T-shirt size" section. You should see a box that looks something like Figure 4-5.

The "Themer info" check box also lists the parents of that themed piece. The parents section is clickable as well, and activating it outlines the group of content that it affects. This kind of feedback is critical when you are trying to find problems with overrides between theming components.

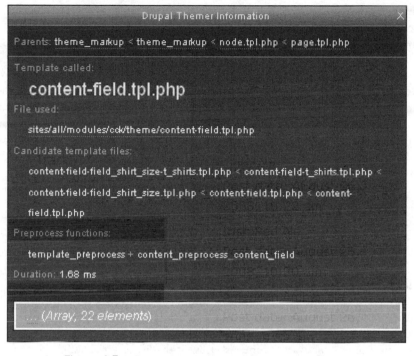

Figure 4-5     The Theme Developer information overlay

One word of warning: The Themer module should be enabled only on test sites or when you specifically need it for theme work. If Themer is enabled, you may see some unexpected behavior in your displays when performing particular tasks. This can be confusing when you are doing something unrelated to theming! Like many great troubleshooting tools, this module should be enabled when you're actively using it, and disabled when you aren't.

To create a more specific file, you can use the files listed by Devel. In fact, once you understand the naming convention, you can easily determine the correct file to change a particular field. If you are looking at the Devel module priority list, you'll see two `content-field.tpl.php` files. There are two of these files in the system: one is the Drupal general file, and the other is CCK's default file. CCK fields use the CCK template, so you are already one step more specific than Drupal's base install.

## Contemplate

Contemplate, also known as Content Templates (http://drupal.org/project/contemplate), is a module that is at the center of much philosophical debate within the Drupal community. As Drupal has continued to move forward, much progress has been made in separating the content from the presentation. In general, many people believe this dichotomy is a good idea because it allows developers and themers to work without absolutely needing to know what the other is doing. A theme that is independent of content does not have to be changed when minor updates to site-wide information are made. Such flexibility reduces maintenance and overhead costs, which is a good thing.

Contemplate represents something of a middle step between theme and content. This module provides visibility into your theme by allowing you to create some template information through CCK pages—which is good. But it also means you are not using the "correct" method of employing a straight template file—which some people think is a bad thing. For a new user, visibility can be the key to understanding. Contemplate also provides theming information only for teasers, the Body field, and RSS feeds, which is the bare minimum of items you may want to theme.

Contemplate adds some new links to your administrator interface: Administer >> Content management >> Content templates or Administer >> Content management >> Content types >> Templates. Either of these paths will take you to the same page, where you may create a new template.

The template gives you three groups of boxes—one each for teasers, the Body field, and RSS feeds. Each provides a check box through which you specify if this part of the template will be used. If your content type is not using a teaser or an RSS feed, it doesn't make sense to create templates for those sections.

The most important aspect of these sections is the list of variables. This list shows you everything that is available to the theming function from the node itself. Figure 4-6 is a brief example of such a list.

Another important thing that the Contemplate module does is to identify fields that may not be secure and are potentially vulnerable to attack. These fields are marked with a double asterisk (**). Drupal provides two functions to sterilize your data so that your users will not cause inadvertent or deliberate problems by using unsanitized data: check_plain() and check_markup(). These functions can be found in the theme

```
▽   Teaser Variables

An example node has been loaded and its properties appear below. Click on the the
property names to add them to your template.

    $node->nid
       11

    $node->type
       batch_brewed
```

Figure 4-6    Partial list of items available to the teaser

preprocessor. If you do use the Contemplate module, it will automatically add `check_plain()` to the types it thinks should use that function.

## Summary

In this chapter you learned about Drupal's theming system and the many ways that CCK interacts with it. Using a range of template files, helper modules, and core UI display options, you should now be able to target, customize, and display any field of content displayed on your site.

# 5

# CCK API

Content Construction Kit includes methods that PHP developers can use to create fields outside the user interface. This creates even more flexibility, but requires a definite knowledge of the PHP language as well as familiarity with Drupal's development style. In this chapter, we delve into the process of integrating CCK with other modules.

## Using the CCK API

The real power of CCK lies in the fact that it is a plugin-based architecture that makes it easy to add new types of fields. Hundreds of CCK modules have been developed, so most of the field types you might need already exist as contributed modules. On some rare occasions, however, custom code will be necessary to fill a very specific need. In addition, the ability to add fields to content types in the browser using CCK's user interface is nice, but sometimes you want to be able to do this programmatically instead—via other modules or other methods.

CCK provides an API to create field types and a number of hooks to allow interaction with the data and data definitions. To effectively use this capability, you should already be familiar with PHP and SQL and the basics of creating a module in Drupal using Drupal's hook system. More information about these topics can be found on the drupal.org Web site. One major reference you may need is Drupal's API reference site: http://api.drupal.org.

There are several ways to use CCK's API and hooks: to create new element definitions, such as field types, widgets, and formatters; to programmatically create specific instances of existing elements and attach them to content types; and to programmatically load and save nodes that contain CCK data.

We've discussed how most of the following information is approached through the user interface (UI). Now we'll look at how these concepts are handled from the code interaction standpoint.

> **Note**
>
> This chapter references many Drupal hooks—the base functions to get data from one place to another within Drupal.
>
> Hooks that contain the words "field" or "content" are provided by CCK. Most other hooks that are mentioned in this chapter are provided by Drupal core. If you aren't sure about the source of a hook, the Drupal API page listing the core hooks can help you out: http://api.drupal.org/api/group/hooks/6.

# The Field Model

CCK fields are composed of a *field* (which describes the way the data is stored in the database), a *widget* (which describes the way a user will interact with the field in a form), and a *formatter* (which describes how the data will be displayed). For example, the core CCK program provides three Number fields—Integer, Decimal, and Float—that store numeric data in those formats. The Number fields can use two widgets, a Textfield widget, in which the user can type in a number (like a phone number or address field), and the Optionwidgets widget, which allows you to provide a list of allowed values that can be presented to the user as a drop-down select list, check boxes, or radio buttons (such as a preset list of postal codes). The formatters for the Number field provide a variety of ways to display the number and define the decimal character and the thousands separator.

Both the field and the widget may also provide validation rules and other settings. The validation operation for the field may include the list of allowed values or a minimum and maximum allowed value. The validation operation for the widget may include checks that the data is in the format required by that widget.

Some settings are common to all fields and widgets. Fields have settings that indicate whether they are required and whether they allow multiple values, for instance. Widgets have settings for the field label and help text shown to the end user, and for a default value to use in a new node.

Formatters have different display settings for each build mode. Thus there can be one display for a teaser, a different display for a full node, and yet another display for the field value when used in an RSS feed. We discussed this issue in Chapter 4; these settings allow you display any given field, or not.

## Creating New Field Types, Widget Types, and Formatters

It is easy to confuse fields with field types. Field types, widget types, and formatters are definitions that describe how these elements should behave and which settings are available or required. All three are really just templates for fields. The templates can then be used to create specific instances of fields, each with its own settings attached to specific content types. For example, you might take the Number field type mentioned earlier, combine it with the Textfield widget type, and attach it to the Story content type to create a specific field instance, providing the specific settings that you want to use for the field and widget in that situation. You could then take an address field and put it in a Story type, giving it specific attributes that are important to the Story.

Many different field types and widget types are available. The CCK module itself provides the following options, and hundreds more are available as contributed modules on the Drupal Web sites:

- Text
- Number: Integer, Decimal, and Float
- Nodereference
- Userreference
- Widget types
- Text: Textfield and Textarea
- Number: Textfield
- Optionwidgets: Select and Checkboxes
- Userreference and Nodereference: Autocomplete

Not every widget type can be used with every field type. For instance, an Autocomplete widget is currently only available for the Nodereference and Userreference fields. The widget type will declare in its definition (in the code) which field types it is appropriate for.

Formatters also declare in their definition which field types they are appropriate for, and then create one or more themes that may be used to display the value of that type of field. Those options appear on the Display fields tab and in the Views module as ways to display the field value.

If you want to create a module to define a new field type, widget type, or formatter, it is best to start with one of the modules provided by CCK. Either the Text or Number module is a good starting point. These modules were designed to be used as examples, and are part of the base installation of CCK. As such, they should be found under `/sites/all/modules/cck/modules`.

## Creating Custom Field Types, Widget Types, or Formatters

A module can define one or more field types, widget types, and formatters. It is not necessary to define all of them. For clarity, our example code will define all three, so that you can see how each is created. For instance, you could create a new widget type or formatter that will use an existing field. Let's look at code for an example module to define a single field type, widget type, and formatter.

The CCK field hooks are defined by field modules—modules that define a new kind of field for insertion in a content type. Field hooks are typically called by CCK using `_content_field_invoke()`. Widget hooks are typically called by CCK when it creates the field form elements in the node form using `hook_form_alter()`.

All modules should declare `hook_content_notify()`. This hook should be implemented inside `hook_install()`, `hook_uninstall()`, `hook_enable()`, and `hook_disable()`, and is used to notify the content module when a field or widget module is added or removed so it can respond appropriately. One use of this hook is to allow the content module to remove fields and field data created by this module when the module is uninstalled and to mark the field and widget as "active" or "inactive." The recommended location for the `content_notify()` hooks is in the module's `.install` file. Following is an example of a `.install` file:

```
/**
 * Implementation of hook_content_notify().
 */
function MYMODULE_install() {
  content_notify('install', 'MYMODULE');
}

function MYMODULE_uninstall() {
  content_notify('uninstall', 'MYMODULE');
}

function MYMODULE_enable() {
  content_notify('enable', 'MYMODULE');
}

function MYMODULE_disable() {
  content_notify('disable', 'MYMODULE');
}
```

This is implemented in a very straightforward fashion in one of the example modules: Text.

## Exercise 5-1

### Examining the Install File for a Module

In this exercise, we examine how the previous code definition is implemented within one of the suggested modules.

1. Open the `text.install` file located under `/sites/all/modules/cck/modules/text` using your favorite text editor.

2. Review the first four hooks defined in the install file. They match up with the example code. Here is the example for `hook_install`:

```
/**
 * @file
 * Implementation of hook_install().
 */
```

```
function text_install() {
  drupal_load('module', 'content');
  content_notify('install', 'text');
}
```

Notice the short comment that states what the function is doing. The function itself declares that you're installing the Text module, tells Drupal that you're loading a module that is a type of content, and then lets the Content module know that you're installing it.

3. Take a few moments to review the uninstall, enable, and disable functions. Each of these behaves very similarly.

The `.install` file for the Text module does a lot more work than this simple exercise demonstrates, but that functionality falls into the realm of general module development.

## Field Type Modules

Modules that define field types should implement `hook_field_info()`, `hook_field_settings()`, `hook_field()`, and `hook_content_is_empty()`. Optionally, you can also implement `hook_content_generate()` to generate dummy field data. These hooks are all provided by CCK.

Field and widget names are truncated to 32 characters in the database and in internal arrays, such as `content_fields()`, so don't try to create names longer than that limit. The `content_icon` value for the field provides the Panels module with information about which icon to use for this field in Panels. Here's some example code, and an exercise where we'll look at the actual implementation:

```
/**
*Implementation of hook_field_info().
*/
function MYMODULE_field_info() {
  return array(
    'example_field' => array(
      'label' => t('example_field'),
      'description' => t('This field will store example data.'),
      'content_icon' => 'icon_example.png',
      ),
    );
}
```

## Exercise 5-2

### Examining the `hook_field` Functions

The `hook_field` functions are fairly long and detailed. In this exercise we look briefly at `hook_field_info` in the Text module.

1. Open the `Text.module` file located under `/sites/all/modules/cck/modules/text` using your favorite text editor.

2. Scroll down to find `hook_field_info`. It should look something like this:

```
/**
 * Implementation of hook_field_info().
 */
function text_field_info() {
  return array(
    'text' => array(
      'label' => t('Text'),
      'description' => t('Store text in the database.'),
      'content_icon' => 'icon_content_text.png',
    ),
  );
}
```

You can see how the function is named in accordance with the module name and which array of informational data it has to return.

Many of the remaining hooks discussed here can be found within the Text module. For the remainder of the chapter, we suggest keeping the `text.module` file open to compare the sample code with its implementation in a real situation.

The code for `hook_field_settings()` provides information to the Content module about which settings are available for this field type and how the settings should be handled in the Manage fields tab of the UI. The value for `$op` is the operation to be performed. The value for `$field` is the current field definition array. Possible values for the operation are as follows:

- `form` We are creating the field settings form. Construct the form elements needed to collect this field's settings.
- `validate` Check the submitted field settings form for errors.
- `save` Provide an array of the settings that this field uses and that should be saved in the field definition.
- `database columns` Declare one or more database columns that the Content module should create and manage on behalf of the field. If the field module wishes to handle its own database storage, this value should be omitted. The values

provided should be in the format used by the Schema API. An additional value for "sortable" is necessary to indicate whether this column is one that should provide a Sort field in Views. The value for "views" indicates whether this column should be exposed as a Views field. If the "views" value is not set and the field has more than one column, CCK exposes only the first column.

- views data Provide data to the Views module for this field. CCK fills in default values automatically, so you need to implement this value only if you want to override the $data array provided by CCK or if you are handling your own database storage.

Following is the default implementation of function hook_field_settings() that incorporates these values:

```
/**
* Implementation of hook_field_settings().
*/
function MYMODULE_field_settings($op, $field) {
  switch ($op) {
    case 'form':
      $form = array();
      $form['max_length'] = array(
        '#type' => 'textfield',
        '#title' => t('Maximum length'),
        '#default_value' => is_numeric($field['max_length']) ?
          $field['max_length'] : '',
        '#required' => FALSE,
        '#description' => t('The maximum length of the field.'),
      );
      return $form;

    case 'save':
      return array('max_length');

    case 'database columns':
      $columns['value'] = array(
        'type' => 'varchar',
        'length' => $field['max_length'],
        'not null' => FALSE,
        'sortable' => TRUE,
        'views' => TRUE);
      return $columns;

    case 'views data':
      $allowed_values = content_allowed_values($field);
          if (count($allowed_values)) {
```

```
        $data = content_views_field_views_data($field);
        $db_info = content_database_info($field);
        $table_alias = content_views_tablename($field);

    // Argument : swap the handler to the 'many to one' operator.
        $data[$table_alias][$field['field_name'].'_value']['argument'].
          ['handler'] = 'content_handler_argument_many_to_one';
        return $data;
      }
    }
}
```

The code in hook_field() defines the behavior of a field type. The value $field is
the complete $field definition array. The value $node is the populated node object.
The $items value contains the values for this field in this node. The value $op is the
operation being performed. Possible values for operation are as follows:

- load  The node is about to be loaded from the database. This hook should be used
  to load the field and should return an object containing extra values to be merged
  into the node object.

- validate  The user has just finished editing the node and is trying to preview or
  submit it. This hook can be used to check or even modify the node. Errors should
  be set with form_set_error().

- presave  The user has just finished editing the node and the node has passed validation. This hook can be used to modify the node.

- insert  The node is being created (inserted in the database).

- update  The node is being updated.

- delete  The node is being deleted.

- delete revision  The node revision is being deleted.

- sanitize  The node is being displayed, so you need to provide a "safe" value for
  the display.

- prepare translation  Used only by the Node Reference field. See the code in
  that module for an example.

The insert, update, delete, validate, and presave operations have no return
value. In most cases, only the validate and sanitize operations are relevant; the rest
have default implementations in content_field() that usually suffice. The odd-looking
handling for $error_field is needed to identify exactly where to set the error in
deeply nested elements. This value is passed into $element so that it will be available
during validation.

> **Note**
>
> Most of the field hooks correlate with related node hooks and are invoked every time the node hooks are invoked. The field's `load` operation, however, is not called on every `node_load()`. For performance reasons, the node and field values are loaded from `cache_content` rather than the database unless the node is being edited or the cache is empty. When the data is loaded from the cache, the field's `load` operation will not be triggered.

The code in `hook_field()` defines the behavior of a field type. The default implementation of this function is as follows:

```php
/**
 * Implementation of hook_field().
 */
function MYMODULE_field($op, &$node, $field, &$items, $teaser, $page) {
  switch ($op) {
    case 'validate':
      $allowed_values = content_allowed_values($field);
      if (is_array($items)) {
        foreach ($items as $delta => $item) {
          $error_element = isset($item['_error_element']) ?
            $item['_error_element'] : '';
          if (is_array($item) && isset($item['_error_element']))
            unset($item['_error_element']);
          if (!empty($item['value'])) {
            if (!empty($field['max_length'])
            && drupal_strlen($item['value']) > $field['max_length']) {
              form_set_error($error_element, t('The value is too long.'));
            }
          }
        }
      }
      return $items;

    case 'sanitize':
      foreach ($items as $delta => $item) {
        $text = check_plain($item['value']);
        $items[$delta]['safe'] = $text;
      }
  }
}
```

In the Text module, you will see that only `validate` and `sanitize` are defined. The handling of the other operations is left to the Content module.

The final required field hook, `hook_content_is_empty()`, helps CCK tell if the values in a field item should be considered to be empty. The Content module removes empty, nonrequired values before saving the data; it needs the information in this hook to determine whether that is safe to do. Following is the default implementation of `hook_content_is_empty()`:

```
/**
 * Implementation of hook_content_is_empty().
 */
function MYMODULE_content_is_empty($item, $field) {
  if (empty($item['value'])) {
    return TRUE;
  }
  return FALSE;
}
```

Within the Text module, this function checks whether the value is empty and the entire field is `$item`. If both are true, then the content is empty.

CCK also provides integration with the Devel Generate module to create dummy data for its fields using `hook_content_generate()`. This functionality is useful to create data in a site that is under construction while you are setting up views and adjusting the theme. If you would like to generate dummy data for your custom field module, implement the following code, using helper functions in the Content module and the Devel Generate module to create dummy data for either single or multiple value fields (see the code in the file `content_devel.inc` for more examples):

```
function MYMODULE_content_generate($node, $field) {
  if (content_handle('widget', 'multiple values', $field) ==
        CONTENT_HANDLE_MODULE) {
    return content_devel_multiple('_MYMODULE_content_generate', $node,
     $field);
  }
  else {
    return _MYMODULE_content_generate($node, $field);
  }
}

function _MYMODULE_content_generate($node, $field) {
  $node_field = array();
  // Generate a value that respects max_length.
  if (empty($field['max_length'])) {
    $field['max_length'] = 12;
  }
  $node_field['value'] = user_password($field['max_length']);
  return $node_field;
}
```

This code is not present within the Text module. Instead, it is most often used on development sites when you have a need to create content but don't want to spend the time adding content. With these hooks and Devel's add-ons via its Generate module, Drupal will automatically create this code for you.

# Widget Type Modules

Modules that define widget types need to implement three hooks: `hook_widget_info()`, `hook_widget_settings()`, and `hook_widget()`. Many of the CCK fields also implement `hook_elements()` for their widgets so as to create reusable elements, and then build them out fully in `#process`, but that's not required. We'll omit this step in our simple example and skip the use of `hook_elements()`, instead creating the full element directly in `hook_widget()`.

In `hook_widget_info()`, we define a name for the widget, specify which fields this widget should be used with, and indicate whether this module or CCK will handle multiple values and the default value.

In earlier versions of CCK, widgets had to test whether a field contained multiple values and provide a multiple-value widget with the proper number of values. This requirement has changed in Drupal 6. Now the Content module handles this task; it asks the widget for one item at a time and builds out multiple values when needed. This approach greatly simplifies the code the widget module must create, although there may be times when this behavior is not desired. A module that prefers to handle this task differently can indicate in `hook_widget_info()` that it will provide its own complete multiple-value element instead.

The following settings may be used with multiple values:

- CONTENT_HANDLE_CORE This module expects CCK to handle multiple values.
- CONTENT_HANDLE_MODULE This module will handle its own multiple values.

The following settings are available for default values:

- CONTENT_CALLBACK_DEFAULT This module expects CCK to handle the default value.
- CONTENT_CALLBACK_CUSTOM This module will handle the default value.
- CONTENT_CALLBACK_NONE This field does not use a default value.

These multiple-value and default-value settings can be omitted if the module intends to let the Content module handle all these values. They are included in the following example for clarity:

```
/**
 * Implementation of hook_widget_info().
 */
function MYMODULE_widget_info() {
```

```
  return array(
    'example_widget' => array(
      'label' => t('Example widget'),
      'field types' => array('example_field'),
      'multiple values' => CONTENT_HANDLE_CORE,
      'callbacks' => array(
        'default value' => CONTENT_CALLBACK_DEFAULT,
      ),
    ),
  );
}
```

Once again, follow along in the `text.module` file. The Text module's implementation of `hook_widget_info()` defines two options for a Text field: text field and text field (multiple rows).

Widgets also need to implement `hook_widget_settings()`. This hook provides information to the Content module about which settings are available for this widget and how the settings should be handled in the Manage fields tab of the UI. The value for `$op` is the operation to be performed. The value for `$widget` is the current field definition array. Possible values for the operation are as follows:

- `form` We are creating the widget settings form in the UI; provide a form element.
- `validate` We are validating the widget settings; check them for errors.
- `save` Provide an array of the settings this widget uses that should be saved in the field definition.

The following code snippet is a sample implementation of `hook_widget_settings()`:

```
/**
 * Implementation of hook_widget_settings().
 */
function MYMODULE_widget_settings($op, $widget) {
  switch ($op) {
    case 'form':
      $form = array();
      $form['rows'] = array(
        '#type' => 'textfield',
        '#title' => t('Rows'),
        '#default_value' => is_numeric($widget['rows']) ?
          $widget['rows'] : 5,
        '#required' => TRUE,
      );
      return $form;
```

```
    case 'validate':
      if (!is_numeric($widget['rows'])
        || intval($widget['rows']) != $widget['rows']
        || $widget['rows'] <= 0) {
        form_set_error('rows', t('"Rows" must be a positive integer.'));
      }
      break;

    case 'save':
      return array('rows');
  }
}
```

Our hook_widget() receives a reference to $form and $form_state, the $field array, an $items array that contains the values for this field in the current node, and $delta, to tell us which delta value of the form is being built.

The following is an example of a simple implementation of hook_widget() for a widget type that is allowing CCK to handle multiple values:

```
/**
 * Implementation of hook_widget().
 */
function MYMODULE_widget(&$form, &$form_state, $field, $items, $delta = 0) {
  $field_key   = $element['#columns'][0];
  $element[$field_key] = array(
    '#type' => 'textarea',
    '#title' => t($field['widget']['label']),
    '#description' => t($field['widget']['description']),
    '#required' => $element['#required'],
    '#default_value' => isset($items[$delta]) ? $items[$delta] : NULL,
    '#rows' => !empty($field['widget']['rows']) ?
      $field['widget']['rows'] : 1,
    '#weight' => 0,
  );
  return $element;
}
```

# Formatter Modules

CCK formatters define how the content of the field will be displayed in nodes and views. Every formatter identifies an array of one or more field types with which this formatter can be used. Most fields have several formatters available that you can choose. Every field should at least define a default formatter.

If you look at the user interface, you'll remember that formatters help determine if the field is hidden, is shown inline with its label or below, and so on.

The "view" operation (handled by the Content module) constructs the $node in such a way that you can use drupal_render() to display the formatted output for an individual field. The field values will be rendered into HTML only at the very last moment, retaining the raw data as long as possible in case other modules want to interact or intervene. Then, when the node has been prepared for viewing, the following function will render the whole field into its fully formatted display:

```
print drupal_render($node->field_foo);
```

The code now supports both single-value formatters, which theme an individual item value, as has been done in previous versions of CCK, and multiple-value formatters, which theme all values for the field using a single theme. The multiple-value formatters could be used, for instance, to plot field values on a single map or to display them in a graph. None of the core CCK modules provide multiple-value formatters; the capability is offered so that contributed modules can use it if needed.

Single-value formatters are the default; multiple-value formatters can be designated as such in formatter_info():

- CONTENT_HANDLE_CORE This is a single-value formatter that will be handled by CCK.
- CONTENT_HANDLE_MODULE This is a multiple-value formatter that will be handled by the module.

You identify formatter information in hook_formatter_info().

```
/**
 * Implementation of hook_field_formatter_info().
 */
function MYMODULE_field_formatter_info() {
  return array(
    'default' => array(
      'label' => t('Default'),
      'field types' => array('example_field'),
      'multiple values' => CONTENT_HANDLE_CORE,
    ),
    'plain' => array(
      'label' => t('Plain text'),
      'field types' => array('example_field'),
      'multiple values' => CONTENT_HANDLE_CORE,
    ),
  );
}
```

When you look at the text.module's example, you will see that it uses three formatters: default, plain text, and trimmed. Each of these should be familiar if you have tried out the formatters in the UI or have tried changing how body fields are displayed (because they also can be trimmed).

If you use a single-value formatter, the resulting formatted value of the field in the node content array will look like this:

```
$node->content['field_foo'] = array(
  '#type' => 'content_field_view',
  '#title' => 'label'
  '#field_name' => 'field_name',
  '#node' => $node,
  'items' =>
    0 => array(
      '#theme' => $theme,
      '#field_name' => 'field_name',
      '#type_name' => $node->type,
      '#formatter' => $formatter_name,
      '#item' => $items[0],
      '#delta' => 0,
    ),
    1 => array(
      '#theme' => $theme,
      '#field_name' => 'field_name',
      '#type_name' => $node->type,
      '#formatter' => $formatter_name,
      '#item' => $items[1],
      '#delta' => 1,
    ),
  ),
);
```

If you use a multiple-value formatter, the formatted value of the field in the node content array will look like this:

```
$node->content['field_foo'] = array(
  '#type' => 'content_field_view',
  '#title' => 'label'
  '#field_name' => 'field_name',
  '#node' => $node,
  'items' => array(
    '#theme' => $theme,
    '#field_name' => 'field_name',
    '#type_name' => $node->type,
    '#formatter' => $formatter_name,
    0 => array(
      '#item' => $items[0],
```

```
        '#delta' => 0,
      ),
      1 => array(
        '#item' => $items[1],
        '#delta' => 1,
      ),
    ),
  );
```

Because the formatter is creating theme elements, your module must declare
hook_theme() for each formatter you create. CCK expects a theme name such as
[*MODULE NAME*]_formatter_[*FORMATTER NAME*], which will receive a single
argument—that is, an element of formatter values. A single-value formatter will
receive the appropriate delta subitem from the field's value in the node content
array. A multiple-value formatter will receive the whole "items" subarray for that field.

In text.module, you can see the multiple implementations of these hooks,
giving each one its own theming function: theme_text_formatter_default,
theme_text_formatter_plain, and theme_text_formatter_trimmed.

Note that it is important—and the responsibility of the formatter—to return "safe"
values rather than raw values for display. The default implementation of hook_theme()
is included here for clarity:

```
/**
* Implementation of hook_theme().
*/
function MYMODULE_theme() {
  return array(
    'MYMODULE_formatter_default' => array(
      'arguments' => array('element' => NULL),
    ),
    'MYMODULE_formatter_plain' => array(
      'arguments' => array('element' => NULL),
    ),
  );
}


/**
* Theme function for 'default' field formatter.
*/
function theme_MYMODULE_formatter_default($element) {
  $element['#item']['safe'];
}


/**
* Theme function for 'plain' field formatter.
```

```
*/
function theme_MYMODULE_formatter_plain($element) {
  return strip_tags($element['#item']['safe']);
}
```

# Creating Field Instances Using Content Copy

You can use existing field types, widget types, and formatters—either those provided by CCK and other modules or that that you create in your own custom module—as the basis for programmatically creating field instances. You might do so to add a specific collection of fields to a content type to make it easier to set up new installations or replicate functionality between one site and another.

A good way to understand the internal structure of CCK fields is to install the Content Copy module that comes with CCK and use it to export a field. You can study that export to see how the field looks to CCK. When you create new field instances, you need to mimic this array. In fact, a really simple method of creating a field without any programming is to create a content type with its fields set up the way you want them, and then use Content Copy to export the definition.

You have two options when importing a Content Copy export. You can create a new content type and import the new type with all the fields, or you can import fields into an existing content type. Thus you can either copy selected fields from one content type to another on the same site or create a content type with all its fields on a new site. You can also use a Content Copy export in installation profiles using the Install Profile API module.

# Creating Field Instances with the CRUD API

Many times Content Copy isn't sufficient for tailoring your site, however. Perhaps you want to create a custom set of field instances and give them some very specific settings and values. To do so, you can use CCK's CRUD (Create, Read, Update, Delete) API.

The $info array passed to content_field_instance_create() should include basic settings to create the field, input either in the field => widget format used by the content module or as an array of form values. The function will add the field instance to the database, create tables to hold the field values, and return the complete, fully structured $field array.

At a minimum, the following settings must be provided in the input array:

- field_name The name of the field to be created.
- type_name The content type of the instance to be created.

If you don't provide any other field settings and a prior instance of this field exists in some other content type, you are creating a shared field; the other settings in the field will then be completed using settings from the other instance. If there is no prior instance to create this from, you need to provide more information. At a minimum, you must provide the following settings:

- `type` The type of field to create.
- `widget_type` The type of widget to use.

For the most reliable results, go ahead and provide additional settings for the field. Any settings specifically set for the `$info` array will override values that might be imputed from another instance.

You can then create a new field instance with `content_field_instance_create()`. The CRUD functions are found in the file `content.crud.inc`, which needs to be included whenever you use it. The following code will create a basic Text field and add it to the Story content type:

```php
<?php
$info = array (
  'field_name' => 'field_text',
  'type_name' => 'story',
  'type' => 'text',
  'label' => 'Text',
  'widget_type' => 'text_textfield',
);
module_load_include('inc', 'content', 'includes/content.crud');
$field = content_field_instance_create($info);
?>
```

The following code illustrates some of the many settings that can be controlled and shows that the input values can appear in the nested field array used throughout CCK. This code creates a complex Text field with allowed values and a default value and adds it to the Story content type:

```php
<?php
$info = array (
  'field_name' => 'field_text',
  'type_name' => 'story',
  'type' => 'text',
  'required' => '0',
  'multiple' => '0',
  'locked' => '0',
  'text_processing' => '0',
  'max_length' => '2',
  'allowed_values' => 'IL|Illinois
IA|Iowa
IN|Indiana
ID|Idaho',
```

```
      'widget' =>
        array (
          'default_value' =>
            array (
              0 =>
              array (
                'value' => 'IL',
              ),
            ),
          'label' => 'Text',
          'weight' => '-3',
          'description' => 'Please fill this in.',
          'type' => 'optionwidgets_select',
        ),
      'display_settings' =>
        array (
          'label' =>
          array (
            'format' => 'above',
            'exclude' => 0,
          ),
          'teaser' =>
          array (
            'format' => 'default',
            'exclude' => 0,
          ),
          'full' =>
          array (
            'format' => 'default',
            'exclude' => 0,
          ),
        ),
);
module_load_include('inc', 'content', 'includes/content.crud');
$field = content_field_instance_create($info);
?>
```

If you tried out Content Copy, you will see that the export from Content Copy looks like the preceding array. In fact, one easy way to create new fields with the API is to export a similar existing field and then adapt the values to make whatever changes are needed.

You may also notice a value in the preceding code that you won't see in the CCK UI—namely, the value called `locked`. Modules that create fields using the API can set locked to "1" to ensure that the field values are not changed. Locked fields will not show up in the UI, so there is no way users can alter or remove them. This approach is appropriate when modules should provide fields with specific settings that should not be altered.

In addition to creating field instances, you can use the CRUD API to read, update, and delete field instances. In these cases, an existing field instance is available; we just need to retrieve it. You would start with `content_field_instance_read()` to retrieve a field instance. This requires only two values to pull up a specific instance—the field name and the content type name:

```php
<?php
module_load_include('inc', 'content', 'includes/content.crud');
$info = array(
  'field_name' => 'field_text',
  'type_name' => 'story',
);
$instances = content_field_instance_read($info);
?>
```

This function is very flexible. It will accept any field settings key/value pairs in the `$param` array and will return an array of all instances that match the submitted criteria. Thus you can use it to find all instances of a single shared field name, or all field instances on a particular content type, or all field instances that are required or multiple, or whatever.

You can then edit or delete the instances with `content_field_instance_update()` or `content_field_instance_delete()`, respectively. For instance, the following snippet would find all field instances on the Story content type and set them to not be required:

```php
<?php
module_load_include('inc', 'content', 'includes/content.crud');
$info = array(
  'type_name' => 'story',
);
$instances = content_field_instance_read($info);
foreach ($instances as $instance) {
  $instance['required'] = FALSE;
  content_field_instance_update($instance);
}
?>
```

The most important thing to note when using the API to alter field instances is that changing some field settings may affect the way data is stored; thus changing these settings could alter or destroy data. For instance, deleting one of two instances of a shared field will change the field into a nonshared field, and will delete the separate shared field table and move the data back into the content type table. Changing multiple values for a field could cause it to require (or no longer require) a separate database table. You will want to be sure that good backups are available whenever you make these kinds of changes; also, make sure you test your changes carefully to confirm that they don't have any unexpected consequences.

# Creating Data for CCK Fields

Once your content type and all its field instances are defined, you can programmatically create or edit nodes to add or update the field data.

One method of injecting data into nodes would be to directly update the database with the desired values. This approach is not recommended for a number of reasons. First, CCK may not be storing data in the table you expect to use. Thus you need to understand how CCK stores data to be sure you are updating the right table correctly.

Second, with this technique, you bypass all the Drupal hooks that normally fire when nodes are created or edited. CCK fields do some of their processing in these hooks, but other modules may try to make other changes during that step. Unless you have a very good understanding of what all the modules on your site are doing during normal processing, bypassing that processing is not recommended. Your nodes will still load normally after a change is made, but when you begin the editing process, you will be presented with the opportunity to add information to any fields you have created.

Another thing to note is that CCK caches the node data. This operation differs from the regular Drupal page cache, which caches content only for anonymous users. The CCK cache is used for all users, even when normal page caching is turned off. The process of creating complex content types and allowing all of the field modules to interact with them is a very expensive process, so it is done only when nodes are created or edited. At that point, the values are stored in `cache_content`.

When you use `node_load()`, the node is retrieved from the cache; it is not re-created from the database. Thus, if you alter the value in the database, you must be sure that you also destroy the cached values. Otherwise, the next `node_load()` operation will bring up the original values rather than your updated values. If that node is then saved, it will write the original values back into the database—and you will lose all of your work.

The two recommended ways to alter data in Drupal are via `drupal_execute()` and `node_save()`. Forms in Drupal are structured arrays of data that are passed through the Form API (FAPI). The `drupal_execute()` function is designed to accept an array of values that is constructed exactly the way the form would be constructed and to automatically submit it to save the values. Nodes in Drupal are structured objects that contain the node's data. The `node_save()` function is designed to accept an object that is constructed in the expected way and to save its data.

When forms are submitted, one set of Drupal hooks is fired: the `hook_form` validation and submission hooks. These hooks allow other modules to interact with the form data. When `node_save()` fires, a different set of hooks is triggered—the `nodeapi` hooks—to interact with the data. Many times the end result will be the same either way, but things can happen differently even when the same data is passed through `drupal_execute()` and through `node_save()`.

The original rationale for using `drupal_execute()` was that the form submission process includes a validation step that doesn't happen during `node_save()`; thus you could use `drupal_execute()` to do validation on the data. However, at the time this chapter was written, there was a core bug in Drupal's FAPI processing that interferes with validation. If you process more than one form programmatically in the same session, the operation doesn't always work as intended because of this bug. If validation is skipped, anything else that should have happened during validation will not happen. For instance, the Date module manipulates date fields from the widget format back to the field format during validation; if validation is skipped, the data is corrupted or missing.

Another problem with using `drupal_execute()` is that you must know exactly how the form is structured. If you are working with deeply nested form elements, which happens with many complex CCK fields, it can be difficult to figure out exactly which format to use. Also, the data must be in the format expected by the widget, not the format used to store the data in the field. As a consequence, complicated widgets like Optionwidgets, which manipulate the data to get it from the field to the form, can have a very unexpected structure in the form.

Because of numerous potential problems in getting `drupal_execute()` to work reliably for complex elements, it is generally best to use `node_save()` instead. If you are passing in data that might not be valid, you will have to clean up the data first, because this method does not perform any validation (although, as noted earlier, because of a core bug there may not be any validation with the other method either).

The format of the node with `node_save()` is much simpler than with `drupal_execute()`. For `node_save()`, you should provide values in the format in which they are stored in the database, not the format used in the form. This format is much more predictable. Each field will have a structure similar to the following array—a structure that does not vary depending on which widget is used:

```php
<?php
array('field_my_field' => array(
    0 => array(
      'value' => 999,
      ),
    1 => array(
      'value' => 999,
    ),
  ),
);
?>
```

You can easily see the structure of the node by creating a node in the UI and then displaying it using `print_r()` or some similar PHP function. You then just need to replicate that structure and send that value to `node_save()`. Similarly, to edit existing nodes, you can use `node_load()` to retrieve the current data, edit the data, and then resave it using node_save(). In earlier versions of CCK, it was sometimes necessary to do a node_submit() operation first, followed by a node_save() operation, to allow some fields to do preprocessing and postprocessing. The Drupal 6 version of CCK handles forms differently, however, and that extra step is no longer required.

# Miscellaneous Helper Functions

Several helper functions in CCK will likely prove very useful in your custom programming. Some of them are discussed in this section.

Use content_format() to format content using a specific formatter. In this function, $field is the field settings array, $item is a single item from the node (for single-value formatters) or an array of all items (for multiple-value formatters), and $node is the node object:

```php
<?php
$node = node_load(99);
$item = $node->field_text[0];
print content_format($field, $item, [FORMATTER NAME], $node);
?>
```

Use content_fields() to retrieve field settings:

```php
<?php
// Retrieve the field settings for all fields
$fields = content_fields();

// Retrieve the field settings for one field, field_text.
$field = content_fields('field_text');

// Retrieve the field settings for the specific instance of
// field_text used in the story content type.
content_fields('field_text', 'story')
?>
```

Use content_database_info() to retrieve information about how and where the field is stored in the database. This data is important, in particular, if you want to know which table the field data is stored in, because the actual table can change if the field is shared or unshared or if the multiple value changes:

```php
<?php
$db_info = content_database_info($field);
$db_table = $db_info['table'];
$db_columns = $db_info['columns'];
?>
```

Use content_clear_type_cache() to clear caches if the field settings change. The CRUD API performs this step automatically, but you may need to use this function if you change things programmatically in other ways.

The function content_write_record() is a CCK-safe version of drupal_write_record(), used because drupal_write_record() will not update the NULL values used in CCK for empty fields.

Use hook_content_build_modes() to let CCK know if other form elements need to be added to the Manage fields tab. Any form elements on this page are available to be rearranged using the drag-and-drop technique. You can see examples of the way that CCK provides these hooks for some of the core modules in functions such as node_content_build_modes() and search_content_build_modes().

## Summary

CCK brings a large number of possibilities for Web site development to the table. With the extensions available through the many modules that have been created by the Drupal community, many people may not ever have a need to create their own fields with other modules. With the strength of CCK's API, however, anything is possible. It's just a matter of understanding how the data is structured internally and how content interacts with Drupal core functionality.

# II

# Views

The Views module is a powerful query builder designed to simplify the task of building custom query displays. It accomplishes this feat by providing lists of all table and field information that it knows of and lets the user assemble items from these lists together. After a complete rewrite for Drupal 6, Views has a brand new interface with more options than ever before. With the addition of a live preview and query display, site builders can nail down their displays in a way that was previously impossible to do without making changes that can affect all users.

# Relational Databases

Drupal relies on an SQL database to store information, and currently supports MySQL and PostgreSQL. Properly using Views requires an understanding of how the database stores data, how the data is related across various tables, and how Drupal works with the database to retrieve data.

This chapter is directed toward newer users and programmers. It covers some of the basics of relational databases: how data is stored, how it goes in, how it comes out, and how pieces are related to each other—most specifically as they relate to using Views later on.

## Drupal, SQL, and the Emergence of Views

Drupal, out of the box, requires a database for everything it does. Drupal supports the use of MySQL or PostgreSQL as an install-ready database. Other databases may work based on drivers developed by members of the community.

### Pronouncing SQL

SQL is an acronym for Structured Query Language. It is properly pronounced as the letters spelled out—that is, "S-Q-L." When people say the word "sequel" they are typically referring to another, unrelated database product. That product is primarily a relic of history, however, and it is often much easier to say the word "sequel." At this point, only database purists really care about the pronunciation one way or the other. MySQL is referred to as "My S-Q-L" or "My Sequel," and you will often hear PostgreSQL referred to as just "Postgres."

Being able to create customized output of database tables once required huge amounts of manual work, which would then be hard-coded into pages. This became a huge maintenance task for sites that needed minor changes. It also required that anyone developing a Web site have experience with writing extensive SQL queries for any type of complex work to show relationships between separate tables. Users looking for a content management system (CMS) that was easily configurable found this approach awkward and unfriendly—another topic that added to the Drupal "learning cliff."

### The Drupal "Learning Cliff"

Over its various iterations, Drupal has made significant changes in its user experience and accessibility. What started as a bulletin board for a group of college students in a dorm is now used by hundreds of thousands of people who don't know each other, or know how to get help.

Because of the flexibility and modularity of the system, new users can sometimes have trouble finding the places they need to go in the system to do what they want. This has frustrated newcomers, especially ones without a strong background in SQL or PHP. What we usually hear called a "learning curve" became known as a "learning cliff"— steep, difficult to traverse, and time consuming. Once people got used to the system, though, suddenly they could fly through setup and configuration.

Views was a major step toward making life easier for new Drupal users. In its current iteration, Views provides a badly needed intermediate step between hand-building queries and having no customized queries at all. Views takes SQL statements and hides them behind a clickable UI that makes it easy to choose particular fields for display. It provides a preview of the query (Figure 6-1) so that users familiar with SQL can see exactly what the query is doing, and then further customize it for performance or other needs unique to their installation.

```
Query   SELECT node.nid AS nid,
            node.title AS node_title,
            users.name AS users_name,
            users.uid AS users_uid,
            node.changed AS node_changed
        FROM node node
        INNER JOIN users users ON node.uid = users.uid
        WHERE SUBSTR(node.title, 1, 1) = 'a'
            ORDER BY node_title ASC
```

Figure 6-1    A query preview provided by Views

The first version of Views was made available for Drupal 4.7. It was later ported to Drupal 5 when that version was released, and maintained through the subsequent point releases of version 5. During the Drupal 6 development cycle, major changes were made to the Drupal core API. These changes, combined with the significant lessons in stability and design that were learned through the development of the first version of Views, created a tough question: Should the developers port Views to Drupal 6 and leave the attendant design flaws, or should they rewrite the module entirely? Time constraints and the complexity of the module led to the latter choice, and Views 2 was born.

## The Basics of Relational Databases

The SQL language was designed to provide a common interface for relational databases, even if they do not have the same engine. It imposes a few definitions upon these systems that we can easily rely on.

## Rows and Fields

All relational databases are composed of one or more *tables*, each of which contains *rows* or *records* of data. Structurally, this resembles a spreadsheet or even a simple table or chart. For example, a table with information about "my cars" might contain information such as that shown in Table 6-1.

Table 6-1    **Table with Rows of My Cars**

| Primary Key | Make | Model | Year |
| --- | --- | --- | --- |
| 1 | Renault | Le Car | 1976 |
| 2 | Toyota | Celica | 1979 |
| 3 | Mitsubishi | Eclipse | 1993 |
| 4 | Jeep | Wrangler | 1997 |
| 5 | Honda | Accord | 2006 |

Each row of the table is made up of a group of *fields*. The definition of these fields is the same for every row, which is the key to what makes databases efficient for storing large amounts of data and retrieving it quickly. Each field has a data type, usually representing a variation on a numeric or string type, and each field has a maximum size of data it can hold. For integer types, this is usually the maximum value the field can hold. For strings, it is usually the maximum number of characters the field can hold.

Each field can be indexed. An *index* is a lookup table that makes it much faster to find and sort records on that field. Indexes can be compound, meaning that they add multiple fields together to get their result. This strategy is most often used to sort on multiple fields simultaneously, such as the make and model of a car, or when using a particular combination of sort criteria and filters at the same time.

Most indexes are named after the field they are based on. One field that is indexed is the "type" field within the "node" table. Figure 6-2 shows a section of the node table's data; the type clearly changes regularly from one node to the next, and an index makes looking data up on a specific content type go much more quickly.

## Keys

Most database tables rely on a *primary key* to ensure uniqueness for the record in a particular table. The primary key is often used to constrain queries by using that unique value to return a single record. Some examples of primary keys in Drupal are the uid (user ID), nid (node ID), vid (version ID), and tid (revision ID). Each of these keys will return a unique record in its respective primary table. Most of the time, primary keys are simply an incremented serial value, meaning that when a new record is inserted, its primary key is 1 + the last value inserted. Table 6-2 shows some of the data from Drupal's user table.

| nid | vid | type |
|-----|-----|------|
| 1 | 1 | story |
| 2 | 2 | story |
| 3 | 3 | book |
| 4 | 4 | story |
| 5 | 5 | beer_recipe |
| 9 | 9 | batch_brewed |
| 10 | 10 | batch_brewed |
| 11 | 11 | batch_brewed |
| 12 | 12 | t_shirts |
| 13 | 13 | beer_recipe |
| 14 | 14 | beer_recipe |

Figure 6-2    Data from the node table

Table 6-2    **User Information**

| User ID/uid (Primary) | Name | Mail |
|-----|-----|------|
| 0 | Anonymous | |
| 1 | administrator | admin@mysite.com |
| 2 | test user | test@mysite.com |

As an example, the Drupal user table uses uid as a primary key. Each user ID is unique to the table, enabling queries against the user table to return a single value for a particular user. This value can be used multiple times by other tables; the node table uses nid as a primary key, but a given uid can appear multiple times for each node created by that user.

A *foreign key* is a primary key from one table that another table uses to establish a *relationship* between records in the two tables. As we've noted previously, the node table uses nid as its primary key, but it also contains uid in each record. The user ID is a foreign key in the node table that refers to data in the user table. It allows the table "users" and the node table to be easily interrelated. The same is true for the node table and the revisions table. The node revision uses vid as a primary key, with nid as a foreign key to the node table. Table 6-3 shows some information from the node table, suggesting how one user ID can create multiple nodes while keeping a unique key for the table.

Table 6-3    **Partial Node Information**

| Node ID/nid (Primary) | Type | User ID/uid (Foreign) |
| --- | --- | --- |
| 1 | story | 1 |
| 2 | beer_recipe | 1 |
| 3 | t_shirts | 2 |

By establishing these relationships, it becomes possible to involve many different tables in a single query. Note that while most SQL databases support explicit declarations of foreign keys to preserve foreign key integrity, Drupal does not make use of this convention. All foreign key relationships are implied only.

# Filtering and Sorting

Two of the most critical functions an SQL query can perform are filtering and sorting. These functions place limits on the amount of data retrieved from the database and make the data easier to read by enforcing an order. Joins are another function that fit some where between filtering and sorting, and are imperative when the data you need is split among multiple tables.

## Filtering

The simplest query against a table will return every result in that table. While this result is sometimes what is wanted, more often some subset of the data is what is required. In other words, you typically want to filter the query. In SQL, filters are implemented through the use of the WHERE statement. WHERE is very simple: It returns rows from the selected table when a particular statement is true, where the statement uses Boolean logic to determine if a particular record matches. If you wanted to query the database for the user ID of a particular username, for example, you could use this query:

```
SELECT uid FROM users WHERE name = '<the username>'
```

In the preceding statement, the user name is the field, the = is the operator, and '<the username>' is the value. This comparison will fetch only the uid where the name is exactly what you have specified.

Filters are extremely useful and necessary to the use of nearly any database. As an example, they can be used to create a list of children's T-shirts or lists of ale versus lager recipes in our two Web site examples.

We'll talk more explicitly about how Views does this in Chapter 7.

## Sorting

Sorting is as important as filtering when you need to see data. Sorting enforces a specific order on the data gathered by a query. Two major types of sorting are performed: *ascending* and *descending*. Ascending order sorts on your key from lowest to highest value, whereas descending order sorts values from highest to lowest.

Numeric fields sort in the obvious manner: larger numbers are always higher. String fields sort a little bit differently, because they aren't numbers. Essentially, each character is turned into a number, where "a" = 10, "b" = 11, "z" = 35, and so on. The actual number used depends on the encoding. This issue matters because symbols may also be sorted, and each also has its own number. When comparing two values for sorting, the first letters are compared. If they are equal, the next two letters are compared. A missing letter will automatically have a lower value than a letter, so shorter phrases will appear before longer phrases. This has interesting effects on numbers when they are represented as strings, as the following ascending sort demonstrates:

```
1
10
2
25
Car
Carriage
Cars
```

As you can see, the numbers do not sort in the order you normally expect (10 does not normally appear before 2), because in this case the numbers are actually strings of text. It's also worth noting that in some databases, (particularly MySQL with the default setup), case is ignored; thus "C" and "c" are equivalent. However, other databases, such as PostgreSQL, consider lowercase values to be smaller than uppercase values.

## Joins

Joins are used to expand a query to include data from multiple tables, joining the tables on established relationships. Although multiple types of joins are possible, Drupal is concerned only with ones that relate data between two tables; it uses only *left joins* and *inner joins*.

The two join types are fairly similar. Given two tables A and B, when you use a left join, all data will be returned from table A, but table B will return NULL values where there is no match. When using an inner join, records will be returned only where there is a match in both tables.

You might use a left join when you wanted to find all nodes posted by a user, and wanted to display the username and node title. For example:

```
SELECT users.name, node.title FROM node LEFT JOIN users ON
node.uid=users.uid
```

This query will display the name of the author and title of every node in the database. If there happen to be nodes without a valid author, the users.name will display NULL, or no value. If the query were an inner join, nodes that do not have a valid author would simply not be returned.

Views will create a query based on what it determines to be the cleanest SQL. It tries to simplify the entire query so that the least amount of database usage time possible is required. However, Views also has to take into account the different uses many sites will put it to, not just "What does my particular site need right now?" Every developer should review the queries based on his or her own knowledge of the Web site under development.

## From SQL to Views to Human Language

Views hides much of the complexity of SQL queries behind its interface. The different groups of fields that Views provides have distinct ramifications for the SQL queries that are created to retrieve data from the Drupal database. Views uses terminology that attempts to bridge the gap between allowing experienced users to quickly understand which SQL statements are being used and allowing newer users to explore the interface without being completely overwhelmed.

In addition, the Views module gives you the ability to see your queries in real time and enables the person building that view to see the exact form the query is taking. As a consequence, you can clearly see what each change to your view is making to your query, which in turn enables you to potentially pinpoint errors and bottlenecks much more quickly. We'll look into this capability in more depth in the next few chapters as we discuss the parts of the user interface (UI).

Views uses three major sections of its UI to deal with building actual SQL queries: fields, sort criteria, and filters. Additionally, the relationships section is akin to explicitly adding a join statement to the query for specific purposes. These effectively create the SQL statements SELECT, ORDER BY, and WHERE. These sections correspond to basic concepts that new users should be able to understand easily. Users who have spent even a small amount of time configuring Drupal should be able to use the fields UI to choose data from different node types to display. By choosing just a few fields, the UI may turn those checks into a basic SELECT statement or a JOIN, depending on which fields are chosen.

For users with a limited understanding of SQL queries, the Views module can provide a cleaner and more easily understood method of retrieving data from the database. Experimentation with field selection, filtering, and other parts of the UI makes it easy for users to see how data is being retrieved, in which order it is being retrieved, and how each piece of data relates to the rest of the system. That said, to truly become an expert and use Views to its fullest potential, it is vital that you develop a good understanding of SQL.

## Summary

This chapter covered some of the basics of relational databases: how data is stored, how it goes in, how it comes out, and how pieces are related to each other. Specifically, tables and fields are used to store data and data is retrieved from rows of data. We also looked at how a collection of fields from various tables can be joined together through relationships that you've defined. Now that you have a better sense of what happens to your data in magical database land, the Views UI should feel easy and natural to use.

# 7

# Creating Views

In this chapter, we talk about the Views user interface (UI) and discover how each function works. We look at how each piece creates part of a query, and how the results of those queries fit into pages and blocks. We also discuss the most important filters you may need and explore how to create relationships between node content that does not otherwise share information. RSS, styles and fields, and the Views Bonus pack are other important topics when determining what you want out of your view.

## Views UI

The Views 2 UI is significantly different from the original Views UI. The rewrite for Drupal 6 allowed for a complete change of the Views control page, bringing the power of AJAX to the Views creation system. The new interface is cleaner, is packed with a large number of features, and gives a distinct clarity to each piece of functionality.

Users of the original versions of Views had to deal with arrows that moved parts of the page around, fields that looked like they might work together but really didn't, and overall an interface that just wasn't very clean. Moreover, when building a query, users really couldn't get a good idea of what the view would ultimately look like unless it was out where other users could see it publicly. This could lead to some ugly or confusing pages temporarily, until the view was completed. For the most part, Views represented a huge step forward over having to custom build your own queries all the time, but there was definitely significant room for improvement.

Several months were spent in the design of the Views 2 UI. The revised UI is compact and clean, allowing users to easily see exactly which part of the view is currently being worked on, which changes have been made, and, most importantly, what the finished view will look like.

When Views is installed, it creates a new menu item under Administer >> Site building >> Views. This menu item is the base Views page. The Views UI consists of four main pages: List, Add, Import, and Tools.

**Advanced Help**

If you don't have the Advanced Help module installed, now is a really good time to add it to your system. Views takes advantage of Advanced Help to give tips and suggestions throughout the UI. It creates a small pop-up window that contains information about the page you are working on, allowing you to keep the working page available. Look for small circle icons containing a question mark; each will take you to a specific topic in the help system.

Advanced Help is not required to use Views, but Views will provide warning notices if Advanced Help is not installed.

There are nearly limitless applications in the real world for Views. Any time you need a list, Views is there. In regard to the examples introduced in this book, you could use Views to create a list of the most recent recipes entered, the most recent batches brewed, shirts available in a particular size, and so on. If you add pictures of a glass of your homebrew, you could use Views to display only the batches for which you have uploaded pictures, and more.

## List

The landing page for Views is the List page. On this page is the list of default views provided with the module install. By default, all of these views are disabled, allowing the administrator to determine which views, if any, might be needed immediately. It also prevents new items from displaying on pages where they may not be expected; the frontpage view, for example, will override your front page. There is also a link to the Getting Started page. It is an example of Advanced Help, and will guide you through the creation of a simple view. Figure 7-1 is an example of what your default Views landing page should look like.

Once you have created views of your own, they will also be listed here in alphabetical order. This list can be modified through the group of drop-down menus found at the top of the list. These drop-downs consist of filters and sorts for the Views themselves.

The first row of list drop-downs are the filters. They filter out any Views that do not match the criteria given:

- Storage: Filters on whether the view is local and in your database (normal), whether default views are stored only in code (default), or whether both code and database are used for storage (overridden).
- Type: Different than the content type. This filter narrows down which sort of content pieces are contained in the view.
- Tag: Lists all tags that are available for currently available views.
- Displays: Lists which type of content sections views can be displayed in.

Figure 7-1    The Views List page

Two types of sorting criteria may be applied in Views. Sort by creates the list by a single particular piece of information about the view, while Order creates an ascending or descending list ordered by the rest of the drop-down choices.

Note that multiple filters as well as both sorting options can be used to change the list of views, narrowing down that list considerably. This makes a case for sites with large numbers of views in use to tag each view with keywords that make it easier to find; this approach allows the Tag filter to be used to minimize the initial returned list. Clicking the Apply button causes your sorts and filters to be executed, returning the list you requested.

The list of default views available is intended to simulate some of the most basic tasks a new Drupal site may need to accomplish. Each view gets a box of its own, displaying the pertinent information about that view. Each view can have many pieces of information, most of which can feed back into the filters.

The next thing to focus on in the Views list page is the title bar for one view. This darker bar contains four pieces of information. In italics is the storage level of the view—normal, default, or overridden. Next is the type of view, which is listed in a normal font and affects the Type drop-down menu. Third is the emphasized text, which is the actual view name. After that, in parentheses, is the tag that is used for that particular view. At the end of the bar is a group of links: Edit, Export, Clone, Delete. For a default view, only the Enable link will be available until the view is enabled. For views that you create, all four links are present at all times. You cannot currently disable a view that you have created.

Inside the box itself are up to four more pertinent Views clues to serve as differentiators for each view. The left column may show the Title, Path, and Display, assuming they have been configured for that view. Title is the human-readable name, much like the Display Name for a field. Path defines the Drupal-specific URL that would take you to a page that displays this information. In italics is the display type, which may contain block, feed, page, or date browser. On the right side of the box is a short description of the purpose of the view or its functionality. This area may also provide prerequisite information on which modules need to be enabled to provide the view with data.

## Add

The Add pages are where all of your view definition takes place. This self-contained, multi-step process keeps the majority of your work on the same page so that you can easily see which parts of the view definition you have changed. The Views UI gives clues as to what has or has not been changed in the display. In the default display for a given view, when a change is made, the changed setting is highlighted and shown in boldface until the changes are saved. Note that if any of the form settings are open for editing in the view, the save button for the overall view will be disabled until the edit itself is saved or cancelled. These pages are also where all of your edits for an existing view will take place.

More clues come at the end of the submenu bar, which contains an italicized note stating whether this is a new or a changed view. This message persists until the changes are saved. The submenu bar is explicit, telling you exactly which view and display type you are editing. At the end of the bar are links to export the view, to clone the view, and, if you are editing, to look at the page in which the view will appear. Exporting a view will give you the code to import the view into another installation. Cloning a view is useful for experimentation. For example, you might want to try some different settings on a view; cloning will let you do that while leaving your original view intact. Cloning also gives you a base to work with if you want to create multiple similar views. For instance, you may have a view of recent comments but also want a view with recent comments for a particular node type. You might clone the recent comments view rather than re-creating it.

# Exercise 7-1

### Enabling and Changing the Default View

In this exercise, we'll enable a default view and make a small change to become familiar with the Edit page.

1. Navigate to Administer >> Site building >> Views.

2. Scroll down to the Glossary view.

3. Click the Enable link on the right side of the title bar.

   It will take a moment for the view to become enabled. When it does, the page will refresh and the view will move up in the list and into the enabled views, which are sorted alphabetically by default.

4. Click the Edit link next to the view (Figure 7-2).

Figure 7-2    Edit: one of the available options for an enabled view

5. Under the "View Settings" box, click the word "default" next to "Tag."

6. Scroll down the page to the "View details" box (Figure 7-3) and change the word "default" to anything else. You can change the tag or remove it all together.

Figure 7-3    Changing the tag for the view

7.  Click the update button.

Your change has not yet become permanent; Views allows you to make multiple edits before saving the view. It will let you know that you've made changes. Figure 7-4 shows you what your submenu may look like after you have updated but not yet saved the changes to the view.

Edit view *glossary*      List    Add    **Edit**    Import    Tools

View *glossary*, displaying items of type Node.   Export      Clone      View "Page"      *New view*

Figure 7-4    Changing the tag for a default view turns it into a new view

You can scroll down to the bottom of the page for a look at the preview; we'll discuss this feature later in the chapter.

8.  Click the Cancel button at the bottom of the edit section. We don't actually want to change the tag.

When you add a display type, all settings appear in a lighter, italicized font until changes are made. If a change is made to a setting so that it differs from the default, that setting will then appear in a normal-weight, non-italicized font. This system enables you to quickly identify exactly which parts of the view have been modified. The "gear" icons indicate styling options are available for that setting. Some boxes for settings have a plus sign (+) in the box title bar (as seen in Figure 7-5); clicking it automatically opens a corresponding add menu that allows you to select and configure a new option for that set of configuration options. For example, click the plus sign next in the Filters title bar to add a new filter to your view. In the same title box, a small up/down arrow icon will appear when two or more options are available in that section. Click this icon to rearrange the items within that group of settings.

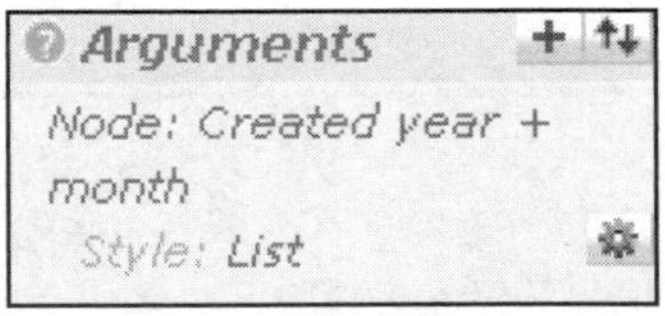

*Arguments*      + ↑↓
*Node: Created year +
month*
  *Style: List*                ✳

Figure 7-5    Icons used to add, rearrange, and configure parts of a view

## Views Add Creation Page

The Views Add creation page is the first page you encounter when you are creating a new view. It requires two pieces of information, view name and view type, and suggests two others, view description and view tag. The view name can be a combination of alphanumeric characters and underscores; names should use all lowercase letters for consistency. The view description is a text field where you should enter a sentence or two to describe the purpose of the view. A view tag is useful for grouping or separating your views if you are using them for specific topics or purposes. Finally, each view must have a type that determines which content it will look at to create the view. The type determines the primary table that Views will access for data.

Here are the types of views:

- Node: Node views are likely to be the most common type of view on a site. The node type creates lists of any node content.
- Comment: Comment lists can be retrieved from nodes, but there may be times when you want only comment information. The view may be faster, but there is a tradeoff in security.
- File: File limits views to information about uploaded files. It is useful for seeing which files are taking up space in your installation.
- Node revision: This limits the view to revision information—useful for determining which users are making changes, and which changes are being made.
- Term: Use this view type with taxonomy; it helps to create lists of taxonomy terms.
- User. This type breaks down user information and helps with showing which users have accounts, and what they are doing.
- Access log: This view can show what your users are accessing, and what they are having trouble accessing. An access log view can help filter down the log so it becomes easier to spot site problems.

Once a view is created, the type of view cannot be changed. If the basic definition is not correct for your needs, the view will have to be re-created. Choosing a particular type means that only certain filters, fields, and other Views functionality will be available once that type is chosen. Figure 7-6 shows the form used to create a new view.

## Left-Side Tabs

Along the left side of the UI is a group of tabs (or drawers). These tabs show which displays the view currently has configured and give you the ability to add new displays. A *display* is a place or way the view may be shown to users of the Web site. All views have a default display. The default display contains the initial and any edited settings for that view. The default display is not actually used anywhere within Drupal itself—something that may confuse new users. It simply is a container, the initial state of the view.

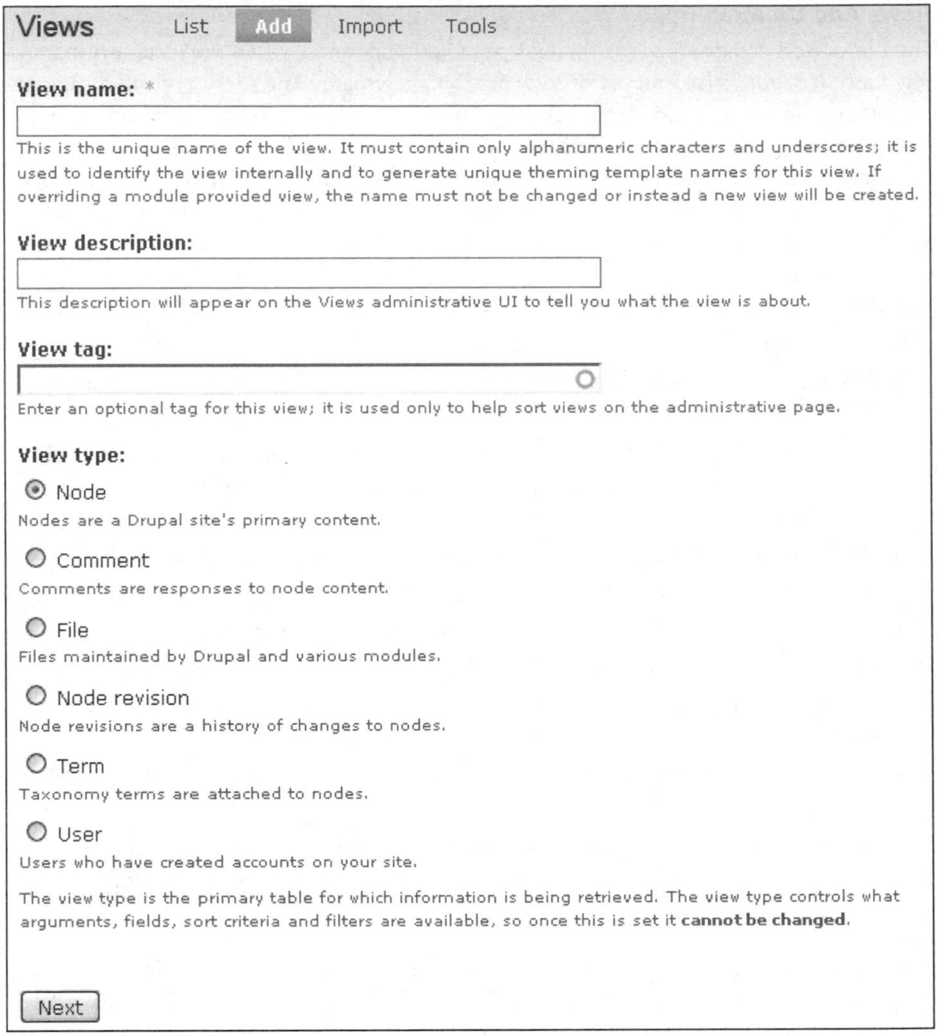

Figure 7-6    Creating a new view

Four display types are used for actual visual placement:

- Page: Displays the view as an entire page complete with a menu and URL.
- Feed: Helps set up the format for an RSS feed.
- Block: Creates a view that will be placed within a block.
- Attachment: Helps to add a view to another view.

The first tab will be the default setting for the view; if you are not sure which display you are editing, the main window will provide this information. Figure 7-7 shows an

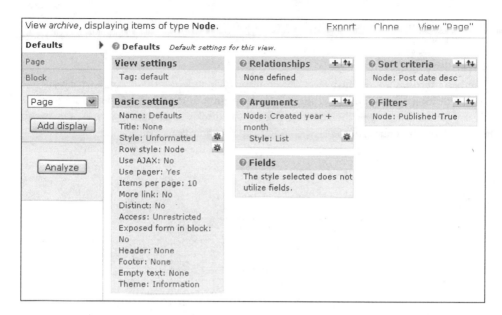

Figure 7-7    The default display for the archive view

example of one of the views included with the Views module. It has been edited; yours may not look exactly the same.

New displays are created by using the drop-down menu and can be an attachment, block, feed, or page. Adding a display allows you to refine the view for that type of display. For example, you may wish to use a view within a block; you could create a display setting specifically to format for a block. You could then create a page display and use the same view, but format it differently to take advantage of the greater space allotted to a page. Choose a display type you want to add, and click the "Add display" button.

The last drawer is the Analyze button. At this time Analyze has only a minor level of functionality, but like the rest of Drupal, it is very pluggable and can be expanded by those developers who wish to do so. Its purpose is to do a low level of error checking on your view to see if anything is obviously wrong. The Analyze feature was originally added to ensure that a view has content that will display. Some members of the Drupal community suggested that a view should contain a filter that required the content being displayed to be published. There are reasons why this approach is not necessarily a good idea, so the filter is not present. Analyze will notice when you have not set a filter that displays some amount of data and warn you of this potential problem.

## View Settings

View settings is the first box in the first column of the main display. It appears only in the default view settings, as it is pertinent to the entire view for all display types. This box contains the Tag field, which can be edited to add or remove tags even after the view is being used. To change the tag, click on the tag itself—this will allow you to change both the tag and the description of the view.

### Basic Settings

The basic settings are the first level of definitions. They define the core of what your view will look like, and may occasionally have slightly different effects depending on the display type. Notice the italicized lettering for the display in Figure 7-8. Most settings for a display will be italicized unless you modify this default behavior.

Name is the name for this particular display. Only the administrative interface sees this name.

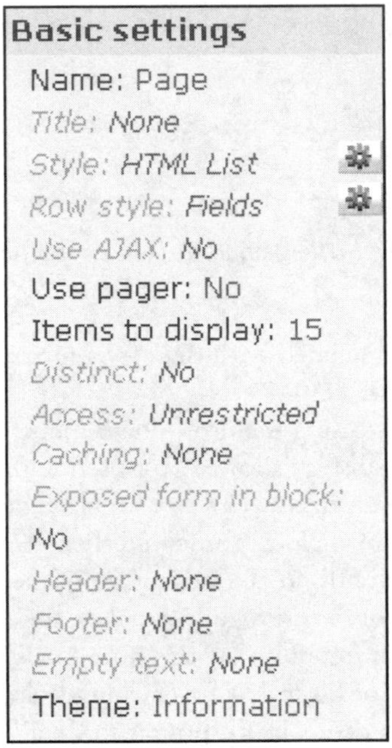

**Basic settings**

Name: Page
*Title: None*
*Style: HTML List*  ✳
*Row style: Fields*  ✳
*Use AJAX: No*
Use pager: No
Items to display: 15
*Distinct: No*
*Access: Unrestricted*
*Caching: None*
*Exposed form in block:*
*No*
*Header: None*
*Footer: None*
*Empty text: None*
Theme: Information

Figure 7-8    Basic settings box for a page display

Title is the displayed title of the view itself and will show wherever the view is. It will be the block title in a block view, or the title of the page if the view is an entire page. You may leave it as "Title" for a default view, but you may want to name it if it is a display, or if you are using a cloned view and the title will be the same wherever it is used on the site.

Style determines how the view itself will actually appear; it does not affect the rest of the page. Your view can be shown in a grid, list, table, or unformatted. Any style other than unformatted will be associated with further settings that customize that style; these options are reached by changing the style or by using the gear icon. Choosing a style determines the look of the view. Each style can be formatted in different ways, from completely unformatted, to a basic list to a neatly stacked grid. Each style type has the ability to group the output by one of the fields that are being displayed; if the post date is in the view, grouping by that date will gather all content added on the same day into one group. Also note that for styles (and for row styles), you can change the look by using template files to specify exactly what you want—more on that topic when we talk about theming in Chapter 9.

The grid style allows you to choose a number of columns that will appear on the view. You may choose to align your view horizontally (top left to bottom right) or vertically (column A from top to bottom, column B from top to bottom).

Lists can be either ordered or unordered. Ordered lists will number the view results. An unordered list provides output similar to the unformatted style. It is significantly cleaner and easier to read than an unformatted view, however, thanks to the bullets that appear next to each entry returned.

Tables are the most complex output format. The table display is clean and easily understandable by most users. By default, each column in a table display contains one field. Columns can be changed to use multiple fields if this formatting is desired. In the style options (which become available when you click the gear icon), choose a field. In the Column drop-down menu next to that field is a list of all other fields available—assuming you have already added fields. Change the drop-down choice to one of the other available fields. This step can be repeated so that all of your fields are in the same column, but only the main column item can be sorted. When multiple values appear in the same column, the Separator field can be used to distinguish between the fields in the column. Separator may use regular characters or HTML. If multiple values are being used, it is highly recommended that you use the   (single space) for separation, if nothing else. Bullets and the pipe (|) character are also common and valid separators, although it is recommended that   be placed around these characters for additional readability.

Tables can also be sorted by column, which creates a clickable header. You may choose a column to be the default column on which the table sorts and specify whether the sort is ascending or descending.

The unformatted style provides a simple, basic list of all items that match the query. Each row is a returned field, but lacks any special spacing or styling. This style is potentially useful for lists of names, but may be hard to read for many users if multiple fields are returned.

Row style determines how each row in the view itself will be styled—as a node or as a field. If the Style setting is using Table, Row style will be missing from the Basic settings box. Row styles may use fields or nodes, with each type displaying one per row. When using fields, you have the option of making each of the fields appear inline rather than stacked, and you can provide a separator just as the full view style does. The node style is exclusive to using selected fields (the fields box), and gives you the option of showing just the teaser instead of the full node. In addition, you can put comment links or comments themselves in the view.

AJAX may be available for use in some cases. The "Use AJAX" option specifies whether you will use AJAX in the view for exposed filters, table sorting, and paging. Be aware that using AJAX will keep the entire page from refreshing, which may cause issues with links.

Pagers make it easy for your users to skip forward and backward in your view, which is a very useful ability within large views. Two types of pagers are available, should they be needed. A mini-pager shows the current page of total pages and uses forward and backward arrows (<< 1 of 6 >>). Mini-pagers are well suited for use within block displays because they fit more cleanly than a full pager. A full pager displays a list of page numbers plus first, previous, next, and last options so that users may easily jump multiple pages. Pager element is a number that can be used to identify a pager within each page. If multiple pagers are used within a page, each one needs to have a different identifier.

Every view needs to have a number of items to return by default. The "Items per page" option sets this number, and can provide a helpful limit. Using a set number can increase the return time of a page—something most Web sites see as a critical function. You can also offset or skip some number of items in your view.

Views can have multiple displays, which may be linked together easily by using the More link. Checking this box will add a More link to the bottom of the view. On a block display, such a link will take the user to the page display version of that view, which may contain significantly more data. This capability could be used to link a teaser to a full article, link the archive of this month's posts to the full archive, or link a short block of recent comments to a full page of recent comments.

Distinct adds the SQL statement DISTINCT to your query, which attempts to remove any duplicated records from the view. Completion of the Distinct operation takes time, which may be considered a performance problem in some cases.

Access places restrictions on what users can see the view, either by user role or by general permissions. You can create roles for users or change user permissions under Administer >> User management >> Roles or Permissions.

Caching is one of the newest features to Views. This pluggable cache is *not* the same as the overall Views caching. Rather, it lets you cache each display separately if you wish, or cache the entire set via the default. The standard options are the ability to cache the query results and/or the entire rendered output. You may cache one and not the other. In addition, you may assign different lengths of time to each cache; the menus provide options ranging from 1 minute to 6 days.

The Header adds a header to the view. A header is simply some text that will appear above the view. It can be set to appear even if the view has no results for display, which helps let the user know that the page did display, even if no actual data was returned. The Footer is essentially the same as the header, except that it appears at the bottom of the view. Either of these elements can be used to provide an explanation of the view or other pertinent information about the view.

Empty text is text that can be displayed if the view returns no results. It lets the user know that the view has completed its processing. Such text is more useful than just returning an empty result, and is clearer than using just a header or footer. In essence, this text lets the user know that the query mechanism did not crash; there are simply no results.

Finally, there's the theme. Theme is not actually a setting; it is informational in nature. It lists template files that the different parts of the view may be using. This display is similar in nature to what you would see if you looked at a page with the Devel module. The template in use by each piece of the view appears in bold font, so you can see exactly which files are being used. You may have display, overall style, and row style themes within the same view. You can also rescan the template files in case you make changes to the names of .tpl files. Clicking the "Rescan template files" button will clear the theme registry.

### Display Specific Settings

Each display type also has a settings box in the first column that appears below the Basic settings box. Figure 7-9 shows one example of display settings.

```
Page settings
Path: archive
Menu: No menu
```

Figure 7-9    Display-specific settings for the archive view

Page has two settings, path and menu. Path is the Drupal-specific path to the page that contains the view. Remember that this path is not a full URL; http://www.example.com/ is assumed to be the base URL, with additional information being tacked on to the end of this URL. When you click on the path setting, you will see the entire base URL but you must enter the remainder of the path. The path statement can take arguments.

Menu gives you options for adding a menu item as a normal menu entry, a tab, or a default menu tab; you can also not add any menu item at all. When creating a menu item link, you should give it a title and determine whether it should have a weight. The menu also has further options that become available when you click the gear icon, which determine exactly where that menu item should go.

Block has only one setting: admin. This simple description of the block is intended to make it more easily findable in the Administer >> Site building >> Blocks page. The admin setting is a name, and should be relatively short and clear.

If your display type is a feed, two options can be changed. Path is the same as it is for page settings; this time it is the path to the XML feed page, whose filename often ends in .xml. The second option is "attach to," which creates the feed as part of one of the other displays. This gives feeds a similarity to attached views.

The settings for attachments also are different from the settings for other displays, as they are not actually changing the display of the attached view. Instead, the attachment settings determine where the attached view will be placed and which information will be inherited from the view it is attached to. Arguments and *exposed filters* may or may not be inherited from the parent view. Exposed filters comprise any of the filters in the view that are made available to the person looking at the view; they can be changed when they are displayed. The attachment can be positioned before the parent view, after this view, or both before and after the view. This group of settings also has an "attach to" option, but it is used to attach the view to one or more displays or to make it part of the default display. Every view built on the default would then have the secondary view attached.

### Relationships

Relationships is the first box in the second column. This and all remaining boxes to set up views have clickable titles. Clicking the title will tell you if that group is using the settings from the default view or if it is using an override. With relationships, you can create links between data that may not be otherwise related. A complex structure can be created by using relationships.

Clicking the plus sign (+) opens the section for adding a new relationship. The different types of content (not content types!) that can be added are grouped together. A drop-down menu allows you to choose which items are available for relationships so that you can more easily find the piece you are looking for. Many groups may be available, and the list changes depending on which content types are available on your site and which other modules you have enabled.

When you add relationships, the number of fields available may increase significantly. For example, you may want users to rate your content. Modules are available to perform this task. However, Views doesn't have a good way to link the various kinds of data together on its own; it needs a relationship. You can create a relationship between voting data and node data, for example, so that they can be displayed together in the list.

### Arguments

The section for adding an argument looks very similar to the section for adding a relationship. The main difference is that many more types or pieces of content can be added as arguments. Arguments act in a fashion similar to filters, but with more exposure to the user. Chapter 8, which is devoted to arguments, discusses this issue in depth.

### Fields

The setup for fields looks significantly like that for arguments and relationships. The fields settings, however, add the actual fields that will be available in your view. This is where you determine which pieces of information will appear in the view and which order they will appear in. Using this feature, you might give a short preview of a group of stories or see a list of recent comments. Fields do not have to be visible to a user to be included in a view.

## Sort Criteria

SQL's sorting mechanisms come into play in the Sort criteria settings. You may sort your view by one or more fields. If you do not specify a sorting criterion, the view will sort itself in ascending alphabetical or numerical order on the first field available to the view. If you wanted to see content posted by users per day, you would add the sorting criteria User: Name, and then Node: Post date, as shown in Figure 7-10. You may also add the criteria in the opposite order, as they can be rearranged using the rearrangement tool.

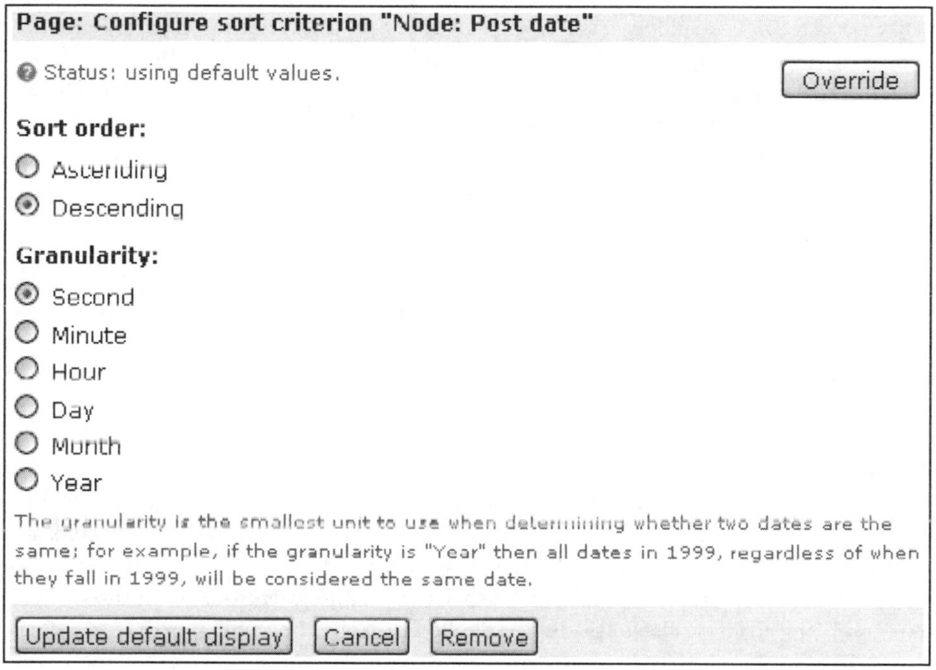

**Page: Configure sort criterion "Node: Post date"**

Status: using default values.    [ Override ]

**Sort order:**
○ Ascending
◉ Descending

**Granularity:**
◉ Second
○ Minute
○ Hour
○ Day
○ Month
○ Year

The granularity is the smallest unit to use when determining whether two dates are the same; for example, if the granularity is "Year" then all dates in 1999, regardless of when they fall in 1999, will be considered the same date.

[ Update default display ]  [ Cancel ]  [ Remove ]

Figure 7-10    Adding a sort by posting date

## Filters

Filters can be used to limit the fields returned for your view. Note that this limit is based on actual data, unlike the "items to display" link in the Basic settings box, which puts a straight limit on the number of fields. This area is where some especially important criteria for your views are stored. If you wish to publish a view for general use, any information obtained from nodes will usually be taken from published nodes.

> ### Warning
>
> By default, the Node: Published filter is not on. In most cases, you need to add this filter. This group of settings is where the Analyze tool is telling you to go when it cannot find data to publish publicly.
>
> It has been suggested that the Node: Published filter be the default. Security concerns dictate that it not be a default filter, however. This is part of the reason why the Analyze tool warns you that no filter is available for published nodes.

## Overrides

Overrides are another part of a change from the default setting. If a setting is changed, it may need to be overridden. Each of the clickable box titles (relationships, arguments, filters, sort criteria, and fields) allows you to override the default display. When you click on the title, the box at the bottom of the configuration screen tells you whether you are using the default display. From here, when you update the settings, the update will be pushed to the default display. If you want this change to affect only the current display, you must override the defaults.

> ### Note
>
> All of these settings can be overridden only as a group, on a per-group basis. An override will take effect for all relationships, for all arguments, for all filters, and so on. Remember that an override is overriding the default!
>
> This behavior may have unintended consequences. Always double-check your results.

## Validation

Many of the parts that you can use to define a view require a setting, especially for displays other than the default. If your view does not have the correct settings selected, a red warning box, similar to Figure 7-11, will appear. It indicates which settings are missing or set incorrectly. In other cases, such as when no content is available to the general user base being made available for display, a yellow warning box will appear to inform you of that fact. Until the validation errors are corrected, the live preview function will be unable to display a view.

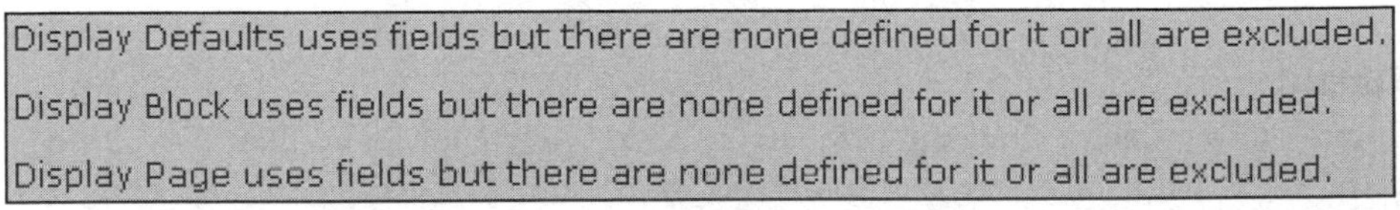

Display Defaults uses fields but there are none defined for it or all are excluded.
Display Block uses fields but there are none defined for it or all are excluded.
Display Page uses fields but there are none defined for it or all are excluded.

Figure 7-11    Validation errors

### Live Preview

The live preview feature represents one of the biggest steps forward in usability for those individuals who are new to using Views. Live preview shows you exactly what your view will look like to your Web site visitors, allowing for changes to be made quickly and easily without needing to click back and forth and constantly reload pages (see Figure 7-12).

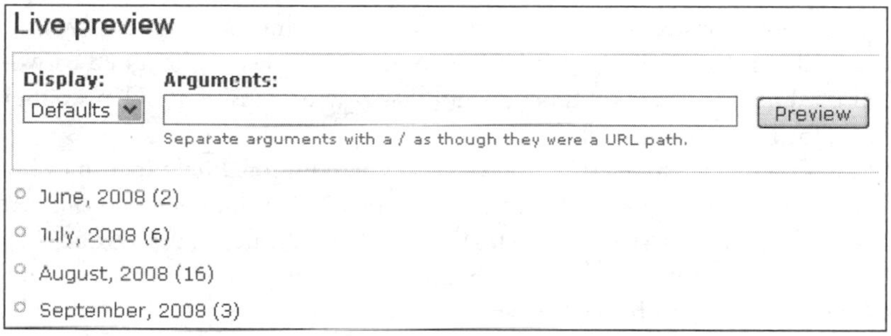

Figure 7-12     A live preview of the archive view

Other basic information about the view is also presented as part of the preview. This information includes the query that is used to create the view, the title and path, and statistics on how long it takes the query to actually build and execute as well as how long it takes the view to fully render.

## Import

The Import page has a simple purpose: to import a view from another site or installation of Drupal. If you have exported a view, you may enter a new name if you wish, or leave the view Name field blank. Remember that the view name must consist of alphanumeric characters, but may use underscores. Paste the exported view into the text box and click the Import button. Views will then attempt to import the view. If this operation is successful, the Edit page will appear, allowing you to customize the view.

## Tools

The Tools pages provide help with troubleshooting and updating your views to the new version. There are two subtabs within the Tools section: Basic and Convert.

## Basic

The Basic tab comprises a list of check boxes that can be selected to enable features that are helpful for performance optimization, troubleshooting, or general placement of some of the query information within the user interface. This page also contains the highly important Clear Views' Cache button. If you are changing your views, and they are not appearing correctly on your actual displayed pages even though they worked perfectly in the preview, you may need to clear the cache. At the bottom of the page is a drop-down menu that allows you to select where the performance statistics should be placed; this location is entirely up to you.

The check boxes on the Basic tab are documented within the page display itself, and should be easily understood in general. Many of these features are designed to work with the Devel module or to turn off functionality that may be causing problems either for the view or for the browser itself.

"Add Views signature to all SQL queries" tacks an additional field that does not need processing onto the SQL query when it is being built. When looking at an SQL WHERE clause, you will see a 'VIEWS' = 'VIEWS' string that indicates Views was used to build the query. When you are searching through an extensive log file to determine which queries may be causing problems, this string makes a Views query easily identifiable. It is recommended that this flag be used only during troubleshooting, even though it does not appreciably change the query. Why process more than you have to?

Views caching can be disabled across your site with the "Disable Views data caching" check box. This setting may be useful during the creation of new views and especially during the retooling of an existing view. Views may cache a tremendous amount of data in an effort to quickly display a view; this data can come from multiple tables, other modules, or other existing views. Trying to maintain this cache can place a significant burden on performance. If the cache is not used, Views is forced to rebuild each view every time it will be displayed on a page. If that view has to call other views and other modules to return information, things can get very ugly, very quickly.

> **Note**
>
> Selecting the "Disable Views data caching" check box does not clear pluggable caches (found under the Basic settings); Views does not know where those caches store their data and cannot effectively clear them.
>
> If you need to turn off the pluggable cache, it is best to do so from the view itself while you are developing the Web site. Turn it on when you're ready to deploy a Web page, and always retest the page to make sure it works correctly.

The next two boxes deal with queries and live preview. We've already seen that the live preview shows you what your view is supposed to look like. Normally, your preview will be displayed and the query used to create that view and its corresponding details will appear below it. These settings boxes allow you to put the query above the preview ("Show query above live preview") and to show all of the queries that are run to create the view ("Show other queries run during render during live preview"). When troubleshooting, these settings can help you determine if a query is being called multiple times when it should not be.

If you have created a view and have the ability to edit it, you may see [Edit], [Export], and [Clone] links over the top of a view that appears in the public section of your site. These are called hover links. You can turn them off by selecting the "Do not show hover links over views" check box. Hover links are useful for quickly reaching the Edit page for the view directly from the view itself. This is much quicker than digging into `admin/build/views/`, finding the correct view, and hoping you've got the right one.

Web site developers should be concerned with the performance of their sites, especially if the site is professional in nature. Views can interact with the Devel module and provide performance and query statistics. Such data helps you determine how long your view and its container are taking to render—again helping you find bottlenecks in system response.

The last check box continues a core tenet within Drupal development—that the entire user interface should work without JavaScript. If you are having problems with using the Views UI because of your browser, or you're just that concerned about JavaScript security, you can turn off JavaScript for views. The interface should degrade and be completely usable without it; it just won't be as pretty or as easy to use.

### Bulk Export

The Bulk export page provides a method for exporting all of the code that creates a particular view. Figure 7-13 is part of this page. Quite simply, you can choose one or more views to export, and have the code available and easy to store in the source control repository.

At the bottom of this page is a box labeled "Module name." This box's purpose is to help you export a view that you can then easily import directly into a module. If you enter a module name, parts of the code will contain pertinent hooks into the module.

### Convert

The Convert tab is likely to greatly interest users of Views 1. Views 1 is not being converted to Drupal 6, and Views 2 is not being backported to Drupal 5. This leaves users in the unenviable position of having to upgrade their Drupal version as well as Views at the same time to maintain a functioning Web site.

The Convert tool checks the database to see if it contains any Views 1 views and then gives you the opportunity to convert each such view to the Views 2 format. It is highly recommended that you use a test site to do so. Using a test bed to convert the view means that you can then export it and later import to the live site once it is upgraded. You have to do the conversion only once, and it can be perhaps ahead of time; this eases the pain of upgrading.

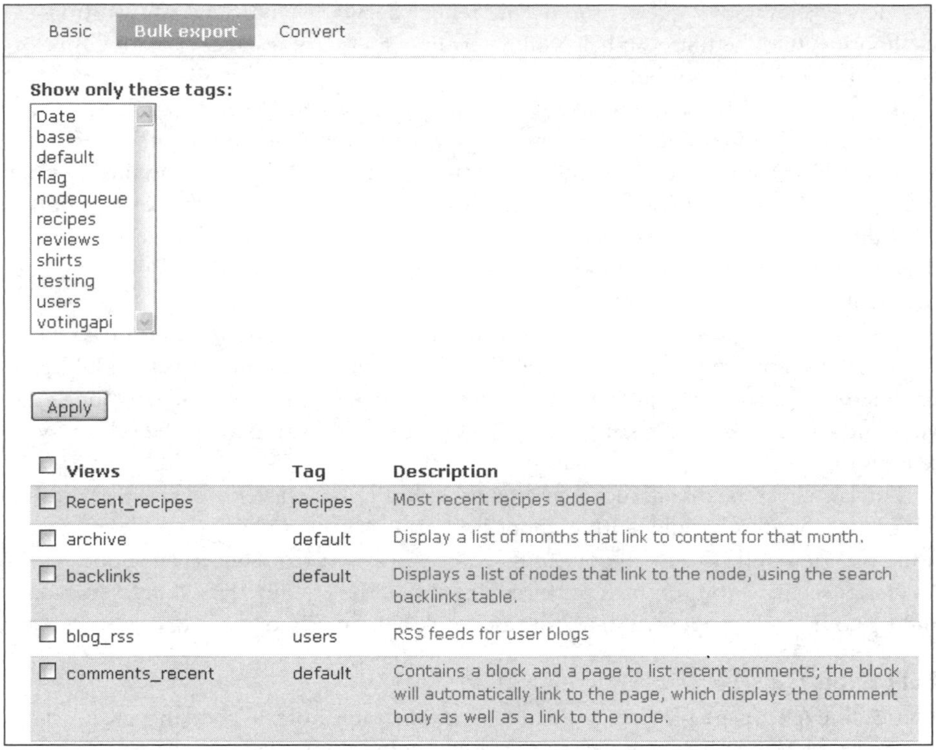

Figure 7-13    Views Bulk export page

Be aware that due to the extensive changes made between Views 1 and Views 2, the actual views are likely to be altered somewhat by the conversion process. You will need to spend some time examining each converted view to ensure that it still shows (or doesn't show) what is expected. If you have not yet upgraded to Views 2, consider exporting your views from the previous version. Once the upgrade is complete, you can import these views via the Import tab. It will take you directly to the editor and give you a clear idea immediately if the view needs work before being made public once more.

With all of these boxes, check boxes, and settings, it's easy to lose track of where you're going. The next exercise takes you through the creation of a new view.

# Exercise 7-2

## Creating a View: Recent Content

In this exercise, you will create a simple view. Before proceeding with this exercise, make sure you have several nodes created for one of your content types. This example will create a default view for use in displaying the most recent content of all types.

1. Navigate to Home >> Administer >> Site building >> Views and click the Add tab.

2. Use the following values to populate the initial view creation page:

| Field | Value |
| --- | --- |
| View name | recent_items |
| View description | Most recent items posted |
| View tag | base |
| View type | Node |

Notice that this data doesn't actually say "shirts" or identify any other content type specifically. We are creating a more generic view that can apply to all content types—giving us something we can clone later to create a view for a specific content type. For now, we'll use the "base" tag to indicate it's a view we intend to start from to create others.

3. Click the Next button to proceed.

4. In the View settings box, notice that our tag "base" is now shown. To change the tag later, come back to this page and click the word "base."

5. Under the Basic settings, do not change Name or Title. When we are doing a display, we might want to change these settings, but not yet.

6. Change the Style to an HTML list and update the settings. This action will bring up the style settings. The default is an unordered list; leave it alone, and update the settings. Notice one of the red warning boxes at the bottom of the page: Display Defaults uses fields but there are none defined for it or all are excluded.

7. Row styles are set to fields by default. For now, leave this setting as is. Attempting to update this choice will also generate an error message.

8. Skip to the Fields box. Click the + sign to add two fields: Node: Post date and Node: Title (you can access the Groups drop-down menu and choose Node to find these fields more quickly).

9. You will be presented with the configuration screen for Node: Post date. Use these values to configure the field, and then update the settings:

| Field | Value |
| --- | --- |
| Label | Clear the label—by default, this says "Post date" |
| Exclude from display | Unchecked (this is the default) |
| Date format | Custom |
| Custom date format | ⌐ j, Y |

10. The UI will immediately take you to the configure screen for Node: Title. Use these values for the fields, and then update the settings:

| Field | Value |
| --- | --- |
| Label | Clear the label—by default, this says "Title" |
| Exclude from display | Unchecked |
| Link this field to its node | Checked |

11. Live preview should now be displaying data. Use the up/down arrow on the Fields box, and switch the order of the field display so that Title is first, followed by Post date. Update the settings, and review how the live preview has changed.

12. Click the + next to Sort criteria and choose Node: Post date. Change the sort order to descending and day. These criteria force the most recent posts to be displayed first.

13. Click the + next to Filters. Choose Node: Published. Checking the box on the configure page means that only published nodes will be displayed in the filter for any user.

Your default display is now complete. Your live preview should now display a list of all nodes and dates on which those nodes were published. Each node title should also link directly to that node.

[Edit]  [Export]  [Clone]
○  shirt 4, size test
   September 24, 2008
○  shirt 3
   September 24, 2008
○  Shirt 2
   September 24, 2008

Figure 7-14   An example of the `recent_items` view

Now that you have completed development of a base view, you can clone the view and set filters so that only one type of node is displayed in the view. At this point, we also need to create displays for the view so that it can be placed into Web pages.

# Showing Your Views to the World: Creating Displays

Now that you have a view, you will want to turn it into something usable that you can place on your Web site somewhere for visitors to see. This requires creating a display, placing it into some type of Drupal container, and positioning that container in a particular place. This operation may sound complex, but it does not have to be. We've already talked about the various display-specific settings that you can set during creation or editing of a display. It's now time to look at those displays and put them to use.

Views provides four types of displays: block, page, attachment, and feed. We've talked about the specific settings for those types already, but we haven't delved into the process of using them to create Web pages or parts of Web pages. In the following exercise, we'll create a display using a block—Drupal provides blocks as part of the core functionality.

---

## Exercise 7-3

### Creating a Block Display

Every view needs a display before it can be inserted on an actual page for use. A block is the easiest type of display to create and understand.

1. Open the view created in Exercise 7-2 (`recent_items`) by going to its Edit page.

2. In the left-hand drawers, change the drop-down choice to Block, and click the "Add display" button. You should now see a new drawer under Default that says Block. Note that if you do not save the view before exiting this page, your new display will be lost.

3. In the Basic settings box, notice the Name field. It says Block, which matches the display type. For the base view that you'll be cloning, you can leave this name alone. For a cloned view (e.g., for Joe's Shirts), you might want to name it something more specific, such as `Block_shirts`.

4. Change the display-specific setting if desired. You can give the block an administrative title, making it easier to find in the blocks administration page. You can also set up caching here for the block. Note that this is Drupal core's block caching, not Views based.

5. Save your changes.

Now you have a display that can be shown as a block. It can be administered from the Blocks page.

---

With the creation of a base view and block display, you are ready to clone that view for use and make it exactly what you want with only a few modifications, rather than having to re-create the entire view every time you want to customize it.

## Exercise 7-4

### Cloning a View to Create More Specific Content

Cloning a view creates an exact duplicate of an existing view. You are required to give a new name to the cloned view to ensure its uniqueness, and you are allowed to change the description and tag. If you haven't created any entries for Joe's Shirts, please do so before continuing with this exercise.

1. Open the `recent_items` view.

2. Choose the Clone item in the menu bar.

3. You will be taken to the Add screen. Change the view name to `recent_items_shirts`.

4. Change the view description to "Most recent shirts posted."

5. Click the Next button.

6. In the Filters box, click the + sign to add a new filter.

7. Choose the filter Node: Type.

8. Choose the Operator "Is one of" and the Node type "Joe's Shirts."

9. Update the settings.

10. Save your changes.

This set of steps creates a view that displays only Joe's T-shirts. The displays from the base view are copied to the new view as well, and are ready to be put onto pages.

---

Now you have a base view and a specific view. Both of these views use the very basics of Views functionality. Of course, having a view defined doesn't do your users any good if it's not shown to them. At this point, we need to create a place for the view to be contained. One of the easiest ways to do so is to create a block.

## Blocks

Blocks are a core Drupal containment system. It's necessary to know about them to use Views effectively, although we cannot hope to cover every use of blocks within this book. Blocks are one of the most common containers for content in Drupal. They can be placed on your page and hold many types of content. For example, blocks can be easily placed within the left or right sidebars, the header or footer, or the main page content. Even more helpfully, the Blocks page under Administer >> Site building >> Blocks has small boxes on the page to show you exactly which region is which.

The process of creating a block display with Views does not just create a display; it also creates the block for you. Blocks containing views are administered just like any other block in Drupal. In some respects, a block looks very much like a node. Blocks were originally used for customization purposes—using them was an easier way to embed custom PHP code into a Web site. As time has passed, this characteristic has become less useful; PHP embedded in blocks is not easily upgraded, nor is it stored in source control. Source control is critical for many organizations, especially those that are doing serious code development work.

To embed a view into a block using the UI, you must create a block display within the Views interface. The blocks UI does not allow you to import a view into a block.

## Exercise 7-5

### Working with Blocks

In this exercise, we will place a block that contains a view in the right sidebar of the page.

1. Navigate to Administer >> Site building >> Blocks.
2. Review the list of available blocks. In the lower section of the page is the Disabled blocks list. Locate the `recent_items_shirts` block.
3. Use the drop-down menu options to choose a placement *or* use the grab handle to drag the block into the region where you want the block to appear. For this exercise, choose the right sidebar. If you use the drop-down menu, the block will immediately jump to the selected region.
4. Save the block. If you forget to save the block and continue working, the block will remain disabled.
5. Choose the configure link to the right of the block name.
6. Change the block title to "Newest shirts!"
7. Save the block.

Observe your page. You should see a section in the right sidebar that contains your new block, and a list of the most recent shirts added.

Using this type of block view can be very useful. Blocks can be configured so that they are shown only to certain users, only to users who are authenticated, only on certain pages, and so forth. With just a few small changes, you could create two similar views and place them in the same location, where site visitors would see a view with an article name and a teaser, but authenticated users or subscribers could have that same view link to a full article.

## Pages

A view can be created as an entire page. We've already created a block view for Joe's most recent items, and one for just his shirts. Users may want to see a full list of shirts, however, and the block view can link to the full page view. The page display automatically creates an alias that can be used in the URL to take you directly to the page containing that view.

Pages are a place where overrides really start coming into play with Views, and it becomes very important to understand exactly how they work. In a block display, a limited amount of information should be presented; presenting too much information crowds the block and overwhelms the user. However, a full page view is where users expect to get a majority, if not all, of the information they are seeking.

# Exercise 7-6

## Creating and Using a Page Display

In this exercise, we will create a page display to go along with our recent shirt block. We want to allow users to see all of Joe's shirts, so we'll need to let them page through the list. We might also want to take a look at the formatting to see if another option would be cleaner for displaying this information on a full page than a basic list.

1. Navigate to Administer >> Site building >> Views and choose Edit next to `recent_items_shirts`.

2. In the default display, under Basic settings, change the More link to "yes," if it is not already set.

3. Change the Items to display to 5; now only five items will be shown on the page.

4. Save the view.

5. In the "Add display" drop-down menu, select Page. Click the "Add display" button.

6. Now you will have a page display available. Highlight the page display so that you can make changes to it.

7. Under the Basic settings, Items to display is set to 5. Click the 5, and look down to the box. Change the setting to 15, and click first Override and then Update. Now, for this display only, 15 items will be displayed. Notice that the status changes to "using overridden values" and the button changes to "Use default," as seen in Figure 7-15.

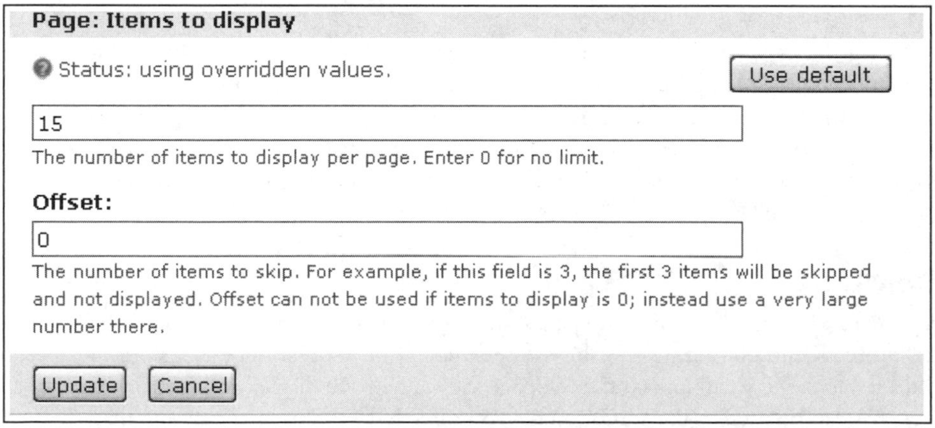

---

**Page: Items to display**

ⓘ Status: using overridden values.                              [ Use default ]

```
15
```
The number of items to display per page. Enter 0 for no limit.

**Offset:**
```
0
```
The number of items to skip. For example, if this field is 3, the first 3 items will be skipped and not displayed. Offset can not be used if items to display is 0; instead use a very large number there.

[ Update ]  [ Cancel ]

---

Figure 7-15    Configuration box changes after overriding the default

8. Now that there are more items on the page, it might be useful to add a pager. Change the Use pager setting to "Full pager."

9. Under Page settings, change the Path variable to "shirts" and update the settings.

10. In the Fields box, you may choose to add extra fields—you may have a purchase price, an image of the shirt, comments about it, and so on. If you add any fields, click Override.

11. Save the view.

If you navigate to http://www.example.com/?q=shirts now, you will see a full page of shirt content. If more than 15 items are available, a pager will appear that helps you to navigate through all of the pages. Thus your users can scroll through all the available shirts easily. If you have enough shirts to pass the block's display limit, your block will display a "More" link that takes you directly to the shirts page.

## Attachments

Attachments, put simply, embed a view within another view. The glossary view is the most obvious example of an attachment. Within the glossary view, the page view is the list of nodes; along the top is the attached view, which summarizes how many nodes begin with a particular letter and number.

Another use for attached views is to embed an archive of recent activity within the content page. Most archive listings appear in sidebars or on their own pages. This format represents a change from the more typical river of news style employed by many sites.

Attachments can inherit arguments from the view they are attached to. This capability gives you the ability to filter the entries displayed.

## Feed

RSS feeds are the most common way to notify people of new content on a site. Most blogs use a feed, which lets their readers follow the blog in their choice of blog reader, lets readers easily keep track of which posts have been read, and, most importantly, lets readers easily get information pushed to them rather than forcing readers to seek it out.

Creating a feed view is almost as straightforward as it gets. Feeds do not allow for field selection, eliminating that list of choices. The feed style gives you two options: use the site's mission statement for the feed description or enter your own. Only the Row style: Node can be used with feeds, and the style options are to use the default RSS settings, send the node title, send the title and teaser, or send the full node. The feed display does not override any of the default options. Feeds are not generally user visible and are certainly not easily readable by the user owing to their XML-based output.

## Summary

This chapter covered the basics of creating a view and developing a display. Views has a large number of options and capabilities packed into a small user interface. By employing the power of Views, you can create lists of almost anything you can imagine, in many different fashions.

# Arguments, Exposed Filters, and Relationships

Supplying arguments to Views is one of the ways this module becomes even more powerful and flexible. Turning arguments into filters changes the dynamic, but exposing those filters allows the user to easily see and change those filters, creating an even more personalized and dynamic experience. Relationships bring data together in new ways, and expand the information available to the rest of Views.

## Arguments

In Chapter 7, we took a brief look at the glossary view. It uses arguments to present a summarized view of all of the nodes on the site. To gain a better understanding of how this really works, we need to go deeper into the structure of arguments and explore how they are supplied to a view.

The most heavily used feature for arguments is to use them in a similar fashion to filters. Like filters, arguments can be used to limit the data returned from a query. Arguments, however, are much more exposed than an embedded filter.

In some cases, arguments in views are used to hide or remove information from the URL. This is the global null variable—its purpose is to take some number of arguments and hide them from the user. The real purpose, of course, is to prevent exploitation of hackable URLs. For instance, if you have a page URL like http://www.example.com/product, in some cases users can enter data after "product" and an invalid choice will return the user to the product page. The global null takes anything after "product" and effectively trashes it, sending the user a "404 – An invalid page" error message.

The other major use of arguments is for taxonomy depth. In other words, you can use arguments to modify exactly how far and how deep your view will search to return a valid result. For example, you can modify your arguments to show specific things out of a group, such as which T-shirts are available in a particular size.

## Arguments as Filters

The use of arguments as a filter that is easily visible and modifiable to the user is one of the most common tactics when using a view on a site. Arguments in most cases act very similarly to filters. The major difference between an argument and a filter is that a filter is built into the view and places a limit on the data the user gets to see. A filter is controlled by the view creator. In contrast, an argument change is often within the user's control—and changing the argument changes the view. This type of argument can be added to other arguments to create depth, and collectively these arguments can be used as the default values for a view.

Like many of the Views configurations, arguments are added via the plus sign (+) in the Arguments box. When you click that button, a configuration screen will open at the bottom of the page. Figure 8-1 shows an example of some of the arguments available for nodes.

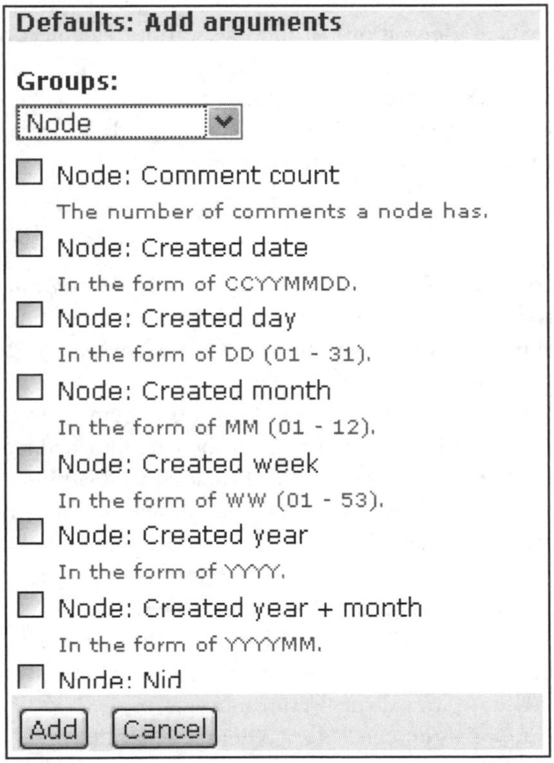

**Defaults: Add arguments**

**Groups:**

Node

☐ Node: Comment count
  The number of comments a node has.

☐ Node: Created date
  In the form of CCYYMMDD.

☐ Node: Created day
  In the form of DD (01 - 31).

☐ Node: Created month
  In the form of MM (01 - 12).

☐ Node: Created week
  In the form of WW (01 - 53).

☐ Node: Created year
  In the form of YYYY.

☐ Node: Created year + month
  In the form of YYYYMM.

☐ Node: Nid

[Add]  [Cancel]

Figure 8-1    Choosing an argument

As an example, suppose you are attempting to determine an argument from the following URL:

```
http://www.drupal.org/node/26419
```

Here "/node" is the default Drupal path, and "26419" is an argument supplied to the path variable. This URL will take you directly to node 26419, the Handbooks overview page. An argument of Node: Type to a node view with a path of "content" dynamically filters the displayed items by content type. In this example (shown with Clean URLs enabled), accessing the view through the path http://www.example.com/content/recipes displays all posts of the type "recipe," the path http://www.example.com/content/t_shirts displays all posts of the type "t-shirts," and http://www.example.com/content displays all posts regardless of type. Each successive argument added further filters the returned results.

## Configuring an Argument

The argument configuration screen offers several options for changing the use of one or more arguments. It is split into three sections: Basic, Validation, and Filtering (Figure 8-2).

Figure 8-2   Configuring an argument

The first group of configuration options handles the most basic argument pieces: Title, Actions, and Wildcards.

The Title is potentially dynamic, allowing substitutions that are evaluated to create a full title for the view. With this option, you could create a title that would print your arguments in order (or create a sentence using the arguments.) For example, Node: Type is a possible argument, and using %1 in that title field automatically substitutes the Name field of the node type into the title of the view.

Arguments may or may not be present. The "Actions to take if argument not present" section gives your view a basis for what to do if the argument defined is not passed to the view. With this set of radio buttons, you can choose to display the entire view (acting as if the argument function wasn't present at all), hide the view (removing it in the case of a block, or displaying a 404 error if it is a page), or display empty text. Alternatively, you can display a summary of all values in an ascending or descending order, which looks very similar to the glossary view. A final option is to provide a default argument, which gives you even more options to provide a fixed entry, to provide a user or node ID, or to enter some PHP code.

Wildcards are a shortcut for all arguments. If the wildcard is set to "All", then any valid value for the argument is accepted. In essence, if the wildcard is set, then either one argument is passed or all arguments are passed. For example, in the recent_items_shirts view, the wildcard value is set to "All," meaning that all shirts pass the test. This choice acts very similarly to ignoring or removing the use of the argument; however, this wildcard is where titles and breadcrumb trails come from. The wildcard title is an option that can be used to substitute into the title; by default, the title uses "All," which may not be useful or accurate for the view.

An argument may use validation to ensure that it is valid and exists within the system. Using validation gives the administrator the ability to decide which arguments the view will accept and what to do if an invalid value is passed. Each validator contains a set of widgets specific to that validation type. An argument may be given to a view, but fail to validate; when validation fails, the widgets let the view know what to do. Validators can check for things like valid node IDs, compare taxonomy terms, or use PHP code. Other modules may work with views to add further validators. For example, when using a node validation, you may choose a particular node type. If the view is called but then fed a node ID of a type that doesn't match the validation, it will fail. When it fails, the same actions are available as in the basic argument settings.

The last group of settings is a set of check boxes that have special functions (Figure 8-3). The first, "Allow multiple arguments to work together," enables multiple arguments to be supplied to the view query as though they were the same argument, thereby enabling users to query for content with multiple taxonomy terms. "Do not display items with no value in summary" is reasonably self-explanatory; in a summary view, it removes items without the value. "Reduce duplicates," the last box, is incompatible with the use of multiple arguments.

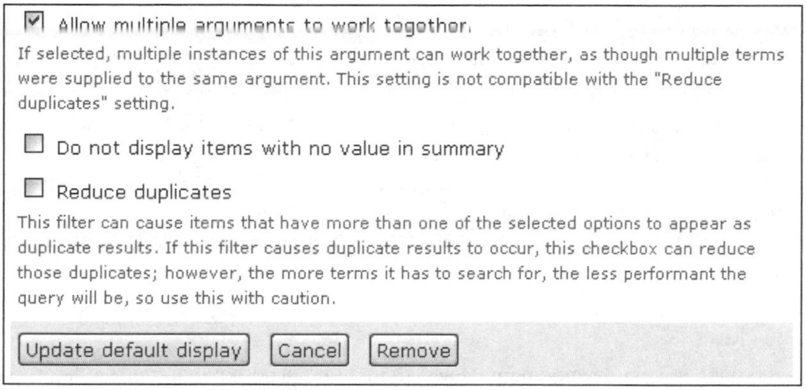

Figure 8-3    Special configuration check boxes for a view

It enforces a single return of any particular piece of content, regardless of how many arguments it may match.

In the next exercise, we'll demonstrate how an argument can be added to a view, and look at how this change affects the view.

## Exercise 8-1

### Adding an Argument to the T-Shirt View

Joe's Shirts has customers who are all different sizes, and they want to see only those shirts that will fit them on Joe's Web site. By using an argument, you can limit which sizes each user sees. Before you proceed, create some shirts with varying sizes.

1. Open the `recent_items_shirts` view (Administer >> Site building >> Views >> recent_items_shirts >> Edit).

2. In the default display, click the + sign next to Arguments.

3. In the drop-down menu, select "Content." This narrows the list so that the field you are looking for is easier to find.

4. Choose Content: Text: T-shirt size (`field_shirt_size`) and then click Add.

5. The Configure screen opens for the argument. No changes are necessary at this time, so save the view.

This set of steps updates all of the display types created for this view. Because our path is already set to "shirts," we can use http://www.example.com/?q=shirts to see all of the shirts. Changing the URL to http://www.example.com/q=?shirts/xs applies the x-small argument, and the view displays only shirts where the x-small size is available. Such a view can be used as a menu link or a bookmark.

**Note**

In most of Views, arguments are substituted in a `%1`, `%2`, `%3` order, allowing the admin user to change the order of the arguments when they are displayed in a title or elsewhere.

Path settings use only `%`; multiple arguments in the path are formatted as `path/%/%/%` for using three arguments in the order that they were passed to the path setting. For example, the arguments might be passed `path/year/month/day`. We'll talk more about this issue (i.e., stacking arguments) later in this chapter.

---

**Saving Views**

Like everything else in development, views should be saved early and often. If something goes wrong before you are able to save your view—if the power goes out, or if you accidentally close your browser window—your view will not appear in the Views List page. That doesn't mean it is lost! Your view will be cached temporarily at http://www.example.com/?q=admin/build/views/edit/viewname.

This view caching may last two weeks or more, unless a second user attempts to edit it. That user will receive a message stating that the view is locked, and will have the option to break it. Breaking the lock will remove the previous view from cache.

---

## Using Arguments as Part of a View

The glossary view is another example of arguments that are supplied directly to the URL, thereby ensuring that users familiar with the system can quickly and easily get to the list that they need. Remember that the glossary defaults to using the letter "A" as an argument; clicking on "A" in the summary does not change the list, but it does change the URL for the page from http://www.example.com/q?=glossary to http://www.example.com/q?=glossary/a. To change the view, it is possible to change the URL itself to feed the new argument to the view; see Figure 8-4 as an example.

4 (1) | A (7) | B (3) | C (2) | I (1) | L (1) | M (1) | P (2) | R (1) | S (3) | T (4) | W (1)

| Title▲ | Author▼ | Last update▼ |
|---|---|---|
| Shirt 2 | uriel | Friday, September 26, 2008 - 14:03 |
| shirt 3 | uriel | Wednesday, September 24, 2008 - 16:41 |
| shirt 4, size test | uriel | Wednesday, November 5, 2008 - 17:42 |

Figure 8-4    The glossary view, using "S": as the argument; the URL is
http://example.com/?q=glossary/s

As another example of using an argument within a view, Exercise 8-2 explains how to create RSS feeds.

## Exercise 8-2

### User Feeds with Arguments

Views provides the ability to create RSS feeds for any view. Common uses for such a feed include the introduction of new products, new blog posts, or publicizing of events. Of course, users may also want to see an archive of previous posts from the feed. Let's create an RSS feed for the site user's blogs. We'll operate with the assumption that all user content consists of blog posts.

1. Navigate to Administer >> Site building >> Views and choose Add.
2. Use these values for the first creation page:

| Field | Value |
| --- | --- |
| View name | blog_rss |
| View description | RSS feeds for user blogs |
| View tag | Users |
| View type | Node |

3. Next to Arguments, click the + sign. Choose the argument User: Name.
4. In the configure screen for the argument, check "Transform spaces to dashes in URL." Drupal allows usernames with spaces, but this convention can cause problems with URLs. This check box prevents errors.
5. Click Update.
6. Next to Fields, click the + sign. Choose Node: Title. In its configure menu, delete the word "Title" from the label (which means the actual node title will now show in the view), and check "Link this field to its node" (so offsite readers can click to view the node itself).
7. Update the settings.
8. Add another field, Node: Teaser. Delete the label, and update the settings. Addition of the teaser will send our short version of the blog post out as part of the feed. Your live preview should now have data.
9. Click + next to Sort criteria. Add a sort criterion of Node: Post date, in descending order, and update the settings.

Now it's time to add a page display. This step will create pages for the blogs—if we add the feed display first, there won't be anything for the feed to attach to and it won't be visible on the site.

1. Change the left-side drop-down menu choice to Page, and click the "Add display" button.

2.  Under Page settings, change the path to "`blogs/%`" and click Update. Our arguments should already be set from the default display.

3.  Save the view.

4.  Now add the feed display. Along the left side, change the drop-down menu choice to Feed and click the "Add display" button.

5.  The live preview has some errors that need to be corrected. First, change the path to "`feeds/%/rss.xml`".

6.  The attachment variable also needs to be set. Attaching the feed to another display gives it a physical place in which it can be located. Click the "Attach to" button, and then click the box next to the page display.

7.  Update the settings.

8.  Under Basic settings, change the Row style to Node; update the settings.

9.  Leave the Row style options Display type as "Use default RSS settings."

10.  Save the view. Any warnings should disappear.

Every user now has a blog display as well as an RSS feed for his or her blog. Because of the argument wildcard, a user can go to http://www.example.com/?q=blogs/username for any user to see that user's blog posts. An RSS icon will appear on the page, allowing easy access to the feed itself.

If you want to narrow down the content that goes onto the feed, you can change the filter to allow only certain node types, only certain users, and so on.

---

Arguments can be expanded and stacked, using multiple arguments to limit or filter on a group of values. The T-shirt view could use genre and then size as a stacked argument, for example. One of the most conceptually easy uses of a stacked argument is the archive. This view is often used with blogs to provide a list of previous posts. Views actually includes an archive view for general use. If you look into this view (you'll need to enable and then edit it to do so), you can see that the argument used is Node: Created year + month. This argument creates a summary list, by month and year. If you want to provide multiple arguments, however, you have to go about it a different way.

Arguments are not passed to blocks! Many arguments are passed to a view via the URL, and blocks ultimately don't care about the page URL. If you need an argument in your block, you may want to provide it directly to the view. In the argument configuration, you can specify an action to take if the argument is not present. When you select "Provide default argument," for example, more form items will appear, allowing you to specify an argument for the block view. You will get several choices in a radio button format (the actual choices will vary depending on which modules you have installed, as this list can be expanded by plugins), but you should always be able to choose Node ID from URL or User ID from URL. If you need something more complex, you can choose PHP code and write a snippet of code to extract the URL. If you simply want to extract it from the URL, you could use the `arg()` function. The `arg()` function will extract a piece of the path based on the number you sent it, counting from zero. For example, if the path is `foo/bar/baz`, then `arg(0)` will return "foo", `arg(1)` will return "bar", and `arg(2)` will return "baz".

Note that `arg()` will use the "real" path, and not the alias. For example, if you have used the path module to create a URL alias that turns "node/1" into "about", `arg(0)` will return "node", not "about".

---

## Exercise 8-3

### Stacking Arguments

Breaking up a blog by month and year is a system with which most users are familiar. This could be done by cloning the archive view and making changes to it. However, we already have a blog view, so we'll add two more arguments to the existing view.

1. Open the `blog_rss` view.
2. Click the + sign next to Arguments.
3. Choose Node: Created month and Node: Created year.
4. Click Add
5. In the configure screen, the wildcard value should be "All" by default. Make sure the action to take is set to "Summary, sort descending," and then click the Update buttons for both fields.
6. Select the List style.
7. Click the "Rearrange" button, and put "Created year" before "Created month."
8. Click Update.
9. Click Save to save the view.

Now you have a view with an archive-style ability. You can pass a username, year, and month to the URL; this stack of arguments will then be passed to the view, retrieving all posts made by that user. Passing only the user argument retrieves all posts; adding a year narrows that result down, and adding a month narrows the list further. This view will use the YYYY/MM/DD format; if you want all entries from August 2008, the end of the URL would look like this: `blogs/<username>/2008/08`.

---

Stacked arguments have myriad applications. With proper use, they represent another way to break down categories of items into smaller groups while allowing the greatest amount of flexibility in your code. When arguments are organized in a stack, it is easy to be as general, or to drill down as deeply, as you want. In the blog sample given earlier, notice that the year view also acts like a summary.

# Exposed Filters

When creating views, the use of filters is very common. Filters limit the amount of data returned—and hide the fact that other data is available that could have been returned if the filter was not present. In some cases, you may want to allow users to see this data and choose which filter to apply to the view at a given time. This setup is most easily accomplished with an exposed filter.

Exposed filters are much more easily understood by the general user than arguments in the URL. Most users are familiar with drop-down menus for choosing a category of items, making them a good choice for groups of things. This arrangement is useful for items that are grouped by a particular category, but have another thing that relates them—for example, recipes for breakfast or lunch that contain cheese. Another example would be books that are historical in nature or fiction, but are also children's books. Exposed filters make it easier to break out subgroups of particular categories.

When you expose a filter by clicking the "Expose" button in the filter configure box, some extra options become available. The configure box expands to show a new group of settings, as seen in Figure 8-5.

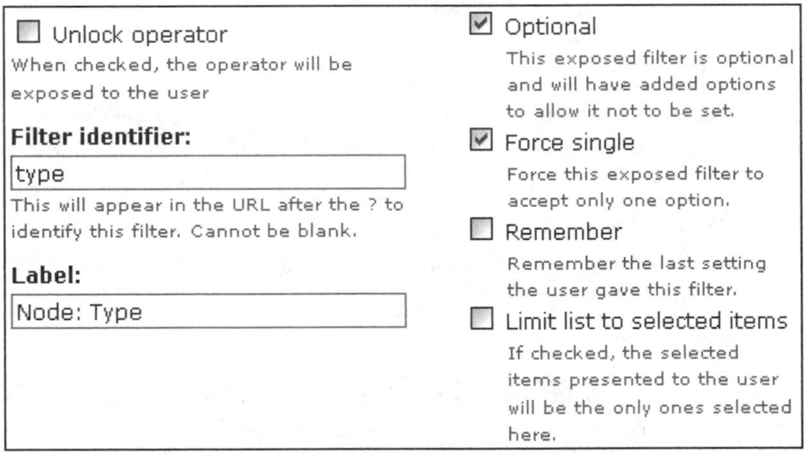

Figure 8-5    Additional settings for exposed filters

Most of the new settings are check boxes, turning a feature for the filter on or off. The "Unlock operator" option makes the "is one/all/none" operator visible to the user as well as the category choices. The "Optional" setting gives the user the choice to not set a filter at all; in this case, the setting will automatically add an "any" filter so that all matching objects are returned. "Force single" disallows the selection of multiple choices for a filter, limiting the user to one selection at a time. "Remember" adds a piece of information to the user's session on the server; this data acts similarly to a cookie but it doesn't touch the user's browser. The final check box, "Limit list to selected items," represents a middle ground between exposing all selections and exposing none; it gives the administrator the ability to limit which choices a user can select.

The remaining settings are text boxes that can be reconfigured by the administrator to be more user-friendly. When you change the "filter identifier" value, the URL is changed when filters are in use. The "Label" box allows you to change the label on the select box or whatever widget you are using to give your users filter options.

Exercise 8-4 will help you understand how to create an exposed filter.

## Exercise 8-4

### Using an Exposed Filter

In this exercise, we'll create an exposed filter using the Joe's Shirts content type. Joe's Shirts has decided to categorize its shirts into genres so that its customers can find things that relate to them. To complete this task, we'll need a new field to use for the exposed filter.

1.  Create a new CCK field for Joe's Shirts, using these values:

| Field | Value |
| --- | --- |
| Field name | categories |
| Label | Category |
| Field type | Text |
| Widget type | Select list |
| Required | Checked |
| Number of values | Unlimited |
| Allowed values list | General |
| | Games |
| | Political |
| | Music |
| | Movies |

2.  Open the `recent_items_shirts` view.
3.  In the default display, click + next to Filters, check the box next to Content: Category (field_categories – Allowed values), and click the Expose button.
4.  Under Operator, choose "Is all of."
5.  Change the label to "Category," and uncheck "Force single."
6.  Update the settings.
7.  Save the view.

Because the default operator is "Is all of", users will be able to pick none, one, or multiple categories. The live preview should now show a multi-select list that offers users the ability to choose none, one, or multiple categories.

# Relationships

Relationships expand the available options for Views to an enormous degree. Each relationship can add one or more fields and filters, creating a complex structure that still can be easily viewed on one page. Modules such as Fivestar and Plus1, for example, make voting data available to Views that let administrators create lists of ratings, giving users a hint into what other users like.

Relationships are the JOIN of the Views–SQL tie-together. Creating a relationship between a node and some other information in the Drupal database joins them by their related fields, and exposes that information to the Views interface. Views only knows about particular kinds of data, and only looks at the basic tables when it is installed. Adding a relationship helps the Views API to understand that additional data is coordinated with the data it already knows about. Exercise 8-5 is an introduction to one of the more popular uses of relationships: voting data.

---

# Exercise 8-5

## Using a Relationship for Voting

The Fivestar module provides voting information to Views via the VotingAPI module. Joe's Shirts wants to know which shirts are the most popular with its customers, and wants the customers to know what's popular, too.

1. Download and enable the Fivestar (http://drupal.org/project/fivestar) and VotingAPI (http://drupal.org/project/votingapi) modules.

2. Navigate to Administer >> Content management >> Content types >> Joe's Shirts >>Edit.

3. A new collapsible item will appear on the Edit page labeled "Fivestar ratings." Open the collapsed field, and check the box labeled "Enable Fivestar rating."

4. Save the content type.

Ratings are now enabled for each shirt, and Views will be able to use that data once a relationship between the nodes and their votes is established. It's important to consider expansion of the site. Adding a new block to Joe's Shirts means that block can't easily be reused for other products. Creating a "top 10" view by itself means each new product needs a display page or block of its own, for filtering purposes. With a little extra knowledge, we can go the second route, and make the site flexible and allow for new content.

1. Navigate to Administer >> Site building >> Views >> Add.

2. Create a new view with the following values:

| Field | Value |
| --- | --- |
| View name | top_ten |
| View description | Top ten items |
| View tag | reviews |
| View type | Node |

3. Under Basic settings, change the Style to HTML List, and the list type to Ordered List. Update the settings. A red box will appear, informing you that no fields are defined. Don't panic!

4. In the Relationships box, click the + sign and scroll down to Node: Voting results. Add this field.

5. In the configure screen, check the "Require this relationship" box. This setting will prevent items without votes from being included in the view. For the Data filters, choose Value type: Percent, Vote tag: Default vote, and Aggregation function: Average. VotingAPI adds additional fields that Fivestar doesn't use, but that are still shown on the view configure page.

6. Click the + sign next to Fields, and add the fields Node: Title and Voting API results: Value.

7. For the configure Node: Title screen, remove the label "Title" and check "Link this field to its node."

8. Update the settings.

9. In the Voting API results: Value configure screen, change the Appearance to "Fivestar Stars (display only)" and the Relationship to "Voting results." Remove the word "Value" from the Label field.

10. Update the settings.

11. Click + next to Sorting criteria. Check "Voting API results: Value and Add."

12. In the configure screen, use the Relationship "Voting results" and a sort order of "Descending."

13. Save the view.

Take some time to add ratings to some content. Once you are done, come back to this view and look at the live preview. You should see a list of 10 items of the Joe's Shirts type (unless you've added Fivestar to other node types!) that appear in order from highest rated to lowest rated. The next step will be to add a display, but we're going to do something that allows for expansion of this view in the next exercise.

---

After Exercise 8-5 is complete, the VotingAPI module is providing information to the view, allowing users to give visible feedback for all content where voting is enabled. This is specific to the node type, and each node will have a rating that users can check. You can even configure the site to allow ratings with comments, so users have even more ability to give localized feedback.

By examining this feedback, site users and administrators can get a good idea of which items are popular with customers. Being social creatures, people like to see what other people are interested in, and to do that, we need a way to show those things. We need a particular display to show the top 10 of any product.

## Exercise 8-6

### Creating a Display for the Top 10 Products

Joe's Shirts wants its T-shirt page to display the top 10 shirts in the sidebar of the shirts page, but also wants to have this display be easily expandable in case the company adds more products later.

1. Open the top_ten view for editing.

2. Add a block display.

3. In the Arguments box, add a new argument. Choose Node: Type.

4. In the Configure screen, use the following values:

| Field | Value |
|---|---|
| Title | Top ten %1 |
| Action to take if argument is not present | Provide default argument |
| Wildcard | all |
| Wildcard title | All |
| Default argument type | PHP code |

5. One more field needs to be filled in, because we chose PHP code for the last option. To make a dynamic block display for each content type, we need to use some code to retrieve the content type.

```
if (arg(0) == 'node' && is_numeric(arg(1))) {
  $node = node_load(arg(1));
  if ($node) {
    return $node->type;
  }
}
```

6. Click Update to change the default value, and save the view.

7. Go to the Blocks page, and add the "top 10" view to the right sidebar (or wherever you're comfortable with it).

Now, when you look at any piece of content, the block we've created will determine the node type, and present a list of the top-rated items of that node type in the sidebar. Remember that this display matters for only content where voting is enabled!

Relationships obviously can add a significant amount of complexity to a view. As noted in Exercise 8-6, there are many times when the relationship provides data that doesn't fit within the context of views or won't make logical sense to users. On such an occasion, an individual module's documentation should be considered before the relationships are put into action.

## Summary

Filters, arguments, and relationships change the complexity of a view significantly. With them, it's easy to add and remove data from a view. With the addition of exposed filters, you can make a default list of arguments available to your users, giving them further ability to control their own experience. Relationships help you bring data together that otherwise would remain separate, and create a rich environment for queries.

# Theming Views

Views can be themed just like anything else in Drupal. Views provides an entirely new level of classes, theming templates, and strategies that greatly surpasses the capabilities of its predecessor. In this chapter, we'll discuss the template files and their contents, change some CSS classes, and consider how we can approach rendering data by multiple methods.

## An Overview

Views cleanly incorporates a CSS class for each piece of data returned by the query. This makes it much easier to pick a class for everything from theming all views to theming the odd-numbered fields for a single view in a specific block display. Views has a reasonably clean integration with the entire theming system of Drupal 6, allowing it to easily take advantage of the standard Drupal theme functions.

In this version of Views, each piece of the view has a template and can be themed separately. The Views user interface (UI) provides significant visibility into the template files used to theme each part of the view display, and each template is designed to be compact and clean.

Views themes are broken up into three major areas: the view area containing the general page elements, the view itself, and the rows of the view. The overall theme contains the entire page, but can be broken down into the smaller parts—specifically, the content area, the view, and the rows of the view.

While you are looking through this chapter, remember the many capabilities of the Devel module. In particular, it enables you to clear your stylesheet cache, which may be useful as you work through the exercises.

## Classes in Views

Views creates classes that can be used for creating thematic parts. Each view is contained within an HTML div of its own, making it easier to assign classes to the entire view. In most circumstances, the div is created using the name of the view as part of the class, which also makes finding the particular class you need to theme easier. The view will also have a class "view," for ease of theming all views.

In addition to the classes that are created for the full view, each field can have multiple classes assigned to it. These classes can help you identify a single field, or tag certain fields to become part of a group of fields.

There are many ways a view class can be named, and each name depends on the function that class is intended to perform. In many cases, these can be divs as well. Each class that is implemented by Views (except for the general "view" class) starts with the word "view." When reviewing a page's source, each class implemented by Views is, therefore, easy to find and adopt into your theme.

Each class name is dependent on the row or view style that is being used. A table view uses the identifier "table" in its class names, while the grid style uses "grid" as an identifier.

One of the most important things to remember is that Views uses two different types of styles. "Style" determines the overall style for the view, whereas "Row style" identifies a style for each row of returned data.

Here are some naming examples from our `recent_recipes` view that we created in earlier chapters:

- `view` The CSS class for all views. It is the most generic class available that encompasses just views.
- `view-recent-recipes` The class for the general view `recent_recipes`. If `recent_recipes` is used in multiple displays, this class could be used to theme all of them the same way.
- `view-display-id-block_1` The view class for this theme in block number 1 only.
- `views-row-4`, `views-row-even`, `views-row-last` Three classes that are part of the row styling for the view, enabling you to style just row 4, just the even rows, and only the last row in the results, respectively.
- `view-dom-id-1` A class that is actually used for Javascript, when certain AJAX functionality is needed.

Views also provides a list of classes that can be used regardless of the actual content of that view. Each of these classes should be easily recognizable from the UI for view creation:

- `view-header` This class provides theme information for the header.
- `view-filters` This class is used to apply theming to filters.
- `view-content` This is one of the more general classes, which is used to theme an entire group of content.
- `view-empty` This class is used only when a view has no results; it returns empty text.
- `view-footer` This class provides theme information for the footer.

- `feed-icon` This provides theme information for the RSS/feed icon.

- `attachment-before` This is used when an "attachment" display should appear before the view.

- `attachment-after` This is used when an "attachment" display should appear after the view.

There are plenty of reasons why you might want to emphasize part of your view. For example, you might change the header to be a cautionary note. You might want the footer to be much smaller and unobtrusive in comparison to the page content. These classes give you a number of places to start working on individualizing your site's theme.

# Exercise 9-1
## Theming Using a View Class

Joe's Shirts wants to use smaller dates for views displayed in blocks, such as the `recent_items_shirts` view. The company believes that this change will place more emphasis on the item, rather than highlighting how old it is.

1. Open the CSS file for your theme. For this example, it may be easiest to continue using the `garland-extend.css` file we used in earlier chapters.

2. Determine which class you need to theme the date appropriately. You can view the source of the page, or look at the text before the example to determine the class to use (`view-display-id-block_1`).

3. Add the following code to the CSS file:

```
div.view-display-id-block_1 {
  font-size: x-small;
}
```

This snippet changes the font size of the entire block. That's close to what we want, but not quite. Joe's Shirts asked for one field in the view to be themed differently, not the whole view.

4. Look again at the page source. If you examine the data to find the created dates, you will see a view class called `views-field-created` that is part of a div. Add it to the class, and you get the following code:

```
div.view-display-id-block_1 div.views-field-created {
  font-size: x-small;
}
```

This gives us the effect we're looking for. We have changed only the "created" field, but it is altered in every view on the site.

Views classes can be used just like any other CSS class. They can be found in divs, used in tables, or deployed as a stand-alone element to affect multiple larger classes. Views classes are extensive, and they can be used for the vast majority of Views theming. In the majority of cases, this level of class availability provides enough distinction for each part of a view, so that template specifications may not even be necessary.

# Template Files

The content or main view area contains the header, footer, and the entirety of the view. We've looked at the different areas that are themable. Each area has a template file that is pertinent to its section of the view. Like CCK theme information, Views works with a set of template files that range from not very specific to most specific, and attempts to use the most specific theme template available. The default theme templates are stored in `/sites/all/modules/views/theme`.

Templates are the base rendering of any layout in Drupal. Nodes, pages, views—you name it, and you'll almost certainly find a `.tpl` file behind it. Templates are mostly HTML files that contain some PHP, enabling Drupal to substitute its own values into the file. Knowing a little PHP can really go a long way here, but you can still do quite a bit without knowing any. Views aims to give you the ability to change everything; the template files are there to do just that.

Theming for Views in many respects is easier than it was in previous versions of Drupal. With the theme system revamp in Drupal 6, Views theming has been integrated tightly with the new system. As with Content Construction Kit theming, all theming work should be done in `/sites/all/themes/<theme_name>/`.

Given the vast number of templates that might potentially be used, some site creators might feel that the theme directory has become too cluttered. To simplify matters, you can create a `views` directory under the `/sites/all/themes/theme_name` directory. The theming system will automatically discover the templates in the subdirectory once the theme cache is cleared. You can also click the "Rescan template files" button in the Views UI under Basic settings >> Theme: Information to find new template files.

> **Warning!**
> Always make a copy of the template file. Do not move the template file itself from `/views/theme` to your theme directory!

To determine which themes a view is using, you can take several approaches. First, the view itself will tell you what each piece is using. In the Basic settings box, the last clickable link is Theme: Information. Clicking this link will display a list of possible template files for each part of the view, in order from least to most specific, as shown in Figure 9-1. Each display may have a slightly different set of files, depending on how you have configured your view and its attendant displays. Further, the name of each part of the view is a link that will open the file that is being used; that filename will also be shown in bold in the UI. Note that you cannot edit the file from here, only review it.

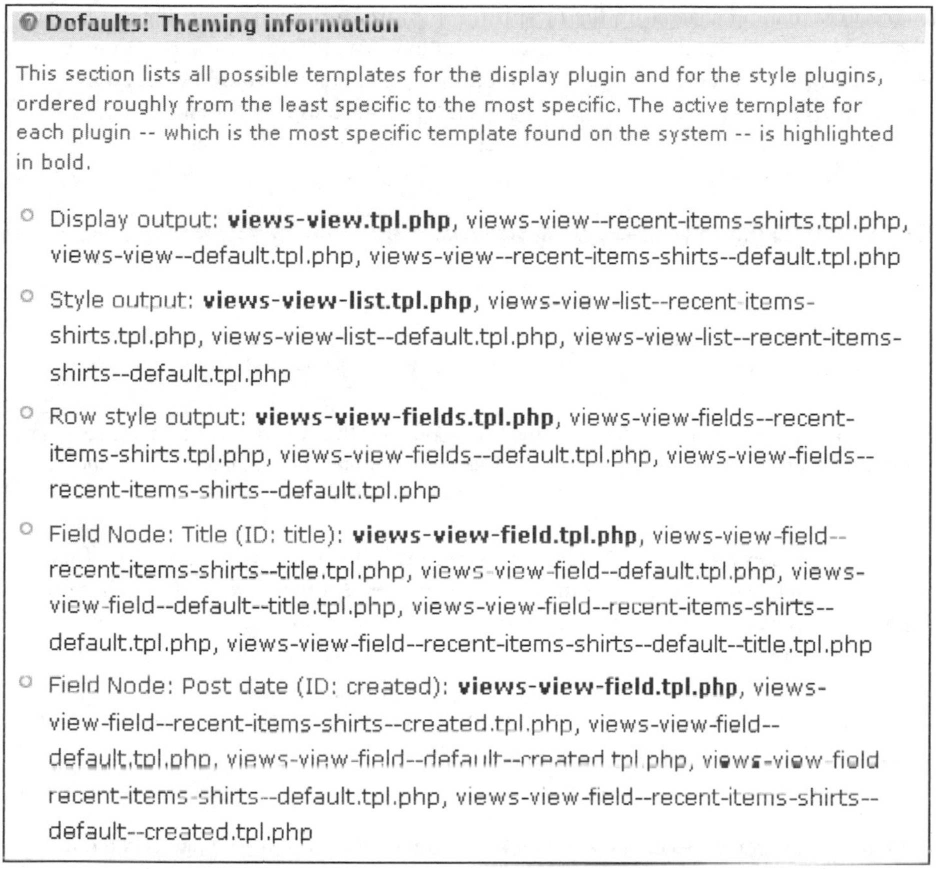

---

**❷ Defaults: Theming information**

This section lists all possible templates for the display plugin and for the style plugins, ordered roughly from the least specific to the most specific. The active template for each plugin -- which is the most specific template found on the system -- is highlighted in bold.

○ Display output: **views-view.tpl.php**, views-view--recent-items-shirts.tpl.php, views-view--default.tpl.php, views-view--recent-items-shirts--default.tpl.php

○ Style output: **views-view-list.tpl.php**, views-view-list--recent-items-shirts.tpl.php, views-view-list--default.tpl.php, views-view-list--recent-items-shirts--default.tpl.php

○ Row style output: **views-view-fields.tpl.php**, views-view-fields--recent-items-shirts.tpl.php, views-view-fields--default.tpl.php, views-view-fields--recent-items-shirts--default.tpl.php

○ Field Node: Title (ID: title): **views-view-field.tpl.php**, views-view-field--recent-items-shirts--title.tpl.php, views-view-field--default.tpl.php, views-view-field--default--title.tpl.php, views-view-field--recent-items-shirts--default.tpl.php, views-view-field--recent-items-shirts--default--title.tpl.php

○ Field Node: Post date (ID: created): **views-view-field.tpl.php**, views-view-field--recent-items-shirts--created.tpl.php, views-view-field--default.tpl.php, views-view-field--default--created.tpl.php, views-view-field--recent-items-shirts--default.tpl.php, views-view-field--recent-items-shirts--default--created.tpl.php

Figure 9-1    A list of default templates

If you click the Theme: Information link and then choose a different display, you will need to click the Information link again; it does not automatically refresh the view. In other words, if you click Theme: Information for the default display, and then change to the Page display, you will need to click Theme: Information to see the template file-names for the Page display. Otherwise, the list of template files will persist from the previous time the link was clicked. This behavior can be confusing. If you're not sure if you are looking at the right templates, click the Theme: Information link.

Views templates use a naming format that is standard throughout the Views system. The pieces of the name are separated by either one or two dashes. Multiple dashes signify a themable part name; for example, `views-view--default.tpl.php` uses two dashes before the "default" part of the name, which indicates that it is applied to the default display instead of being the default file for the view. This convention helps ensure that the user making changes to the template can more easily figure out which template is the correct one to modify. This point becomes important if you have, for example, a view named "list." If the double-dash distinction is not made, it would be much more difficult to tell `views-view-list.tpl.php` (the default template for all list row styles) from `views-view--list.tpl.php` (the default template for a view named "list"). Template names can use the double-dash format for secondary pieces of a theme as well, such as `views-view-field--recent-items--default--created.tpl.php` for just the "created" field within the "recent items" view.

> **Note**
>
> Don't be confused by the terms "default display" and "default template." The default display is used to define all of the base fields, row styles, sorting, and so on. It is part of the Views UI.
>
> In contrast, default template files are the back-end files that Views uses to determine how and where items ultimately are rendered. These files cannot be changed through the user interface.

Views templates are designed to be very cautious in regard to the possibility of namespace conflicts. It would be a very simple matter to create a view with a CSS class that matches another class in the system. For this reason, view CSS classes start not only with "view," but also add more information about which part of the view they target: `views-field` and `views-label` are two examples of this naming scheme. Remember that any field ID that include an underscore in its name will have the CSS ID converted to use a dash.

> **Note**
>
> There is a difference between the field name and the field ID. The field name is the user-friendly name that you know and see in the user interface. It is not the same thing as the field ID in the database! Navigating to Theme: Information will show you the field ID needed if you plan to modify template files to print out specific fields.
>
> For example, Field Node: Post date (ID: created) is the "Post date" field taken from the node. The field ID is "created." When printing this field, adding a CSS class, or performing a similar operation, use the field ID.

The main view area contains the entire page, or display of the view. The default template file that it looks for is `views-view.tpl.php`. This view contains basic information that can be used to theme the entire view for all views on the site. In particular, it provides information for the header and the footer, as well as general theming information for the entire view.

The `views-view.tpl.php` file contains the simple, stripped-down theming information that determines which parts of the view are being shown. At the top of the file is a list of available variables to the theme, defining their purpose clearly to the user. The `views-view` template checks which regions of the page are present and must be printed, based on which variables are passed to it.

To do so, the template creates an initial div, then uses PHP `if` statements to check which variables are set on a one-by-one basis. If the variable is set, the theme is processed and the data is then rendered on the page.

Views templates are, unfortunately, inconsistent. The template variables are not necessarily the same from one template type to the next. Likewise, identical variable names do not necessarily mean the same thing in each template.

## The Display Templates

We've already noted that Views comes with a set of templates in its default install. Each of these templates serves a specific purpose: to theme one thing, whether that's the entire view, a view's style, or the fields within the view. Display templates cover the most general level—theming the entire view.

### views-view.tpl.php

This display template uses a group of variables, each of which may contain variables that are used by more specific templates. The default template may style all views, or may be renamed to include the specific view name you are trying to theme (`views-view--myview.tpl.php`). You can find all the potential template names next to "Display output" after you follow the Theme: Information link.

- `$css_name` The name of the view, using dashes instead of underscores for use by CSS when you are creating classes.
- `$header` The view's header information, if any.
- `$footer` The view's footer information, if any.
- `$rows` All of the data that is returned by the query that the view has performed.
- `$empty` If the view is empty, text is displayed in this variable.
- `$pager` If a pager is being used, this contains information on which pager it is and how it should be used.
- `$exposed` If any filters are exposed to the user, their information is displayed in this variable.
- `$feed_icon` If this view display is for a feed, which icon should be used for that feed, if it exists?
- `$more` If the view uses a "More" link, this variable is set.
- `$admin_links` The fully rendered list of administrative links for the view.
- `$admin_links_raw` A list of administrative links suitable for the theme ("links"). In most cases, raw data is not safe to use, but it is up to the administrator to determine whether the administrators can be trusted to use clean data here!

### views-view-rss.tpl.php

This template is the default template for the XML page that is needed for RSS created by a view. The template itself is simple. It prints XML, with the base required information for an RSS feed. It doesn't have any special variables, and it is generally unlikely that this template will need to be modified.

## View Styles

The next step down from the most general template in the theme is the view style. The view style owns the overall look of the view output, determining how the returned data is presented. The template file used is determined by what was chosen under the Basic settings in the view, next to Style.

Four view styles are available: grid, list, table, and unformatted. The `views-view-list.tpl.php` file contains the base information for views that use a list style, while `views-view-unformatted.tpl.php` is the default file for an unformatted style. The view style does not use any variables that are explicit to its template.

### views-view-grid.tpl.php

The grid style is a very basic style that puts the results of the view query into a grid. The only variable defined by the template is `$rows`, which is a nested array of rows, each containing columns of results. Additional classes for this style are `row-<row number>` and `column-<column number>`. Other styles do not contain columns, but rather use even or odd rows.

Each iteration of the PHP `foreach` loop prints a piece of the `$rows` array with the row and column data. Each of these items is encapsulated in HTML `td` tags as the loop progresses, which builds the grid.

### views-view-list.tpl.php

The list style is also very simple in concept. It prints either an ordered list (HTML `ol` tag) or an unordered list (`ul`), depending on the configuration you chose when you created the view. This template uses an "options" variable that stores which type of list is being used.

The list style does very little besides printing rows. Each loop of the `foreach` structure assigns a member of the general `$rows` variable to a `$row` variable inside the template. That `$row` variable is then printed. Beyond printing the data, this style uses only two CSS classes: `list-view` and `views-row-<number>`, which comes from the `$id` variable in the `foreach` loop.

### views-view-table.tpl.php

A table may seem in some respects to be similar to a grid, but the two actually have some major differences. The table template is the most complex of the style templates. One of the unique things it does is change the title of that view to the table caption. This behavior makes it very simple to change, but also emphasizes the table rather than the grid.

The table template has the largest number of predefined variables:

- $title The title of this group of rows. It can be empty.
- $header An array of header labels for each column, keyed by field ID.
- $fields An array of CSS IDs to use for each field ID ($field). Recall that the field ID is not determined by the field name; it is the machine name.
- $class The actual CSS classes to apply to the full table, based on settings made during the view creation.
- $row_classes An array of classes to apply to each row, indexed by row number. It matches the index in $rows.
- $rows An array of row items. Each row is an array of content. $rows are keyed by row number; fields within rows are keyed by field ID.

Like the grid style, the table style provides for a caption. This template cycles through the headers, then through each of the fields to be printed for those headers. The CSS classes are created in the same foreach loop that creates the headers, and again for the fields as they are created. The template itself uses two different loops to print the contents. This is the first template that uses views field as a class, enabling the use of this template to actually theme field data alone, rather than requiring use of a more specific row template.

### views-view-unformatted.tpl.php

This template is the least difficult in terms of complexity. In essence, it says, "Print some data." It prints the title, if present; gives a row number to create a CSS class; and then prints the contents of each row in the $rows array.

## The Row Templates

The next most specific template in a Views theme is the row style. Qualifying as a deeper format level than the previous templates, it is based on the row style set up in the Basic settings box. This is really where the styling for fields takes place.

The row style box in the UI gives "field" and "node" as options. When you choose a row style of "node," the style does not utilize fields, and the number of possible templates is minimized. When this style is selected, the view generally passes the responsibility for theming off to Drupal's core system; in many cases, it gets handed off to node.tpl.php.

However, when you use the "field" style, every field in the view has a possible template. The name of that template will be based on the field ID, which you can easily find under Theme: Information.

There are two real row style template files: fields and RSS.

### views-view-fields.tpl.php

The base field template is views-view-fields.tpl.php. This template deals with everything around the field, in the field, and being done to the field.

One of the templates that designers most often want to change is the fields template. There are reasons why this kind of modification can be easy, and reasons why it may be complicated. First, such a change involves simply applying a style to a list of fields, and only fields. Matters are more complex than that, though, because the template doesn't know what those fields are, and it has to figure things out by querying the array for those fields.

This template has many variables:

- `$view` The entire view that is being used.

- `$fields` An array that stores of all of the `$field` objects. It contains more variables inside it.

- `$field->content` The actual rendered data output for the field.

- `$field->raw` The raw data for the field, if there is data. As always, this data is neither clean nor output safe.

- `$field->class` The CSS safe class name. Once again, dashes are used instead of underscores.

- `$field->handler` The Views field handler object controlling this field. This object references itself, so if you make the mistake of using `var_export` to dump this object, the result will be a white screen or some other problem.

- `$field->inline` A setting that determines whether the field is displayed inline. If the field is not inline, then it is automatically a block.

- `$field->inline_html` Based on the `$field->inline` setting, set to either an HTML div (block display) or span (inline display) tag.

- `$field->separator` Stores the separator, if your view is using one.

- `$row` The raw result object from the query, with all data it fetched. The data is not sanitized, so be careful with the output.

The template itself is not terribly complex. In turn, it renders the field separators, the CSS classes, and then the actual field content. The `views-view-fields.tpl.php` template uses the `views-field` class, but appends the class ID, so it is more specific than the table template that uses `views-fields`.

### views-view-row-rss.tpl.php

The `views-view-rss.tpl.php` template populates the XML page that becomes the RSS feed for a reader, and actually prints the fields that will be in the feed. It has no classes of its own. It just says, "Here's your title, here's your link to it, and here's whatever you've added to the feed." It is possibly the simplest template in the Views system!

## Other Templates

The `/views/theme` directory includes a number of other templates that we haven't already mentioned. These templates may have special purposes or in some cases are rarely used.

## views-ui-*.tpl.php

One group of templates' names start with `views-ui`. These templates are the theme templates for the Views user interface itself. Within the Views UI, these templates are what ultimately determine the look of what you're seeing. They can be used as an example of how to work with a template, but it's not a good idea to change them. If you make a simple mistake, you can hide entire sections of the Views UI or render it entirely unusable—and if you don't remember that you changed the CSS, reinstalling Views will not fix the problem.

## views-exposed-form.tpl.php

For such a theoretically small part of the page, this template is mid-level complex. It deals with the exposed filters. If any filters were exposed to your users in the view, this template determines how they are placed and printed. Within the template, filters are called widgets. Widgets are part of a form. Other modules can create plugins to be used with views; these would also be widgets. The `views-exposed-form.tpl.php` template tries to make it obvious that we're using a widget, which does not have to be a filter.

This template includes the following variables:

- `$widgets` An array of exposed form widgets.
- `$widget->label` The visible label to print. This may be optional, and is determined by the view or plugin that created it.
- `$widget->operator` The operator for the widget. Its presence depends on which type of exposed widget is involved. When we created the `recent_recipes` view, we used "is one of" to set the filter.
- `$widget->widget` The widget itself.
- `$button` The submit button for the form.

This template has its own classes as well, which are specific to the template. The `view-exposed-form.tpl.php` template also makes liberal use of nested div tags:

- `views-exposed-widgets` class Themes the entire widget, including the button.
- `views-exposed-widget` Themes the widget, operator, and label.
- `views-operator` Used if you want to theme the operator separately.
- `views-widget` Used for just the drop-down menu itself.

The submit button also uses the `views-exposed` widget. If you want to theme the button separately, this is a good place to change the class.

## views-more.tpl.php

This template is used only if the "More" link is turned on for your view, and you have enough entries for that view to trigger the link to be printed. It has the `more-link` class; thus, if you want to make changes to the "More" word, you can.

### views-view-summary-unformatted.tpl.php

This template and the `view-summary` template deal with summary views only. The `views-view-summary-unformatted.tpl.php` template uses the same inline variable that `views-view-fields` uses to determine if the summary should be in a div or a span tag.

Beyond that, this template prints each row with a separator, a link, and a count. Only two classes are provided to theme these items: `views-summary` and `views-summary-unformatted`. This template and the regular `view-summary` template interact with arguments—because summaries require an argument to work.

### views-view-summary.tpl.php

This template creates a summary with an unordered list format. Beyond that, its output is much the same as the unformatted summary. The entire summary is wrapped in a div that gives it the `item-list` class, but it still contains the `views-summary` class underneath that.

### views-view-field.tpl.php

This template really isn't designed to be used; rather, it is provided as an example more than anything else. If you wish to print a single field in a view, you can use this template. Use of the `views-view-field.tpl.php` template is really recommended only if you have a very few places you want to print a single field.

If you want to print single fields, Views provides a theme function with which to do so: `theme_views_view_field`. If you need to print out multiple single fields, using the template not only means that you have a lot of extra files to keep track of, but also can affect performance detrimentally. Use the function if you need to perform this task repeatedly.

### views-view-row-comment.tpl.php and views-view-row-node.tpl.php

Both of these templates are provided as courtesy examples, and both point to the templates you should be using in their stead. Comments should be handled by a comment template (`comment.tpl.php`) that is specific to the view; nodes should be handled by node templates (`node.tpl.php`) specific to the view. Neither of these types is a Views template, and neither is found in the `/views/theme` directory.

Node and comment templates work very similarly. You can append `-view-VIEWNAME.tpl.php` to each for theming a specific view. This approach will also work with `-view-VIEWNAME-displayid`.

## Working with Templates

An important part of the Views template system is the ability to use the preprocessors that are employed by the overall theme system. Preprocessors are functions within the theming system that allow you to further modify how your output will be rendered based on specific conditions. As an example, you might have a view that has a particular value in one row. If that row with that value is present in the display, you can use the preprocessor function to add a CSS class or a property to it (e.g., "sticky").

This is another place where using the Devel module can be extremely helpful. Within Devel, you can use its dsm() function to print your variables out within the template. Without Devel, there are still ways to perform this task, but they take more time to use.

The theme.inc file is the one file in the /views/theme directory that is not a template. It contains all the preprocessors that the theming system uses to prepare data before the template system prints it.'

Fields within a view may already have rendering information with them when they are passed to the view. HTML conveniently provides a tag (<pre>) to deal with this pre-formatted data.

> ### Note
>
> Being able to make changes to your template is part of what makes Drupal so flexible. It also means that you have to be responsible for maintaining your templates when changes and updates occur.

## Rescan the Template Files

We mentioned the "Rescan template files" button that appears under Theme: Information earlier in this chapter. When you create a template file that is more specific than the very first level file (for example, more specific than views-view.tpl.php), you need to rescan the template files so that the theme system knows which template it should be using. Figure 9-2 illustrates Views using a more specific template after a rescan.

```
○ Field Node: Body (ID: body): views-view-field.tpl.php, views-view-field--
   body.tpl.php, views-view-field--recent-items-shirts.tpl.php, views-
   view-field--recent-items-shirts--body.tpl.php, views-view-field--
   page.tpl.php, views-view-field--page--body.tpl.php, views-view-field--
   recent-items-shirts--page.tpl.php, views-view-field--recent-items-shirts--
   page--body.tpl.php, views-view-field--page-1.tpl.php, views-view-field--
   page-1--body.tpl.php, views-view-field--recent-items-shirts--
   page-1.tpl.php, views-view-field--recent-items-shirts--page-1--body.tpl.php

   [ Rescan template files ]
```

Figure 9-2　Using a more specific template

If your template filename does not become bold, there are a few things to check:

- Make sure your template file has the correct name. Count all the dashes, remember that they should be dashes and double dashes, and check for underscores.
- Make sure you are running the most recent version of Views. Versions before 6.x-2.6 had problems finding the correct templates if you used a different theme for the administrator than was used for the general site.

• MUST BE NAMED AFTER THE Block 11 VIEW

- Make sure your template files are in the right place:
  `/sites/all/themes/<theme_name>/<template>` or
  `/sites/all/themes/<theme_name>/views/<template>`.

- Make sure you have highlighted the correct display when you are trying to determine if Views sees your template. If you added a page template, but you are looking at a block display, the theme information will not show what you expect.

## Exercise 9-2
### Looking Inside a Template

In this exercise, we'll look at how to print out the variables separately, using `drupal_set_message`.

1. Open the `recent_recipes` view for editing. Under Basic settings, notice that the style is set to "HTML List."

2. At the bottom of the Basic settings box, click Theme: Information. We will work with the style settings, so we'll want to use the file whose name appears in bold next to that label: `views-view-fields.tpl.php`.

3. Copy `views-view-fields.tpl.php` from `/views/themes` to your custom theme directory (for example, `garland_extend`). Again, this practice keeps our original template safe from being broken in case we need to revert to the original. If we use this code within a loop, it should return an array of the variable values for each row that's in the table:

   ```php
   <?php drupal_set_message('<pre>' . var_export($row, true) . '</pre>'); ?>
   ```

4. To add this snippet to the loop, look for the following code within the template:

   ```php
   <?php if ($field->label): ?>
     <label class="views-label-<?php print $field->class; ?>">
             <?php print $field->label; ?>:
     </label>
   <?php endif; ?>
   ```

   Insert the `drupal_set_message` code in between the `label` and `php endif` lines.

5. Save the template, and reload the view edit screen.

6. This array should return only two values that match the fields from the view: Node: Title and Node: Post date. The array should look something like this:

   ```
   array (
   'nid' => '27'
   'node_title' => 'Light Ale',
   'node_created' => '1219774932'
   )
   ```

Knowing what this array looks like can help you determine the identifier that is available for CSS to use. The $row variable contains both of those fields for each row. Thus, by determining which row you have and what the field title is, you can style each field in each row differently by using its unique identifier. This possibility enables you to use the following snippet to print just the title (although in the fields template, that's not really recommended):

```
<?php print $row['title']; ?>
```

## Debugging

Understanding how to enter the dsm() function into a template file is one of the first steps to debugging a theme that is not working the way you expect, especially if you aren't sure if the page, node, or field is actually receiving the data from Views.

There are some reasons you might choose to use drupal_set_message() rather than the Devel module and dsm(). On the one hand, drupal_set_message() is quite a few characters to type over and over again. When you're trying to solve a problem, the last thing you want to do is spend extra time typing debug messages. Looking at this name once or twice is one thing, but after you've had to type or copy-and-paste it for the fortieth time in the last half-hour, you don't want to do it again. That makes dsm() much more friendly for some levels of troubleshooting.

On the other hand, drupal_set_message() hands off the entire contents of the field. This can mean nothing, or it can mean a lot. If your field contains rendering information, drupal_set_message() prints all of that rendering information so you may see some amount of HTML printed along with the field value. The dsm() functions works a little differently. It runs a check_plain() operation on the field data before passing it along to be printed, which provides for data safety.

Between the two debugging approaches, you have the ability to make sure that your view is actually printing data. With theming, it's possible to accidentally (or intentionally!) screen out fields from display, which this lets you confirm that the values are really there and working. One of the great things about the theme system is the ability to make tweaks to the theme to place items exactly to your specification.

## Printing Default Messages for Empty Fields

One of the easiest things that can be done with a template file is to print a default message when a particular field is empty. This capability can be useful when a field is available, but is not required to have any data, and you want to indicate that the field is present. On a product Web site, for example, you may have photos of your items, but a photo may not be available for every item. With this Views feature, you could add a default image so that it's obvious to your users that there could be an image. Such a message keeps your page looking consistent, and is much more user friendly and professional than simply displaying a blank spot or everyone's favorite little red X.

As of this writing, Views allows default text to be used only if all rows are empty. If you want a default output for one field, or one row that is blank, it has to be themed within a template.

## Exercise 9-3
### Creating a Template with a Default Message

In this example, we'll modify the Recent Shirts view template to show some text if the body is not present in the node. The Body field is a default with nodes, so it doesn't come with a lot of extra markup. Also, it's not a required field by default, so it may not be filled in! Even so, we don't want this field showing up everywhere; it's most useful on the full page list of shirts.

1. Open the `recent_items_shirts` view for editing.

2. Choose the Page display.

3. Under the Fields box, click the + sign to add a field.

4. Add the field Node: Body.

5. Click the Override button.

6. Save the view.
   Now the Page display contains the node's Body field. All other information remains inherited from the default display.

7. Click the Theme: Information link in the Basic settings box. At the bottom of the information box, notice the list of template files available next to the "Field Node: Body (ID: Body)" link. These templates range from the general `views-view-field.tpl.php`, which is a template for all fields in all views, to the highly specific `views-view-field--recent-items-shirts--page-1--body.tpl.php`, a template for the Body field in the `recent_items_shirts` view on page 1 of the view. We want the Body field for this view, but it doesn't matter which page it is on in the list. That means that our best option is to choose one potential template: `views-view-field--recent-items-shirts–body.tpl.php`. If we had added this field to other displays, we would create yet another template file.

8. Navigate to the `/views/theme` folder, and find the `views-view-field.tpl.php` file.

9. Copy this file to your site's theme directory, and rename it `views-view-field--recent-items-shirts--body.tpl.php`.

10. Go back to the Theme: Information box for the Page display. Click the "Rescan template files" button. The name of the `views-view-field--recent-items-shirts--body.tpl.php` template should become bold. If it doesn't, something is wrong.

11. Open the `views-view-field--recent-items-shirts--body.tpl.php` file. It has some comments surrounded by PHP open and close tags, and one bit of code that prints the output that is fed to it:

```
<?php print $output; ?>
```

12. You want to print a default value if there is no text in the Body field, so you need to change this template. A simple PHP `if` statement will do the trick nicely. Delete the original line, and enter this code snippet:

```
<?php
if (empty($output)) {
echo '<p>No body text present.</p>';
}
else {
 echo $output;
}
endif;
?>
```

This code is called for only one part of the page: when the Body field is being rendered in this view. The `if` statement determines whether the field is empty. If it is empty, it prints the text; otherwise, it prints the field. We surround the text with paragraph tags because when the field contains data, it also has surrounding tags; this keeps the look consistent.

13. Save the file.

14. Go back to the view, and scroll down to the preview bar.

15. Change the Display drop-down menu choice to Page.

16. Click Preview. You should see copy of the view, with your text added wherever there is an empty Body field.

At this point, your view will now print that default text on your Page display. You can theme it further using the regular CSS classes for that field provided by Views and the other theme templates.

## Grouping in a Template

The major purpose of templates, at least for Views, is to do things that you simply cannot do with CSS. One of these things is grouping. CSS modifies output properties: It has to be told where that output will go. CSS has to be told what a group is, and then it can decide what to do with it.

In some situations, you may need a particular set of data to be rendered together, but in a different place than the rest of the view. Perhaps you have an image, an image title, and a post date that should all appear on one side of the display, while the image description and location where it was taken should appear on the other side. You could use CSS to float each of these fields individually to one side or the other, thereby accomplishing this goal.

None of these fields has a connection to the others in terms of rendering their data. CSS will do some of the job, but what happens if you want to do something else, such as draw a box around the fields? Then you need to add some template structure, because the fields won't be able to perform this feat on their own. With a template, you can render the left- and right-side fields within their own div; from there, boxes and specialized decoration become much easier to create.

## Exercise 9-4

### Grouping Fields

For our user blogs, we'd like to make it easy for visitors to see when posts were made. It would be even more useful to see when the last changes were made to those posts either by update from the blog author or by a comment. In addition, we want to keep the dates together and on the right side.

1.  Open the `blog_rss` view for editing.

2.  In the Fields box, click the + to add a new field.

3.  Choose the field Node: Updated/commented date and click Add.

4.  In the field configuration screen, change the Label from "Updated/commented date" to "Last change." This doesn't have any real effect except to give us a shorter label to work with and it might make our work easier later.

5.  Save the view.

6.  Click the Preview button.
    You should see the new field in your list of returned items for your view. For a test site, chances are that the post date and the last change date are the same. In contrast, for a production site, they may be vastly different.

    Now we have to decide how to theme the view. This view already has two displays: page and feed. We want to change the way the fields themselves are displayed.

7.  Choose the Page display for the view, and click Theme: Information in the Basic settings box. In this case, we want to change the way the fields are laid out, but just for this view. Given this constraint, we'll most likely want to change the "Row Style output" setting and create the appropriate template file for it. The most appropriate file for this purpose is `views-view-fields--blog-rss--page.tpl.php`, which is the unformatted list style for the `blog_rss` view, with the Page display.

8.  Copy `views-view-fields.tpl.php` from your `/views/theme` directory to your working theme directory.

9. Rename the file in your working theme directory to views-view-fields-blog-rss--page.tpl.php.

10. Go back to the view page, and click the "Rescan template files" button. Your new file should change the bolded filename after Style output.

11. Open your new views-view-fields--blog-rss--page.tpl.php file.

    Here is where things get tricky. This theme can be created in two ways: by creating two new classes for the left and right sides, and by rendering each field and placing it separately. Let's look at both strategies. We begin with separate groups.

12. Replace everything below the comments and ending ?> with the following code:

```php
<div class="clear-block">
 <?php foreach ($fields as $id => $field): ?>
  <?php
 /* To group items, we're going to rely on this field ordering: title,
  * teaser, created, last_updated. When we see one of the fields that
  * starts a group, we'll place the div before the field. When
  * we see a field that ends a group, we'll place /div after the field.
  */
  ?>
  <?php if ($id == 'title'):
/* If title, start the left-side group: */
  ?>
    <div class="views-left">
  <?php else if ($id == 'created'):
/* If created, start the right-side group: */
  ?>
    <div class="views-right">
  <?php endif; ?>
  <?php if (!empty($field->separator)): ?>
    <?php print $field->separator; ?>
  <?php endif; ?>
  <<?php print $field->inline_html;?>
    class="views-field-<?php print $field->class; ?>">
    <?php if ($field->label): ?>
      <label class="views-label-<?php print $field->class; ?>">
        <?php print $field->label; ?>:
      </label>
    <?php endif; ?>
      <?php
      // $field->element_type is either SPAN or DIV
      // depending on whether the field is
      // a 'block' element type or an 'inline' element type.
      ?>
      <<?php print $field->element_type; ?> class="field-content">
```

```
        <?php print $field->content; ?></
        <?php print $field->element_type; ?>>
  </<?php print $field->inline_html;?>>
  <?php if ($id == 'teaser' || $id == 'last_updated'): ?>
    </div>
  <?php endif; ?>
<?php endforeach; ?>
</div>
```

This template starts rendering on the left, and then changes to the right. It also places a clear-block (`clearfix`) around each group of fields so that they are also grouped clearly. See Figure 9-3.

13. Save the file.

```
┌──────────────────────────────────────────┐
│ Light Ale                                 │
│ Post date: Aug 26 2008 - 11:22            │
│ Last change: Aug 26 2008 - 11:22          │
│ Irish Red Ale                             │
│ Post date: Aug 26 2008 - 11:20            │
│ Last change: Oct 29 2008 - 17:51          │
│ American Amber ale                        │
│                                           │
│ One of the first beers I ever brewed.     │
│                                           │
│ Post date: Aug 26 2008 - 10:52            │
│ Last change: Aug 26 2008 - 10:52          │
│ Pale ale with a twist                     │
│ Post date: Aug 26 2008 - 10:47            │
│ Last change: Aug 26 2008 - 10:47          │
└──────────────────────────────────────────┘
```

Figure 9-3    The view after applying the new template

14. We also need the supporting CSS to place the fields where the template has provided new classes. Open the CSS file for your theme (`garland_extend.css`).

15. Enter the following code at the end of your CSS file:

```
div.views-left {
 float: left;
}

div.views-right {
```

```
float: right;
width: 30%;
}
```

This snippet fixes a width for the date fields, and allows the Title and Teaser side to be flexible, as shown in Figure 9-4. If the teaser is one long sentence, however, it runs into the area where the dates are displayed and interrupts the clean flow of those fields. You can add a width—70% into the `div.views-left` rules—to force the teaser to wrap.

| | |
|---|---|
| Light Ale | Post date: Aug 26 2008 - 11:22 |
| | Last change: Aug 26 2008 - 11:22 |
| Irish Red Ale | Post date: Aug 26 2008 - 11:20 |
| | Last change: Oct 29 2008 - 17:51 |
| American Amber ale | Post date: Aug 26 2008 - 10:52 |
| One of the first beers I ever brewed. | Last change: Aug 26 2008 - 10:52 |
| Pale ale with a twist | Post date: Aug 26 2008 - 10:47 |
| | Last change: Aug 26 2008 - 10:47 |

Figure 9-4    The view after applying the first template and CSS

As mentioned in Exercise 9-4, there is a second way to solve this problem. This second version of the template renders each field separately. With the previous template, fields can be added, and will render to the left or right based on where they are positioned within the view with respect to the Title and Created fields. Anything between Title and Created will be positioned on the left; anything after Created will be positioned on the right. These items can be rearranged with the Views UI Fields box.

Rendering each field separately, while certainly more complex and longer in terms of time spent in creation and overall code length, has the advantage of making it very obvious where each field is placed. This approach is superior when considered in terms of future maintenance by persons who did not originally create the template (or sometimes even by the person who did!).

# Exercise 9-5
## Using a Second Grouping Method

Let's try the same exercise using another template, just to get a feel for how it works. This version of the grouping method ignores a lot of the settings, because you can have finer control in the theme. Thus considerations such as inline, separator, field labels and the ordering of the fields are moved into one area, allowing you to control them all in one place.

Note now the teaser field is wrapped in a div while other fields are wrapped in a span. This approach is used because the teaser is a "block"-level element, meaning it contains tags like p or other div tags; thus a span would be invalid HTML.

1. Back up the `views-view-fields--blog-rss--page.tpl.php` file used in Exercise 9-4 if you want to keep it!

2. Replace the code in the previous example (anything that's not the initial comments and their surrounding PHP tags) with this:

```php
<div class="clear-block">
 <div class="views-left">
  <?php /* Title field */ ?>
  <div class="views-field-<?php print $fields['title']->class; ?>">
    <label class="views-label-<?php print $fields['title']->class; ?>">
    </label>
    <span class="field-content">
      <?php print $fields['title']->content; ?>
    </span>
  </div>

  <?php /* Teaser field */ ?>
  <div class="views-field-<?php print $fields['teaser']->class; ?>">
    <div class="field-content">
      <?php print $fields['teaser']->content; ?>
    </div>
  </div>
 </div> <!-- views-left -->

 <div class="views-right">
  <?php /* Created field */ ?>
  <div class="views-field-<?php print $fields['created']->class; ?>">
    <label class="views-label-
      <?php print $fields['created']->class; ?>">
      Posted:
    </label>
    <span class="field-content">
      <?php print $fields['created']->content; ?>
    </span>
  </div>

  <?php /* last_updated field */ ?>
  <div class="views-field-<?php print $fields['last_updated']->class; ?>">
    <label class="views-label-
      <?php print $fields['last_updated']->class; ?>">
      Last updated:
    </label>
```

```
    <span class="field-content">
      <?php print $fields['last_updated']->content; ?>
    </span>
  </div>
 </div>
</div>
```

With our previous CSS file still in place, the rendered page looks just like the previous template (see Figure 9-5).

| Light Ale | Posted: Aug 26 2008 - 11:22 |
| | Last updated: Aug 26 2008 - 11:22 |
| Irish Red Ale | Posted: Aug 26 2008 - 11:20 |
| | Last updated: Oct 29 2008 - 17:51 |
| American Amber ale | Posted: Aug 26 2008 - 10:52 |
| One of the first beers I ever brewed. | Last updated: Aug 26 2008 - 10:52 |
| Pale ale with a twist | Posted: Aug 26 2008 - 10:47 |
| | Last updated: Aug 26 2008 - 10:47 |

Figure 9-5    The revised output appears the same as Figure 9-4 but displays the custom label of "Last updated" instead of the Views UI label text "Last change."

The major caveat with this grouping method is that whenever you add a field to the view, you will also have to update the template file; without that update, the field won't appear on the view.

The Views module provides an almost unlimited amount of flexibility. With templates and displays, the provided CSS will enable you to create almost any type of page you want.

# Summary

The Drupal template system, along with Views' strong base in that system, provides a number of ways for anyone—from a beginner with minimal knowledge of Cascading Style Sheets, to an expert in CSS and PHP—to create and change the way a Web site looks. With simple CSS changes, and through manipulation of the templates available following its installation, Views enables you to readily change the look of your entire site, all the way down to just one field. It gives you the tools you need to find the template being used, and it gives you the opportunity to easily change that template however you deem necessary.

# 10

# Query Optimization

One of the biggest questions that arises with a software installation of any kind is "How much time will each part of this application take?" Entire software packages exist to measure this kind of information. For some people, optimization is the key to a well-run and well-maintained site. For others, it's a giant hassle. In this chapter, we provide a few suggestions about when and why it might be appropriate to do some customization to your Views-generated queries.

## Balancing Development Time Against CPU Time

Views is a query builder; at the end of the day, passing data through the Views system is never the absolute fastest way to retrieve data. What you as the user or administrator have to decide is this: is that small savings in speed worth the hassles that come with updating queries manually when the needs of your site change, or the time spent crawling through each piece of each query?

Views includes tools to help you determine what the speed of your query is. These tools can be used within the view creation and general UI pages. The Devel module may also provide useful insights into your queries.

There are a few ways to speed up the process of running queries. One option is to embed a created query directly into the template for display. Within the Views UI, you can work to create the slimmest query possible. SQL itself contains support for working through queries.

When it comes down to speed, one question is key. Which time is worth more: your time or CPU time? More often than not, CPU time is cheaper than your time, at least when you need to get a site running and keep it running.

## Sticking with What Views Gives You

There are many reasons you might not want to worry about query optimization. Perhaps your site isn't very big or doesn't have lots of traffic, you're not using Views to a major extent, or you have aggressive caching. Another big reason is one of the simplest. Maybe you don't want to spend a lot of time digging through SQL statements and clauses, and you don't have a need to be intimately familiar with the site database.

Views has some detractors who point out that each view can have a very large query. Some people believe that Views queries are too large, or too general, or make it too easy to pull too many options. All of these criticisms may be true for any particular view. While you as a user may know exactly which data you are looking for and exactly where to find it, Views doesn't have that luxury.

Views does its best to create the minimal-size query you need to retrieve the requested data. The benefits of reusing those views—including being able to easily export and store them in a version control system—and the ease of maintenance may vastly outweigh any other considerations.

# When You Need More Than Views

Sometimes, Views just isn't enough. Perhaps your query needs more speed, takes too much time to load, or otherwise just needs some help. That's when you need to start looking into the various tools available for optimization. These methods range from the very simple—embedding the query into your module code—to the complexities of advanced SQL optimization techniques.

## Determining Query Performance

Views includes an important performance tool for determining the speed of your queries, which works in conjunction with the Devel module to provide performance statistics. To enable this tool, navigate to Admin >> Site building >> Views >> Tools. Scroll down to "Enable views performance statistics via the Devel module" and check the box. Near the end of the page is a drop-down menu that enables you to select where the performance data will be placed. When testing queries, it may be most useful to place these results in the footer; because the footer appears below your preview data, you'll be looking in that area to check your view for accuracy.

One of the biggest, most important tasks you can perform when building a site is testing. This step includes benchmarking as well. Checking each query is the ideal, but reviewing performance data for larger queries or queries doing complex data manipulation can mean the difference between a user-friendly and useful Web site and a Web site where your visitors get annoyed and never return.

---

# Exercise 10-1

### Viewing Performance Data

The first step to determining which, if any, queries are causing slowdowns in performance is to look at how long those queries are taking.

1. Make sure that Views performance statistics are enabled.
2. Open a view (`recent_items_shirts` is a good choice).

3. Click the Preview button at the bottom of the page.

4. Below the view output, review the data returned for the query.

Here's a suggestion of what you might see as part of the performance data:

```
Query build time 4.07 ms
Query execute time 0.39 ms
View render time 24.45 ms
```

These three pieces of information can assist you in breaking down where a given view query is taking the longest. In this case, rendering time is the most significant factor in the display of the view. This information can help you determine if you can—or even want to try to—reduce the time to produce a display.

## Embedding Queries

One of the easiest ways, code-wise, to speed up the processing of a query is to embed that query directly into code. There are certain advantages to this approach. The first is that the Views system is entirely bypassed, so any processing it would do is completely stripped out. You get the bonus of using Views to easily create a query, without needing to keep its functionality enabled all the time. This has benefits in terms of both memory usage and speed. Embedding a query can be very useful if you intend to create a static page, displaying the same type of information on a permanent basis; the information contained may change on such a page, but the containers remain.

Embedding a view query within a module is relatively simple if you have a basic understanding of PHP. Using the query handlers built into PHP, you can insert the query into the handler, and presto! Problem solved. As an example, let's look at the query that's used by the `recent_items_shirts` view. This is a fairly simple view, with a small query. Embedding it just requires feeding the query to (in this case) MySQL's query function:

```
mysqli_query = "SELECT node.nid AS nid,
 node.title AS node_title,
 node.created AS node_created,
 DATE_FORMAT((FROM_UNIXTIME(node.created) + INTERVAL -28800 SECOND), '%Y%m%d')
AS node_created_day
FROM node node
WHERE (node.status <> 0) AND (node.type in ('t_shirts'))
 ORDER BY node_created_day DESC"
```

By embedding the query directly into your module or page, you are cutting out the query building time entirely. In the case of Exercise 10-1, that won't save much time. With a more complex query or on a server that is slow or heavily used, however, you may get response times of several seconds.

> **Tip**
>
> Remember the live preview section of the Views UI. You can get the straight query right from that preview.
>
> Note that embedding a query in this fashion gives you only the data. It doesn't provide all the styling or CSS information that you get with the full view.

On the other side of the "to embed or not to embed" question is the issue of maintenance. If your needs change, you must manually change the query. This tweaking could take anywhere from a few minutes to several hours, and potentially might require that you temporarily bring down production Web sites to make the changes. It also means that your code is significantly less flexible.

## EXPLAIN

EXPLAIN is an SQL statement supported by most SQL databases. Its purpose is to "explain" how the database will process a query, and to return information that shows how each table is fed into the query, which order the tables are called in, and how they are joined together.

When using MySQL, EXPLAIN can be used in place of DESCRIBE when you wish to review the structure of a table. Its more useful purpose arises when it is used to precede a SELECT statement.

If you know that your query execute time is longer than you'd ideally like it to be, EXPLAIN is where you can start to figure out where and how to speed it up. One of the major purposes of this SQL function is to help determine where an index might be useful. Adding an index to a table can speed up the query retrieval time for that table significantly. This faster performance can be of major importance when using CCK, as CCK fields and their associated content types do not carry any indexing when they are created.

The following is an example of a query using EXPLAIN. This query is the same one we used in the previous section where we talked about embedded queries, so it's a simple version.

```
----+---------+-------+------+----------------------------+
| id | select_type | table | type | possible_keys              | key
| key_len | ref   | rows | Extra                       |
----+---------+-------+------+----------------------------+
|  1 | SIMPLE      | node  | ref  | node_status_type,node_type |
node_type | 14       | const |    4 | Using where; Using filesort |
+----+-------------+-------+------+----------------------------+--------+--------
-+-------+------+----------------------------+
1 row in set (0.00 sec)
```

Due to the simplicity of this query, we see that there is only one select statement being made. The EXPLAIN results agree with what we already know; this is a simple query.

There are two important pieces of information we should look at here: `possible_keys` and `Extra`. We discussed keys when we talked about relational databases in general; keys are often used to ensure uniqueness of data. In some cases, keys may be usable as an index.

The `Extra` column denotes secondary clauses that the `select` statement is using when attempting to return data. In this case, we're using two additional clauses with the statement. First, we're performing a `WHERE` operation, narrowing down the data retrieved to a particular set. Next, we're performing a `filesort` operation, indicated by the `ORDER BY` clause within the query.

Any one of these things may be an indicator of a good use for an index. Before you get "index-happy," however, take some time to consider the other queries that you're using. It rarely makes sense to index one field if that field isn't being used somewhere else. At the other extreme, if a table contains a large number of records, it may be necessary to use an index for the sake of expediency.

Let's take a look at another query that's more complex: our `top_ten` items view, which we used with Fivestar to handle ratings. We created this view in Chapter 8, in Exercise 8-5.

```
SELECT node.nid AS nid,
    node.title AS node_title,
    votingapi_cache_node_percent_vote_average.value AS
votingapi_cache_node_percent_vote_average_value
  FROM node node
  INNER JOIN votingapi_cache votingapi_cache_node_percent_vote_average ON
node.nid = votingapi_cache_node_percent_vote_average.content_id AND
(votingapi_cache_node_percent_vote_average.content_type = 'node' AND
votingapi_cache_node_percent_vote_average.value_type = 'percent' AND
votingapi_cache_node_percent_vote_average.tag = 'vote' AND
votingapi_cache_node_percent_vote_average.function = 'average')
  WHERE node.type = 'beer_recipe'
    ORDER BY votingapi_cache_node_percent_vote_average_value DESC
```

This query has multiple levels. It has a `SELECT`, a `WHERE`, and an `ORDER BY`, so we can expect `EXPLAIN` to show those results. In this case, however, there's the added level of the `JOIN`.

```
| id | select_type | table   | type | possible_keys     | key     |
key_len | ref     | rows | Extra
+----+-------------+----------------------------------------------+-------
|  1 | SIMPLE      | votingapi_cache_node_percent_vote_average | ALL
|
content,content_function,content_tag_func,content_vtype_tag,content_vty
pe_tag_func | NULL    | NULL   | NULL |    5 | Using where; Using
filesort |
```

```
|  1 | SIMPLE     | node  | eq_ref | PRIMARY,node_type
   | PRIMARY | 4       |
logrusbrewing.votingapi_cache_node_percent_vote_average.content_id |
1 | Using where        |
+----+------------+-----------------------------------------------------------+--------
-+---------------------------------
```

This query has two parts, both of which are simple. They use different tables, but both use a WHERE operation to reduce the amount of data returned. In this case, optimizing the voting average might speed up the query.

### Resources for EXPLAIN

If you need more detail on the exact syntax and usage of EXPLAIN, you may refer to these sites:

MySQL documentation for EXPLAIN:
http://dev.mysql.com/doc/refman/<version>/en/explain.html

PostgreSQL documentation:
http://www.postgresql.org/docs/current/static/sql-explain.html

## Indexing Versus Caching

Drupal contains a number of caching mechanisms. There are many situations where performance may be improved by using a cache instead of forcing tables and fields to do a dance to satisfy your whims. The most important caching mechanism for general site usage is anonymous page caching. Anonymous page caching builds and stores a copy of each page; when anonymous (not logged in) users visit the page, they are provided with this version of the page. This feature, more than anything else, can greatly reduce the amount of time it takes to process a request and supply a page in return.

Page caching is enabled at Administer >> Site configuration >> Performance. Selecting "Normal" under the Page cache turns on anonymous page caching. The page cache is updated whenever the content within a given page is updated. For a majority of Web sites, this strategy is sufficient to speed performance without taking additional steps into query optimization—enough so that it is the recommended setting for Drupal production Web sites.

Drupal also has a caching mechanism for blocks, located on the same page as the page caching mechanism. This feature is either enabled or disabled, and otherwise is handled internally by the block itself.

Additionally, Views has its own pluggable caching mechanism that can be enabled for each view.

Caching is at a different level than indexing. When something is cached, it's usually an entire rendered piece of content (e.g., a page, a block). Once a query is built and displayed, it's cached. Building the query quickly and efficiently? That's what indexing is all about.

# Experimenting with Your Site

Like many things in Drupal, or any other activity, there is often more than one way to accomplish a goal. Just because you can build a query, it doesn't mean that approach is the best or most efficient way to accomplish a task. The simplest queries are built with data from a single table. There are many times when the simple query will be more than sufficient for the needs of a given page. As long as that table is well structured and organized, it may be difficult to come up with changes that can optimize the query.

With more complex queries, including those using multiple tables and their associated JOIN clauses, there is often more than one way to create a query that will return the data you need. Starting a query with a well-indexed or small table may speed things up because that first step will quickly pass the results to a larger table.

As an example, consider two tables. One contains a username and user ID; the other stores user ID and a list of shirts that user has entered into the system. There are two obvious ways to construct a query accessing these tables. First, you can use the username to find the user ID. Armed with that result, you can use PHP or a SQL stored procedure to take that value and find which shirts that ID has entered. The second method would be to sort the shirt table by user ID, and then compare that result with the user ID table. Knowing that the user ID is likely to come from a smaller table, and that it is likely to be a foreign key for the shirt table (and possibly an index as well), it makes much more sense to perform the query to retrieve the ID first.

Views utilizes a "base table" concept. When creating a view, the view type determines the base table (e.g., user, node). All views are tied to this concept. Because of the base table, a query may sometimes be reversed from its optimal direction. -

There are also relationships to think about. When you add a relationship between some data for a view, Views loads all of that data to make it available, even if you need only one field. You may need to do more analysis to narrow down specific fields you want, instead of letting Views load the data all for you.

# Summary

When we discussed the process of creating content types in Chapters 1 and 2, we talked a little about your site and data structure. Ultimately, optimization is about making the best use of your data structure, capitalizing on your database's strengths, and being smart about putting it all together. Many resources are available on the Internet to assist you with optimizing data, constructing queries, and using your chosen database with your own Drupal installation.

Testing your Web site under load conditions, reviewing your performance data, and understanding what you really want your user experience to be like are the key factors in creating a truly optimized experience for your users.

# Views API

In this chapter, we explore the nuts and bolts of how Views is put together, and we get our hands dirty talking seriously about PHP code. Each view consists of a staggering number of moving parts, all of which have to be assembled in the right place at the right time to give the user the final output. In addition, all of these parts need to support a user interface where each piece could need its own configuration. The cost of this flexibility, of course, is a long list of parts that are included, plus a broad ability to extend this list by other modules. In essence, Views follows the Drupal core model of modularity but uses a very different architecture than the Drupal core itself uses.

## Data Architecture

The Drupal core uses a procedural architecture, meaning that the code primarily focuses on functions. To be extensible, it provides a large list of known events, and it lets modules use specially named functions—*hooks*—to respond to these events. And while Views does take advantage of these events, mostly for data gathering and in process modification, this is not actually the model that it uses for most purposes.

Instead, Views uses an object-oriented architecture, which means it is more about classes and methods than it is about functions. In addition to providing new functionality via hooks, it allows modules to add code via *extending* the objects. Also, instead of a model where anyone can use a specially named function to add to the flow, Views requires registration of objects, which are then given supreme authority to handle particular operations.

The procedural model is often said to allow extension horizontally, whereas the object-oriented model allows extension vertically. What this means is that in the procedural model, siblings can modify each other's behavior; in contrast, in the object-oriented model, the extension is from parent to child, and siblings aren't really allowed to get involved. The difference is that siblings generally can only add to another sibling's behavior, whereas a child can completely control what a parent does to the point of disallowing the parent from running any code at all. Because a large part of Views' code exists in parent objects, children objects registered by other modules can, therefore, override large portions of Views' behavior completely if the parent object's code does not do what the child object needs.

## Object-Oriented Programming

Some of the core principles of object-oriented programming differ greatly from the procedural model. Some may cause confusion in newer developers, especially if they are already familiar with the procedural approach but are unfamiliar with the new codebase. While we do not have the space to provide an exhaustive treatment of object-oriented programming here, we will start off with a few basics to set the stage for understanding how Views is put together.

Object-oriented programming is built on the principles of *abstraction* and *encapsulation*. Abstraction means that particular areas of functionality are meant to know as little as possible about other areas of functionality; encapsulation means that functionality should be kept with the data. To illustrate these concepts, let's compare two ways of doing the same thing. First we will establish a piece of data that we are working with:

```
class vehicle {
  var $color;
  var $seats;
}
```

Here we have a simple piece of data with a few well-known properties. Setting and retrieving those properties is straightforward and is the same for both procedural and object-oriented code. However, performing actions on or with these objects is the first place that the two methodologies differ considerably.

Suppose we want to write code that will "start" the vehicle—that is, code that will handle the simple task of setting a property on the vehicle to let us know that it is running:

```
function start_vehicle($auto) {
  $auto->running = TRUE;
}


$car = new vehicle;
start_vehicle($car);
```

In the object-oriented paradigm, we would use a *method*, which is a function attached to the object:

```
class vehicle {
  // ...properties...
  function start() {
    $this->running = TRUE;
  }
}
$car = new vehicle;
$car->start();
```

The key difference in the object-oriented model so far is that when you have a method, which is a function attached to a class, you automatically get the special variable $this, which represents the object being worked on. Otherwise, it seems that what we're working with is the same, except for some syntactic sugar to make the program go down easier.

Let's add another layer of complexity to this example. We want to add a person object that can then be used to drive the vehicle:

```
class person {
  var $gender;
  var $height;
  var $weight;
}
```

Of course, we also need a way to have the person drive the car:

```
function drive_vehicle($person, $vehicle) {
  // ...
}
```

or, as you might expect in the object-oriented manner:

```
class person {
  // ...properties...
  function drive($vehicle) {
    // ...
  }
}
```

Again, there's nothing too terribly different between these two programs yet. But when we start adding variations on the same data, the object-oriented model really begins to shine.

Suppose we want to have a few different types of vehicles: a car, a motorcycle, and an airplane. We want to have licenses to see which people can drive each vehicle. Here is one way a procedural program might attack this version of the problem:

```
class vehicle {
  var $type;
}

class person {
  var $license;
}

function can_drive_vehicle($person, $vehicle) {
  switch ($vehicle->type) {
```

```
    case 'car':
      if ($person->license != 'driver') {
        return FALSE;
      }
      break;
    case 'motorcycle':
      if ($person->license != 'motorcycle') {
        return FALSE;
      }
      break;
    case 'airplane':
      if ($person->license != 'pilot') {
        return FALSE;
      }
      break;
  }

  // If this switch did not return, then this person has permission
  // to drive this vehicle.
  return TRUE;
}

function drive_vehicle($person, $vehicle) {
  if (!can_drive_vehicle($person, $vehicle)) {
    return;
  }
  // ...
}
```

Object-oriented developers hate this kind of code, because there is no clarity to whether the person or the vehicle is really responsible for the data determining whether a vehicle can be driven. In addition, you have to modify this code directly to add new vehicle types. Let's look at how the object-oriented developer might have done the same thing:

```
class vehicle {
function can_be_driven_by($license) {
    return TRUE;
  }
}

class car extends vehicle {
function can_be_driven_by($license) {
    return $license == 'driver';
  }
}
```

```
class motorcycle extends vehicle {
function can_be_driven_by($license) {
    return $license == 'motorcycle';
  }
}

class airplane extends vehicle {
function can_be_driven_by($license) {
    return $license == 'pilot';
  }
}

class person {
  var $license;
function drive($vehicle) {
    if (!$vehicle->can_be_driven_by($person->license)) {
      return;
    }
    // ...
  }
}
```

Whoa! Don't let your head spin on that one too much! First, this example demonstrates encapsulation. Clearly, a person is responsible for the driving. The vehicle is responsible for testing whether it can be driven by a person with a given license; it doesn't need to know anything about the person holding the license. The person just knows that the vehicle has a method it can use to find out if it can be driven. The functionality is encapsulated with the data it is most relevant to, and the two objects know as little about each other as is necessary to do their jobs.

In addition to satisfying the object oriented developer's need for abstraction and encapsulation, we introduced two really unique principles to object-oriented philosophy in the preceding example. They are really the two things that make object-oriented development what it is: *inheritance* and *polymorphism*. Inheritance means that we have children classes that inherit all of the properties and methods of their parent class. Polymorphism describes the scenario in which an object can be treated as though it were the parent object. In this case, we have four distinct classes: vehicle, car, motorcycle, and airplane. However, as far as the person::drive() method is concerned, it just receives a vehicle. If $vehicle happens to be of class airplane, the person object doesn't really care. It runs the appropriate method and gets the appropriate response.

How does all this work? Under the principle of inheritance, when a child object extends a parent object, the child object gains all of the methods and properties of the parent, plus the child is allowed to define additional methods and properties of its own. In addition, the child object is allowed to provide methods and properties that have the same names as those on the parent object. This practice, which is called *overriding,* is one of the key principles that makes object-oriented behavior possible. In our driving example, if we added a fourth vehicle, `bicycle`, and did not add a `can_drive` method to it, then `bicycle::can_drive()` would *inherit* the method from the vehicle object, meaning any person could drive it regardless of his or her license. In addition, we don't need to modify any of the previously developed code to add this new class. We just instantiate a bicycle and try to drive it:

```
class bicycle extends vehicle {
  var $motorized =  FALSE;
}

$person = new person;
$vehicle = new bicycle;
$person->drive($vehicle);
```

Believe it or not, that is just about all of the object-oriented programming paradigm that anyone really needs to understand to work with the Views API. There is just one more piece of the puzzle that needs to be mentioned. Once you get all of this information, you should be armed with the tools necessary to succeed.

What if you don't want to actually override a parent's method, but instead want to extend it? You have two options. First, if necessary, you can cut and paste the method directly from the parent into the child and modify it. Sometimes, that just has to happen if the parent's method is complex or needs to be split apart. At other times, however, we just need to do something before or after the method runs, and use the same code as the parent. We can do that quite easily:

```
class some_class extends some_other_class {
function some_method($args) {
   do_some_setup();
   return parent::some_method($args);
  }
}
```

In this case, we were able to do a little setup, and then we called the immediate parent object's method. In this case, `parent` is a keyword that allows this method to reach other methods that are normally completely inaccessible.

### Constructors and Destructors

One other important part of object-oriented design that is (surprisingly) not all that relevant to Views is the concept of constructors and destructors. In PHP, constructors are special functions that are executed automatically when an object is instantiated (with the `new` keyword); destructors are run when the object goes out of scope and can no longer be referenced. Views uses these functions rarely, because how they are used changed between PHP4 and PHP5, and Views is intended to be compatible with PHP4. If you run across an object with a method that has the same name as the object, you should recognize that it is a constructor and will be run when the object is created.

## Base Tables and Relationships

Fundamentally, Views is about fetching a group of objects of a given type. Originally Views was restricted to just nodes. Later, innovations in Views 2 allowed this object type to be any table, with one important restriction: the table being used must have a single (i.e., not compound) primary key. In practice, Views provides a list of some group of first-class objects in the system. This usually means users and nodes, but it also includes taxonomy terms, comments, files, and whatever other tables a module might provide that need Views. In the UI, this is called the view type.

Whatever table is used for this purpose, internally Views refers to it as the *base table,* and it is the key to how Views ties data together. When adding other tables to a query, Views will automatically figure out how the new table joins to the base table and add the joins to the list. In the configuration provided to Views, every declared table contains information about how that table relates to one or more base tables. These are occasionally referred to as *implicit relationships* because Views knows about them and creates them automatically.

### What Are Base Tables?

Base tables are the core objects that someone building a Drupal site might want to use to make lists. The canonical example of a base table is the node table, and the users table is a close second. Less frequently used tables may also be good base table candidates, such as node revisions, comments, and taxonomy terms. Items that might be listed specifically in an administrative UI are also good choices, such as watchdog entries and view statistics. Tables that are not really primary data—such as roles, permissions, and profile fields—are not good candidates for base tables.

For example, suppose we have a node view, and the user adds the Node: Body field. In the schema, this field is not stored in the node table; it is actually stored in the `node_revisions` table, and is related to the node table using the `vid` field. Views knows about this relationship. Thus, when the field is added, Views automatically joins the `node_revisions` table to make its fields available, and then adds the field.

When describing a join to Views, there are three critical pieces of information:

- Base table: Each table can have one implicit join to any base table.
- Field: Which field to join on. Usually this is a key of some sort.
- Left table: If we think of the path the join takes as starting from the table and traveling to the left until it gets to the base table, this would be the table to the immediate left on the way to the base table. It may link directly to the base table, which means the journey will be done after one hop. Alternatively, it could be some intermediary table, in which case that intermediary table will then be added. It, too, will look to the left, adding tables until finally the base table is reached.

In addition, other modifiers may be used. For example, there can be operators and extra fields in describing joins, which can be used for more complex joins, such as deltas used to pick just one item when there is a many-to-one relationship.

This data is limited to just one implicit join per base table. But what if multiple paths can be followed to reach the base table? A great example in Drupal is the files table, which can use many paths to get to the node table. The Upload module has a table that it uses to link uploaded attachments to nodes, but the Image module also has a table that IT uses to link uploaded attachments to nodes. Views won't let you have both.

The solution to this dilemma is the creation of an *explicit relationship*. These relationships are detailed enough to be added in the UI, where they set up the right paths and make certain that the right tables are available. Because all fields selected in the UI are considered to be attached to base tables, all relationships must provide a base table. This can be the same base table used for the view, or it can be a different base table.

In the preceding example, a relationship is provided on the upload table, "Upload: Attached files." This adds a relationship to the files table. As a consequence, all of the fields associated with the files table become available. The Image module provides a similar service.

Internally, where items selected in the UI do not matter as much, relationships can be used to add individual tables. One useful application of relationships is to add a sense of hierarchy. By chaining relationships together, you can create a simple loop that gets information up or down a parent/child tree.

## The Objects Involved in a View

The pluggable nature of Views means that a large number of objects are utilized to figure out the data needed. These objects are generally classified into three categories: the *view* object, *plugins,* and *handlers.* A fourth object, the *query* object, is owned by the view. In the future, this object will actually be a plugin. Finally, the query object needs *join* objects that describe how to join tables together—a capability needed to handle some of the more complex joins.

The view object represents the view as it is stored in the database (or in a module's code). It is also used to execute the view—that is, to build the query, execute the query, and render the results. It is based on the `views_db_object`, which contains methods for reading, writing, and exporting a view.

Plugins are objects that control most of the real behavior of the view. The most important plugins are *display, style,* and *row style.* You can think of the display plugin as a way of telling the view where to display its content—that is, as a block, as a page with its own URL, or as an RSS feed. Display choices also can be more esoteric. Some displays simply attach themselves to other displays, essentially letting you run multiple views in the same view. The Panels module includes its own display plugin to create views as panel panes. A given view must always have a display to function, even if it is just the default display that does not put the view anywhere in particular (but does allow the view to be accessed from code elsewhere, which is a method known as *embedding* a view).

Style plugins answer the question of how to display the view—that is, as a table, as a list using `<ul>`, or as just each row one after another. Again, many other styles are added by other modules.

Row styles are subordinate to styles, and inform Views how each record from a view is rendered. Row styles are not used by all styles. For example, the table style has to handle the HTML for the table, row, and cell items, so it does not use row styles. Most other styles simply care that they are displaying one blob of data after another, and they let the row style handle what each blob of data will look like. As with the display plugin, all views must utilize a style plugin or the view will not know how to render anything.

Other types of plugins include the *access, argument default,* and *argument validator* plugins. These special-purpose plugins are less visible than the display and style plugins, but are often just as important. Access plugins determine whether the logged-in user can even see the results of a view. The argument default plugins allow views that use arguments to extract the data for the argument from their environment rather than having the argument passed directly (e.g., a view as a block gets no arguments, whereas a view as a page gets arguments from the URL). Validator plugins allow views to ensure that the argument data is useful and may also be used to transform the data. While an access plugin is required, the argument plugins are not required for a view to function.

All plugin objects are derived from the `views_plugin` object, which primarily contains UI methods for telling Views about forms. The `views_plugin` object is, in turn, derived from `views_object`, which handles properties for the object and smoothes the process of getting defaults and translations.

At the time of this writing, there were several more plugin types in development, including plugins for caching; view translation; swapping out the query back end to generate interfaces with other APIs such as REST APIs or dedicated search engines; new pager types; and replacements for the header, footer, and empty text intended to make them more interactive with view data.

Handlers are very similar to plugins, but they are tightly coupled to the query of the view. Handlers provide all of the data necessary to build the query, and then extract the needed data from the query results. Five types of handlers exist, which correspond very closely to the SQL structure. Fields represent the fields used in the SELECT portion of the statement. Filters represent the WHERE clause. Sort criteria represent the ORDER BY clause. Relationships represent JOIN statements, and arguments are generally WHERE clauses that obtain their data from an external source.

The handler objects are all derived from `views_handler`, which contains most of the interface necessary to use a handler. That includes UI information as well as stub methods for interacting with the query at the right moment. Like `views_plugin`, the handler object is derived from `views_object` to provide a mechanism for property storage.

## Plugin and Handler Naming Conventions

Given the vast array of these objects, the naming convention used by Views for plugins and handlers is not actually enforced. Nevertheless, you will find that Views sticks to it rigidly, and most modules implement it pretty closely. This naming convention can help you figure out which object a given thing will use and tells you a lot about what the object does. For plugins, the naming convention looks like this:

*MODULENAME*_plugin_*PLUGINTYPE_PLUGINNAME*

*MODULENAME*, then, is the owning module. This module is often Views, but when the plugin is provided by another module, it is simply that module's name. This is a common practice within Drupal to prevent namespace collisions. *PLUGINTYPE* is display, style, row, access, or something else, as per the type of plugin it is. Finally, *PLUGINNAME* is the simple name of the plugin. For example, the table style is simply known as table. Thus `views_plugin_style_table` is the object for the table style plugin; `views_plugin_display_page` is the object for the page display plugin.

### Properties and Methods for views_object

`views_object` is the base class for all plugins and handlers, and primarily provides a common component for configuration. What follows is not a complete list of methods and properties, but rather a selection of those methods and properties containing information that is important to users who might be creating their own plugins and styles.

```
var $options = array();
```

The `$options` array holds all of the options for a view after they have been translated. The exact options available depend on the object, and will be defined by the `option_definition()` method.

```
var $definition = array();
```

The `$definition` array contains data from either `hook_views_handlers` or `hook_views_plugins` associated with the object, which is used to define what the object works on. For handlers, this data includes the table and field it is attached to, plus any options that the handler may require. For plugins, it includes parentage and theme information. For example, the table style plugin has the following definition in Views' `hook_views_plugins`:

```
'table' => array(
  'title' => t('Table'),
  'help' => t('Displays rows in a table.'),
  'handler' => 'views_plugin_style_table',
  'theme' => 'views_view_table',
  'uses row plugin' => FALSE,
  'uses fields' => TRUE,
  'uses options' => TRUE,
  'type' => 'normal',
  'help topic' => 'style-table',
),
```

Each of the above items will be available in `views_plugin_style_table` once that plugin object has been fully initialized.

```
function option_definition() { return array(); }
```

This method is meant to be overridden by the specific class, and is used to explain to Views which properties the object needs. In particular, it ensures that all properties will have a default, and that Views will try to only save only items whose settings are changed from the defaults. It also helps Views determine which items are translatable.

This function returns an array with the following settings:

```
'option_name' => array(
  'default' => default value,
  'translatable' => TRUE/FALSE (wrap in t() on export if true),
  'contains' => If this item is not actually a property but an
    array of properties, this will be array of items, each with
    its own defaults, etc. If contains is set, 'default' will be
    ignored and assumed to be array().
),
```

Because PHP4 and PHP5 have different styles for constructors, Views uses a construct method that simulates a more PHP5-style constructor.

```
function construct() { $this->set_default_options(); }
```

This method is used almost immediately after a handler or plugin has been instantiated, and should be used to perform any initialization prior to learning about a view or display object that it might be attached to. Any object-instantiating construct should always call `parent::construct()` to make sure that options get their default values.

```
function destroy()
```

Much like the construct method, the destroy method is a fake destructor. This method was created because PHP prior to version 5.3 has trouble automatically destroying objects with back references, owing to the fact that the reference counters never go to zero. As a consequence, a view object contains a reference to a display object, and a display object contains a reference back to the view. Because these two objects contain references to each other, even if nothing else references these two objects, they will not be destroyed and, therefore, will continue to eat up memory. The primary use of this method is to clean up references that might cause this problem. The parent method automatically removes any references to the view or display. Child objects are responsible for dealing with anything that is left over from this cleanup operation.

## Properties and Methods for the Query Object

The query object is responsible for taking the data of the view and turning it into an actual SQL SELECT statement. It contains methods to add tables to JOIN, fields, WHERE clauses, ORDER BY clauses, and other SQL goodies. When the object is instantiated, it is given the base table and the primary field for that table. Handlers and some plugins then add their data needs to the query. When all of this processing of the view is complete, the `query()` method is called to create the actual SQL statement to be executed.

```
var $table_queue = array();
```

The table queue contains all the tables that will be made into JOIN statements, plus a little bit of information about each table. The key to the array is the alias of the table. The array contains the following data:

```
'table_alias' => array(
  'table' => "Real database name of the table",
  'num' => "Instance number of this table if it is in the query
     multiple times. This field is more or less legacy and not really
     used.",
  'alias' => "Alias of the table, matching the key",
  'join' => "Views_join object describing how to create a join. "
  'relationship' => "ID of the relationship this table belongs to",
);
```

During query processing, the table queue is used to create the actual JOIN statements.

```
var $tables = array();
```

This array is related closely to the table queue. Instead of holding the actual list of tables added to the JOIN statement, however, it holds information keyed by relationship so that the query object can figure out if a table already exists during the path finding step. This array is a two-dimensional array.

```
var $relationships = array();
```

The first dimension of the array is the relationship. Every relationship in the table (of which there will always be at least one, the base relationship) is represented here. Each table that relationship needs will then be represented here with the following data:

```
[$relationship][$table] = array(
  'count' => "number of times this table appears in the query",
  'alias' => "The alias of this table used in the table_queue",
);
```

Each relationship represented in the query will be contained in this array. The data contained in each item looks like this:

```
[$alias] = array(
  'link' => "All relationships except for the 'base' relationship
    chain from another relationship. This points to that relationship
    or NULL if it is the base relationship.",
  'table' => "The actual table added by this relationship",
  'alias' => "The same alias used in the key",
  'base' => "The base table that will be provided by this
    relationship. This is usually the same as 'table'.",
);
```

By default, a query will not be set to use the DISTINCT flag. When setting this field, however, it will change the primary field to DISTINCT, causing the database to try to pull only unique records.

```
function set_distinct($value = TRUE)
```

It's worth noting that databases are finicky about whether this flag will truly pull distinct records. Sometimes it ignores this setting and creates duplicated records anyhow.

```
function set_count_field($table, $field, $alias = NULL)
```

When using paging, the query has to generate a query to count how many records are present so that it knows how many pages to produce. It will do this automatically, but it does need to count on a field. By default, the primary field is used, and nothing needs to be done here. Special queries, such as the summary queries, need to page on different data, however.

```
function add_relationship($alias, $join, $base, $link_point = NULL)
```

This method adds a relationship to the query. It will attempt to adjust for alias collisions, but use caution with this function: it is known to fail to adjust properly and break the query. The instantiated join object is required here, and should contain a join that links to a table that already exists in the query. It may be necessary to call the ensure_table() method prior to making the add_relationship() call. The add_relationship() method will return the alias of the relationship actually used.

```
function add_table($table, $relationship = NULL, $join = NULL, $alias = NULL)
```

The add table function is one of two ways to get a join into the query. Its use ensures that all intermediary tables are included in the query. This method then adds the table regardless of whether it already exists in the query, and adjusts for alias collisions. If not otherwise specified, the relationship is assumed to be the base relationship. The $join object will be found from the views data, but can be specified to join the table differently. The auto-generated alias may have a number appended to it to avoid alias collisions. This method returns the actual alias used, and that value should always be kept: It is needed to refer to the data in the query results.

```
function ensure_table($table, $relationship = NULL, $join = NULL)
```

This is the second method of adding a join to the query. However, this approach will not actually add the table if it already exists, which is the most common case. It then becomes much easier for handlers to cooperate with each other, because they do not need to make assumptions about the existence of a table. The $join parameter allows you to specify a join other than the default, but in general should not be used with ensure_table(). Instead, use add_table() if $join needs to be specialized, as other items using ensure_table() will not realize that the intended join is different than the default. This method returns the actual alias used, and that value should always be kept: it is needed to refer to the data in the query results.

```
function adjust_join($join, $relationship)
```

The normal method for adding a table traces a path back to the base table and adds each table directly to the query. When every table is part of the base relationship, this approach works out well. However, when relationships come into play, all of the names change, because the tables could easily already be in the query and we do not want to have naming collisions. Ordinarily, adding a table through the normal means will adjust the joins automatically, with the actual aliases to use being looked up in the `$tables` array. However, in certain very rare circumstances, it may be necessary to make this adjustment yourself and add this specification into the query. You can safely do so using this method, which will mark the join so it won't be erroneously readjusted a second time.

```
function add_field($table, $field, $alias = '', $params = NULL)
```

If your field is being added through a simple database column, the `$table` parameter will automatically be run through `ensure_table()` to make sure it is valid, and then the field will be added. The alias will be `$table_$field` by default.

When you are adding a field that is not a simple database column, `$table` should be NULL; `$field` can then contain the formula. The formula should be complete and use table aliases provided only by previous calls to `add_table()` or `ensure_table()`. It is important to never refer to a table by anything other than an alias provided by the query object, because relationships can cause those aliases to be something completely unexpected. *Even if you provided the alias to `add_table()`, that alias may have been modified prior to being used.*

The `$params` parameter can contain an array of additional data about the field. Currently, it supports `distinct`, a Boolean flag to tell the query generator to add DISTINCT to the field. The `count` flag turns the field into the COUNT function. Finally, `aggregate`, if set to TRUE, means that this field is an aggregate function and, therefore, remains a normal field in a GROUP BY clause. If GROUP BY is enabled in the query, fields that are not aggregate are automatically added to the GROUP BY to ensure ANSI SQL compatibility.

```
function set_where_group($type = 'AND', $group = NULL, $where = 'where')
```

When adding WHERE and HAVING clauses to the query, be aware that they must be added in groups, which allows a simple one-level tree for creating some amount of OR logic. While Views does not support this feature fully, the WHERE group can be used externally to create a simple OR structure.

```
function set_group_operator($type = 'AND')
```

All top-level groups will, by default, be combined with AND. To combine them with OR instead, use this function to change that setting.

```
function add_where($group, $clause, ...)
```

```
function add_having($group, $clause)
```

These two functions are identical, except that one adds the clause into the WHERE portion of the SQL statement, and the other adds it into the HAVING portion. HAVING is used only when GROUP BY is part of the query; it restricts grouping to items matching the stated comparisons. The $group should have already been defined with set_where_group(), but it can also be NULL, which is the default "ungrouped" condition. All filters in Views will have a $this->group setting, defining which group to use. All mentions of tables in this clause should use aliases provided by add_table() or ensure_table() to be relationship safe. All arguments following the clause should match up with Drupal's standard for query substitutions used by db_query() to ensure the safety of possibly user input data:

- %d Any numeric, integer value.
- %f Any numeric floating-point value.
- %s Any string.
- %b Any binary blob data.
- %% A literal %.

```
function add_orderby($table, $field, $order, $alias = '')
```

To add sort criteria to the query, use this method. The $table, if specified, will be automatically ensured. All ORDER BY statements will be automatically added as fields to meet ANSI SQL standards. When ordering on a formula, use NULL for the table and use $field for the formula. The $alias will then be required, so the field can be added safely. $order should be either ASC or DESC. Use proper capitalization, as case will not be translated.

```
function add_groupby($clause)
```

This method adds a simple GROUP BY clause. As with WHERE clauses and ORDER BY, make sure to only use aliases of tables assigned by Views to ensure relationship compatibility. Once a GROUP BY clause is added, any fields that are not aggregate fields will automatically be added to the GROUP BY clause to satisfy ANSI SQL requirements.

```
function query($get_count = FALSE)
```

When all of the data has been added to the query object, this method can be used to generate the final query. It will process everything and return a SQL statement that can be sent to db_query() (and should be passed through db_rewrite_sql() for access control). If the argument is true, a COUNT query will be generated to return the number of records the main query would have used. If possible, this query will strip out the fields; it will not strip these fields if GROUP BY or DISTINCT is used.

# The Views API

As mentioned previously, the Views API uses an amalgam of Drupal's normal procedural hooks and its own inheritance based object-oriented approach. You use hooks to tell Views about your objects, and then your objects are called upon to do the real work. You can also use a hook to change the execution of the application.

### Hooks in Drupal

Drupal uses a method for responding to events called hooks. A hook is a specially named function that a module can implement. When hooks are invoked, all modules with a function matching the specified name have their implementations called. They can do whatever is necessary for that event—sometimes modifying objects passed and sometimes returning data.

Hooks are named `hook_HOOKNAME` in documentation. They are implemented by creating a function and replacing the word "hook" in the function name with your module's name. For more information about modules and hooks in Drupal, refer to the Drupal API documentation at http://api.drupal.org.

All hooks that Views implements start with the word "views" so that there are no namespace conflicts with other modules. With one exception, Views expects the hooks to be stored in a *MODULENAME*.`views`.`inc` file that will be stored with the module. That exception is the hook used to tell Views whether it implements the Views API, where your files are stored, and which version of the API the module is compatible with. That hook is called `hook_views_api` and it returns a small array of data. Typically it looks like this:

```
function hook_views_api() {
  return array(
    'api' => 2,
    'path' => drupal_get_path('module', 'modulename') . '/views',
  );
}
```

The API returned is the minimum API version the module can support. This means that if the API version of the installed Views module is older than that, Views will not try to run the module's code. If the module is older than what Views thinks it can use, it also will not try to run the code. The path can be left out if the file to include is found in the module's directory, but it is often recommended to create a `views` or `includes` directory and keep code there, as Views can end up using many files and it is important to keep them organized.

The objects that Views uses are implemented one per file. Each object must be registered with the proper hook, and it must be registered with the parent chain. Because Views can utilize so many objects, and because any given view needs to use only a fraction of them, Views uses this system to try to reduce the amount of code loaded. PHP has limited memory available, and loading code still takes time off the page. By loading class definitions only on demand, Views tries to mitigate some of the performance costs inherent in a generic query builder. It is important to reiterate that without this hook, Views will not try to call registration hooks for a module, even if the hook appears to be implemented properly.

It is also important to note that Views does not routinely check for registration hooks on every page load. Instead, these hooks are cached to improve performance, because they rarely change. During development, however, the hooks change frequently. Fortunately, there is a setting at Administer >> Site building >> Views >> Tools that can disable this caching entirely. It is highly recommend that this setting be used only during development.

# The Life Cycle of a View

Views goes through a relatively long process from starting a view to finally presenting rendered output to the user. First, the view has to be loaded and argument input given. Then, handlers and plugins have to be instantiated, pager data loaded into the view, and the exposed forms executed to get the input. After that, the build process will go through all of the handlers, which can add their own data to the query. The query is executed, and finally the style and handlers render the view. Along the way, hooks are called to allow modules to modify the view during the process to let them do all manner of crazy things to the query if necessary.

## View Execution Cycle

The first step in the view execution cycle is to load the view using `views_get_view()`. This function will search the database for a view, by name, as well as check for *default views* provided by modules. If a view is both in the database and in code as a default view, the database version is considered to override the in-code settings. This action loads the `$view` object as well as any associated displays, but does not instantiate any handlers. All handler settings are stored with the associated display, which is either the default display or the specific display if they are overridden.

Once the view is loaded, arguments are loaded into it. The view itself never really knows where the arguments are coming from, although the display plugins get to make some assumptions about that. For example, page displays know that they will come from the URL, and block displays know that they don't normally get arguments. Arguments are given as a simple array via the `set_arguments()` method. The first item in the array will correspond to the first argument in the list in the UI, and so on until there are no more arguments.

### Initialization

Initialization is a two-step process. First, the display plugins are instantiated. Each plugin object is created, the `construct()` method run, and the `init()` method run. The `init()` method ties the view and display object (which just holds database information) to the display plugin. The options are read from the display object and unpacked into the `$options` array on the display plugin, and a pointer to the default display is kept so that options can easily be retrieved from the correct place.

### view::pre_execute()

The `pre_execute()` method sets the view for use in `views_get_current_view()`, storing the last view there in case views are embedded within views. It calls the `views_pre_view` hook, makes sure the arguments are set, and then loads pager data from the display onto the view, if applicable. If this step is skipped, Views will default to 10 items per page if `pre_execute()` is not called. Failing to call the `pre_execute()` method is a common oversight often missed by users when trying to run a view manually.

### view::build()

`hook_views_pre_build` is called to let modules make modifications to the view prior to running it. This is where modules could add or remove handlers if they have a need to do so. These handlers could create very specialized queries if necessary.

Next, the build method initializes all objects in the display, if they are not already initialized. `$view->build_info` is created, which will ultimately hold the query and arguments, plus assorted data about the query as needed, such as breadcrumbs and title information. The objects initialized in this step include the query object, all display plugins, and all field, sort, filter, argument and relationship handlers. The one handler that is not initialized immediately in this phase is the style plugin; its initialization is delayed until after arguments are processed, because arguments can change which style is used if they put the view into summary mode.

Once all of the handlers are initialized, `pre_query()` is called on all handlers. The exposed form is built, processed, and rendered, and data from it is extracted into `$view->exposed_input`, which will be used for filter input when filters are processed. If exposed filters fail the validation test, the abort flag is set.

The normal build process for handlers is to first pass exposed input into the handler, set the handler's relationship if it is using one, and then run the `query()` method on the handler. First relationships are built, because all handlers will need them, and then filters are built.

Argument building is much more complex, however, because arguments can make decisions that change the nature of the view. Each argument is processed by extracting the data from `$view->args` for the argument and passing it in. If the argument is not available, the default action for the argument is called. If another argument is passed after this happens, the argument is validated. Both the default action and the validation can cause the view to abort entirely, as well as put the view into summary mode. If the view goes into summary mode, sorts and fields are removed from the view, the style plugin is changed, and the argument takes over what happens. Well-written argument plugins have total control over the view at this point. Arguments can also decide that they will not participate in controlling the view, either because they have no argument or because they received the wildcard argument. Finally, arguments can modify the breadcrumb and the title, which is stored in the build info array. At the end of argument processing, substitutions are run on the title so that `%X` can be translated into argument data.

After arguments are processed, the style is initialized, the fields are processed (if the style uses them), and the sort criteria are processed. At this point, the display plugin and the style plugin are both allowed to add to the query.

Finally, the query object generates the actual query. The display asks any other displays on the view if they wish to attach to this display, which could cause another display to run through the entire process of building and executing a query, and allow icons and links to be added to get to other displays, such as attached RSS or atom feeds.

### view::execute()

The `hook_views_pre_execute` hook is called to allow modules to modify the view. The execute process then runs the query through `db_rewrite_sql()`, and checks whether it needs to change the active database. It modifies the query for any pager values that might be needed, runs the query, and changes the database back to the default if necessary. Results of the query are then stored in `$view->result`.

If caching is enabled, execution may be skipped to use cached results, and Views will offer the caching plugin the opportunity to store the result if it executes it.

### view::render()

The render process begins with a caching check, similar to execute. Then `pre_render()` is called on the style and, if the style supports it, all fields. Next, `hook_views_pre_render` is called. Rendering is delegated to the display plugin, which will call a theme function. Each display plugin can now do its own thing, although most will call the associated theme function for the display, which in turn will delegate tasks down to the style, row style, and individual fields.

### Teardown

When a view has finished the rendering operation, the view and all handlers will call the `destroy()` method. Technically, this method does not destroy the view, but it does unset most of the data on the view and remove any handlers. The primary reason for calling this method is to prevent PHP circular reference problems, because PHP cannot tell when objects that reference each other are no longer used; thus the objects will never get cleaned up without this teardown step.

## Executing a Views Display

There are three primary methods of executing a view, once it has been loaded. For displays that are executed where they are meant to be—that is, in the menu callback for page views, or in the block hook for block views—the `view::execute_display()` method is called. This method always returns data in the manner that the caller would expect. Thus, for blocks, instead of getting the view data, an array is returned containing the output that `hook_block` needs. A page view will set the page title and page breadcrumb. For this reason, `view::execute_display()` must be used with caution when a display is used outside of its intended location.

In this case, the `view::preview()` method is the superior choice. The preview method assumes absolutely nothing about the environment. It returns only the actual rendered output of the view. Any title or breadcrumb work can still be done by the caller by using `view::get_title()` and `view::get_breadcrumb()`. The following method is used by the `views_embed_view()` function:

```
function views_embed_view($name, $display_id = 'default') {
  $args = func_get_args();
  array_shift($args); // remove $name
  if (count($args)) {
    array_shift($args); // remove $display_id
  }

  $view = views_get_view($name);
  if (!$view) {
    return;
  }

  return $view->preview($display_id, $args);
}
```

This code is generally the minimum necessary to execute a view. When rendering a view via code, however, this function is often not enough, because it creates the view locally and isn't available at the end. Sometimes the title is needed, and sometimes a few other tricks are needed.

For example, Views will always use the path set in the view, if there is one, for the target on exposed filters, more links, summary links, or any other links that it generates. When a view is embedded, sometimes this behavior is desired—but sometimes it is not. It is easy to change this behavior by setting `view::override_path` prior to executing it. It is also possible to call `$view->set_display()` and then set options on the display to change how the view will appear, if the caller has specific needs, such as to always turn AJAX on or off, or always turn the pager off, or to always make sure that a given field is available.

Furthermore, the preview method can be broken down to make changes along the way. If necessary, the methods called in the view life cycle can be called on an as-needed basis. So long as the caller understands the ramifications of skipping steps, or making changes in between steps, there is a great deal of flexibility to be had. One very common approach is to skip the rendering phase entirely and use a view to fetch results. CCK uses this method for node reference input, where a view is used to select which nodes a reference can link to, and select options are given on the form.

## Execution-Related Hooks

There are many hooks that can modify or react to a view during the process of executing it. Data can be added, removed, or extracted from these views. Other things, such as blocks, can use this data for other purposes, as necessary. Usually these requirements are very specific to a given site, such as adding sidebars to Views to display related data, or adding restrictions to Views queries to do things that the existing filters cannot do.

`hook_views_pre_view` is called almost immediately, when no processing will yet have been done on the view:

```
hook_views_pre_view(&$view, $display_id, $args);
```

Almost anything about the view can be manipulated, and additional output can be added to the view by placing text on `$view->attachment_before` and `$view->attachment_after`. For modules that need specific headers on a view, this is a good place to add them.

`hook_views_pre_build()` is called before the build process, but displays are attached and the display performs its `pre_execute()` phase afterward:

```
hook_views_pre_build(&$view)
```

If there are attachments, they will already have completed their execution cycle, including calls to this hook. This hook may examine `$view->current_display` to see which display is being executed. As with `hook_pre_view`, text may be placed on `$view->attachment_before` and `$view->attachment_after`.

```
hook_views_query_alter (&$view, &$query)
```

This hook is called after all of the data for the query is known, but before this data is assembled into an actual SQL statement. The query object can be used to add or remove a wide array of items from the query. It is important, however, that aliases in the SELECT portion of the query are carefully preserved because they are used during the render process to retrieve the data. Removing them will cause PHP warnings to appear.

```
hook_views_pre_execute(&$view)
```

This hook is called right before the execute process. The query is now fully built, but it has not yet been run through `db_rewrite_sql()`, which may add items to the query for access control or whatever modules want to do. See the Drupal `hook_db_rewrite_sql` for more information.

```
hook_views_pre_render(&$view)
```

This hook is called right before the render process. The query has been executed, and the `pre_render()` phase has already happened for handlers, so all data should be available. This is a good place to do postprocessing on a view, such as making replacements via regular expression or the like.

```
hook_views_admin_links_alter (&$links, $view)
```

The last change that a module can make to a view is to add or remove administrative links from the hover tooltip that appears over a view. One fine example of this behavior would be a view that shows a list of items, such as from a node queue, and contains a hover link to go directly to the administrative interface for that list of items.

# The Database Schema and Data Hook

`hook_views_data()` is the single most important part of the Views API for module developers, because it is the method used to tell Views about a module's schema. All of the Drupal core is described to Views through a series of implementations of this hook. In fact, those implementations are the best place to look for existing examples of how this hook is used, because the schema used by Drupal is well known; it is a good place to understand how Views sees this data.

## Relating Tables to Each Other

To understand how the data in this hook is structured first requires realizing that Views does not see the data as a traditional relationship diagram. In particular, typical relationship diagrams will contain every relationship on each table to every other table in the schema. While Views may be interested in that information, there are two particular ways that Views sees this arrangement. When considering these two types of relationships, it is important to recognize that all relationships are to base tables, which correspond to the view type on the UI, although there are base tables that are not in the UI.

First, there is the *implicit relationship*. Such a relationship is so fundamental that you can always depend on it existing, so Views can simply assume that it's true. In general, implicit relationships can be used only if the records are tightly coupled and there is no ambiguity involved. For example, all users have zero or more roles that are stored in the `users_roles` table. The relationship between users and roles can, therefore, be considered implicit because they are tightly coupled and referring to a role when the view that is listing a user is unambiguous. Each user has one set of roles, and all roles are bound specifically to users.

In contrast, *explicit relationships* must be specified in the UI, because the system cannot rely on that relationship to be always true. For example, files are related to nodes ambiguously, because every module that attaches files to nodes needs to include a table to perform the attaching. The files table does not contain a node ID, just a user ID. Thus, when listing nodes, to list files attached to that node a user must specify the relationship in the UI to use; otherwise, Views will be unable to determine how the file relates to the node.

When calculating which tables and, therefore, which fields are available to the user, Views uses these relationships to build a path to the base table (view type) that is defined in the UI. This path tells Views how these tables will be joined in the query. Every table that is declared to have a join to the base table in the view will automatically have its fields available for use.

Explicit relationships create new or alternate base tables in the view. For example, when using the user reference CCK field, a user reference allows a relationship to be created from a node to a user based on this field. This adds a new base table to the view, such that all fields from the users table (and all fields declared to the users base table) become available. Likewise, the node reference CCK field allows a relationship to be created from one node to another node. While this does not add a new base table to the view, it does mean that every field within the view must now specifically declare which of the two possible nodes it is using. This choice appears as a select widget within the UI for each field.

## Declaring Tables in hook_views_data()

The hook_views_data() method returns an array of tables to Views. Each table in this array should be owned by (that is, implemented in the schema of) the module implementing hook_views_data(). What this means is that modules should not return data about tables not owned by the module. For example, only node_views_data() should return information about the node table, and only user_views_data() should return information about the users table. When modules need to make alterations to the data provided by other modules (and it is common to need to make additions to the node table), hook_views_data_alter() should be used instead. Attempting to return data about tables defined by other modules could actually corrupt the data when PHP tries to merge the data arrays together.

Each table array contains a definition array, which is accessed using the table key, and every other key in the array corresponds to a field within the table. The table array contains default text information about the table, and all of the implicit relationships available for that table. Tables that do not have implicit relationships (the join section) will not appear in the UI unless a relationship is added that refers to this table as a base table. Tables can also use this section to declare that they are base tables, meaning they will show up as view types.

In the next example, we demonstrate the two methods in which implicit relationships are usually created. When listing records from the bar table, the foo table is directly available by a join on the bar_id, which is part of the foo table. This is considered a one-hop join because the two tables join together directly:

```
// Definition of the 'foo' table
$data['foo'] = array(
  'table' => array(
    'group' => t('Foo'),
    'join' => array(
      // Simple one-hop join to the 'bar' base table
      'bar' => array(
        // The field on the bar table for the join
        'left_field' => 'bar_id',
        // The field on the foo table for the join
        'field' => 'bar_id',
      ),
      // More complex multi-hop join to the 'baz' base table
      'baz' => array(
        // We join to the baz table by way of the bar table
        'left_table' => 'bar',
        // The field on the bar table for the join
        'left_field' => 'bar_id',
```

```
        // The field on the foo table for the join
        'field' => 'bar_id',
      ),
  ),
  'field1' => array(
    // Information about the field1 field.
  ),
  'field2' => array(
    // Information about the field2 field.
  ),
);
```

Most schemas are not quite this simple, however, and relationships often take more than one join to complete. These are multi-hop joins, because they incorporate one (or more) intermediate joins to include the table when listing the base table. Views can actually include as many hops as necessary, as long as the hops follow a straight line, and each hop is defined. In the preceding example, we do not know how many hops are between the foo table and the baz table, and we don't have to. What Views knows is that to join foo to baz, it must first join bar. It will then check the bar table to see how it joins to foo. If it contains intermediary joins, Views will keep checking until it finds the path. Note that it is the developer's responsibility to ensure that all declared paths actually exist. Creating the previous example without also including a valid definition for the bar table would lead the Views UI to contain fields that could not properly be joined, and would likely end up creating invalid SQL.

> ### Tip
> Joins do not have to be simple field-to-field joins. In fact, Views contains a special type of object (which for legacy reasons is referred to as a handler, but does not actually behave as a handler) to control the behavior of joins. Views' default join handler can create many joins, but very complex schemas can have very complex joins and may require customized code. Explaining how to create these join handlers is beyond the scope of this book, but a quick perusal of the `views_join` object in `includes/handlers.inc` is an excellent starting point for exploring this possibility. A complete list of data used by the default join object can be found in the "Describing tables to Views" section of Views' Advanced Help module.

The declared tables do not have to be real tables, unless they are base tables. In fact, they can be aliases for existing tables. This approach is primarily used with complex joins, where the same table might be implicitly joined in multiple ways. For example, the history table in Views implicitly joins with a clause restricting the history records to the current user. In so doing, it creates an alias so that the real history table could also be joined in alongside it. For example:

```
// Explain how this table joins to others.
$data['history_user']['table']['join'] = array(
  // Directly links to node table.
```

```
    'node' => array(
      'table' => 'history',
      'left_field' => 'nid',
      'field' => 'nid',
      'extra' => array(
        array('field' => 'uid', 'value' => '***CURRENT_USER***',
          'numeric' => TRUE),
      ),
    ),
  );
```

By utilizing the table and extra key, this more complex join can be defined directly within Views. Note that this operation can't be completely dynamic, so it uses a special keyword to grab the current user ID (which is defined elsewhere by hook_views_query_substitutions()). Thus there are significant limitations when employing this method.

If a table is to be declared as a base table, which means it will show up as a view type, it will include the base keyword, with an array. This array includes only a small amount of data: a primary key field, a title, a help description, and an optional weight, which can be used to ensure that the most important view types are listed first. This data is necessary only for the most important tables, and should be used sparingly. The node table is the canonical example of a base table, and its declaration is included here as an example:

```
// Advertise this table as a possible base table
$data['node']['table']['base'] = array(
  'field' => 'nid',
  'title' => t('Node'),
  'help' => t("Nodes are a Drupal site's primary content."),
  'weight' => -10,
);
```

## Declaring Fields on Tables

Each field on a table can appear in as many as five parts of the UI: fields, filters, sort criteria, arguments, and relationships. All of these possibilities have already been described in this book. In general, these fields will correspond directly to database fields, but they do not always have to. Sometimes fields will perform secondary queries to collect the data, and sometimes they are special versions of a field.

For example, when listing users, each user can have multiple roles. If you simply added that data as a field, then each role would duplicate the user record, which is rarely the desired result. Therefore, the user roles field actually performs a secondary query to collect all of the roles for the users listed and merge them together as a single field.

Other unusual fields, such as the node edit field, have no corresponding data in the database. They do, however, need to collect data from the node to perform access checks. Such a field adds the data it needs to the query and utilizes this data as necessary to print its link. From the perspective of Views' data, however, it is just another field—it is just not a field in the schema.

# Handlers Versus Plugins

For the most part, handlers deal with data; you can have many handlers for each view. In contrast, plugins deal with the structure of the output; you can have only one plugin of each type. When you write the code to describe a table in the database to Views, you use handlers to tell Views how to deal with fields, filters, arguments, and sorts (there are *many* things you'll need to tell Views about). When you decide how you would like to format the data that is returned from a view, you use a plugin to affect the "shape" of the output. For example, a view can be displayed as either a simple HTML list or a calendar, but not both; you can choose only one output style for your information.

## Handlers

In Views, a handler is an object that is part of the view and is part of the query building flow. Much of the time, the base handlers will work for your purposes, but often you'll need to override the handler for something. One typical handler override is `views_handler_filter_operator_in`, which allows you to have a filter select from a list of options; you'll need to override this behavior to provide your list.

Handlers have two distinct code flows; the UI flow and the view building flow. For the query flow:

- `handler->construct()` Creates the initial handler. At this time, it is not yet attached to a view. It is here that you can set basic defaults if needed, but there will be no knowledge of the environment yet.
- `handler->set_definition()` Sets the data from `hook_views_data()` relevant to the handler.
- `handler->init()` Attaches the handler to a view, and usually provides the options from the display.
- `handler->pre_query()` Runs prior to the `query()` stage to do early processing.
- `handler->query()` Does the bulk of the work to all the handler to add itself to the query. Fields, as the only handlers concerned with output, also have an extended piece of the flow.
- `handler->pre_render()` Called prior to the actual rendering. It allows handlers to query for extra data. The entire result set is available here, and this is where items that have *multiple values* per record can do their extra query for all of the records available. There are several examples of this at work in the code.
- `handler->render()` Does the actual work of rendering the field.

Most handlers are just extensions of existing classes with a few tweaks that are specific to the field in question. For example:

```
/**
 * Filter by node type
 */
class views_handler_filter_node_type extends views_handler_filter_in_operator {
  function get_value_options() {
    if (!isset($this->value_options)) {
      $this->value_title = t('Node type');
      $types = node_get_types();
      foreach ($types as $type => $info) {
        $options[$type] = $info->name;
      }
      $this->value_options = $options;
    }
  }
}
```

The handler `views_handler_filter_in_operator` provides a simple mechanism to set the list used; the rest of the handler is perfectly fine for performing this task.

Handlers are stored in their own files. For these files to be loaded by Views on demand, they must first be registered. Because Views core handlers are also loaded this way, it's imperative that your module implement this pattern to prevent code crashes when your handler's parent class is not yet available.

To register handlers, you must implement `hook_views_handlers()`. This hook returns an array with two keys. The first key consists of *info*, which contains the module name (necessary only if you're registering handlers on behalf of another module, such as what Views does), and *path*, which is the search path to find the files. This path is necessary only if your files will not be stored in the same directory as the `.module` file. The other key is *handlers*, which contains a full array of handlers and the information for each handler. The key to each handler array is the name of the handler class. It can contain:

- *parent*: The class that this handler extends. It is important to make sure that the parent class is included before your handler class. Otherwise, you may cause people's sites to crash in a difficult-to-recover state. Be sure you get this right!

- *file*: The filename the handler is in. By default, it will be `classname.inc`. However, you can have multiple similar handlers together in one file. Because there is only one parent, you must make sure that the parentage on these handlers matches. Otherwise, you will run into white screens, as not all parents will be loaded.

You can see examples of this function in any of the various `module.views.inc` files in the Views modules directory. Appendix C contains a selection of sample handlers from the Views API online reference site at http://views.doc.logrus.com/. Understanding how `views_handler` and its child classes work is handy, but you can do a lot just by following these models. You might also want to explore the files in the Views module directory, particularly `node.views.inc`. Note that while all handler names in Views are prefixed with `views_`, you should use your own module's name to prefix your handler names to ensure namespace safety. The basic pattern for handler naming goes like this: `[module]_handler_[type]_[tablename]_[fieldname]`. Sometimes `tablename` and `fieldname` are not appropriate, but something that resembles what the table and field would be can be used in their stead.

## Plugins

In Views, a plugin is a bit like a handler, but plugins are not directly responsible for building the query. Instead, they are objects that are used to display the view or make other modifications. Six types of plugins are used in Views:

- Display: Controls *where* a view lives. Page and block are the most common displays, as well as the ubiquitous "default" display that is likely to be embedded.
- Style: Controls how a view is displayed. For the most part, object wrappers are placed around theme templates.
- Row style: Handles each individual record from a node.
- Argument default: Allows pluggable ways of providing arguments for blocks. Views includes plugins to extract node and user IDs from the URL; additional plugins could be used to carry out a wide variety of tasks.
- Argument validator: Ensures arguments are valid, and even does transformations on the arguments.
- Access: Controls access to the view.

Plugins are registered by implementing `hook_views_plugins()` in the file `module-name.views.inc` and returning an array of data. The array will look something like this:

```
return array( 'display' => array(
// ... list of display plugins, ), 'style' => array(
// ... list of style plugins, ), 'row' => array(
// ... list of row style plugins, ), 'argument default' => array(
// ... list of argument default plugins, ), 'argument validator' => array(
// ... list of argument validator plugins, ), 'access' => array(
// ... list of access plugins, ), );
```

Each plugin will be registered with an identifier for the plugin, plus a fairly lengthy list of items that can define how and where the plugin is used. Here is an example from Views core:

```
'node' => array(
    'title' => t('Node'),
    'help' => t('Display the node with standard node view.'),
    'handler' => 'views_plugin_row_node_view',
```

```
      'path' => drupal_get_path('module', 'views') . '/modules/node',
// not necessary for most modules
      'theme' => 'views_view_row_node',
      'base' => array('node'),
// only works with 'node' as base
      'uses options' => TRUE,
      'type' => 'normal',
),
```

Of particular interest is the *path* directive, which works a little differently from handler registration; each plugin must define its own path, rather than relying on global info for the paths. Also, there is an optional *parent* directive, which is automatically filled in to be the base parent for the plugin type. Usually this default is sufficient, but if your plugin derives from something other than the base, it must be filled in. For example:

```
'feed' => array(
      'title' => t('Feed'),
      'help' => t('Display the view as a feed, such as an RSS feed.'),
      'handler' => 'views_plugin_display_feed',
      'parent' => 'page',
// so it knows to load the page plugin .inc file
      'uses hook menu' => TRUE,
      'use ajax' => FALSE,
      'use pager' => FALSE,
      'accept attachments' => FALSE,
      'admin' => t('Feed'),
      'help topic' => 'display-feed',
),
```

Unlike handler registration, where parentage is referred to by object name, with plugins it is referred to by the unique plugin identifier.

> **Tip**
>
> Be sure to prefix your plugin identifiers with your module name to ensure namespace safety. After all, two different modules could try to implement the "grid2" plugin—and that would cause one plugin to fail completely.

# Summary

This chapter covered the nuts and bolts of how Views is put together. You learned about the data architecture of Views, the life cycle of a view, and the database schema. You were also introduced to the plugins and handlers you will need to use to control how you get data out of Views and how that data can be formatted. This chapter wraps up our section on Views; however, there is additional information in Appendix C that covers the many functions you can use to hook into the Views API.

# III

# Panels

# 12

# Introducing Panels

The core functionality of the Panels module is layout; when it is used, the Web site starts to look polished. With an understanding of Panels, administrators can create a style that easily applies to every page of a site, or they can develop a different style for every page. This chapter provides an introduction to how Panels works.

## Introduction to Panels

The purpose of the Panels module is to enable administrators to easily create entire page *layouts* without complex manipulation of HTML or CSS. A layout is a design of your own page regions. You can redefine the default regions, creating your own headers, footers, sidebars, and columns within the page with a width determined by you. Through a simple drag-and-drop interface, many kinds of content can be added to a panel: Views, blocks, and nodes are just the beginning.

### A Brief History of Panels

For Web site development, earlier versions of Drupal relied on experienced administrators who had enough time and ability to fuss with placement of content. With the increasing time pressures in today's environment, however, developers needed an easier way to move sections of content.

Panels was created to enable the quick design of one or more page styles that could be applied easily and allow for a consistent look, without having to manually change code on each page. Panels is, in essence, the bigger and stronger sibling of Drupal's block system. With blocks, we can place pieces of content within predetermined regions of the whole page; we did this with the block display example in the Views chapters. With Panels, you can do all the things that blocks can, and some things that blocks can't.

The Panels module was first written for Drupal 4.7, and was intended to provide an easy way to create a styled layout for a news-like site. Previously, Drupal had not included any serious layout tools, and users were forced to rely on their own HTML and CSS skills for placement. To create a place where specific types of content would always be, Panels became a necessary addition to the Drupal universe.

Panels was ported to Drupal 6, and later largely rewritten to take advantage of the lessons learned from problems with design in the first version. Panels 2 worked more cleanly with Views and other areas of Drupal, and had a significantly more robust amount of functionality than its predecessor.

Panels is currently on its third iteration. When the Panels module was being updated to Drupal 6, it became dependent on the Views module due to some functionality that was useful for Panels that was already present in Views. Rather than forcing developers to reinvent the wheel or copy-and-paste code resulting in duplication, the dependency on Views was required. After some further work was done, some flaws came to light in the overall porting process to Drupal 6.

Because of these problems, Earl (one of the authors of this book) and the Panels co-maintainer, Sam Boyer, decided to scrap some of the work that had been done to update Panels 2 to Drupal 6. From this decision, the CTools (Chaos Tool Suite) module was born. It generalized many of the tools that Panels and Views were using, making these tools available without requiring the much larger Views module, and removing the Panels dependency on Views. These changes were large enough to warrant the Panels version being numbered as Panels 3.

## Push and Pull: How Panels Is Different

Drupal core is optimized for one grand, master layout that controls the appearance of your Web site. If you don't know any code, you are limited to this single layout. Although Drupal's theming engine allows you to refine (and even replace parts of) this layout, you have to learn the code needed to do so—and custom code is often a risky proposition. Inefficient code can significantly affect Drupal's page rendering time and can even expose your site to security risks.

In Drupal core's page rendering process, all of the regions must be defined ahead of time by the theme. To customize where blocks appear, you have to change the block visibility settings for every single block on your site—one at a time. When Drupal is preparing a page, it renders every single block for display and *then* checks whether the block will be displayed on the page that is being rendered. *If* the block is being used, the rendered block is *pushed* into the page template (Figure 12-1). This logic is both upside down and inefficient.

Figure 12-1    Drupal core renders all blocks and then pushes only some
into a page template.

Figure 12-2    Panels pulls in only the content it needs for any one
particular layout.

Panels takes a different approach. One of the major advantages of Panels is that it uses a series of pluggable layouts, so you are no longer limited to one master layout for your whole site. Panels offers a series of sample layouts for your use, or you can create your own layout. These layouts can be filled with panes that pull in blocks of content. When they are rendered, Panels will first look to see what's needed for that layout and then *pull* in *only* the necessary content (Figure 12-2). As you're assembling your Panels layouts, you can adjust the cache settings both for the individual panes and for the entire panel display. Nothing else in Drupal gives you as much fine-grained control over how each of your pages, and the various embedded page elements, are cached.

## Point-and-Click Layout

Panels are made up of three major functionality pieces:

- Displays: Overall layout of the panel.
- Panel regions: Individual regions where you can place content.
- Panes: Individual pieces of content (including blocks, views, and just about anything else) that are placed into your panel.

When you view "a panel" on a Drupal Web page, you are really looking at a panel *variant* that has a specific *display* that is divided into *panel regions* that contain *content*. Figure 12-3 shows how each of these pieces fits together. The variant isn't labeled on Figure 12-3 because you can see only one variant at a time.

You can put virtually anything you want into a panel:

- A single node
- A view of lots of nodes
- Any part of a node, such as the comments for a specific node or even part of a node editing form
- Related categories for a given node
- Any block that is available to Drupal core—menus, who's online, user login, and more
- Custom content (such as a warning, or a notice) that you create from within the panel itself

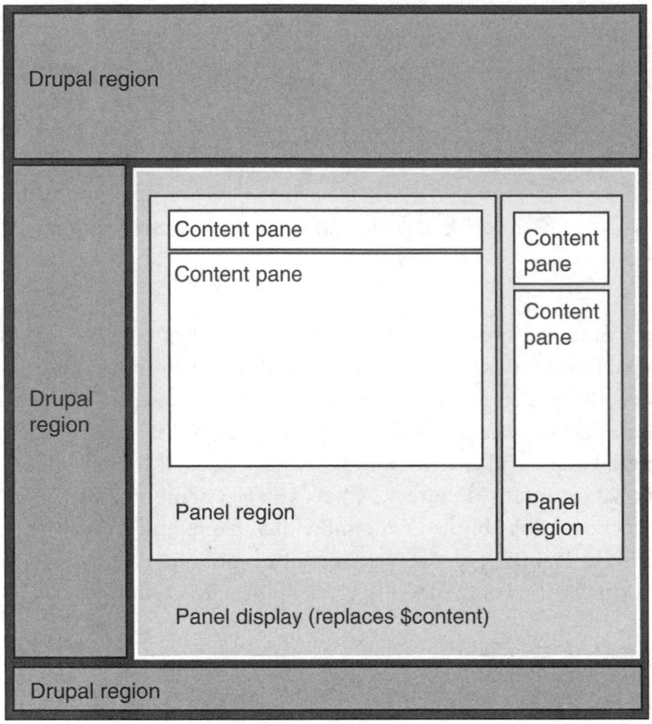

Figure 12-3    Drupal regions (dark gray) surround the panel. This variant
has two regions, each of which contains content.

The panes that you place into a panel can be easily moved up or down, made larger or smaller, and themed. You'll learn more about theming panels in Chapter 15.

Panels can also be used to hold items smaller than pages. Suppose you have a normal sidebar, and you have two pieces of content that waste a bunch of space because they're really too narrow. Your design would look significantly better if those pieces of content appeared side by side. Unfortunately, that change is complex to make in Drupal. You have to create a custom block with custom code to display these two pieces of content, or use some pretty sophisticated CSS. With Panels, you just create a *mini-panel* with a two-column layout. Add one block to the left, add one block to the right, and finish. This mini-panel will then be available to your system as an ordinary block, or as panel content to go in the other panels.

In addition to creating panels to hold units smaller than pages, you can use Panels to take over your entire site layout. Panels Everywhere (http://drupal.org/project/panels_everywhere) replaces Drupal's restrictive blocks system and replaces it with the Panels Layout system to control how your Web site looks. Panels Everywhere modifies the page as it is being rendered to "wrap" the content in a display and can even take over your whole page theme file. To get a sense of how this capability works, check out the theme Tinsel (http://drupal.org/project/tinsel) that is available with your Panels installation. Although it looks like Drupal's default theme of Garland, it uses Panels Everywhere to control the layout of the site.

## Context

In a panel, you can create contexts, which represent the objects being displayed. For example, when displaying the node view, the `nid` argument on the page is converted into a context through the "arguments" system. You can then create a relationship from that node to, say, the node author or, if you have a node reference from CCK, a related node. Once the contexts are in place, content specifically about those contexts can be added. For the node context, you can add CCK fields, the node body, attached files, and a host of other information that can be provided by plugins. For the user context, you can display items such as the user's photo or profile.

In addition, these contexts can be checked for specific types of information, which they can then use not only to make content available to be displayed, but also to choose which layout to display. For example, if your site is geared toward an international audience, you can use a context to see if the node being viewed is set for a particular language and choose to display it one way if it is in French or another way if it is in English. You can also select display characteristics based on attributes such as node type, whether the user has access to edit the node, and more. This system is also pluggable, so that you can add your own custom criteria with just a small amount of code. Want to display nodes differently based on how a custom CCK field you've added to a node type is set? That code is very simple to write, and you can use it to change the presentation entirely.

## Pluggable Architecture

The Panels module supports styles, which can control how individual content panes, regions within a panel, and the entire panel will be rendered. While Panels ships with few styles, a plethora of styles can be provided as plugins by modules as well as by themes.

The layout builder is nice for visually designing a layout, but a real HTML guru doesn't want the somewhat weighty HTML that this process will create. Modules and themes can provide custom layouts that can fit a designer's exacting specifications, yet still allow the site builder to place content wherever he or she likes.

Panels includes a pluggable caching mechanism. A single, time-based cache type is included, known as the "simple" cache. Because most sites have very specific caching needs based on their content and traffic patterns, this system was designed to let sites devise their own triggers for cache clearing and implement plugins that will work with Panels. Panels can be cached as a whole, meaning the entire output of the panel can be cached, or just individual content panes that are heavy can be cached.

# Modules

In reality, Panels isn't just one module, but rather a group of modules that do the same kinds of work. We've worked with displays for Views; some panels work directly with those displays to create layout. Other panels work within each other, or more generally with content types. Each type of panel is generally controlled by a different Panels module, making it easier to enable just those panel types that you need. This system also allows for easier troubleshooting of problems.

Understanding what the different modules are and what the basic purpose of each module is will allow you to choose the correct functionality. Panels modules are (more or less) split into two groups:

- Display modules: Actually place content on a page.

- Helpers: Help the display modules function more smoothly and allow for code to be moved from one site to another.

To enable the relevant modules for your site navigate to Administer >> Site building >> Modules.

> **Warning**
>
> You should have already downloaded the Panels package from http://drupal.org/project/panels and the Chaos Tool Suite from http://drupal.org/project/ctools. If you haven't already done so, go ahead and do it now.

## Panels Package

The following modules are available from the Module page fieldset, "Panels":

- Mini panels: A display module. It is an adjunct to the higher-level Panels modules for nodes and views. Mini panels allows you to embed a panel within a larger panel. It also can create blocks for use by Drupal's core engine.

- Panel nodes: Creates nodes that are divided into areas with selectable content. This module does not have a separate administrative UI of its own. Instead, it uses the regular "Create content" menu item to create a new node as a panel. Users with administrative privileges also can use the "Administer nodes" menu to create new panel nodes.

- Panels: The engine. It contains the core display functions, but does not provide an external user interface. To be useful, at least one other module should be enabled.

- Panels In-Place Editor: Provides a UI for managing some panels directly on the front end, instead of forcing developers to use the back end. This module depends on the contributed module jQuery UI (http://drupal.org/project/jquery_ui). Be sure to read the documentation carefully on how to enable and use this module.

> **Note**
>
> Panels In-Place Editor is not covered in this book; however, you should enable the other modules to be able to complete all of the exercises in this book.

## Chaos Tool Suite

CTools (Chaos Tool Suite) is an abstraction of some of the tools developed for use with Views and Panels. For panels usage, the most important thing to know is that CTools includes secondary modules that are not obviously part of the project. CTools appears in the "Other" group on the Drupal modules page, and only one of its modules is visible in that group. For all of the panel types to be available, CTools, Page manager, and Views content panes must all be enabled.

Chaos Tool Suite also provides the following modules that will be used by Panels:

- Bulk Export: Performs bulk exporting of data objects known about by Chaos tools.

- Chaos Tools: A library of helpful tools by Merlin of Chaos (the mastermind that other CTools modules will hook into).

- Custom content panes: Creates custom, exportable, reusable content panes for applications such as Panels.

- Custom rulesets: Creates custom, exportable, reusable rulesets for applications such as Panels.

- Page manager: Provides a UI and API to manage pages within the site.

- Stylizer: Creates custom styles for Panels.

- Views content panes: Allows Views content to be used in Panels.

Page manager provides a user interface and the API for managing panes and pages throughout the site. For this reason, the Panels and CTools packages must be updated at the same time. If you try to upgrade just one of the modules but not the other, the entire suite will fail.

Page manager also handles tasks defined by other modules. As you move through the Panels interface, you will notice a series of displays, each of which has features. Viewing a page is a task; returning that rendered page is done by Page manager. This module checks for features and the display type as well.

When you are creating panels, Page manager handles any panels that are full pages. It helps establish features and contexts to build those pages and create relationships to data. The decisions made at this point are essentially yes-or-no questions such as "User is authenticated" or "User: role." Based on the results of each question, content is then rendered.

Page manager can be used by other modules to handle the transition from request to rendered information. In other words, its use is not restricted solely to Panels.

# Summary

Panels and CTools make a nearly infinite number of layouts available for use with your site. By taking advantage of the different types of panels, multiple purposes can be fulfilled quickly and with relative ease—whether you need just a node, one page, or many pages. The default layouts in the Panels module give a beginning user a preset, painless group of regions to work in, while the flexible layout provides a helpful tool for developers who want to do something unique as well as for advanced Web designers.

With the core modules installed, it's time to create your first panel. Let's move on.

# Creating Panels

In this chapter, we explore the Panels user interface (UI), including how each part fits together to create a wide range of panels. You will learn how to create your very first panel, add content to a range of panel types, and override the core display pages for each of your site's content types.

## Your First Panel

Once the Panels (the main module), Page manager, and CTools modules have been enabled navigate to the Panels Dashboard at Administer >> Site building >> Panels. There will also be several new Administrative links added to your management menu under Administer >> Site building (Figure 13-1).

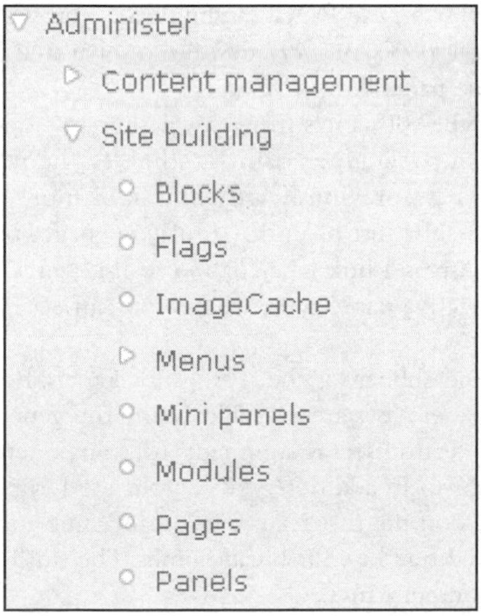

Figure 13-1    Administrative menu links for Mini panels, Pages, and Panels

## The Panels Dashboard

The Panels landing page has been completely revamped in the release of Panels 3. With this revamp comes the Panels Dashboard (Figure 13-2), which is intended to be a clean and simple landing page on which you can start creating panels.

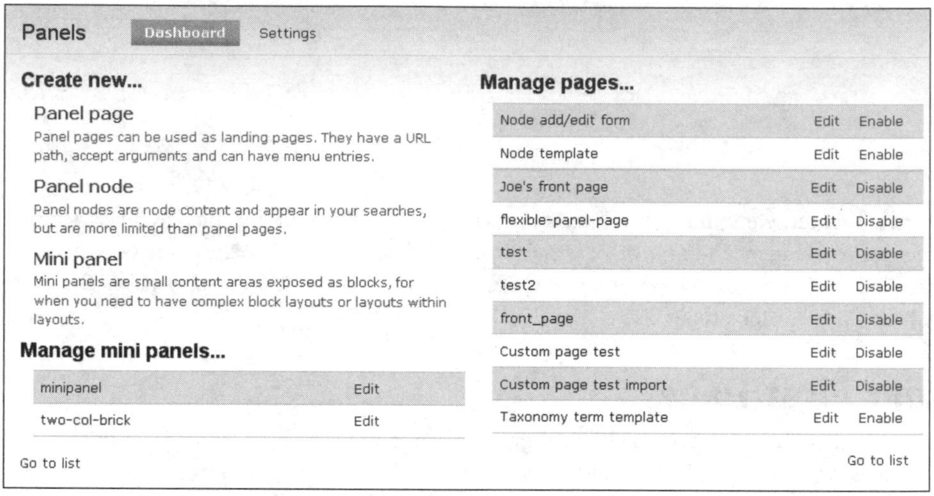

Figure 13-2    The Panels Dashboard

When you review the list on the Panels landing page, you will see three types of panels you can create: panel pages, panel nodes, and mini-panels. This page also briefly reviews what each of these panel types does.

You can create most types of panels from this dashboard page, the exception being Views content panes. Each panel type's name is a link to the page to create a new panel of that type. If you have previously created one or more panel pages or mini-panels, you will also see a short list of up to 10 of your pages or mini-panels. At the bottom of each of these lists is a link labeled "Go to list"; clicking it takes you to the landing page for the respective panel type, where you can access the entire list of pages or mini-panels.

The second tab on the dashboard is the settings for Panels. Both general settings and settings for some of the panel types are available. Using the general settings, you can limit the number of taxonomy terms used as arguments to a single term. (Drupal defaults to allowing multiple arguments.) In addition, you can change Drupal's breadcrumb trail, by injecting a hierarchy based on the first term into breadcrumb trail. This enables you to have a more easily followed trail in your breadcrumbs. The third check box enables all views to be available as content panes.

> **Note**
> If you do not check this box, only views that have a "content pane" display type will be available to Panels.
>
> If you want to make all your views available, check the box. If you want to limit which views can be added to panes, uncheck this box and create content pane displays for those views.

The other three tabs under the Settings tab control which data and layouts can even be made available to users wishing to create panels and panes. These tabs are Panel pages, Mini panels, and Panel nodes. These settings pages (Figure 13-3) comprise a long list of check boxes, covering whether new content can be created as blocks, views, panels, and so on. The Settings tab pages also permit you to control which data is added into a pane from blocks, views, or other content. Finally, they enable you to specify which layouts are available to that panel type.

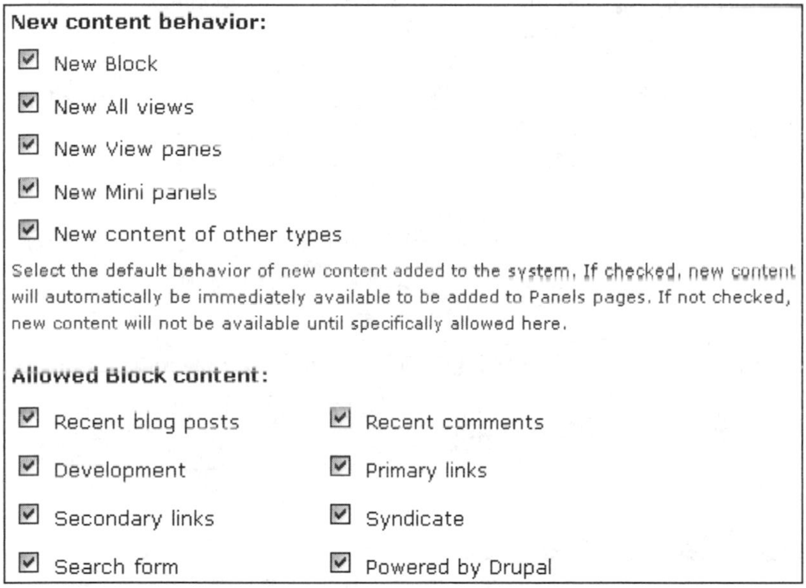

---

**New content behavior:**

☑ New Block

☑ New All views

☑ New View panes

☑ New Mini panels

☑ New content of other types

Select the default behavior of new content added to the system. If checked, new content will automatically be immediately available to be added to Panels pages. If not checked, new content will not be available until specifically allowed here.

**Allowed Block content:**

☑ Recent blog posts          ☑ Recent comments

☑ Development                ☑ Primary links

☑ Secondary links            ☑ Syndicate

☑ Search form                ☑ Powered by Drupal

---

Figure 13-3    Panel settings for New content behavior and Allowed Block content

These settings will become clearer as you start creating your own panels later in this chapter.

## Panel Pages

Panel pages are one of the easiest types of panels to understand. When a panel page is created, it can be accessed at its URL—whatever the path is leading to that panel page. A list of pages created by Panels appears under Administer >> Site building >> Pages.

This resulting list also includes existing system pages that can be overridden by Panels layouts. You will do a significant portion of your editing through the Pages settings, and most if not all of your actual panel creation.

The list of pages that are panels based are broken up into two groups of pages: system and custom. System pages are pages that people may want to override on a case-by-case basis. With these plugins, you can change the look of nodes, user profiles, and so forth. We'll talk more about overriding these characteristics later in this chapter. Custom pages are pages that you have created. These individually created pages have their own names, contents, and layout. They can do just about anything you want.

> **Tip**
>
> Drupal continues to render other blocks unless you tell the panel pages not to do so. In the Page settings, selecting the check box labeled "Disable Drupal blocks and regions" removes all of the preconfigured blocks or regions that the page would have otherwise had, enabling you to follow some radically different directions in theming. Disabling Drupal-provided blocks and regions removes any sidebars on the left and right sides, and any widgets that you might have otherwise added.

On the landing page for panel pages (the List page), notice the group of filters (see Figure 13-4). They are intended to help you sort your pages, making it easier to find a particular one. These filters look much like the Views sorting filters found on the Views List page.

Figure 13-4    Filtering panel pages

There are three additional tabs on the landing page: Wizards, Add custom page, and Import page.

## Panels User Interface

When you have a panel page—whether it's one you have created or one you have customized based on an existing system page—you must then take all of your actions on that panel through the Panel page user interface (Figure 13-5).

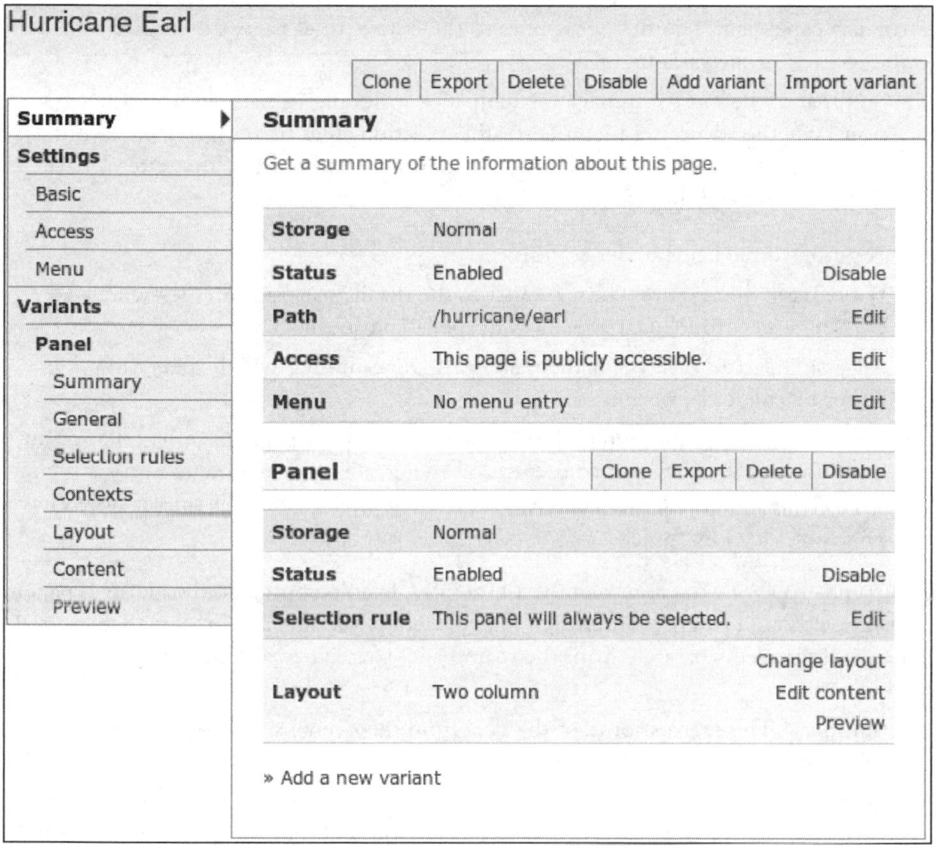

Figure 13-5    Panel page user interface

Along the top of the UI, the following options are available:

- Clone: Like the clone function in Views, it creates a duplicate copy of your panel page.
- Export: This directly prints out the code to create this panel page.
- Delete: From here, you can delete the panel page. In addition, you can delete the panel page from the panel pages list.

- Disable: Clicking the disable button immediately disables the panel page. The disable function is available for both system and custom pages.
- Add variant: Variants are a collective group of displays and permissions. You can have multiple variants for a given page, depending on what you want to let your users see.
- Import variant: This enables you to import a variant.

Along the left side of the UI is a group of tabs that deal with the configuration details of a particular panel page. The first set applies to the entire panel page; the second set is specific to each of the variants.

- Summary: The short summary for the panel, including its path, its access permissions, whether there is a menu entry, the selection rules (if any), and the layout. To the right of each of these items is an Edit link, and most of these items have their own tabs on the left.

Settings groups three items underneath it:

- Basic: Basic information comprises all of the details you had to enter when creating a new panel page—name, title, path, and so on.
- Access: This creates rules for the panel page, determining which users can see it either by role or by permission.
- Menu: This determines which kind of menu item your panel page has, if any. You can choose not to have a menu entry, or else create a normal menu entry, a menu tab, or a default menu tab. The creation of these menu entries is similar how Views produces menu items.

Variants may have one or more members listed. By default, you can only add new panels as variants, although plugins can change this restriction. Variants can be cloned, exported, deleted, and disabled separately from the main panel page. They also have their own group of settings:

- Summary: This repeats some of the data from the overall summary—namely, selection rules and layout.
- General: These details are specific to the variant. Here, you can create a title for the variant, decide to disable Drupal-provided blocks and regions, give the variant its own CSS ID, and add some CSS styling in the CSS code box if you wish.
- Selection rules: Selection rules are another form of access rules, and are specific to this variant. If you are using multiple variants (for example, authorized users see one variant of the page, while anonymous users see another), the selection rules check whether they match. If they do match, the page is displayed in accordance with those rules. If not, the checks move on to the next variant.
- Contexts: Contexts allow you to add data and relationships to your panel to enhance the base data with which the panel was initially created. (More about this in Chapter 14.)

- Layout: This is where the different layouts are set up. If your current layout isn't doing what you need, change it here.

- Content: This setting provides your actual display, where you can add content.

- Preview: This setting enables you to see a live preview of your page in progress. The Panels module incorporates a live preview, much like the preview that appears with the Views module. This preview link can give you a very good idea of what a page will look like to your users. It does have a limitation in that you must use the permissions that the logged-in user (you) has; any other permission set must be tested manually.

Most of these settings are easily understandable from their names, and the functionality is much like you already have seen in Views.

### Creating a Panel Page

When you create a new panel page, a configuration wizard guides you through a series of configuration screens for the options described in the previous section. Before starting the wizard, make sure you have a clear idea of how your page will be used and what it should look like. This will help you to choose the right options throughout the panel page creation process. To create a new panel page, navigate to Administer >> Site building >> Pages and click the tab at the top of the page titled "Add custom page." Exercise 13-1 walks you through the step-by-step instructions to create a new panel page.

---

# Exercise 13-1

### Creating a Panel Page

Joe's Shirts wants a new front page, with a new shirt on one side, and a list of people who are currently online at the company's site. Panel pages make it easy to create and display a new front page.

1. Navigate to Administer >> Site building >> Pages. Click the link "Add Custom page" from the list of tabs at the top of the list of the Panel pages screen.

2. On the Basic settings configuration screen, enter the following values:

| Field | Value |
| --- | --- |
| Administrative title | Joe's Shirts front page |
| Machine name | joes_frontpage |
| Administrative description | Joe's Shirts front page |
| Path | joesfront |
| Make this your site home page | Select this check box |
| | (Note: Your front page will remain blank until you add content to this panel. Leave this *unchecked* if you are working on a live site.) |
| Variant type | Panel (This is currently the only one available.) |
| Optional features | Leave unchecked |

3. Click Continue.

4. Choose a layout. We want a simple two-column layout. Change the category to "Columns: 2." Select the radio button above "Two column" and click Continue.

5. On the Panel settings configuration screen, enter the following values:

| Field | Value |
|---|---|
| Administrative title | Default front page |
| Renderer | Standard (selected and the only option available) |
| CSS ID | joes-frontpage-default |
| CSS code | Leave blank for now |

6. Click Continue. You are passed to a page with two boxes, a left side and a right side, as shown in Figure 13-6.

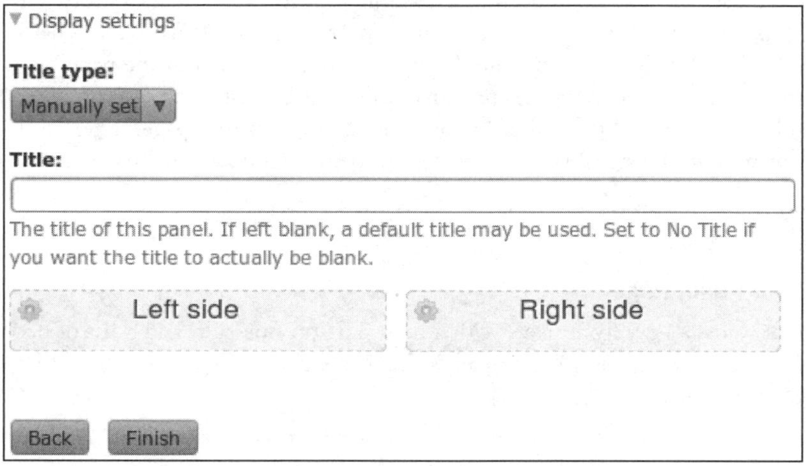

Figure 13-6    Two-column panel content page. Content will be added to the two light gray boxes labeled "Left side" and "Right side."

Now we have a basic layout ready for content.

7. Click Finish to begin the process of saving the panel page.

You are now taken to the main Panel page edit screen. As with Views, an indicator in the upper-right section of the screen identifies whether the panel is new or changed, as shown in Figure 13-7.

8. Click the Save button at the bottom of the screen to finish saving the page.

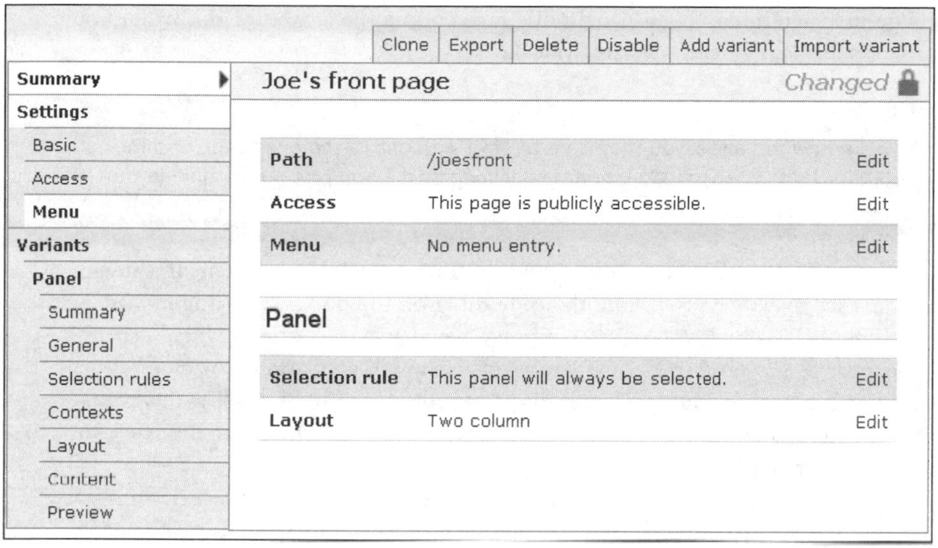

| | Clone | Export | Delete | Disable | Add variant | Import variant |

**Joe's front page**                                    *Changed* 🔒

| Summary ▶ | |
|---|---|
| **Settings** | |
| Basic | |
| Access | |
| Menu | |
| **Variants** | |
| **Panel** | |
| Summary | |
| General | |
| Selection rules | |
| Contexts | |
| Layout | |
| Content | |
| Preview | |

| **Path** | /joesfront | Edit |
|---|---|---|
| **Access** | This page is publicly accessible. | Edit |
| **Menu** | No menu entry. | Edit |

**Panel**

| **Selection rule** | This panel will always be selected. | Edit |
|---|---|---|
| **Layout** | Two column | Edit |

Figure 13-7    Panel page edit screen showing the panel currently has
unsaved changes

When you return to the panel dashboard, you will see the new front page for Joe's Shirts listed under the Panel Pages heading. When you choose the Edit link next to a given panel page, you will return to the Panel page edit screen as shown in Figure 13-7.

## Panel Nodes

Panel nodes are fairly self-explanatory. These panels take the place of nodes and act like nodes. Panel nodes and panel pages may serve similar functions; nevertheless, they have some key differences. For example, each panel node can have a custom layout—you are not forced to use a common content type template. Panel nodes are indexed by the Drupal core search module and will be returned in relevant search results.

When you are creating panel nodes, you will notice that the initial configuration screens are similar to those for panel pages. However, the edit screens that appear after creation of panel nodes and panel pages can differ significantly.

### Creating a Panel Node

Panel nodes are created from the Create content >> Panel menu; their creation page is very similar to the general node creation page. Choosing this menu option starts you along the path to creating as clean or as crazy of a design as you can imagine for a particular node.

The first step in creating a panel node is to choose the layout for this panel node. All of the default Panels templates are available.

> **Tip**
>
> If you're new to panels, you may want to start with one of the one-, two-, or three-column layouts so that you don't become overwhelmed by the setup of the Flexible layout, which is selected by default.

Choose your layout based on the needs of this particular panel node. If a stream of news articles or blog posts will be the only thing on the display, you might work with a single-column layout. If you're working on a newspaper and articles will alternate between large and small sizes, or if you want to show lists of articles or pictures, you could use the two-column brick, a layout that looks like a brick wall, with alternating rows of wide content and rows of two narrower regions. Click on the desired layout to proceed to the next screen.

The second configuration screen is the Create Panel screen (Figure 13-8). Once your panel is created, the Edit screen appears; it is where you would make changes if

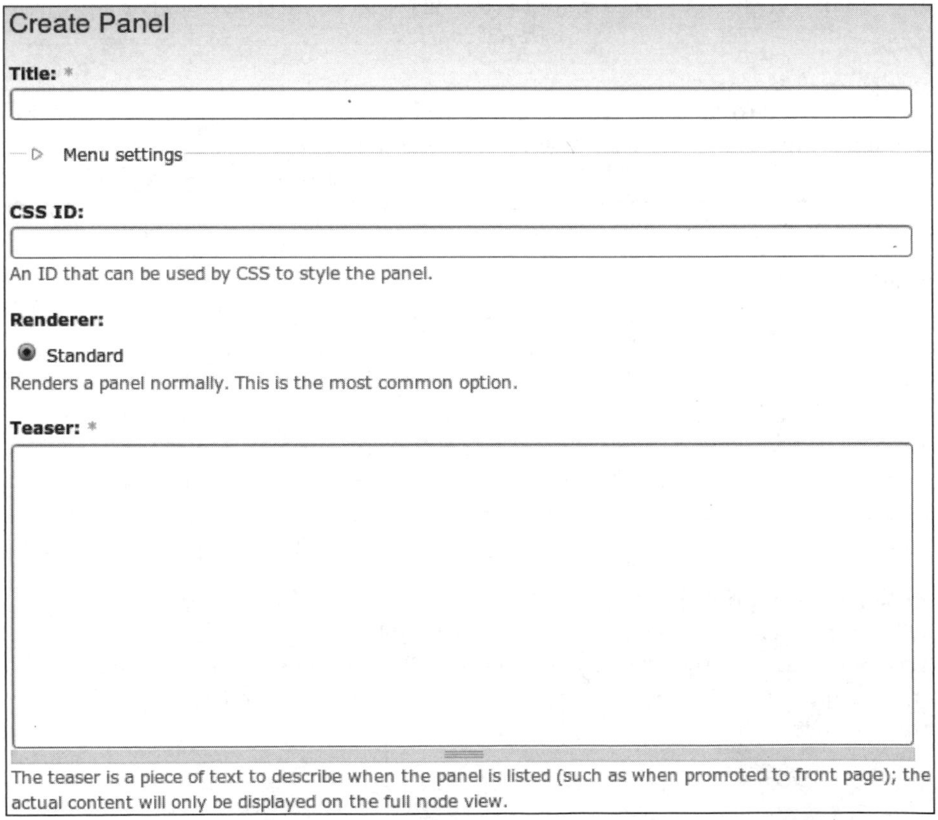

Figure 13-8    Creating a new panel node

needed. The Create Panel screen has the following panel node–specific fields exposed:

- Title: Name for the panel display.

- Teaser: Short description that will take the place of the entire plane if that panel is not shown in its entirety.

- CSS ID: Gives you the option to create a deliberate and specific class identifier for use by CSS when theming this particular panel. No verification is performed to ensure this is a unique ID, so you need to be careful when creating the new ID.

The remainder of the fieldsets are the same as if you were adding a new node to your site with a core, or custom, content type:

- Menu settings: "Menu link title" is the text that becomes the name of the link on the site menu. "Parent item" determines the major section of the menu under which the link will appear. Should it be top level? Is it part of a group of information that will have its own subsection? "Weight" determines where within the menu section the link will reside. Items with a lighter weight will be listed higher on the menu. The default weight for any item is zero.

- Book outline: Book outline is available only if you have enabled the core Drupal Book module on your site. The Book drop-down menu gives you the option to include this panel within an existing book, or to create a new book. You can also assign a weight to the panel within the book, although it is important to note that both weight and alphanumeric title affect where the page will fall within the book. Weight, then title, determines placement.

- Revision information: This simple check box determines if a new version of the panel is created when it is edited, and if an optional log message will be used to track what was done during that edit.

- URL path settings: These paths are similar to the paths we saw in Views, but allow for less complexity. Panels path settings support a straight, simple path such as http://www.example.com/locations. They use relative path settings. Thus you should be sure not to add a trailing slash; if you do add this character, your path will not work.

- Comment settings: Comments can be enabled, read-only, or read/write. You can't change any other settings or filters from here, unlike with other content type comments.

- File attachments: This setting enables attachments to the panel if you have enabled the core Drupal module Upload. By default, it allows you to attach only files that are 1 MB in size or smaller. When multiple files are attached to a panel, only the first one is listed in an RSS feed.

- Authoring information: The "Authored by:" field is an auto-complete box that will search your system's users and help you find names faster. By default, it uses the name of the logged-in user. This group also contains a field called

"Authored on:" that consists of the time of initial creation (when the panel create form is submitted), unless the submitter manually changes the date.

- Publishing options: Again, as with content creation, you have some options in terms of where this panel will land. Will it be published? Should it be promoted to the front page? Should it remain sticky at the top of lists? By default, "Published" and "Promoted to front page" are checked.

Once you've determined how you want to set all of these form fields, you can save, preview, or throw the whole panel node out by deleting it.

### Editing a Panel Node

Once a panel node is created, it is administered like any other node, by navigating to Administer >> Content management >> Content. Panel nodes have a content type of "Panel." You may use the content type filters to refine the list to show only panel nodes. To edit a panel node, click the Edit link next to the appropriate panel node. After navigating to the panel node you wish to edit, use the following tabs to change it:

- View: Takes you directly to the page the panel is on. This simple link provides a reasonably real-time view of your work, but does require actual changes to your site, unlike Views' live preview feature. If you don't save your panel, changes will not appear on this page.
- Edit: Takes the place of the screen used to create the panel and the panel layout page where the general panel setup can be changed.
- Panel layout: Allows you to edit the layout template assigned to this panel node.
- Panel content: Allows you to add, remove, and alter the settings for each content pane in your panel node. We'll talk more about these configuration screens later in this chapter, as all types of panels use the same content configuration screens.

## Mini-Panels

Mini-panels are panels that you can embed throughout your site, either as content panes within a panel or as blocks. They can be used to perform a wide range of functions. Unlike panel pages and panel nodes, however, mini-panels are reusable. You can use mini-panels to:

- Create a multi-tab panel with a group of searches or lists, where each tab represents a view.
- Create a multi-component block that is placed into one of your theme's page template regions—in other words, *outside* the panel's layout.
- Show information that is either site-wide (for all users) or narrowed down to the specific logged-in user.

To access your mini-panels, navigate to Administer >> Site building >> Mini panels. You will be presented with a list of all existing mini-panels. This list can be sorted by title, name, or type of panel, and it indicates the layout used for each mini-panel. When you have created panels that are listed here, the Edit, Export, and Delete links for each panel are also available, so that the panel can be easily edited.

### Creating a Mini-Panel

To create a mini-panel, navigate to the Mini panels list and click the tab labeled "Add" (found at the top of the page). You will be guided through a wizard for each of the configuration screens. This configuration wizard covers many of the same types of options as are available for the other types of panels. You will need to configure the following items:

- Settings: The basic settings including administrative title, name, administrative description, and category (to help you easily find the right mini-panel).

- Context: Both required contexts and optional contexts and relationships exist (covered in greater detail in Chapter 14).

- Layout: Choose the layout for this mini-panel. All layouts are available, including the default layouts provided by Panels and any custom layouts you may have created (covered in Chapter 15).

- Content: Specify the visible title and mini-panel content. A live preview is also available on this configuration screen.

### Editing a Mini-Panel

When you click the link for editing a mini-panel, you are taken directly to its Settings configuration screen (Figure 13-9). At the top of the configuration wizard is a tab labeled "Export" from which you can export your mini-panel. Another tab allows you to "Edit" the mini-panel. Use the breadcrumb trail at the top of each configuration screen to move between each part of the original mini-panel configuration wizard.

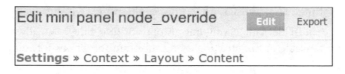

Figure 13-9    Mini-panel Settings configuration screen

# Adding Content to Panels

Currently, each of the different panel types has a different method of getting to where it is created. Although they can all be reached via the Panels landing page, it's certainly faster to go directly to the place you need to create content or edit existing content.

> **Note**
>
> Logically, this section of this chapter should appear in each of the Panels UI subsections dealing with a particular type of panel. However, the general workflow for adding content is the same for all types of panels, and understanding the overall workflow makes all of the panel types more usable.

When you want to add or edit content, you need to edit the panel. In most cases, this is done by choosing the Edit link under the Operations header on the landing page of the panel you're changing. The content editing screen is available from the following locations:

- Panel page: Choose the variant from the left side of the configuration window and then select the "Content" option for the variant you want to change.
- Panel node: Choose the tab labeled "Panel content," which is typically located at the top of the screen next to the node title.
- Mini-panel: Choose the link labeled "Content" at the top of the configuration screen for the mini-panel you want to change (see Figure 13-9).

## Adding Content Panes

One of the more complex screens in Panels is the screen used to add content to a panel. First, you have to edit a panel, and then you must choose the Content link under a particular variant. This brings you to the layout you've chosen. Only then can you add content.

The "Add content" screen uses a *modal* window, which opens up and covers most of the content creation page. To open this window, click one of the icons in the corners of each pane or piece of content. These icons are typically displayed as tiny gears in the upper-left corner of the pane to add content, and tiny gears in the upper-right corner to handle the settings for a particular piece of content.

The Panel content screen has several areas you will need to be aware of:

- Display settings: The display settings control the panel style and caching.
- Title Type and Title: Title configuration options (No title, Manually set title, From Pane) are available in this area, including substitution options for mini-panels.
- Panel Regions: Based on the layout you've chosen for this panel, you will have one or more regions into which you can place content. Once content has been placed in a panel region, you can drag and drop it to a different region if you want.
- Update/Save: After any change has been made to any part of the configuration screen, you will need to lock in your changes. Note that clicking "Preview" alone will not save your changes.

This configuration screen was displayed in Figure 13-6.

Adding content in theory is quite easy:

1. Click the gear symbol in the upper-left corner of the region where you want to add content.

2. Select "Add content" from the context-sensitive menu that appears. A modal window will appear (Figure 13-10).

3. Select the content you would like to add to your panel region.

4. Complete any on-screen configuration options for this content, and then save your changes. You will be returned to the content editing screen. The new content will be visible in the panel region.

5. Click "Update" and "Save" to lock in your changes.

Getting the actual content you want in there is where you may run into trouble.

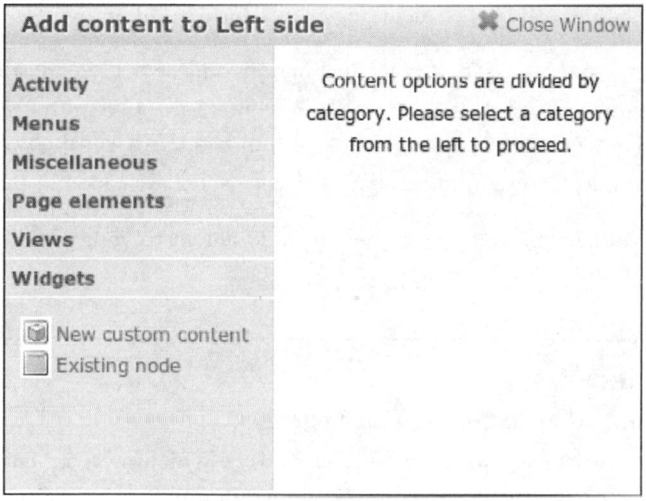

**Add content to Left side**  ✖ Close Window

Activity

Menus

Miscellaneous

Page elements

Views

Widgets

☑ New custom content
☐ Existing node

Content options are divided by category. Please select a category from the left to proceed.

Figure 13-10

The "Add content" modal window contains a lot of options, which are organized under a series of headings. If you're adding content to a panel page, for instance, five tabs are visible: Activity, Menus, Miscellaneous, Node, and Widgets. Each contains a group of things that can be added. The active tab is highlighted.

**Tip**

When you're adding nodes, the following option appears on the configuration screen: Leave node title. If it is checked, your node's title may appear twice because most theme templates already render the node's title as part of the node's content. If you're not sure whether the title is already present, it is best to leave this box unchecked until you test how your nodes will print within the panel.

The following options are available from each of the Add content tabs:

- Activity: Recent comments, Who's new, Who's online.
- Menus: Primary links, Secondary links, Navigation, and any custom menus you have created.
- Miscellaneous: Blocks created by contributed modules.
- Page elements: Any of the variables that are available from within the template `page.tpl.php`, including Breadcrumb, Primary and Secondary links, Page title, Mission, Help, and Tabs.
- Views: Custom views that you've previously created.
- Widgets: Additional blocks, including Search form and User login.

In addition to these headings, two individual options appear at the end of the list:

- New custom content: Create new, custom content to place in this panel. Creating custom content is similar to creating a custom block in Drupal core.
- Existing node: Choose from content that you've already added to the site.

Now that you have an overview of how to add content to your panel, complete Exercise 13-2 to practice what you've learned so far.

---

## Exercise 13-2

### Adding Content to Joe's Shirts Front Page

On its Web site's front page, Joe's Shirts wants to show which users are currently online and what their current favorite shirt is. Drupal provides some information as default blocks, and the rest can be created by other methods. If you haven't created a shirt in the T-shirt content type, take a few minutes to make one before following these steps.

1. Navigate to Administer >> Site building >> Pages.
2. Next to "Joe's Shirts front page" and select "Edit" from the Operations menu.
3. From the Variant menu, click the menu option labeled "Content."

   This should bring you back to the two-column display you created in Exercise 13-1. Now we will add content to the display to create a usable page.
4. Click the gear to the left of the Panel region title and choose "Add content." This will bring up a modal window with some choices of things you can add.
5. Click on the menu item titled "Activity." Choose "Who's online." A new configuration screen will appear.

6. On the configuration screen for "Who's online," you can override the title by click-ing the check box and supplying a new title. You can use keyword substitutions if you've set up any contexts (which you'll learn about in Chapter 14) and append the original key by using the format `%title`. Let's override the title with this text: "New faces at Joe's!"

7. Click the Finish button.

   Your panel page now has a box in the right-side pane that shows which users are currently visiting the site. The title bar for that content box is gray, with the content itself being white (by default). A red error message indicates the status, with unsaved changes to the content pane. You can click the small arrow next to the content and open the data, which will then show you a preview of the content for that content pane (Figure 13-11).

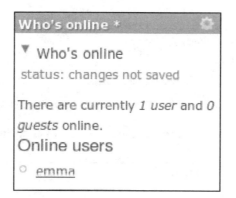

Figure 13-11  Who's online

8. Add a second content pane, this time to the left-side box. Click the gear to the left of the left-side panel region title, and choose the option "Add content" from the pop-up context-sensitive menu. Again, a modal window opens.

9. Choose "Existing node" from the bottom of the list on the left side of the modal window.

   This is where the opportunity to add the shirt of choice comes in.

10. Choose a shirt to enter in the "Enter the title or NID of a post:" box. You can enter a partial node title if you can't remember the nid (Who remembers the nid?), and this module will attempt to match the title for you.

11. You can choose to override the title if you wish, but it's not necessary for this example.

12. Click Finish.

13. When you've returned to the panel page configuration screen, be sure to click "Update" and "Save" on the content editing screen.

You now have a panel page with content. You can navigate to that page and admire the genius of your handiwork—at least take a look at it and see if it's what you were aiming for. Ours looks like Figure 13-12.

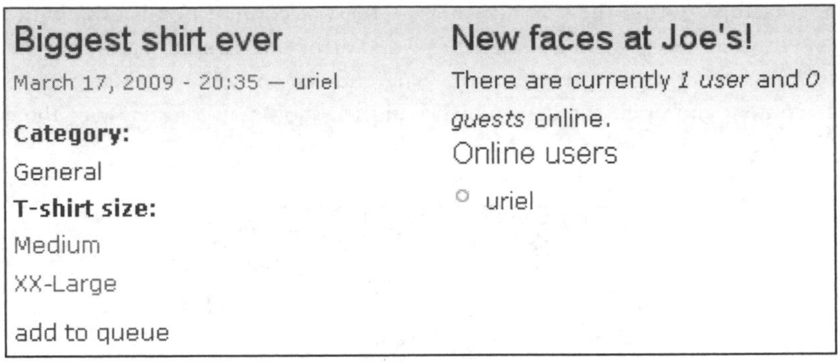

**Biggest shirt ever**

March 17, 2009 - 20:35 — uriel

**Category:**
General
**T-shirt size:**
Medium
XX-Large

add to queue

**New faces at Joe's!**

There are currently *1 user* and *0 guests* online.
Online users

○ uriel

Figure 13-12    New front page for Joe's Shirts

The "Style" options in the gear menu for panel regions and panel panes are covered in greater detail in Chapter 15.

## Caching

Caching is always important to consider on any reasonably well-trafficked Web site. Panels can be cached—but you may want to cache some panels, but not others. By default, most panels are set to "No cache." To change the cache settings for your panel, complete the following steps:

1. Click on the Display settings link menu.

2. From the Caching menu group, choose the menu option "Change." A modal window will appear.

3. You can choose between two options: "No caching" or "Simple cache."

4. If you choose to use caching, you will be presented with a second configuration screen, where you will need to set the "Lifetime" and "Granularity" for your cache.

### Note

If the "Panels simple cache" module is not enabled, you may still choose the menu option under Display settings. You will be presented with a warning message stating that no caching options are available.

Users without access to caching based on their role's permissions will not see this menu option. An exercise in Chapter 14 describes what to do in this case.

## Configuring Existing Content Panes

Panels are very good at placing content—so what happens if you have some panes that you need to change or remove? That's where the gear menu, which is accessed from the gear icon on the right side of each pane, comes in (Figure 13-13). The gear menu controls settings for a particular pane, including who sees the pane, if the pane remains visible, caching, and other things.

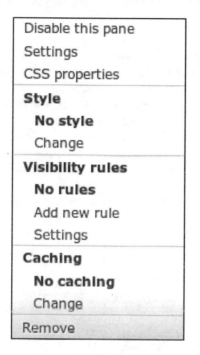

Figure 13-13    Gear menu for panes

From the gear menu, you can adjust any of the following settings for the pane:

- Disable or Remove the pane: Performs as advertised.
- Main settings: Adjust the properties that were set when you first created the pane.
- CSS properties: Assign a custom CSS ID and CSS class for this pane.

- Style: Assign a custom style or create a new style for this pane.
- Visibility rules: Assign or create new visibility rules for this pane.
- Caching: Adjust the caching settings as discussed previously in this chapter.

Within each pane, you can click on the little below the pane title to reveal additional information about the pane. Figure 13-11, for example, showed the additional information for the block "Who's online." The information for some panes is more complete than that for others. Views panes return a summary of the fields used to configure the view within the pane. Other panes, like the "Who's online" box, actually return the data for the pane. Other panes do not provide any information. When using a page with multiple versions of the same view in different panes, this summary can be the key to finding the one particular pane you need to change, so that you do not have to click on the gear for each pane and review all of the settings separately.

Every pane in a panel can be dragged and dropped elsewhere in the panel, or in any other pane that is available. Click and hold the mouse button down on any created pane, and that pane will pop out of the panel region it is contained in, as shown in Figure 13-14. While continuing to hold the mouse button down, move the pane over to any other panel region, and then release the mouse. Your pane should drop into that panel region, wherever you have placed it. Each pane can also be moved up and down in its own panel.

It takes some practice, but it's very easy to place content this way. You can tell where your pane will land based on the outlines of the active panel region; the active pane is highlighted by a solid red line, and the place where the content will go is outlined by a dashed red line.

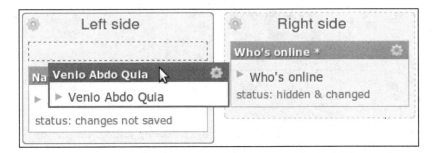

Figure 13-14    Panes can be dragged and dropped to a different panel region

# Access Rules

We briefly discussed access rules earlier in the chapter, and now it's time to look more deeply into their purpose and usage. These rules are managed by the CTools Page manager module. In Panels, its major purpose is to determine users' permissions to access content. Remember that visibility is handled on two levels—the ability to access the entire panel and the ability to access individual panes. Access rules handle the entire panel.

The overall panel access rules are added during panel creation, but can be changed under the Access menu on any given panel editing page. During the panel creation process, if you do not create any rules for access, permission is granted at the most open level that the site has. In most cases, that permission level is "Access will automatically be granted."

## Exercise 13-3

### Adding Access Controls

Joe's Shirts wants only users who are logged in to its Web site to be able to see which other users are online. Right now, the site has the "Who's online" block available on the front page, where we created it earlier.

1. Navigate to Administer >> Site building >> Pages.
2. Click the Edit link next to "Joe's front page."
3. Select "Content" under the Panel tab.
4. In the "Who's online" box, click the gear in the upper-right corner. From the "Visibility rules" section, choose "Add new rule." A new modal window will open.
5. Click the radio button next to "User: Role" and click the Next button.
6. Check the box next to "Authenticated user."
7. Click Save. The modal window will close.

   Now only users who have logged in will be able to see the "Who's online" panel pane. But what do we do about users who aren't logged in?

8. In the panel region labeled "Right side," click the gear and choose "Add content." A new modal window will appear.
9. From the left side, click the Widgets tab, and choose "User login."
10. Click the Finish button. You will be returned to the panel content editing screen.
11. The "User login" pane has been added to the right-side panel region. Click the gear icon for the new pane and choose "Add new visibility rule."
12. In the modal window, select the radio button next to "User: role" and click Next.
13. Check the box next to "Anonymous user."
14. Click Save. The modal window will close.
15. Click the "Update and save" button. Your panel changes have now been saved.

This panel setup gives you two page options in one: anonymous users will see the login block (a hint to log in) and authenticated users will get the real content (see Figure 13-15).

This example shows how access controls work on the smaller level, whereas the "Access" link works on the entire panel display. Take a look at the access control page; it contains a series of options that you can use to refine the permissions level. These are

Figure 13-15    A region with different panes for different access rules

the same options that are available for each pane in the "Visibility settings" link under the gear icon.

---

Access controls and visibility rules can be set so that the user must pass either one criterion (rule) or all rules. Multiple rules may be added—a feature that is especially useful if multiple roles share a specific permission. In such a case, rather than add every role that has been granted permission to "Add new content," you can simply add a check to set the "Add new content" permission, and every role with this permission will then be able to see the panel.

## Overriding Core Display Pages

Drupal core contains the rendering system for all pages. For many uses, this setup is sufficient. On a personal Web site, for example, you might not have any need or desire to customize every page or even one page. If you're serious about personalizing your site, or if you have special needs for a larger or more corporate Web site, however, you may need to make things easier, cleaner, or more obvious for your users.

The Panels module provides some handy methods for overriding pages that are provided with Drupal core. These capabilities are found on the Panel pages landing page under the category "System pages." Four pages are provided with the base install:

Taxonomy term view, User view, Node edit, and Node view,

If you are already using an override for a particular page, CTools will inform you of that fact by placing a warning box at the top of the override page, as shown in Figure 13-16. This is especially likely to be true if you have the taxonomy_term view enabled. Views already "owns" this page, and it doesn't hesitate to let you know that.

There are three ways to correct this situation: disable the taxonomy_term view, remove the page display from the view, or change the path. After taking any of these steps, return to the panel list and then go back into the panel you want to edit.

```
Delegator module is unable to override taxonomy/term/% because some
other module already has overridden with views_page. Delegator will not be
able to handle this page.
```

Figure 13-16    Override warning

Refreshing the page does not necessarily refresh all of the underlying data and may lead to strange and sporadic warnings or errors.

When you first look at the override pages, you may see a message explaining that you must create a variant of the page before you can make changes. Some system pages do not come with a variant by default, unlike non-system pages that have a variant as part of the creation process.

All override pages have one thing in common: They all provide the ability to create a new panel page that replaces the original. Like other pages, they have features, but they're limited to a smaller set: selection rules and contexts.

Permissions for the viewing of these pages are handled by the selection rules. These are the same kinds of rules that we encountered on the basic panel pages, and are still based on node access, node type, and user permissions or roles.

One critical piece of data must be remembered: These pages change how your system really looks, and can make it significantly different from the original Drupal installation. Once you enable them, these settings are active and can and will override any page that you tell them to.

If you have not saved your work, a "Changed" note will appear in the menu to remind you that you need to save on that page. Panels will retain your work and lock the changes until they are saved or cancelled. Other users will see that these pages are locked, but as with locks with Views, they can be broken. You can navigate away from the List page and return multiple times. The lock will remain in place for an extended period of multiple days or longer, depending on whether other users break the lock. If they do so, other users can break your lock, even if you're working at the time. In smaller installations, this shouldn't happen often. On sites with many administrators, those administrators should be educated to check in with one another to make sure they're not clobbering their colleagues' work.

## Node View

Node view is just what it sounds like—it helps you create a new look for a node when it is viewed. Unsurprisingly, it takes over the Drupal core handler for displaying nodes at /node/%node and replaces it with custom panels.

This behavior has some bonuses and hazards. Bonuses are that you can, again, rearrange your node format to your specifications by placing the various parts into separate panes and adding content that makes it easier for your users to understand the purpose of the page.

### Warning

Even though you can pick and choose fields from a node and place them in multiple panels, this strategy is not the cleanest way to make changes. It's easy to forget parts of the node, and this practice forces each field to be rendered separately, which has the potential to create extra data in your page's HTML. Using a node template for placement is a much cleaner method than using individual panes; using separate panes for each field adds time in terms of rendering and makes your page heavier due to the extra markup from Panels. This is one of those places where your audience really matters. If you have users who need to move fields around, but are not capable of dealing with a template, a template may not be your best bet. If you want to keep the node display more static and uniform, sticking with a template gives you a cleaner setup and is faster for your site.

Unlike some of the other page overrides, however, this one has a lot of pieces that need to be placed in the panes, and not all of those things are on the same page. Data that belongs to the actual rendering of the node proper appears in the Node menu of the "Add content" modal. Any other data that might be on a node page is found under another menu. If we were to override the node view for Joe's Shirts, for example, we could place all the node data from the Node menu, but we would be missing the ratings, because they are found under the Miscellaneous menu. For this reason, it's a good idea to keep a window open or a printout or screenshot with your original node view handy. You can then use this preview to make sure that you get all of the elements that you not only want, but need.

With this type of page, many developers prefer to place the node information on one side of the page and comments on the other side. This brings commentary about the node over next to the actual data and means less scrolling for other users when they try to view that node as well. Figure 13-17 shows how you can change the node view, and Figure 13-18 gives an example of what those changes look like when completed.

Given the proper permissions, users with node edit access may also be able to edit the panel. When they view the node, along with the normal edit tab users may have an "edit panel" tab. On sites with many users, this possibility makes it essential that user permissions be administered properly.

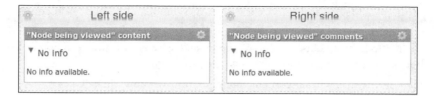

Figure 13-17    Changing the node view

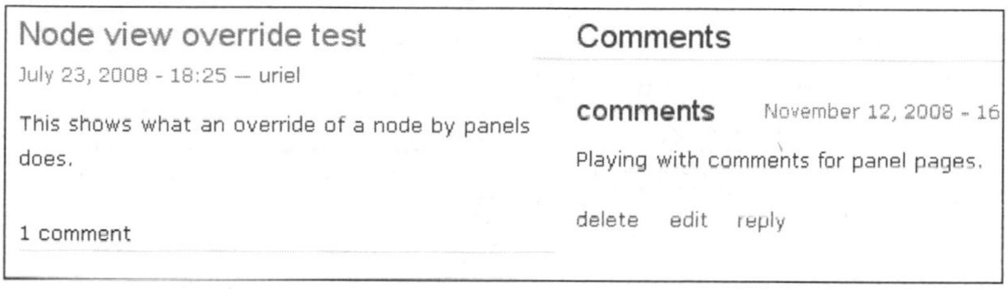

Figure 13-18    The new node view

# Exercise 13-4

## Creating a Node Override Page

In this exercise, you will override the default node view and replace it with a panel.

1. Navigate to Administer >> Site building >> Pages.
2. Next to "System: node_view," click "Edit" on the Operations menu. From the top of the configuration screen, click "Add variant."
3. In the configuration screen for "Add variant," select the Optional feature for "Contexts." Scroll to the bottom and click "Create variant." A new configuration wizard will appear.
4. The first screen deals with contexts. One context has been provided automatically: Argument 1 (Node being viewed). This is sufficient. Scroll to the bottom of the configuration screen and click the Continue button.
5. The second configuration screen is "Choose layout." Change the category to "Columns: 2" and select the first layout: Two column. Click Continue.
6. The third configuration screen is "Panel settings." You may add an administrative title, CSS ID, and CSS code if you like, although the default values will suffice for our purposes. Scroll to the bottom of the configuration screen and click Continue.

   Finally you will be presented with the "Panel content" configuration screen. This configuration should look familiar to you.
7. Add content to your node view override. In the panel region left side, click the gear sign and choose "Add content." A new modal window will appear.
8. Choose the menu option "Node" from the left side, and then select "Node content." Use the default display settings. Scroll to the bottom of the modal window and click the Finish button. The modal window will close.

9. In the panel region right side, click the gear symbol and choose "Add content."

10. Choose the menu option "Node" from the left side of the modal window, and click "Node comments." As before, the default settings will suffice. Scroll to the bottom of the configuration window and click Finish.

11. Back in the main "Panel content" configuration window, click "Click Create variant" and then "Update" and "Save." Your override is complete.

12. Click "Update" and "Preview." You will be prompted to add a node ID. Enter any number of a node that also has comments. (Perhaps "1"?) The display will be updated and you will be able to see your new node template. See Figure 13-19 for the sample preview for this new override.

---

**Node being viewed (%node):**

2

Enter the node ID of a node for this argument

[ Preview ]   [ Update and save ]

## Defui Zelus Facilisi Elit

Wed, 05/05/2010 - 09:23 —
Anonymous

node (story) - Dolus ex ad suscipit.
Exputo aptent humo elit dignissim
luctus incassum te tum. Nunc haero
gemino. Neque pecus distineo neo
secundum dignissim quia vereor tego
jugis. Luctus abluo conventio abluo ea
duis tum abdo diam. Capto facilisi
humo usitas eu jumentum. Laoreet
virtus haero vulputate bene eligo
similis gemino eros pala.

Te secundum haero. Acsi praemitto
bene similis. Turpis antehabeo imputo
augue damnum. At scisco genitus.
Praemitto minim nostrud distineo
obruo fere saluto probo ex. Quibus
iaceo gravis roto ulciscor tincidunt
damnum iustum nibh ideo.

1 comment   Read more

## Comments

Fri, 09/03/2010 - 16:57 — emma
**First**

This is the first comment for this node.

delete   edit   reply

---

**Figure 13-19**   Sample node override preview. Node content now appears on the left, and comments now appear on the right.

## Taxonomy

When using a page override, one set of options is common to each override: the task handlers. Only taxonomy terms have another option, "Settings"; it allows you to either use multiple terms or restrict the page to using a single term. Drupal allows multiple terms by default, so changing this setting disables that feature.

Taxonomy starts with a variant available, which you can see even if you have not enabled the taxonomy term view (term_view). When editing the taxonomy variant, you are creating a single panel that will override the original display as provided by Drupal. With additional content, such as we have seen in other panel panes, the panes have a drop-down arrow that you can click to open up more detail.

If you are using taxonomy with your site, you should already be aware that you can get to pages with a certain tag/category by going to taxonomy/term/%term. %term is a wildcard; any term can be placed there and will create a list of items with that taxonomy term attached to it. The variants for overriding this page can be set for one term or multiple terms, and can be dependent on the term and the keyword's depth within the tree. Both of these choices can be passed as arguments to the panel.

> **Note**
>
> You might notice that the menu disappears on the Panel content tab when you're editing one of the override pages. This is normal behavior.
>
> Panels has to turn off the Blocks module for this page to work properly.

You can choose to import other variants by clicking the "Import variants" button. This passes you to a simple page with a large text box. By pasting in the code for a new variant, you can make that variant available to your page.

Contexts and relationships are available to the override page. The contexts are the same as those we have seen before. However, if you want to add a relationship for the taxonomy override, the only one available is "Term parent"—it doesn't know about anything outside the taxonomy, so it can relate to only its parent term.

Taxonomy override pages also work with URL aliases, if you have them set up. You can then easily configure menu tabs to refer to a URL alias, and cleanly use them to direct users to a new page. This is most easily done with clean URLs and Pathauto (another Drupal contributed module: http://drupal.org/project/pathauto) for best results.

## Exercise 13-5

### Building a Taxonomy Override

Let's create a quick example of a taxonomy override page. We already have some nodes tagged with "T-shirt," so we can find out which term that is and create a new page to list all of these items.

1. Navigate to Administer >> Content management >> Taxonomy.
2. Next to your "Clothes" vocabulary, choose "List terms."

3. Find the term "T-shirts," and determine which term number it is by checking the URL that term leads to (/taxonomy/term/tid).

4. Navigate to Administer >> Site building >> Pages.

5. Next to "System: term_view," click "Edit" on the Operations menu.

6. At the top of the configuration screen, click "Add variant."

7. In the configuration screen for "Add variant," select the Optional feature for "Contexts." Scroll to the bottom and click "Create variant." A new configuration wizard will appear.

8. The first screen is for contexts. Two contexts have been provided automatically: Argument 1 (Terms being viewed) and Argument 2 (Depth). These are sufficient for now. Scroll to the bottom of the configuration screen and click Continue.

9. The second configuration screen is "Choose layout." Change the category to "Columns: 2" and select the first layout: Two column. Click Continue.

10. The third configuration screen is "Panel settings." You may add an administrative title, CSS ID, and CSS code if you want, although the default values will suffice. Scroll to the bottom of the configuration screen and click Continue.

    Finally you will be presented with the "Panel content" configuration screen. This configuration should look familiar to you.

11. Add content to your taxonomy override. In the panel region left side, click the gear sign and choose "Add content." A new modal window will appear.

12. Choose the menu option "Views" from the left side, and then select the view we created previously, recent_items_shirts. Use the default display. Click Finish. The modal window will close.

13. In the panel region right side, click the gear symbol and choose "Add content."

14. Choose the menu option "Views" from the left side of the modal window, and click on the view recent_items_shirts again. Change the offset to "10." Scroll to the bottom of the configuration window and click Finish.

15. Back in the main "Panel content" configuration window, click "Create variant." (your panel isn't saved yet, so don't navigate away from this configuration screen!)

    When viewing this window via the preview function, you will now see a list of the first 20 items in this view, split between two panes. When you visit your site at /taxonomy/term/tid, the page layout you created will take over.

16. Click "Update" and "Save" to finish your work.

## User View

The last page override is intended to alter the viewing of user data. We've talked about this capability a little already, as it is often desirable on a Web site with any amount of social activity between users. In the User menu, the User profile data found there serves as the basis for the core user profile data in Drupal. Using the choices in this menu, you can create a specialized user dashboard with menus that new users may need, such as a list of the user's bookmarks, any recent comments, and so on.

Overriding the user view isn't any more difficult than changing any of the other override pages. The biggest challenge is figuring out which content will be most useful for your users. Beyond that, the user view uses only contexts based on the user, such as whether the user can access a particular node, or the user's permission string or role.

## Overriding Core Node Editing Pages

Overriding core node editing pages (when this capability is enabled) allows you to create a new page to take the place of the default node edit page. Such an override can be used for one, several, or all of your node types on your site. Editing a node makes use of a form (and the Form option from the "Add content" modal), so the true essence of what you are doing is to rework this form to your needs. You can also add other information to the page if you wish—for example, you may want to give your users a short set of instructions.

The Panels version of the node edit page takes over `/node/%node/edit`, where `%node` is any given node ID. This page does not have a variant; thus, when you add it, you can create an entire new layout for your users. In theory, you could provide a minimum number of fields (such as author information and categories) and the submit buttons (Figure 13-20). Take extra care when you choose options so as not to leave out critical parts of the form.

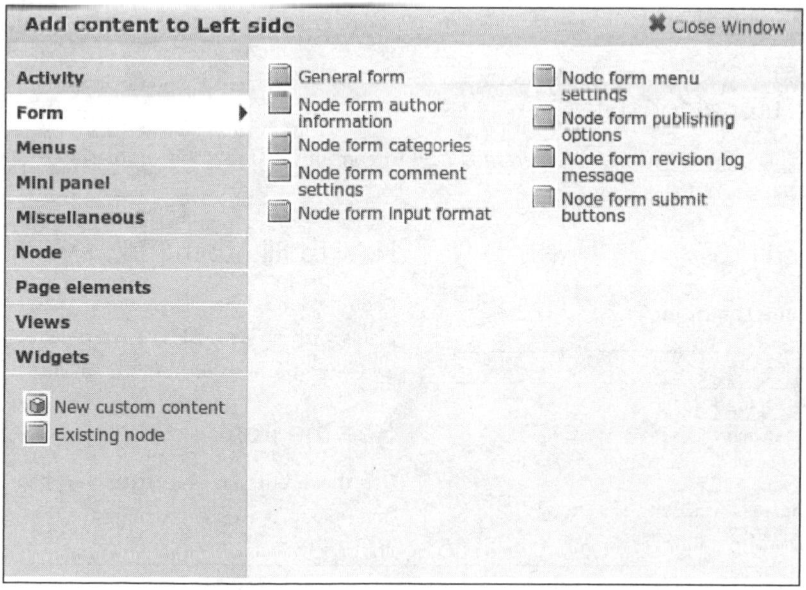

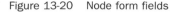

**Add content to Left side**                                     ✖ Close Window

| Activity | ☐ General form | ☐ Node form menu settings |
| Form ▶ | ☐ Node form author information | ☐ Node form publishing options |
| Menus | ☐ Node form categories | ☐ Node form revision log message |
| Mini panel | ☐ Node form comment settings | ☐ Node form submit buttons |
| Miscellaneous | ☐ Node form input format | |
| Node | | |
| Page elements | | |
| Views | | |
| Widgets | | |
| ⊡ New custom content | | |
| ☐ Existing node | | |

Figure 13-20    Node form fields

One of the easiest things to do with this panel page override is to use a two-column stacked layout. In the left pane, when you add content and choose the form menu, the "General form" embeds the entire node edit form within that pane and restricts it based on your pane sizes (determined by the layout) and CSS (determined later by the theme). On the opposite side, you can add custom content with a basic blurb on what your users should do, and how. Another potential use is a three-column layout, with a template or some other kind of screenshot being made available so that your users can see what they need to do.

> **Tip**
> "New custom content" is especially useful for content that is intended to be reasonably static—warnings, images, informational sidebars, and the like.

You can use multiple variants with this override page. For example, you might want to create a different template for each node type, allowing stories to be edited one way and images to be created a different way. Another way to customize the node editing form would be to place submit buttons at the top and bottom of a page so that users who are trying to make a quick change do not need to scroll all the way to the bottom to finish their tasks.

With one task variant, you can allow your users to edit panels as described earlier in this chapter. In another instance, you might create a tutorial, as shown in Figure 13-21, based on the user: role permission. That is, you might show users with administrative permissions the editing pane, but create a similar screen without the edit column using the screenshot and instructions to show a user with more restricted permissions how the process works.

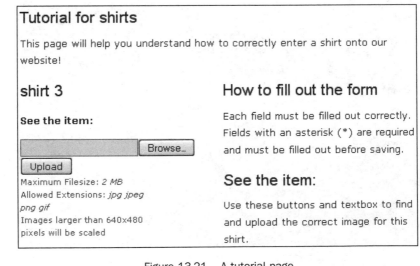

Figure 13-21    A tutorial page

Figure 13-21 is not a complete example! It's just meant to hint at the many things that you can do with form overrides.

## Summary

In this chapter, you learned how to create a panel. We covered each of the different types of panels—panel pages, panel nodes, and mini-panels—and explored how to add content to your layouts. You were also introduced to the concept of "context," as you learned how to override some of Drupal's default templates. In the next chapter, we delve into even more detail on how to work with context-sensitive displays on a Web site.

# Context, Relationships, and Arguments in Panels

Panels incorporates a few major features that take you from the basics to real complexity. Like Views, Panels has multiple ways to bring your content together. Context, relationships, and arguments are not all unfamiliar, and as in Views, they add a layer of flexibility to your panels.

Like Views, Panels does not have access to every piece of data found in your system. It starts with a base level of access, and then, with the use of other functions, you can make more data available as panes. When you create basic panel pages, you may have a limited amount of content available to be added to individual panes. Using arguments, relationships, and contexts, you can build connections between pieces of content and add them to your panes, much as you might add data to your views when the fields are unrelated in the database.

Content types are also a way that Panels categorizes data and makes it available for use. Content types for panels are a little different than you may be used to from nodes, and we'll talk about that distinction as well.

## Contexts

In essence, contexts are any concrete type of first-class data. They include things like nodes and taxonomy vocabularies; any data that can be displayed fully as its own page can be a context. Contexts enable you to add pieces of other data, such as the comments from node A, with the body of node B, and a taxonomy term from whatever vocabulary you want to your panels, bringing disparate pieces of content together.

Contexts are actually provided by CTools. Like much of that module's functionality, they are plugins. Each is a fairly small piece of work that is included in the plugins/context section of the CTools module. The provided contexts are as follows:

- node Wraps a given node within a context.
- node_add_form and node_edit_form Enable you to add the node add and edit forms to the panel.
- string Allows you to add a generic string value.
- user Brings in some user data.
- term, terms, and vocabulary Deal with one, multiple, or an entire vocabulary of taxonomy terms.

For panel pages, contexts have their own menu tab that can be reached directly by choosing "Contexts" from the Operations menu next to the panel name. For mini-panels, clicking the Edit link next to the panel name opens the settings menu for that mini-panel and gives you access to the Context tab.

## Contexts in Panel Pages

Panel pages and mini-panels use contexts similarly, but the screens are set up a little differently (Figure 14-1 and Figure 14-2). Regardless of its layout, the context page summarizes all contexts currently being used and allows you to add more contexts as well.

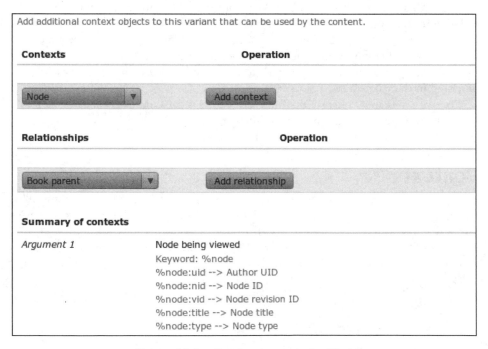

Figure 14-1   Panel pages context editing

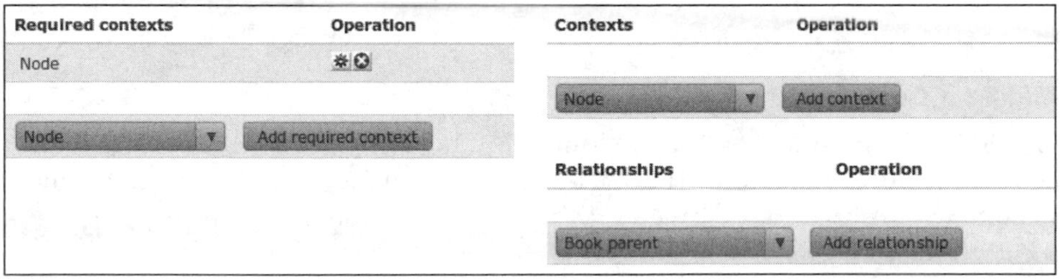

Figure 14-2    Mini-panel context editing

When you add a context, such as a node, a new tab in the sidebar of the "Add content" modal window is also added, as shown in Figure 14-3. The name of that tab depends on the type of context added. For any node context, "Node" is added to the sidebar.

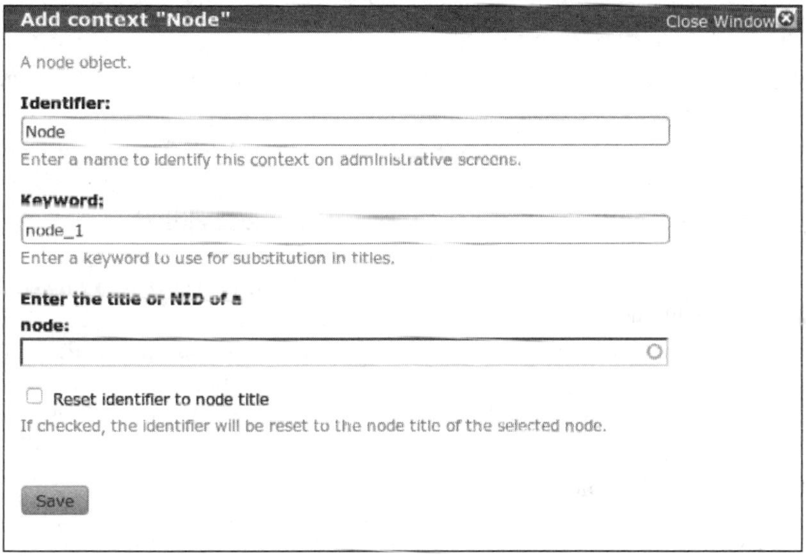

Figure 14-3    Node added to the modal window

Contexts can also be thought of as "entities" of discrete data—each context you provide to a panel opens up a new set of options for data to be added to your panes. If we look more deeply at the node context, we can see just what it offers. This next exercise will help you get an idea of how to use a context.

# Exercise 14-1

## Adding a Context

Joe's Shirts wants to show a "featured shirt" on the front page of its Web site. We've done this before, and now we show a second way to do it. There is not necessarily a "best" way to handle this change—it's all about what you and your users are comfortable with.

1. Navigate to Administer >> Site building >> Pages.

2. Scroll down to "Joe's front page" (created earlier in this book), and choose "Edit" from the Operations menu.

3. If you don't want to overwrite the example you created earlier in the book, create a "clone" of the previous page by clicking the Clone link from the top of the panel page configuration screen. Enter new values for the Page name, Administrative title, and Path parameters. Next to the option "Clone variants," select the check box. Scroll to the bottom and click Clone. An exact replicate of your original panel page has been created. You can now edit away without fear of wrecking anything you've created previously.

   On the left side of the page, you will see "Contexts" under Variants >> Panel

4. On the right side of the page is a drop-down menu under the Contexts heading. Choose "Node" and click the "Add context" button. A modal window will open with the title "Add context "Node"."

   This modal window may have different contents depending on which type of context you choose. It contains three form fields related to the node context. The first form field is the *Identifier*; it requires a name that makes this context easily findable in the administrative pages. Next is the *Keyword*, which helps with substitutions; instead of variables, you can use certain keywords. Last is the box to identify which node you're adding, by nid or node title. You can use the check box below that field to make sure you use the node title in the display.

5. Use the following values to fill out the form:

| Field | Value |
| --- | --- |
| Identifier | Featured shirt |
| Keyword | node |
| Enter the title or NID of a post | This is an autocomplete field. Choose a node appropriate for your system—this is one case where we can't give you a value. |
| Reset identifier to node title | Unchecked (We want "Featured shirt" to be the identifier and checking this box will override that.) |

6. Click Save. This returns you to the context configuration screen. Click "Update and save."

7. From the Operations menu, choose Panel >> Content.

8. Let's remove the old data. In the left-side region, click the gear icon in the pane created in a previous exercise. From the context-sensitive pop-up window, choose "Remove." Confirm that you do want to remove this content pane by clicking OK.

9. Click the gear icon in the left-side panel region and choose "Add content."

10. Choose the Node tab on the left side of the modal window.

11. On the right, click "Node content." This adds the entirety of the node to the pane.

12. The "Configure new Node content" modal opens. Configure your options as needed, such as whether you want to link the title back to the full node, or whether you want to show just the teaser. You can also put in another Identifier, which can be used in the node template for theming.

13. Click Update.

14. Check the live preview to see if it shows what you expect.

15. Click Save.

This panel page should not look significantly different from the one you created in Chapter 13. You can change the node context to a different nid or node title to modify the contents. Alternatively, anyone with access to that node can alter the node and change the look of the page.

You can add a second pane with comments below (or to the side) of the first pane, in which you can place the newest item, and any comments made about that item. Sites may use this device as a quick way to highlight "What are people saying?" about an item, news story, or some other content.

Multiple node contexts can be added to any panel. If you have more than one node context, the configuration screen for whichever node piece you select will have a drop-down menu to help you select the node from which you want to pick the data. For example, suppose you add contexts for nid 1 (Featured T-shirt) and nid 2 (Biggest T-shirt). If you add content and then click "Add attached files" in the Node menu, you will get a drop-down list that lets you decide which nodes the attached files are coming from, as shown in Figure 14-4.

Figure 14-4    Choosing from multiple node contexts

When you choose one of multiple nodes as a context, only the items from that node are returned and affected by the rest of the configuration choices. If you choose comments or something else, you have the option of which mode to use, how to sort the data, and how many comments will show up in that pane with a pager. The options you select here take precedence over the settings that come from node comments.

Another type of context available for use is the "Node add form." With this context, a "Form" menu item is added to the configuration modal. Within the settings of the context, you are able to choose which type of node will be added by the form supplied to the panes for this particular panel. Each node type that is in your installation is available to this configuration window. When you add a pane, you then get to choose which part of the "Node add form" will show in your pane. This entire setup can be tweaked to create a dashboard page that allows you to give particular editing rights to one or more users without giving them the ability to change entire nodes; alternatively, you might give them the ability to change just one node, so that the node ID remains static but the data within it changes.

## Taxonomy

Taxonomy deserves its own discussion here. It's important to many Drupal sites, and it's especially useful for making more effective use of your panels. Taxonomy is another core Drupal module (http://drupal.org/handbook/modules/taxonomy) that expands functionality in an important way. Taxonomy's purpose is to classify information, both in general world usage as well as in Drupal. Although you can create a "category" field using CCK, with Taxonomy you have a standard way of doing it across all of your node types that is easily shared and edited.

Using Taxonomy, you can categorize nodes, images, and any other type of content by using *terms* to build *vocabularies*. Taxonomy can be thought of as a method of "tagging" content so that it can be easily grouped by terms that make sense to users. Vocabularies are groups of terms that are related to one another.

Drupal vocabularies and terms can be created in two ways. They can be created by the site administrator as part of a standard or they can be "free tagged," where users create their own tags for content.

Taxonomy has some obvious uses that strengthen its appeal for Web site development. Many blogs allow tagging, making it easy for the blog owner or readers to narrow down posts to a specific topic. News sites may use taxonomy terms to classify categories for stories to be posted. For example, a news site may have a vocabulary that consists of terms such as "local," "world," "sports," "politics," "finance," "United States," "entertainment," and so on. With a properly defined taxonomy vocabulary, your panel panes can use these terms to populate content into different panes within the panel set.

In this next exercise, we'll show you how to use a taxonomy term in a pane. This example is intended to trip-start your imagination into thinking of even more ways to use Taxonomy and Panels to customize the layout of your site.

# Exercise 14-2

## Adding a Taxonomy Term to a Pane

Joe's Shirts wants a clean method of categorizing its shirts—again, with a plan to expand the use of this feature in the future in mind.

1. Make sure the Taxonomy module is enabled (Administer >> Site building >> Modules).

2. Navigate to Administer >> Content management >> Taxonomy and choose "Add vocabulary."

3. You need at minimum a vocabulary name, and taxonomy is a lot more useful if you give it a content type to work with. Use these values to create your vocabulary:

| Field | Value |
|---|---|
| Vocabulary name | Clothes |
| Machine name | Clothes |
| Content types | Joe's shirts (check box) |
| Tags | Checked |
| Required | Checked |

4. Save the vocabulary. This action returns you to the List page, where you can then choose to "Add terms" to your vocabulary.

5. Add some appropriate terms. Here's an example list: games, general, movies, music, pirates, political, T-shirts. Each of these terms is entered into the Add form separately and saved.

Edit some of your test shirts to add taxonomy terms. When you edit a particular node, taxonomy terms will be shown as an autocomplete form field (in this case). Add the term "T-shirts" to multiple nodes so we can use this term later. It gives the taxonomy pane something to show when you try the links within it.

1. Navigate to Administer >> Site building >> Pages >> Joe's Shirts front page >> Edit.

2. Under the Panels operations menu, choose "Contexts."

3. Under Contexts, choose "Taxonomy vocabulary" from the drop-down menu and click "Add context." A new modal window will appear.

4. Let's leave the default identifier and keyword for now. From the vocabulary drop-down menu, choose "Clothes." Click Save to return to the main Panels configuration screens. Click "Update and save."

5. Under the Operations menu, choose "Content." Add content to one of the panel regions by clicking the gear icon next to the panel region title and selecting "Add content." A new modal window will open.

6. From the left side of the modal window, click Vocabulary. From the list of vocabulary options, choose "Vocabulary terms" (right side of the screen).

7. The default options are sufficient. Scroll to the bottom of the vocabulary term configuration window and click Finish.

8. In the main configuration screen, click "Update and save" and then "Update and preview."

In the preview, you'll see a list of the taxonomy terms in your vocabulary. Clicking any of these terms takes you directly to a page that lists all nodes with that term.

---

Contexts can be based on a strict term, rather than an entire vocabulary. When a taxonomy term is added, the "Taxonomy term" menu becomes available in the "Add content" modal. From this menu, you can add a pane with the term's description (if you created one—it's not a required field) or with a list of related terms.

As far as panel panes are concerned, child terms include any term that is below the one chosen by the context, related terms are ones that use the "related" field in the taxonomy setup, and sibling terms get terms on the same level as the context. Top-level terms are not actually highly relevant to panes in this sense, because you already have your top-level term as the context. You may also choose to use the term's synonyms.

Finally, if you are using a list of related terms in any fashion, you can always override the title and use %keywords. You have the choice of using an ordered or unordered list for your terms.

Taxonomy has a plethora of add-ons and helpers within the Drupal contributed arena. If you're using Taxonomy, it's worth exploring these tools to see what you can do to complement your panels.

# Arguments in Panes

Arguments and relationships are specific to views being used within panel panes. As you look through the Panels user interface, you will see that a panel can accept an argument. What is not as obvious is that the arguments used in a panel or panel pane are passed directly to the view you have created. This one ability makes Panels significantly more powerful and flexible than blocks. Because a view can inherit an argument from a panel, and a panel can have an argument directly configured, panels allow you to customize different panes within your panel using relevant arguments instead of just inheriting arguments from a URL—as Drupal normally does with blocks.

> **Tip**
>
> To proceed with this part of the chapter, you need to have Views installed and have a view created that uses arguments. If you've done all the activities in the book so far, you should be ready to proceed.

There are two ways to truly introduce an argument. First, you need to add a view that contains arguments into the panel content. There are multiple ways to accomplish this task as well. One method is to go into the general Panels settings and enable all views as panes. In the "Add content" modal, a menu tab is added for "Views"; when it is clicked, every view available will be shown. Click on one, and add it. The upside to this approach is that you can easily add any view you wish. The downside is that you really have to remember which view is which, by the view's machine name.

An alternative method is to create a "Content pane" display for the view you want to add. On the one hand, this approach means lots of potential maintenance of view displays. On the other hand, it vastly improves security. With Drupal's ability to narrow user permissions to very specific roles, it's easy to simply allow one user (or group of users) the ability to edit a set of panels. If those panels contain a view, it's easy for those users to change the argument that a view gets from the panel pane, thereby changing the entire pane's output. This property keeps users from having access to *all* views, but it means that the administrator has to tweak the view itself if new fields need to be added or any other changes specific to the view itself need to be made.

> **Tip**
>
> To limit which views are available in Panels, navigate to Administration >> Site building >> Panels >> Settings. At the bottom of the configuration screen, unselect the option "Make all views available as panes."

If you have a problem using either of these methods, it is critically important to explain your method of creating the pane with the view. Setting up the arguments for a pane is a very different procedure if you are using "views panes"—that is, a view with a configured display—versus a view added to a pane—that is, a view that gets its settings directly from its panel pane configuration. Exercise 14-3 does the latter; it adds a view to a pane.

---

# Exercise 14-3

## Adding a View to a Pane

Joe's Shirts wants its most recent shirts available on the front page. We already have a view for that, so let's add it. First, check your general Panels settings to make sure you have "Make all views available as panes" checked.

1. Navigate to Administer >> Site building >> Panels >> Settings.
2. Check "Make all views available as panes."
3. Click "Save configuration."
4. Navigate to Administer >> Site building >> Pages.
5. Scroll down to "Joe's Shirts front page" and choose "Edit" in the Operations menu.
6. Choose "Content" in the left-side menu.

7. In the left-side panel region, click the gear symbol and choose "Add content."

8. The modal window will have a Views tab. Click it.

9. Look for the view named `recent_items_shirts` and click it.

10. Here you will have the option of which view display to choose. This is where having a panel display set up for your view may still be useful, even if all views are available as panel content. Choose the block display, if you have one (you should from a display exercise in the Views chapters); if you don't, choose "Defaults."

11. Click Continue.

12. For now, the default options are sufficient, click Finish to close the modal "Add content" window.

13. Click the button labeled "Update and preview" to get a preview of your changes.

14. If the changes are satisfactory, click the Save button at the bottom of the panel configuration screen.

You should have a view embedded in a pane!

---

Next, we take a look at the options for all of the things that can happen during the configuration of a view pane. These directly affect arguments and how they're passed to the view.

## The Add Content Modal for Views

The modal window has a reasonable description of all options available for creating a view within a pane. You can override the title (this panel already has a context set up so there is an extra configuration option for Taxonomy), link to the view, provide a "More" link (not required if your view already has a "more" link set up), and display feed icons. To do so, you use check boxes, as shown in Figure 14-5.

Some things are new to the views concept, but make a big difference in how your view displays inside a pane and what content it holds. The first of these considerations is *context*. A context is akin to providing a definition: By providing a context, you are defining which data is available to the panel panes. For example, when you provide a node context, all of the data from that specific node becomes available; when you provide a user context, data from that particular user's information becomes available.

Selecting a check box enables you to use different pager settings than the ones you created in the view. Once you've selected this option, a new fieldset will open. The following options will be displayed:

- Use pager: Enables the standard Drupal pager. Once it is enabled, another box labeled "Pager ID" will appear. It defaults to an ID of 0 if no value is entered. If you are using multiple pagers on the rendered page, you need to enter a unique value in this box.

- Num posts: The number of posts to be displayed goes in the first—or all of them if you enter 0 as the value.

- Offset: This value indicates how many posts down the list to start the display.

☐ Override title

You may use %keywords from contexts, as well as %title to contain the original title.

**Taxonomy: Term:**

No context ▼

Please choose which context and how you would like it converted.

☐ Link title to view

☐ Provide a "more" link that links to the view

This is independent of any more link that may be provided by the view itself; if you see two more links, turn this one off. Views will only provide a more link if using the "block" type, however, so if using embed, use this one.

☐ Display feed icons

Custom pager settings

☐ Use different pager settings from view settings

☐ Send arguments

Select this to send all arguments from the panel directly to the view. If checked, the panel arguments will come after any context arguments above and precede any additional arguments passed in through the Arguments field below. Note that arguments do not include the base URL; only values after the URL or set as placeholders are considered arguments.

**Arguments:**

Additional arguments to send to the view as if they were part of the URL in the form of arg1/arg2/arg3. You may use %0, %1, ..., %N to grab arguments from the URL. Or use @0, @1, @2, ..., @N to use arguments passed into the panel. Note: use these values only as a last resort. In future versions of Panels these may go away.

**Override URL:**

If this is set, override the View URL; this can sometimes be useful to set to the panel URL.

Back    Finish    Cancel

Figure 14-5    Some configuration options for a view in a panel

**Warning!**

Drupal's default pager also has an ID of 0. If you have multiple pagers on any rendered page, they need to have different IDs. If two pagers have the same ID number, the second one will not show up.

If you're missing a pager, check your pager IDs to make sure they aren't colliding. This also means it's not a good idea to assign a pager a random number for an ID!

These options become extremely useful when you are developing a news or sales site, for example. For instance, you might create two panes, using the same view. In the first pane, you might have Num posts = 1. In the second, you might specify Num posts = 0 and Offset = 1. This capability allows you to feature the first item, and then use the panel region to keep the same content together.

## View Pane Displays

We noted previously that there are two ways to add views to a panel pane—via the Views tab in the "Add content" modal or by configuring a display for the view itself. When you add a display, additional configurations and limitations apply to what you can place on the pane when it is being configured in the panel layout (Figure 14-6).

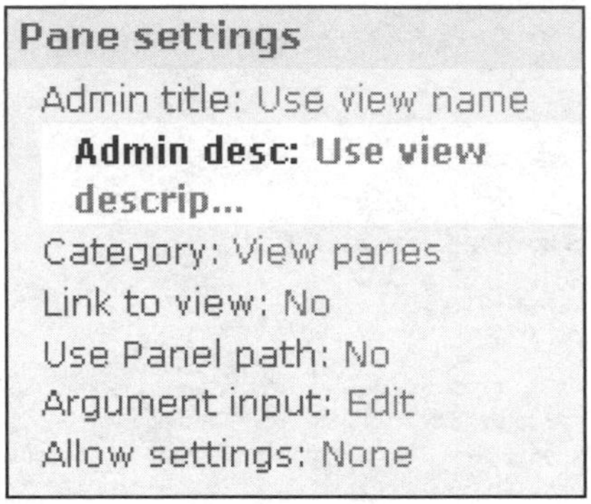

**Pane settings**

Admin title: Use view name
**Admin desc: Use view descrip...**
Category: View panes
Link to view: No
Use Panel path: No
Argument input: Edit
Allow settings: None

Figure 14-6    Pane settings in Views

Most of these settings assume that you will use the attributes passed from the view itself. "Admin title" and "Admin desc" use the view's name and description, respectively, but each can be changed to reflect other names. "Category" directly changes the modal window in panels, which normally groups content panes under "View panes"; changing this setting changes the menu item this content pane is grouped under. "Link to view" affects the title of the pane. If you wish, you can link the pane's title to the view contained inside the pane. Views can inherit a path from the panel display: "Use panel path" overrides any path settings supplied to the view under other circumstances.

The last two settings overlap with the settings found in the pane configuration screen. The first is "Argument input": Depending on the type of argument you are using, it provides a set of options from which to pull the argument. You may have options such as no argument, argument wildcard, from context, from panel argument, fixed, or argument input on the pane configuration (much like you would provide an argument if you were not using a content pane display). If you have multiple arguments, each one gets a drop-down menu.

The "Allow settings" menu is a set of check boxes that lists the majority of options that are available when you just add a view to a pane—minus the argument data. It lets you enable a limited set of permissions, which is useful if you are giving your users only a limited set of update permissions.

One last thing you can do in the configuration screen (aside from provide arguments) is to override the URL for the view. By doing so, you can force the view's URL setting to a particular place, aside from the path provided by the view itself. In this way, you can force a specific term into a URL as well.

Arguments may also be configured within the view configuration screen for a pane. There are two pieces to sending an argument from a pane to a view. The first is the check box for "Send arguments" that passes all of the panel's arguments directly to the view. This setting is lower in priority than any limitations set by a context.

The second piece is the Arguments text box. It enables you to manually enter an argument such as a nid, node type, or username as if they were coming from the URL. Alternatively, you can use the same type of arguments used by a view, by substituting %0, %1, and so on; those values do come directly from the URL.

The Panels module easily handles basic arguments. Other arguments can be handled by creating new plugins for CTools, if necessary.

## Exercise 14-4

### Using an Argument in a Pane with a View

Joe's Shirts likes having votes on its site for everything! The company wants a page of "most popular items" with a spot for each kind of thing offered for sale on the site. We can accomplish this goal with a view, an argument, and some panel panes.

First, we need a view that implements votes in a reasonably generic fashion so that we can implement an argument. We already have a view like that— the "top 10" view we created in Chapter 8. All we need to do now is organize it into panes with the appropriate arguments. Second, you need to rate some T-shirts. Enable voting on your "Joe's Shirts" content type, and add some votes to a few test shirts.

1. Open the top_ten view. Take a look at the argument; it uses Node: Type.

2. Navigate to Administer >> Site building >> Pages and scroll down to Joe's front page. Choose "Edit" from the Operations menu.

3. In the right-side panel region, click the gear symbol and select "Add content." A new modal window appears.

4. Click the Views tab along the side of the modal window.

5. In the right pane, click "top_ten."

6. Select a display type. This is a place where, if you had a display set up just for panels, you could choose to use it instead of the default display. Choose the style "Defaults" for now.

7. Click Continue. The configuration screen opens. Enter the following values:

| Field | Value |
|---|---|
| Override title | Unchecked; leave the text field blank |
| Node: Type/context | No context |
| Link title to view | Checked |
| Provide a "more" link | Checked (Our view is not using one, so we'll add one here.) |
| Display feed icons | Checked |
| Use pager | Unchecked |
| Num posts | 5 |
| Offset | 0 |
| Send arguments | Checked |
| Arguments | t_shirts (Use the machine name for the content type you created in Chapter 2.) |
| Override URL | Leave blank |

8. Click Finish.

9. Click the "Update and preview" button to make sure your changes are working.

10. Click Save.

Your new panel page is saved. With this setup, you can use the same view over and over in multiple panes, each time with a different argument. For example, if Joe's Shirts expands the store to include wristbands, stickers, or other products with their own node types, the view can be added to a new pane with the new node type as the argument.

There are multiple ways to achieve the same ends in Panels. Instead of using an argument with a view, you can use a view pane—a display from Views—to create a similar set of panels. This has one real advantage: you can give users the ability to administer a pane, without giving them the ability to change the view.

# Exercise 14-5
## Using a View Pane Display with an Argument

Some sites may not want to administer views to handle multiple versions of the same type of display. Instead of creating multiple views, you can use one view, and use panes with different arguments. To do so, we have to go back to Views.

1. Navigate to Administer >> Site building >> Views.

2. Edit the top_ten view.

3. In the display drop-down menu, choose "Content pane" and click the "Add display" button.

A new configuration region opens, labeled "Pane settings." There are a few changes here that we haven't seen in previous views. For example, the basic settings have a name of "Content pane"—something you want to customize if you use more than one display of this type for this view. Also, the Pane settings box, unlike most other settings boxes, affects only this display type. Finally, the Update button does not make changes to the default display.

4.  In the Pane settings configuration box, enter the following values:

| Setting | Value |
|---|---|
| Admin title | Top 10 shirts |
| Admin desc | Top 10 shirts |
| Category | Leave current settings |
| Link to view | Yes |
| Use Panel path | No |
| Argument input | Fixed: t_shirts |
| Allow settings | No changes |

5.  Click Save.

When you try to preview this display, you will see the message, "No query was run." At this point in the processing of the view, it doesn't know about the argument, because it is actually processed by Panels. When you add a panel pane, and look under "Views panes"; you'll see this display there. If you add it, it will be shown in the same fashion as in Exercise 14-4.

# Relationships

Relationships are an addition to Panels contributed by Drupal core. Views relationships function similarly to those found in Drupal core: Drupal core's relationships are built on relating content types to one another, while Views' relationships are based on relating one table's data to another table's data. As in Views, creating a relationship tells Panels that "these items fit together, even though there's no formal relation within the database."

## Using Relationships

Within Panels, relationship information appears on the Contexts tab and has a drop-down menu and submit box of its own, found on the lower-right corner of the page. Relationships in panels can be things like a Book parent, a term that's on a node, or a node's author. When you add a relationship, you make the content that's associated with the relationship available to panels as well.

Every type of relationship has another modal window that helps configure its details. These settings include identifiers so that each relationship can be easily identified, keywords for substitution, and in some cases other specific details. For example, "What level of parent is this book?" might be specified in the case of book relationships, and "What is the exact vocabulary term that is being used?" might be specified in the case of terms on a node.

Taxonomy relationships don't change much within the modal windows. If you've already added a taxonomy term as a context, your menus may already be present. Of course, this point depends on whether you've added a term or an entire vocabulary.

Book parents are a little different, and not commonly used. They are also based on having a node context available. To use this relationship type, the configuration requires that a node be chosen via a drop-down list, in which each node is given as an option. You can then determine whether the relationship is to its immediate parent or to the top level of the book. In the "Add content" modal, this setting falls under the Node menu.

When you use a relationship for the node author, you open up the possibility of bringing data from that author's information into the panel panes as well. Another Drupal contributed module called Content Profile (http://drupal.org/project/content_profile) turns user profiles into nodes. With this module, you can use CCK to expand and enhance your profile pages, and you can use panels to create layouts for your user profiles with more interesting and useful data than the default user profiles.

### Note

While using a node author relationship can bring in user data, it may not actually be the best choice for re-creating user profiles. Like so many things in Drupal, there's a module for that: Advanced Profile Kit (http://drupal.org/project/advanced_profile). It uses Panels as the basis for its layout tools.

When you add a node author relationship, you need at least one node context for that relationship to be built on. The user data is pulled from that node, and then the relationship finds the appropriate user in the user table and brings it to the panel. It is made available via the "Add content" window under "User."

## User Reference and Node Reference

Content Construction Kit offers a pair of plugins to Panels that provide new contexts based on our old friends Node Reference and User Reference. Like other contexts, they bring in additional data to your panel content options. We bring this point up here instead of in the discussion of contexts because it's important to understand the difference between what these plugins provide versus what data comes from a relationship.

Unlike all of the CTools-provided contexts, CCK's Node Reference and User Reference contexts examine the current node being provided, and then look at the reference fields. Each then looks at that node or user and makes that data available to be added as content in a pane. This task is carried out in two parts. If you are working with nodes and node references, you must add a node context. After that, a relationship must be added: node from node reference for nodes, or user from user reference for users.

When a node with a Node Reference field is added as a context, the Content menu has additional information within the "Add content" modal. This menu's items will include each CCK-created field that was added to the content type, including Node

Reference fields pointing at other nodes. If any of these fields are placed within a field-group, that fieldgroup is also available if you don't want to use the individual fields.

In Figures 14-7 and 14-8, a context was added for a node that was created in the Batch brewed content type. Figure 14-7 shows the node before the context, while Figure 14-8 shows it after the context and relationship are added. Every node type will have its own fields here for placement.

| Activity | Batch brewed: (Computed) field alcohol by volume | Batch brewed: (Float) field final gravity |
| --- | --- | --- |
| Content ▶ | | |
| Menus | Batch brewed: (Computed) field alcohol by weight | Batch brewed: (Float) field original gravity |
| minipanel | | |
| Miscellaneous | | |
| Node | Batch brewed: (Datetime) field brewing date | Batch brewed: (Node reference) field recipe used |
| View panes | | |
| Views | Batch brewed: (Email) field mail brewer | batch_brewed: (fieldgroup) Alcohol level |
| Widgets | | |

Figure 14.7    Fields available using a node with CCK fields

Figure 14.8    Content from two different nodes available with Node Reference

User Reference fields can be used in the same fashion. By adding a node context, relationships become available. Choose the "user from reference" relationship, and content that is part of the user's profile can be added to the display of that panel. This marks the real beginning of the quest to create specialized user profiles.

## Summary

Contexts and arguments represent powerful additions to the Panels arsenal. They serve similar functions—bringing more data into your panels content—but they do so in very different fashions. Contexts make almost anything you want or need available. Arguments in Panels work with Views to provide specific information.

"Content type" is just another name for a container for data. Panels works with these containers to determine which parts of the container can be placed in a pane, to decide which parts will be made visible to particular users, and to bring together multiple types of data that normally would not be easily shown on the same page. Content types are critical for other modules to hand off information to Panels as well, bringing data into your site so that it can be placed within panes in whatever fashion Panels will allow.

# Panels Theming

We've come to the final step—theming panels. This puts the last touches on a Web site and brings everything together. This chapter covers styling that can be done from within the Panels user interface (UI). You will also learn how to apply custom CSS selectors that you can hook into from your own CSS files. Prepare to be amazed at the level of control Panels gives you for theming your site.

## Layout

The Panels module ships with eight different layout styles, including one-, two-, and three-column options. You can apply these layouts to create any variants that you need, and you can even place these layouts inside one another. If your needs change, you can change the layout that was previously applied to a panel. In this chapter, we cover some of the more "advanced" concepts of dealing with layouts in Panels.

## Flexible Layout

So far in this book, we've recommended that you use one of the one-, two-, or three-column layouts instead of the Flexible layout. When you choose Flexible as your layout style, you are asking for the ultimate in customization for your panel regions. This layout enables you to put regions within regions, modify panel sizes down to the pixel level, and choose fluidity versus fixed sizes for each region. Each panel type can use the flexible layout.

---

### Informational Messages

Flexible layouts use their own directory for storage and style. The first time you create a panel using the Flexible layout, you may see informational messages such as these:

- Panel *flexible-test* has been created.
- The directory *sites/default/files/ctools* has been created.
- The directory *sites/default/files/ctools/css* has been created.

These messages let you know that the directories are created. If they appear in red, indicating failure, you may need to create the directories manually.

---

You can create a Flexible layout as you are creating a new panel, or you can create your layouts ahead of time and choose from these prepared layouts as you are creating your new panels. Let's go ahead and create a Flexible layout without having to also worry about creating a whole new panel. To start, navigate to Administer >> Site building >> Panels. Click on the link for "Custom layouts" and select the tab "Add flexible layout." You will be presented with the screen shown in Figure 15-1.

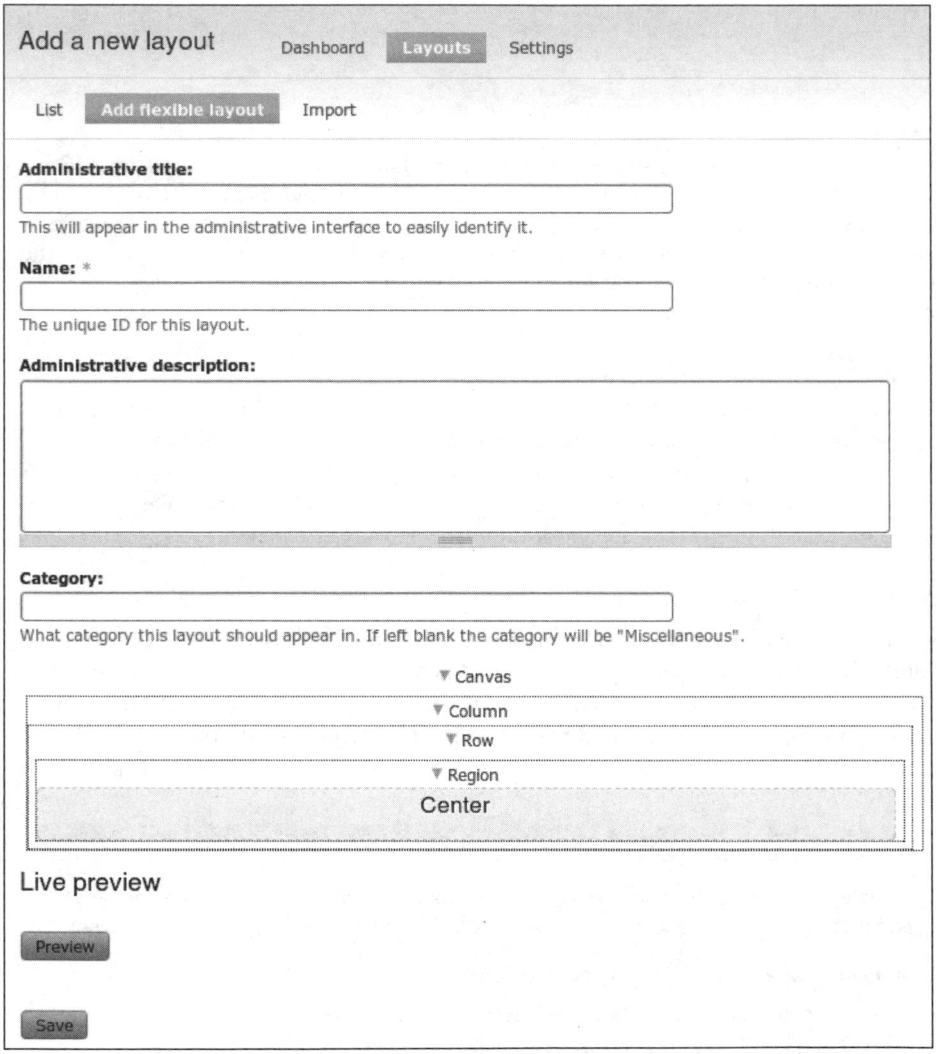

**Add a new layout**     Dashboard   **Layouts**   Settings

List   **Add flexible layout**   Import

**Administrative title:**

This will appear in the administrative interface to easily identify it.

**Name:** *

The unique ID for this layout.

**Administrative description:**

**Category:**

What category this layout should appear in. If left blank the category will be "Miscellaneous".

▼ Canvas
▼ Column
▼ Row
▼ Region
Center

Live preview

Preview

Save

Figure 15-1   The layout manager

The layout manager is visible in the bottom half of the screen. You will create the Flexible layout through the controllers:

- Canvas: Affects the entire layout. With this menu, you may add panel regions to the left or right side of the already available center.
- Column: Affects the left, right, and center columns, allowing you to add rows to the top or bottom of each. Adding columns is what enables layouts such as Brick. The columns may be either fluid or fixed.
- Row: Adds regions to each row, to the left or right side of that row.
- Region: Determines if the region itself is fluid or fixed.

A Flexible panel layout starts with one region: Center (visible at the bottom of the stack of controllers). With this setup, you have a panel that mimics the single-column format that Panels creates at install time. To enable you to add new panes and regions, each container has a down arrow next to its name. Clicking on the container name or arrow opens a menu with multiple choices.

The Canvas menu allows only column containers to be created. You have the option of adding columns to either the left or right side of the panel.

Opening the Column menu presents a variable menu list that contains a set of these items. Column settings has one configurable item: width. This setting determines whether the column is fixed or fluid. Three versions of the new row variant are available within columns. "Add row" is available if no rows exist; "Add row to top" and "Add row to bottom" will be available if another row is already present. "Remove column" does just that: it removes the column from the panel. Note that you can only remove a column if all panels, regions, and rows within the column have been removed.

The Row menu allows you to add actual panel regions. You can also use this menu to add more columns. Regions may be added to either the left or right side of the column that contains the row. If you look at the Row settings in the default Flexible layout, you will see that this page provides only one option, which tells you what the row contains: a column or a region. If there is content within the row, you cannot change the row container's type. If you add a region, you must give it a title and a width setting (fixed or fluid). If you add a column, the Row menu makes the same options available as the Canvas menu has.

The Region menu has only two options: the region title and the width. The title is a required field, and the width has the same fluid or fixed options we have seen for all other containers. Once you create a region, you can change its title and width from the Region menu.

The last player in the Flexible layout scheme is the slider bar, which allows you to control the width of a region. If the layout includes two or more columns, a bar separates each pair of columns (see Figure 15-2): In a two-column layout, there is one bar in the center; in a three-column layout, there are two bars; and so on. Every column set may have its own set of sliders.

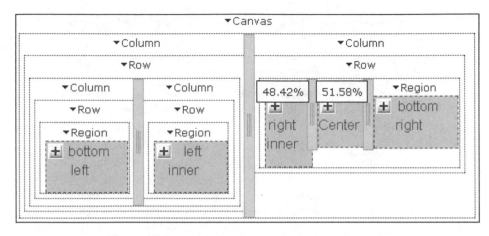

Figure 15-2    Using the slider to determine column size

Notice the hover box containing percentages. Both of these regions are fluid, and when the slider is clicked, the hover text shows what percentage of that container is to the left and right of the bar. If one side is fluid and the other is fixed, the fixed side will show a number counted in pixels (150 px, for example). If both sides are fixed, the slider shows both sides with a pixel count. This makes setting region sizes very quick and easy.

One final trick: Hold down the shift key while grabbing and moving the slider bar. Doing so causes the slider to move by 1%, or 10 px. This quickly gets you very close to where you want to go, and allows you to make the fine adjustments by hand.

> **Note**
>
> In this case, we have no specific exercise in mind for the Flexible layout. Consider this some "free play" time. Create your own Flexible layout and then use it to create a new panel.

Now that you know how to create your own Flexible layouts, you can skip the plan-ahead step if you want and create your layout when you create your panel.

To create your own panel layout, select the default layout option, "Flexible layout," when you are asked to choose a layout by the panel creation wizard. When you are on the "Content" editing screen for your panel, you will have the option to "Show layout designer." When you click this button, the layout designer discussed earlier in this section will appear. When you are finished adjusting the layout, click the button labeled "Hide layout designer." You will be returned to the "Add content" version of the page, where you can add, alter, or remove panel panes if necessary. If you would like to save this layout, click the button labeled "Reuse layout." A modal window will open and you will be prompted for an administrative title and machine name for your new style.

## Changing Layouts

It is possible to substitute one layout for another after you have created a panel page with content. Changing a layout will not cause any of your content to be lost. When you choose the new layout and click "Continue," you will be presented with a new screen that shows the layout change and gives you the opportunity to do a general placement of content (Figure 15-3).

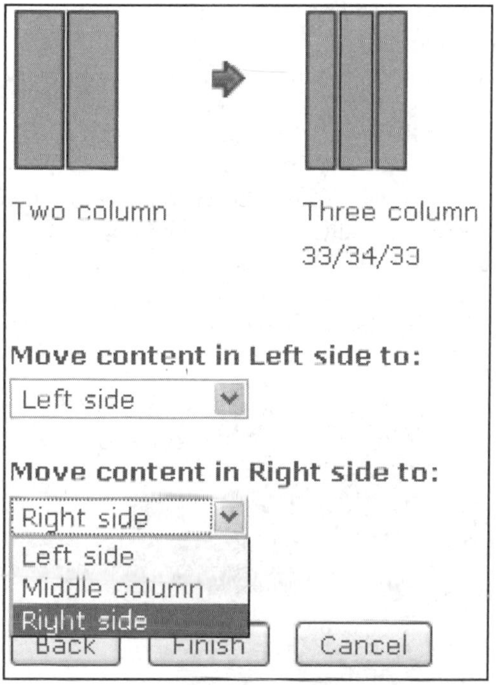

Figure 15-3    Changing layout and placement of content

Each region will have a drop-down menu with a list of the regions available in the new layout. All of the content from the original region will move to the new one. The layout manager attempts to match previous regions with new ones, so any left-side content stays left, right-side content stays right, and so on. If the regions do not have matching names—such as would happen when you move content from a two-column left/right layout to a stacked layout, or vice versa—all content will move to the first region in the list. In most layouts, this will either be top or left. Regardless of the initial placement of content on this page, the draggable nature of panes makes it easy to tweak the new regions appropriately in the panel content screen.

When you take advantage of relationships and contexts (which you learned about in Chapter 14), the possibilities for designing page content and layouts are practically infinite. Once you are comfortable with the way these things build on each other and how to arrange your content in the fashion you want, the Panels system will provide you with significantly greater flexibility and strength in controlling the look of your site. And it does so while allowing you to define multiple rules for a single type of page so that you have less administrative overhead.

With a custom layout in hand, it's time to further style your panel.

## Stylizer

Fonts, colors, padding—oh my! This section covers the process of creating custom styles for entire panels, each region, or individual panes within your panel. The Panels module makes absolutely no value judgment about the styles you create. Figure 15-4 is an awful mess of styles—and an example of what you should *not* do. Ideally, you will use the Stylizer for good—not for big piles of yucky.

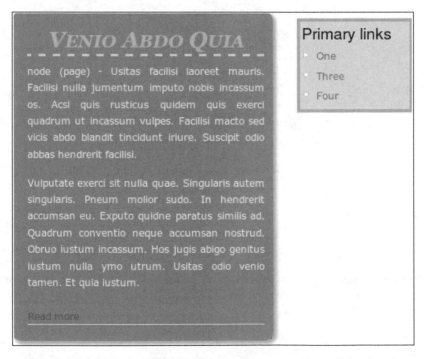

Figure 15-4    The Stylizer does not help you to create beautiful styles. It just allows you to set the CSS properties for elements within your panels.

With no additional customization, you can create custom styles incorporating the following design elements:

- Basic style: Rounded shadow box or Plain box
- Colors: Background, Text, Header text, and Header border
- Header font and Text font: Font family, Size, Letter spacing, Word spacing, Decoration, Weight, Style, Variant, Case, and Alignment
- Header border: Thickness and Style
- Padding: Top, Right, Bottom, and Left

Figure 15-5 shows the configuration screen for a panel region. The options you see will vary slightly depending on whether you are creating a style for a whole region or a content pane.

Styles can also be shared with others through the Import/Export tool, which works much the same way that Views Import/Export works.

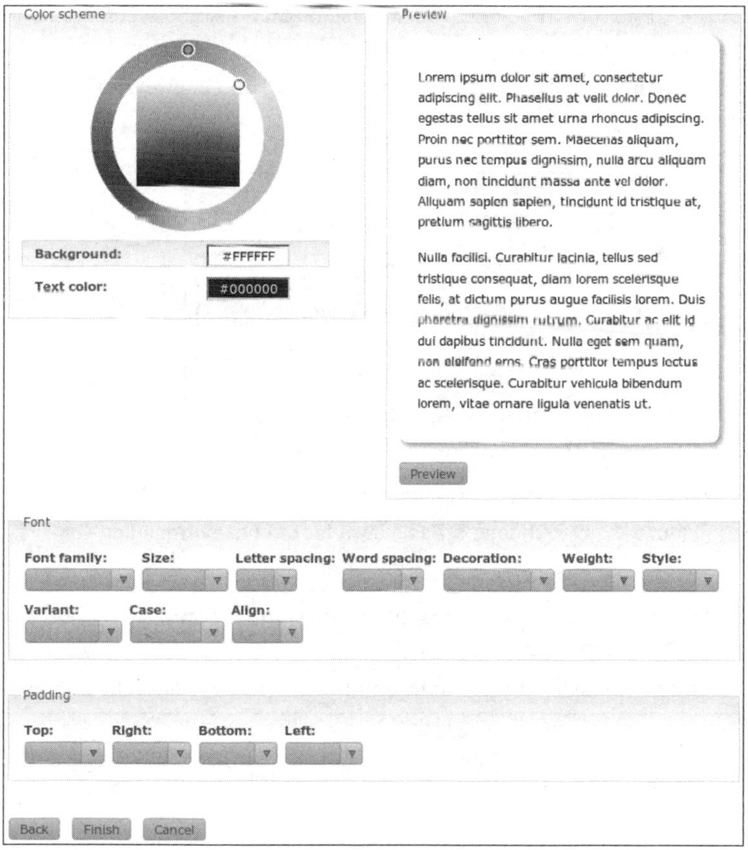

Figure 15-5    Settings configuration screen for panel regions

## Working with Styles

Panels styles are merely a set of CSS properties that are applied to a panel region or a panel pane. Check your current CSS files to see which properties you can "abstract" and apply using the Panels point–and–click UI instead.

# Exercise 15-1

### Creating a New Style

With your CSS properties in mind, navigate to Administer >> Site building >> Stylizer and complete the following steps:

1. Click the tab labeled "Add" at the top of the Stylizer summary page.

2. Enter an administrative title, name, and administrative description for your new style and then click Continue. You may choose to name your style based on its attributes ("Big brown") or its role within your design ("Second sidebar, blocks"). Click Continue.

3. Select the "Type" for this style. You will need to choose between a panel region (like a region) and a panel pane (like a block). Click Continue.

4. Choose a Basic style: Rounded shadow box or Plain (Figure 15-6). Click Continue.

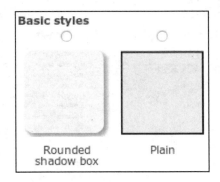

Figure 15-6    Choose a Basic style for the box surrounding your custom style

5. The final settings screen will now appear for your custom style. Adjust each of the properties to your liking.

6. When you've configured your style, scroll to the bottom and click Finish.

To apply your styles, you need to pick the element within your panel that you want to change:

- Display style: Changes an entire panel display.
- Region style: Changes the bounding box for a panel region.
- Style: Changes an individual pane.

The default for all types is "no style." If you change the style for the display or any lower-level part, the menu will update to show that style, as shown in Figure 15-7.

```
Add content
Style
    Big Pink Region
Change
```

Figure 15-7    Display settings menu after choosing the style
"Big Pink Region"

## Exercise 15-2

### Applying Your Styles

Once you've created your new styles, you can apply them to relevant panel regions and panel panes using the following steps:

1. Navigate to the Pages summary: Administer >> Site building >> Pages. Next to the panel you want to customize, click the Edit link.
2. Navigate to the Content summary for the appropriate panel variant.

Proceed with the following steps to apply your custom *panel region* styles:

1. Click the gear icon to the left of the panel region name. A context-sensitive pop-up menu will appear with the option "Add content" and then a summary of the style currently applied to this panel region. Select "Change" at the bottom of the list. A new configuration screen will appear.
2. Select the name of the custom style you would like to apply to this panel region. Click Next. You will be returned to the Content summary screen. At this point, you can also choose to create a new "Custom style."
3. Click "Update and save" to lock in your changes.

Proceed with the following steps to apply your custom *panel pane* styles:

1. Click the gear icon to the right of the content administrative title for the panel pane you want to change. A context-sensitive pop-up menu will appear. From the subsection that starts with "Style," select the menu option labeled "Change." A new configuration screen will appear.

2. Select the name of the custom style you would like to apply to this panel region. Click Next. You will be returned to the Content summary screen. At this point, you can also choose to create a new "Custom style."

3. Click "Update and save" to lock in your changes.

To see how your new styles will look, click the "Update and preview" button on the Content summary page.

# CSS in the Panels UI

The default panels styling comes from the Panels module. Panels itself has a number of places within the user interface where classes and styles can be supplied and edited. This module also has a low level of actual styling that can be applied to regions and panes singly or as a group.

In addition, Panels has a number of places where you can add CSS classes and definitions into your displays without having to edit the stylesheet itself. This ability is helpful for testing some levels of styling without needing to make changes to the actual .css file; it may be especially useful if you don't have permissions to access the CSS file, or if any changes to code or CSS require revision control for your installation. Panels itself isn't generally affected by such modifications, but permanent CSS changes should always go into the CSS files, not into the panel settings.

The first place you can add CSS information is the page settings, if you're using a panel-based page. Use the text box to create a CSS ID for the entire page should you decide you need one. You might have a particular ID you want to use for all override pages, for example, or just for pages that are using a view so that they can be styled similarly.

The second place that you can make changes is the large text box labeled "CSS code." Notice that the help text on the page for this box makes it clear that this should be used for minor tweaks only.

You may also make CSS additions to individual panes. Under the gear menu, you can add CSS IDs and CSS classes to a given pane by accessing the CSS properties selection. This step is not required, but it may again make particular panes easier to call out. For example, you might want to make the font in your featured item a little bigger than the rest of a page, or de-emphasize some other feature on the page.

Individual panes can use special identifiers as well. The identifier has a simple purpose: it is a partial name that a specialized template file can use for theming nodes embedded in panels. When configuring certain types of content, such as a node, the Identifier field is available under the Settings menu for that pane. Nodes are the only type of content that has this Identifier field by default.

## Exercise 15-3

### Adding Custom CSS Selectors

Follow these steps to customize the CSS selectors for content within each pane:

1. Navigate to the Content settings page for the panel pane you want to adjust: Administer >> Site building >> Pages >> (Choose your page) >> Variants >> Content.

2. Find the content item you want to alter. Click on the gear icon to the right of the Administrative title. From the context-sensitive pop-up menu, choose "CSS Properties." A new window will appear.

3. Enter the CSS ID and CSS class you would like to apply. Click Save when you've finished.

4. Upon returning to the Content configuration screen, click "Update and save" to lock in your changes.

Your new selector has been applied. Update your CSS stylesheets with your new properties, dump Drupal's cache, and enjoy your new styles.

---

### Tip

CSS can be cached. If you're looking for a cached stylesheet and can't find it, try checking under /ctools/css.

# CSS in Source Code

There's also plenty of styling that is not supplied or editable within the user interface. For instance, the Panels stylesheet is found in panels/css/panels.css. In addition, several plugins incorporate their own stylesheets. This proliferation of stylesheets means that there are a number of places any given piece of style can come from, but also provides a very good way of compartmentalizing each component's pieces.

Panels comes with the following stylesheets:

- panels.css
- panels_admin.css
- panels_dnd.css
- panels_page.css
- panels_dashboard.css

Each of these stylesheets handles a different area of the user interface. Most are quite straightforward. The panels_dashboard stylesheet handles the dashboard interface located at Administer >> Site building >> Panels. The panels_admin stylesheet handles the rest of the general administrative interface. Any section of the interface that can be altered by the drag-and-drop technique is styled by panels_dnd. The remaining pieces, which mainly focus on the actual display of panels, panes, and regions, are handled by `panels.css` and `panels_page.css`, depending on which type of panel you are using. Because of the way these files are named, and because of the way Drupal calls for theming, your stylesheets should not run into conflicts with one another; panels stylesheets are relatively specific. This is especially true given the other stylesheets within Panels.

There is also a secondary set of stylesheets that Panels may use, with the selection made available depending on your current layout. When you are using a given layout or when you are creating your own layout, each layout is a plugin for Panels. If you look in the `panels/plugins/layouts` directory, you will find other directories named for each layout that is available. Each of these directories includes a stylesheet named for that layout: `flexible.css`, `onecol.css`, `threecol_25_50_25_stacked.css`, and so on. Each stylesheet contains a minimum of class formatting for its respective layout. The single exception is the Flexible layout, which also contains a `flexible_admin.css` stylesheet to style the administrative page where you create a customized layout.

Panels starts out with a group of classes that are very general, beginning with the layout type of that panel. Using these classes enables the theme to easily imprint the same features on all panels of one type, regardless of their content. Earlier in this book, we discussed this set of CSS classes for the node view override page where we used a two-column stacked display.

```
panel-2col-stacked clear-block panel-display
```

Other than `clear-block`, the classes that come from the Panels module are obvious: `panel-2col-stacked` invokes styling just for the specific layout, and `panel-display` is the most general Panels styling in the system.

## Identifying a Particular Pane

So far, we've looked at several places where you can view the classes for Panels. Now let's see how we identify one particular pane and its associated elements. Each pane has contents, the pane style, any region style it has inherited, and the general display style. It also may have separators between it and other panes if you are using one of the list formats.

Nearly all of the stock areas of a panel, regardless of whether it is a region, block, pane, or page, are identified with multiple CSS classes, all of whose names start with `panel-`. In some cases, a pane will need to be identified using multiple classes to pinpoint the correct one. Using identifiers and classes will help you identify the right pane on the right page.

## Exercise 15-4

### Identifying Panel Panes for Styling

Suppose you want to style one pane in a layout differently than the rest. How do you find it? Let's look at some of the panes on the front page of the Joe's Shirts Web site to see the different classes being used for the page areas, and change the featured shirt's style so that it's a little more prominent.

As shown in Figure 15-8, these elements are currently in play. There are two columns, the left column has rounded corners around the panel region and uses separators, and the right column has corners around the individual panes.

Figure 15-8    Part of the current front page for Joe's Shirts

1. Examine each area in the source code. There are many panel styles that provide a breakdown for panes in groups.

2. Find the area in the page for the featured shirt. Around it, you'll find a number of panel-based classes that could be used for theming: `panel-display`, `panel-2col`, `panel-panel`, `panel-col-first`, and `panel-pane` are all viable classes for this page.

   If you want to theme one particular pane differently than the others in that page or region, these classes aren't enough. You'll be able to theme one column differently, or the panes, or the entire display, but you need more specific classes to find just one pane.

3. Navigate to Administer >> Site building >> Pages and select "Panel content" on the Operations menu next to the Joe's Shirts front page.

4. In the "Featured shirt" pane, click the gear icon and choose "CSS properties."

5. For clarity, we'll use obvious names: `featured-shirt-id` for the CSS ID and `featured-shirt-class` for the CSS class.

6. Click Save and then Continue. This will take you to the Page settings display.

7. For the CSS ID of the page, make sure you have something entered, such as `joes-frontpage`. This will make it easier to distinguish the featured shirt on this page versus the same panel being used anywhere else.

8. Click Save.

Figure 15-9 shows a group of classes that are handling the featured shirt. With this group of classes, you can make the featured shirt do anything you want. In essence, you can style the node output for the panel without affecting the node itself when it is viewed by a user.

```
iv><div class="panel-display panel-2col clear-block" id="joes-frontpage">
<div class="panel-panel panel-col-first">
  <div class="inside"><div class="rounded-corner">
<div class="wrap-corner">
  <div class="t-edge"><div class="l"></div><div class="r"></div></div>
  <div class="l-edge">
    <div class="r-edge clear-block">
      <div class="panel-pane featured-shirt-class" id="featured-shirt-id">
```

Figure 15-9    Classes handling the featured shirt

9. Open your CSS stylesheet. If you're still using the garland_extend theme, it appears in /sites/all/themes/garland_extend as garland_extend.css.

10. Add the following snippet to your stylesheet and then save it:

```
#featured-shirt-id {
  font-size: large;
}
```

11. Refresh the front page and review the changes.

This is one of the simplest changes you can make to theming for Panels.

---

You can also identify mini-panels with relative ease. Each mini-panel is granted a class with a standard name: mini-panel-*panelname*. This naming system allows you to very quickly isolate one mini-panel from another within a page.

Remember that changing styles within a panel has to be done with care and caution. This is especially true if you have also used panels to override system pages. If you're just using something like div.panel-pane and changing the font color to green, all of your panels across all of your pages will have their text in green—not just your front page, or your node edit pages. Put simply, everything will change.

Following is a short list of Panels-based CSS classes:

**Display Type**

- `panel-flexible`  Provided for panels developed with the Flexible layout.
- `panel-onecol`  Provided for panels developed with the single-column layout.
- `panel-3col_stacked`  Provided for panels developed with the three-column stacked layout.
- `panel-2col`  Provided for panels developed with the two-column layout.
- `panel-2col_bricks`  Provided for panels developed with the two-column brick layout.
- `panel-2col_stacked`  Provided for panels developed with the two-column stacked layout.

**Region**

- `panel-col-first`  Handles the first column in any layout.
- `panel-pane`  Styles all panes within a panel.
- `panel-col-last`  Handles the column labeled "last" in a layout.
- `panel-col-top`  Styles the "top" region.
- `panel-col-middle`  Styles the "middle" region.
- `panel-flexible-region-inside`  Provided for any region in a Flexible layout that is inside the others.
- `panel-flexible-region-inside-first`  Provided for the first region inside a Flexible layout.
- `inside`  Handles any region labeled "inside."

**Other**

- `panel-separator`  If your panel panes have separators, this determines how they will look.
- `panels-flexible-row`  If you use rows within the Flexible layout, this will style them.

Take time to explore the CSS files for each layout style. In them, you will find a generalized list of attributes for each panel and its regions.

## Other Stylistic Changes

Each pane has a multitude of settings that can be changed and themed. Each panel, each region, and each pane has its own div, singly and in groups. This lets you go beyond just fonts, enabling you to float images to one side of a pane, or change link colors for just one region.

You can create your own style plugins for Panels as well. As an example, you might want to use corners other than rounded ones. Perhaps you have a signature stylistic figure that can be incorporated into a corner easily. A plugin could be added to bring that element in, producing rounded corners around separate panes. The rounded corners style is found in the `/panels/plugins/styles/corners` directory and consists of a template, an include file, and a group of `.PNG` files containing the images that are used for the corners.

With the plethora of classes available to panels and panes, in addition to the many different styles that can be added onto the core of the Panels module, it's largely a matter of spending the time and finding the right classes to get your panels looking just the way you want them.

## Summary

Panels, like Views, provides a number of theme pieces as part of its default installation. Minimal changes are required to evolve the default panels and panes from the standard into something a little more unique. With the addition of the multiple levels of Cascading Style Sheets that can be employed with Panels, your site can easily be styled in just about any fashion you want.

# 16

# Site Deployment

$O$nce a site is built, it must be deployed and made available for use. In this chapter, we touch on some of the challenges and changes that come with moving a site from the test stage to production.

## Configuring Your Development Environment

At this point, you have built your site and set up your theme the way you want it, and your users are ready to embrace your handiwork. (Okay, maybe they aren't, but we can dream, right?) In other words, you think you're ready to go live.

Are you, though? There are a lot of things to consider when you move from a development site to production. Are your production site and server ready to handle the volume of users who may be active? Is there a solution for backups (there should be!)? If there is one, does it cover just the code or the entire site?

In addition, you have to consider how the site will be updated: content and structure are different factors. Should you export your structures? What ones are important?

### Content Versus Structure

One of the most significant splits you may have to make, especially for sites with a larger potential deployment for users is the separation of content versus structure. Ultimately, your goal is to have a site structure that makes it easy for your users to create and/or find content.

With this goal in mind, now could be a good time to take another look at the people who will be responsible for maintaining your site. For smaller sites, it is entirely possible for one or a few people to do it all. On bigger sites, it may be more important to split out the duties of those who administer users and data, and handle interactions with the end users, from the duties of dealing with the structure, stability, and maintenance of the site in general. This results in some level of specialization, but ultimately may help both sides of the maintenance coin accomplish their jobs better.

## Source Control

Source control is the single most important thing you can implement for the development and deployment of a Web site. Some developers don't see the benefits of source control, claiming that it costs too much money or time. The simple truth is that source control does take some time, but it doesn't have to cost much real money—and the time you save by having it can far outweigh the amount of time required to rebuild a Web site that isn't under source control.

Many solutions for source control are available through open source projects and supported by those projects' user communities. Drupal.org uses CVS for version control for all of the modules and themes contributed to the community. Its use is so essential that there are some who quip, "If it's not on cvs.drupal.org, then as far as I'm concerned, it doesn't exist." Because Drupal uses CVS, we can create a vendor repository in Subversion (SVN) that includes not only the CVS files, but also site-specific files or data in SVN. This allows for SVN updates to be used in deployment and all update scripts to be run directly from the server.

Many other choices for repositories exist as well: Git, Bazaar (bzr), and so forth. Each system has benefits and issues that can make or break your decision on which to use. Many members of the Drupal community initially use one version control system for their personal sites and development platforms, and later commit to Drupal.org's CVS system.

### Finding Source Control Software

There are many, many source control projects available for your use. The open source community supports a number of projects, some of which are listed here and are popular within the Drupal community:

- Git: http://git-scm.com/
- CVS: http://www.nongnu.org/cvs/
- Subversion: http://subversion.tigris.org/
- Bazaar: http://bazaar-vcs.org/

Along with the many open source projects, myriad packages have been developed by companies that make their living creating and maintaining their specialized repositories. Even if Drupal is the best Web site builder, an open source repository might not be the best option for you or your company.

Source control provides two critical functions. First, it provides a general backup for your site's codebase. Second, it serves as a means of revision control in case a change someone makes goes horribly awry in strange and unexpected ways. CCK data structures, as well as Views and Panels code, can be exported and stored in a version control system. If someone changes or deletes any of those files, it's a relatively simple task to restore that piece of data to your site, without relying on the potentially faulty memory of the site builder to return the site to its unblemished state. Even worse, if the person who built your site is now gone, you have no real way to rebuild something that's broken—unless you have source control, that is.

The other major benefit of using source control is that multiple users can edit the codebase at the same time without overwriting one another's changes. Version control keeps track of which user is editing which file, which changes the user made, and how the changes have to be merged with existing code once those changes are checked in. This makes every developer accountable for his or her work, and can provide insight into which changes caused a major breakdown much more quickly than the "hunt and guess" method that might otherwise be used.

The bottom line: use source control.

# Moving to Production

Your site is built. You've tested it as thoroughly as you can. You think you're ready to unleash it on the unsuspecting masses. In some cases, you can move your development site directly into production—particularly if the site has undergone a complete overhaul and it's all new code.

## Keeping Development Separate from Production

Of course, it's still the absolute best practice to keep a development environment that's entirely separate from your production site.

Separate platforms are useful for an overwhelming number of reasons. The first and most important reason is that if you have two sites, and you push from development to production, and production breaks, you can back out of that process (You do have a backup in source control, right?) and restore your site to service more quickly. Outages might not be a big deal for personal Web sites, but for almost any other kind of site, an outage is a business-critical problem that can cost the Web site's sponsor customers and hundreds to thousands of dollars.

## Testing Your Changes

The second major reason to have separate sites is simply because it's easier to test on a non-production site. Maintaining a development site allows developers to try new configurations, test new code, and make other changes without risking problems for users on the production site. It allows for major changes to be made, tested, and reviewed in whole or in part before being moved over to a production site.

Always, always test your changes before they go live. The one time you forget to test is the one time you will make a small typo that deletes the administrative user's account, or you will forget to confirm a row was present before deleting data, causing all of your user traffic to be directed at the anonymous login.

Anyone who has ever had to do a site migration, or move code and data from a development server to a live server, knows all too well some of the hazards that come with this sometimes treacherous territory. Paths may not match, data may fail to be copied or be copied to one server but not another, items may be missed in testing, and so on. With any luck and a lot of work to set up your structure—both hardware and software—properly, it's possible to alleviate and plan for most potential problems.

One of the bigger challenges in moving from development to production is the need to update content types and fields. Changing even one thing can have an enormous impact on the rest of your content and the way in which it is displayed. Consider what is involved in changing the name of a field. This change has the potential to affect any views that use that field name, theming centered on that field name, any panels using that specific field for content placement, and so forth.

Moreover, changing a given piece of information may not remove the data from a table, but changing it from one type to another may represent a significant challenge. Converting one type of data to another can increase the time needed to make changes as part of an update operation. On a development site, you may be able to simply remove a field, change it and re-import; in production, it is often not feasible to bring the site down for several hours to make this kind of change.

One thing Content Construction Kit (CCK) does not currently support is the migration of an existing field's settings. As a result, making changes to your field settings can turn ugly very quickly. In some cases, it may be better to re-create the data on your development site and then move the entire site into production.

## Documenting Your Work

In a small to moderate-size company, it may be just you or you and one or two other people who really know how your Web site works. Everything is great and runs wonderfully, as long as you're there to put content up and show people how it works. But you can't always be there; especially if you're a contractor: your role is to build and let go. To achieve this goal, you need to document how your site works.

Something always happens when you are unavailable—that's just how things work. Someone will need to put up a critical news article, change the color scheme, or do some other thing that just cannot wait. If you have created a basic workflow document, left comments in your CSS code, and so on, it's much easier for others to change things they need to without making panicked calls to you.

# Exporting Your Structures

Structure isn't just about how your data is put together; it's more than your tables. Each of the major modules discussed in this book has export functionality that enables the work that was done once on a site to be essentially copied and saved for later use, backed up, and potentially imported on other sites.

Some modules are available that can help you with import and export tasks. Several of these modules are mentioned in Appendix A. Use them wisely; they can make the whole job go significantly more quickly and smoothly.

Views, Panels, and CCK all come with functionality to aid in the exporting of your data structures, and all offer specialized handling for those modules. Exporting your structures enables you to keep them in source control as well, adding an extra level of safety for your Web site's internal workings.

## Exporting CCK

In Part I of this book, we briefly discussed exporting CCK fields, content types, and so on. Content Construction Kit provides an export mechanism for one or more fields from a selected content type, as shown in Figure 16-1.

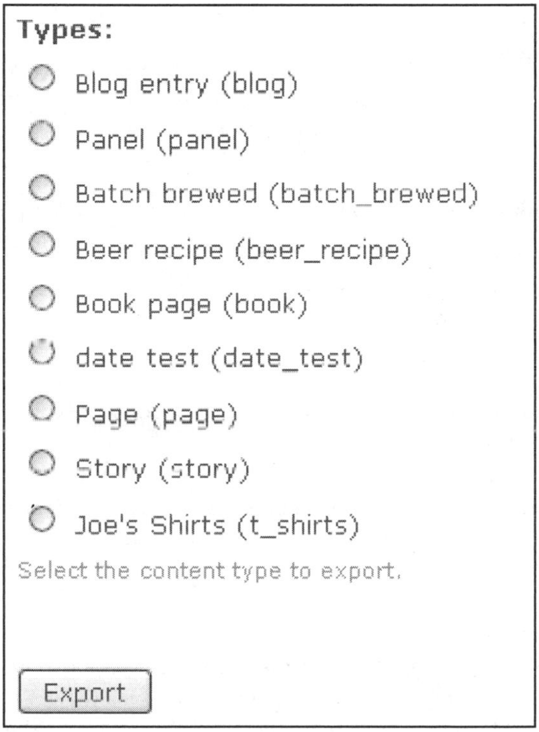

**Types:**

- ○ Blog entry (blog)
- ○ Panel (panel)
- ○ Batch brewed (batch_brewed)
- ○ Beer recipe (beer_recipe)
- ○ Book page (book)
- ○ date test (date_test)
- ○ Page (page)
- ○ Story (story)
- ○ Joe's Shirts (t_shirts)

Select the content type to export.

[ Export ]

Figure 16-1     Available content types for export

The export page for CCK is located at Administer >> Content management >> Content types >> Export. From this page, you must choose one content type to export from—each choice is a radio button, so you can not choose more than one at a time.

Notice in Figure 16-1 that "Panel" is an available content type for export. Exporting this content type is not the same as exporting panels, so don't be fooled by it. This export is actually the structure for a panel node, not for any of the various panels themselves.

When you choose to export from a node type via the CCK interface, you are given a choice of fields to export, and you may choose one or multiple fields. Because node types are built upon nodes, the export operation does not pull out the entire structure of the node type. Drupal core already contains this hierarchy; when you are importing node types, you'll just be returning the field data to an association with a node type. So there is no purpose to exporting the node structure every time.

Exercise 16-1 walks you through an export for Content Construction Kit. Note that this process is a little more complex than an export for Views or Panels.

---

# Exercise 16-1

## Exporting CCK Fields

Suppose you've got a content type that you want to use on another site. You could create a new content type with fields, or import one from a current installation. You may need only some of the fields, not all of them.

1. Navigate to Administer >> Content management >> Content types >> Export.
2. Choose "Joe's Shirts" and click the "Export" button.
3. Check one or more items. Multiple items may be checked by default, so uncheck any you do not want exported.
4. Click the "Export" button.

You're presented with the entire data structure for that content type, with default settings for every part of the structure, as well as the type of structure it was, such as a node. This entire structure can be uploaded to a source control system. If changes are then made to the original, the revised structure can also be exported and added, enabling differences to be easily spotted.

---

## Exporting Views

The reasons for exporting views mirror all the reasons for exporting content types. There's also a bonus reason for exporting views: exported views can be placed into code. Views in code have performance benefits over views that reside in the database.

Exporting a view is a fairly simple process. Each view has the ability to be exported, and the title bar for a given view indicates which one is being exported. However, unlike with fields or entire content types, each view must be exported separately. Views also must be enabled to be exported. In most cases that should not be an issue, as any created view is enabled by default; any view that is disabled by default is a view that was created during the installation of Views or one of the modules that integrates and provides a new view.

To export a view, navigate to the Views landing page at Administer >> Site building >> Views, and choose the Export link next to the view you want, as shown in Figure 16-2.

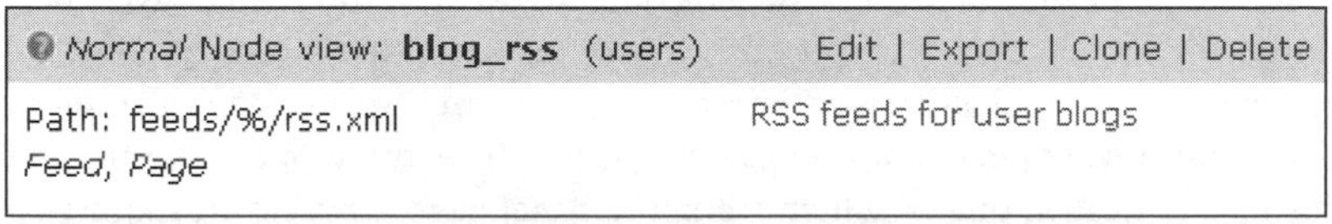

**Normal** Node view: **blog_rss** (users)     Edit | Export | Clone | Delete

Path: feeds/%/rss.xml     RSS feeds for user blogs
*Feed, Page*

Figure 16-2     Export a view by using the link on the title bar

An exported view consists of code. It looks in many ways similar to the content type code from a Content Construction Kit export. This is especially true when you examine data about the fields for a view. Each field used is followed by data that explains the purpose within the view, the way it relates to other data, and so on. By reading through the export details, you may be able to change certain features that you need for another site, so that your new import works immediately. This is what the beginning of a view definition in export looks like:

```
$view->name = 'blog_rss';
$view->description = 'RSS feeds for user blogs';
$view->tag = 'users';
$view->view_php = '';
$view->base_table = 'node';
$view->is_cacheable = FALSE;
$view->api_version = 2;
$view->disabled = FALSE; /* Edit this to true to make a default view disabled
initially */
$handler = $view->new_display('default', 'Defaults', 'default');
$handler->override_option('fields', array(...
```

Exported views can be placed directly into code—into a module, or into any other method that you wish to use to place the view. The major advantage of this approach is that larger sites may realize enough performance boosts, especially during heavy traffic times, to outweigh concerns over updating the view manually. Also, with an appropriate design, a view can be tweaked, exported, and pushed out to a site without needing to run with the overhead of the Views engine. Additionally, if you are using separate development and production sites, you may not need to enable any of the default views on the production site, saving just that little bit more.

Views does not provide a bulk export mechanism with the base module. The Views Bonus Pack (http://drupal.org/project/views_bonus) module provides this functionality and more.

## Exporting Panels

Panels has a slightly different export mechanism than Views or CCK. Unlike Views' "one view at a time" approach or CCK's "single content type at a time" strategy, Panels offers two options for getting the code out of your system: bulk export or single export.

Single export functions not unlike Views and CCK; each panel page or mini-panel can be exported from its respective List page. Mini-panels have three options available under their Operations header, one of which is Export; panel pages provide an Export option under their Operations menu. Some panels are not exportable, however. Notably, panel nodes cannot be exported as a panel; they are essentially nodes with extra markup for layout. System pages also cannot be exported; they are best defined on a per-site basis.

Bulk export is easily reachable from the main Panels landing page, as a Bulk export tab is found along the top of the content area. When you click this tab, you are presented with a page where you may choose one or more panels, or an entire group of them. Bulk exports need to be sent to a particular module, as shown in Figure 16-3.

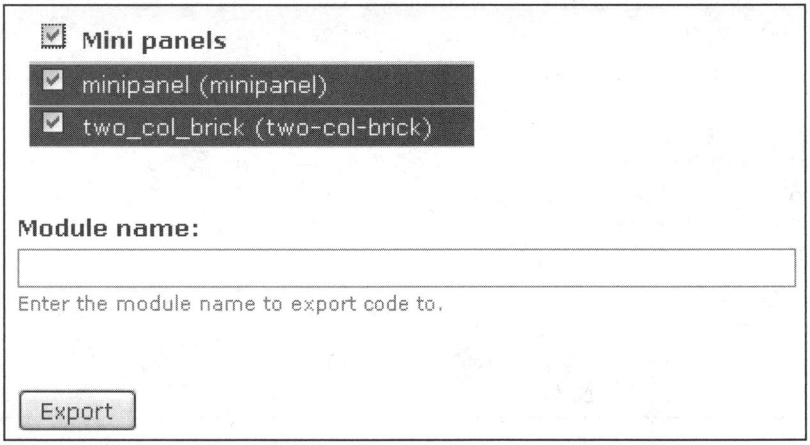

Figure 16-3    Panels bulk export

If a module name is not provided at the time of export, Panels replaces the module name in code with "foo":

```
/**
 * Implementation of hook_default_panel_minis()
 */
function foo_default_panel_minis() {
  $mini = new stdClass;
  $mini->disabled = FALSE;
  $mini->name = 'minipanel';
  $mini->category = 'minipanel';
  $mini->title = 'minipanel';
}
```

By providing a module name, you can use the bulk export function to create default layouts for new modules or, if you're clever, you can plug them into existing modules. You can easily search and replace based on a module name to use the same layout for multiple modules, or you can just perform a bulk export using each module name.

# Helper Modules

The following modules may prove useful in your site's migration from development to the production environment.

## Deploy

The purpose of Deploy (http://drupal.org/project/deploy) is to bring together all of the pieces you need to move a site from development to testing. This includes content as well as configuration information, meaning that you can use this module to move everything—images, users, and uploaded files, as well as your content types and views. At the time this book was written, Deploy was still undergoing active development.

The Deploy module also helps you manage new and existing content by enabling you to push new content or make changes to existing content. Deploy currently supports CCK and Views. It will examine nodes; if it finds a node reference on one node that is being pushed, Deploy will also push the referenced node, keeping your references intact.

## Features

The Features module (http://drupal.org/project/features) enables the capture and management of features in Drupal. A feature is a collection of Drupal entities that, taken together, satisfy a certain use case. Features provides a UI and an API for taking different site-building components from modules with exportable items and bundling them together in a single feature module. A feature module is like any other Drupal module except that it declares its components (for example views, contexts, CCK fields) in its .info file so that it can be checked, updated, or reverted via source control applications.

## Drush

Although it is not technically a module, Drush is definitely a helper! Drush is a command-line shell and scripting interface for Drupal. It is designed to make life easier for Drupal hackers who spend some a lot of time at the command prompt. It can be downloaded from http://drupal.org/project/drush.

# Summary

Taking care of your site after its creation is just as important as taking care of it during its development. Source control is an important function no matter what the size of your site or operation, and it becomes critical if more than one person is doing development.

Keeping your data structures in code as much as possible is a crucial step toward helping keep your site under source control and, therefore, more well protected from a disaster. Views, Panels, and CCK all have the ability to export their structures, giving you the most leverage in site control.

# IV

# Appendices

# A

# Other Useful Modules

The modules we've discussed previously are far from everything available to complement Drupal development; they're really just ways to start creating a Web site. The modules described in this appendix will extend the usability of your site and help you do things you didn't realize you needed until you got deep into your development.

## Extending the Use of Your Modules

One of the greatest things about the Drupal community, and open source projects in general, is the willingness of the community to contribute fixes and improvements back to the project for others to use. This generosity enables the entire community to benefit from every person's learning experience.

Developers can't think of every use case for their software, and this is especially true when it comes to the larger modules. Drupal's extensibility is another of its great strengths, enabling other contributors to extend the functionality of the modules they are using. Sometimes these extensions are added into the project, though often they are left as their own modules.

These modules are maintained by individuals who are generally not the Views, Panels, and Content Construction Kit maintainers. When using these modules, remember to post questions or problems into the correct issue queues. It makes the maintainers' lives a lot easier, and it's much more likely you'll get an answer or a fix!

## General Modules

These modules don't necessarily provide specific plugins to add functionality to a particular module, but they definitely can make things easier for you and your site.

### Pathauto

http://drupal.org/project/pathauto

Pathauto helps users create more readable and memorable URLs automatically. It works with multiple types of site content, such as nodes. This module makes it easy to add a secondary path to images, recipes, blog posts, and so on, without having to manually create a path to it.

With Views and arguments, you can make a hackable path that defaults users to an index page that you can customize, rather than dropping them to a 404 error page and losing them from your site when they get annoyed.

The earlier example involving the `blog_rss` view demonstrates one of the things that Pathauto can make easier for you and your users.

# Views

These modules specifically have some level of integration with Views. They may provide new styles, new filters, or other functionality that makes Views easier to use.

## Views_or

http://drupal.org/project/views_or

The base Views module functions by using the Boolean AND for all fields and filters. The Views_or module adds two functions: it combines filters using OR, and it provides the ability to combine fields with COALESCE. These functions give developers significantly more flexibility in terms of the data that can be retrieved with Views alone.

Views filters currently assume there is no OR capability, only AND. As a consequence, a number of Views filters have difficulty working with the Views_or module. Eventually, this functionality is destined to be included in the greater Views module, and this module will be deprecated. However, this will not happen until the filters are rewritten to accept both the Boolean OR and the Boolean AND. This is no small task. Many of the simpler filters will work, but the more complex Views filters will have problems.

Views_or also enables functionality for nested queries. For instance:

```
if field_a AND (field_b OR field_c)
```

This kind of query can be used with taxonomy, node types, or any number of other pieces of node information. For example, you could filter on a node type, and then use the OR query to find ones that are unpublished or contain a taxonomy term such as "recipe." Views_or increases the flexibility of all of your filters—exposed or not—giving you and your users one more way to find the data you need.

## Nodequeue

http://drupal.org/project/nodequeue

Nodequeue was created for the original purpose of queuing news articles so that they could be published in a timely fashion with minimal need for administrative oversight once the queues were created. Nodequeue is part of content management.

Nodequeue integrates with Views in a reasonably clean fashion, and Views is extremely useful for displaying the queues in use. On the surface, Views and Nodequeue might look similar because both are focused on lists. Nodequeue helps you create arbitrary lists of whatever sorts of content you want. Once a queue is created, the queue maintainer can add items until the queue is full. Items go to the back of the queue and fall out of the front. Using Views also enables Nodequeue to pick content out for display in a more complex fashion.

## Flag

http://drupal.org/project/flag

The Flag module includes functionality that was previously included in the Views_bookmark module. Flag provides data to Views, and adds a new view to the list of available views, called "My Bookmarks." With this functionality, each user can "flag" content. With the bookmark view enabled, each user can quickly access the list of items he or she has flagged.

This capability is potentially useful for constructing many types of lists: staff favorite picks in a store, a wish list of items, favorite articles, and so forth.

## Views Slideshow

http://drupal.org/project/views_slideshow

Views Slideshow is a module that adds a style plugin to the Views UI. It is a jQuery-based module that enables you to create slideshows of any content. It adds an option to the Views style options called "Slideshow." Views Slideshow has its own group of settings that are reachable by clicking the normal gear icon. Slideshows can be enabled as page displays or as blocks.

A slideshow is often thought of as a rotating group of images, but it can be used for whatever content you want. Using Views Slideshow, you might, for example, create a rotating list of recent news stories or images. Business sites may use slideshows as a showcase for new products or newsletters. You can also integrate a slideshow with an image gallery to show off pictures of your favorite activities, such as kitten shows or your most recent costumes for Talk Like a Pirate Day.

## Views Bonus Pack

http://drupal.org/project/views_bonus

Views Bonus Pack is a slightly misleading name for an add-on module that contains multiple utilities that Views and Panels users may find handy. Some of these add-ons are tools; others provide additional views or plugins to use with your views.

One of the major features of the Views Bonus Pack is the export capability. This addition exports views as CSV files for use in spreadsheets, as `.doc` files, plain `.txt` files, and provides XML support.

Another major feature within Views Bonus Pack is a series of pre-created panel layouts, complete with templates for theming use. These layouts will automatically split a view into multiple columns. At the time of this writing, there were three different three-column layouts and two different two-column layouts available. Although this kind of formatting can be done with Views and Panels alone, the beauty of the open source community is that the Views Bonus Pack maintainers have already done the work for you, so why reinvent the wheel?

## Views Attach

http://www.drupal.org/project/views_attach

The Views Attach module is capable of some pretty nifty stuff. Views already has the concept of an "attached" view; Views Attach expands on that concept to create more dynamic use of those attached views. The power of this module is that it allows you attach views to nodes, not just to other views.

One of the most useful parts of this module is that attached views get to use the arguments passed by the main view, even though they have no path of their own. As a consequence, you can create a specialized view that has related information to the original view. For example, you might create a view that will accept a taxonomy term as an argument, and produce a list of articles that are related to the currently viewed one.

## Views Import

http://drupal.org/project/views_import

Views Import is a brand-new module, modeled somewhat after the idea underlying Image Import. This module is, again, not strictly necessary. Even so, if you have sites with multiple installations and you are using the same views on each of them, its functionality could be a huge time-saver.

Views Import relies on views that have been exported to text files, which were then placed in this module's subdirectory. It provides a link to import all files in that directory. Views already provides an import page that is simple and effective enough for a small handful of views, or for small groups of sites. For repetitive tasks or large-scale multisite deployments, however, the Views Import module can be invaluable.

## ApacheSolr Views

http://drupal.org/project/apachesolr_views

Another very new module, ApacheSolr provides Views integration for the Apache Solr search platform. Its purpose is to integrate a new search engine into Drupal and potentially replace the current core search engine.

Note that this module does require installing non-Drupal software, which can detrimentally affect the performance of your hardware (though part of its purpose is to speed performance over the core engine). This possibility is especially likely for installations on hosted sites where you may not have the ability to install third-party software.

## SimpleViews

http://www.drupal.org/project/simpleviews

SimpleViews is not really a module for anyone who has managed to read this far through the book. It is, however, something you might want to have around for your less technical or less trained users who might be nervous about handling the full Views interface.

SimpleViews provides a small and simple user interface designed to create basic views. Users answer a few simple questions about the type of view they want to create, and SimpleViews uses the Views API to create them. Because it uses the Views API, more advanced users can then use the regular Views UI to modify, clone, or export those views.

## Views Bulk Operations

http://www.drupal.org/project/views_bulk_operations

Views Bulk Operations (VBO) allows you to perform actions on multiple nodes that are being displayed by a view. It provides a series of check boxes that allows the user to select the nodes that will be operated on. It also provides a list of operations that can be performed.

Using VBO, you can publish or unpublish nodes, change their authors, or take any of several other actions. This module uses a style plugin to expose the node information to the bulk operation. It is also expandable, allowing other modules to plug their information into VBO as well.

## Views Datasource

http://www.drupal.org/project/views_datasource

Views Datasource comprises another set of plugins for the Views module that output Views content into several formats like JSON, XML, and XHTML. Some readers may find it easier to use one of these formats, especially those in the mobile Web site area.

## Sheetnode

http://drupal.org/project/sheetnode

Sheetnode is a module that enables you to create nodes as spreadsheets, feeding field contents from Views directly into the sheet. If you wish, you can create spreadsheet templates for Views as well. This module also works with several different spreadsheet types, so you can more easily import your data from other files or file types. There are many, many potential uses for this type of feature. Note that this module does require installation of an additional piece of software; details can be found on the project page for Sheetnode.

# CCK

We discussed a number of the Content Construction Kit modules in Part 1 of this book. There is one other module that we didn't mention there that's also a major player in the CCK contribution space: Calendar.

## Calendar

http://www.drupal.org/project/calendar

Calendar is one of the most important uses of the combination of the Content Construction Kit and Views modules. Calendar requires that the Date module be installed, as well as Views. Working in concert, this group of modules can modify the display of Views date fields, wherever they come from. The display items that can be altered include dates created by nodes, files being uploaded, or dates input as part of a content type's required field.

Calendar also takes advantage of Advanced Help to provide updated, context-based help for the module's functionality. It includes a dozen template files to help tune its display to your needs. Note that Calendar is not the same as the Event module (http://drupal.org/project/event), which has a calendar setup of its own.

# Panels

Panels does not yet have a significant number of add-ons: its purpose is layout, and its main additions are styles or layouts. Each of these components is often unique to a given site, and it may not be appropriate to contribute back to the larger Drupal project. Nevertheless, two major projects use Panels to a significant extent.

## Advanced Profile Kit

http://drupal.org/project/advanced_profile

The purpose of Advanced Profile Kit (APK) is to create specialized and specific user profile type pages for sites where the user profile is a significant portion of important content. This requires Panels to be enabled. APK uses panels and the Panels interface as part of a point-and-click system to add content to user pages.

With the Panels integration, APK can create highly modular user profiles containing items such as buddy lists, recent posts made, personal information, and other statistics that a social site might find useful.

## Total Control Admin Dashboard

http://drupal.org/project/total_control

Total Control Admin Dashboard gives you visibility into what's really going on with your Web site. It creates a new administrator's dashboard with an eye toward a number of items that are important to a site administrator. It provides views for multiple types of data (such as activity, users, and comments), and Panels content panes with further details on your commonly needed data. It requires both Views and Panels to work.

# B

# Reporting Issues

$O$r how to help module maintainers and supporters help you—a best practices guide.

> *"It's an issue queue, not a social club."*
> —*Jeff Eaton*

Reporting issues and asking questions are two of the most important things any user of any software can ever do. One of the most critical things you can do when looking for help is to *do it right.* There are many keys to getting the help you need in a timely fashion, and even in a terrific community like Drupal's, there are multitudes of users who don't understand how to fashion a question, or submit a bug report or request for support. Here's a quick rundown.

Trust us. We know. Each of the authors has had more than a decade of experience in software development and support, and these are the things that we have seen over and over again that cause us and so many others in our fields to tear our hair out in frustration.

We hope this guide educates and illuminates the process. If it does, then all of us will have saved both time and a few handfuls of antacids!

## Submit a Complete Report

There is almost nothing more frustrating to someone in a support or development role than a one-line report offering little or no detail about the actual problem. Ninety-nine times out of 100, the "one-liner" report can be distilled further to "BROKE. FIX IT." If you want to watch a support representative or a developer's eyes bug out, utter that sentence to them. Then run, fast, before they can catch you. If you submit a one- or two-line issue (especially a bug report), you should not be surprised when the maintainer says he or she can't be bothered to answer.

Check the issue submission page for the module you are working with. *Read the guidelines.* Module developers don't put them there because it's fun to make you read more; they do it to save time, yours and theirs. These guidelines contain important information about which data you need to provide in your issue. If you fail to provide it, the developer is forced to read your issue, and tell you that you didn't submit enough data, and then you both have wasted time.

Also, *search the queue before submitting a new issue.* Give it an honest shot or two or three. A complete report includes things like these details:

- The version of Drupal you are using. Yes, the issue page requires it. Put in the right one.

- The version of the module(s) you are using. Make sure your module is actually compatible with the version of Drupal you're running. This prevents nasty surprises when your module fails to install correctly.

- A list of the modules involved with the problem. That means that not only should you say "CCK," but also that you should note things like "I have a Node Reference field." Again, the submission fields for issues have drop-down menus for these, so try to use them as accurately as possible.

- Step-by-step instructions on what you did—every click, every box, every field you filled out, every page you touched, and every file you modified.

- What you expected to have happen.

- Exact error messages. If this means you have to type the entire message in by hand, do it. You never know which tiny scrap of information might lead to the solution.

- Supporting files. Provide exports of Views, Panels, and Content types with CCK fields. Give screenshots. Drupal issue queues let you attach files; don't be afraid to do so. It's a million times easier for us to help you when we can see what you're doing.

There's no better way out there to get help faster than to provide as much data as you can. Even if your problem turns out to be difficult or even unsolvable, other members of the community will remember you as someone who does good work in reporting issues. At the very least, you won't be someone who made the developer angry. Either of those results means you're more likely to get good help when your issues are solvable.

## Read the Documentation

We all know that some modules are better than others at providing documentation. It's a sad fact of life that most developers hate writing documentation. If they liked writing documentation, they'd be doc writers. They're not—they're developers. If we're very lucky, a given developer is good at and feels obligated to write documentation for his or her work (or works with a person who meets that description).

Every project on Drupal.org has a link on its project page to the available documentation. This could be a text file, some handbook pages on Drupal.org, and some projects that are taking advantage of the Advanced Help system.

Every project release also has release notes. Again, some of these documents are more complete than others. Some release notes will have a list of bugs fixed, whereas others will list known problems. Read them anyway. Don't report problems that are listed as known!

Overall Drupal documentation starts with the handbooks. On Drupal.org, the Documentation link (http://www.drupal.org/handbooks) is one of the very first links you will see. Following this link opens up a wealth of user-created pages geared toward developers of all experience levels, from new users to senior developers. Every registered member of Drupal.org has the ability to create and edit most handbook pages.

As a site maintainer or content creator, you have a responsibility to at least attempt to find the information in the documentation. Few things will earn you the disdain of a module maintainer more quickly than asking a question that is clearly outlined in the documentation.

# Check Other Sources

There are many, many resources available to people seeking help with Drupal and its contributed modules. These resources are there to help you, and you'll find a lot of answers and new ways to do things, especially early on in your experience with Drupal.

We've already mentioned looking in the documentation. If your answer isn't there, the next thing to check is a Web search. Drupal.org has a search implementation on the site. If you start asking a lot of basic questions, you may be directed to do a general Web search. Sometimes it will be a polite suggestion; sometimes you will be asked to head over to a particular consumer-wide search engine with a multicolored logo.

There are vast numbers of tutorials, screencasts, and podcasts available that cover multitudes of topics. Look for them! You may be surprised at what you find.

Another place to get help is IRC. The Drupal community maintains a set of IRC channels, which is a great place to get to know the real people behind the queues and commits. It's also a place where people are doing real work in real time. For more information on the various IRC channels and ways to get connected and use them effectively, visit http://drupal.org/irc. Remember to respect the channel topics and be polite—that gets you the best response!

There are also forums that can be accessed through links on the front page of Drupal.org. The forums are a general place to ask all kinds of questions Drupal related. More people see the forums than a specific issue in the queues, and you may find support help there faster.

Finally, there are the issue queues. You can always submit a request for support. Some of the queues are very busy and don't have as many people answering questions as the queue needs. The modules covered in this book are the focus of some of the highest-trafficked queues in the entire Drupal project (see http://drupal.org/project/issues /statistics for full details).

# Know the Difference between a Bug and a Support Request

When a developer reads an issue, his or her first hint of the severity of a problem are the "priority" and "category" of that issue. Bug reports that are marked critical will almost always receive the highest level of attention. That's because these reports have the potential to affect multiple Drupal sites—if not hundreds or even thousands of sites. If your problem causes white screens, it's critical. If a submit button blows PHP and SQL back at you instead of a page, it's probably critical.

You don't understand how to do something? That's a support request. You want to know how to theme a particular field/row/block/panel/box/button? Support request.

There are two other kinds of categories: tasks and feature requests. Tasks are placeholder issues for people to provide feedback, patches, or reminders. Feature requests are functionalities that you would like to see added to a module. If you start an issue with "Wouldn't it be cool if . . ." or "I'd like to see. . . ," you probably want to mark it as a feature request.

# Stay on Topic

When you have a question or a problem and you open an issue, do your absolute best to *stay on topic*. Even more importantly, when you add comments to another person's issue, make sure they are relevant to that issue! Don't hijack issues for your own purposes. It makes everyone angry.

If you have an issue on a different version of code than the one the original issue was for, open a new issue. Link the issues in a comment. It saves sanity.

# Understand the Life Cycle of a Bug

Fixing problems has its place in the great circle of software life. The life of an issue is a smaller circle within the full development cycle. Have a look at http://drupal.org/node/317 (use the issue queue). If you need to know what an issue status really means, read http://drupal.org/node/156119.

When a developer looks at a bug, he or she assesses the problem to determine whether the initial category and severity are appropriate, as well as to make sure that the issue is even in the correct queue (see the submission guidelines!). If an issue is in the wrong queue, the maintainer will punt it to the correct one, if he or she is feeling generous. Most of the time this is the case, but everyone has a bad day, and after the fifth time in an hour when a maintainer has read an issue that's not categorized correctly, or has been fixed in a current release, that person gets tired and unhappy.

If the issue is in the correct queue and has a correct category and priority, the developer digs into the problem and tries to determine where the issue lies. This is where a complete report of every single step taken to create the problem, file exports, and screenshots make all the difference.

---

### One Tiny Piece of Data

Listing everything really is that important. One issue recently had more than 50 replies. Multiple people were unable see the option to hide the title for a panel. The maintainer was unable to reproduce it. This dragged on for weeks, until one person mentioned they were creating a panel node. To that point, the maintainer had assumed everyone was using panel pages! Node titles are controlled by the node system, not by Panels, so there is no option to hide the title. One tiny piece of information changed the entire picture.

---

If the maintainer can find the problem, great! If it's feasible, the fix can be checked in to the next build. Users with the problem have the option of running a dev (development) release if they have to. If the maintainer can't track down the problem, he or she may postpone dealing with it and ask for more information, or just postpone fixing the problem entirely.

It's even better if the submitter is able to track down the problem and provide a patch. Patches can be attached to issue submissions or comments; this really speeds up the time needed to fix a problem. If you submit a patch, you may be asked to do more work on it. It may be reviewed and tested by other members of the community. This is a good thing! It means that you gain some understanding, the maintainer gets a problem fixed, the community notices "This is a person who contributes" and you're more likely to get help on other problems later, other people can help you figure out where you went wrong on a fix so your skills improve, and so on.

Once a fix is in place or an answer is given to a question, the issue is considered fixed and gets closed after two weeks of inactivity. If you open an issue, it is your responsibility to provide feedback!

Finally, be aware that some issues can't or won't be fixed. Some of these are intentional, some are too difficult to fix within the architecture, and some are related to the software platform. That's just how it goes.

## Be Patient

Most projects have only one or two maintainers. For big projects like Views, Panels, and CCK that are used by a significant percentage of Drupal sites, the number of requests for help of any sort can be overwhelming. Views is second only to Drupal core in terms of issue activity. At the time of writing, CCK was third, and Panels sat at seventh. For software that has a few thousand modules that can be plugged in, that's a very high percentage of the issue traffic.

# Remember That You're Asking for Someone Else's Time

Yes, there are a lot of people out there getting paid to work on Drupal. There are also a great number of people who work on Drupal because it's their passion. In the great scheme of things, unless you have a Drupal consultant that you're handing a paycheck to, nobody is getting paid to do things for you. They're getting paid by other people, or they're not getting paid to work on your problem at all.

Treat your maintainers courteously, even when you disagree with them. Don't insult them when you post in the queues, no matter how frustrated you are. Drupal's strong community means that when you insult one person, lots of people find out about it. *Especially* do not start out in an argumentative fashion. Nobody likes coming in on the defensive, when they've spent tens or hundreds or sometimes thousands of hours of time to create software that they are giving to you for free. It's a real gut wrencher to put in that kind of time and have someone say in the issue queue, "This UI sucks!" Yes, it's really happened.

# Contribute Back

The Drupal community thrives because there are so many people who love doing what they're doing. They want to take what they have been given and make it better. When someone takes the time to help you, pay that person back by doing something for the community. There are so many ways to contribute! Patches aren't the only way. If you learned how to do something, write a handbook page. Spend a few hours in #drupal-support and answer some questions. Skim the forums and issue queues and lend a hand when you can. Your maintainers will appreciate it, and it will free them to work on the next great piece of code—or at least it might give them 10 more minutes to work on a bug fix.

Don't take it personally when a maintainer says he or she can't or won't fix your problem. Don't keep posting comments to the issue when it's closed. Try not to confuse rudeness with efficiency. People think differently, and most of the time, developers are just trying to get issues answered as quickly as possible with as much help as they can give at the time.

Do work with your maintainers, whether they are focusing on code, documentation, or some other capacity. Thank them. When you do cool stuff with their work, let them know! That's what helps drive the next iteration. If you're really feeling the love, send them something, donate to a cause in their name, or name a kid after them (okay, maybe not that one). These are the small things that move mountains.

Every one of us is a builder. Together, we can build the best community and the best software that can be had. We just need to use our blocks right!

# C

# Views API Handlers and Plugins

This appendix is meant as a reference only. It contains the class names for Views API handlers and plugins. An in-depth description of each of these classes is available from within the code base itself or at http://views.doc.logrus.com.

## Views Handlers

Handlers are used to interact with data. They are grouped according to: field, sort, filter, arguments, and relationships.

### Field Handlers

- `views_handler_field` Base field handler that has no options and renders an unformatted field.
- `views_handler_field_broken` Special handler to take the place of missing or broken handlers.
- `views_handler_field_file_size` Handler that renders a numeric value as a size.
- `views_handler_field_xss` Handler to run a field through simple XSS filtering.
- `views_handler_field_boolean` Handler to provide proper displays for Boolean values.
- `views_handler_field_custom` Handler to provide a field that is completely customized by the administrator.
- `views_handler_field_date` Handler to provide proper displays for dates.
- `views_handler_field_markup` Handler to run a field through `check_markup`, using a companion format field.

- `views_handler_field_numeric` Handler that renders a field as a numeric value.
- `views_handler_field_prerender_list` Field handler to provide a list of items.
- `views_handler_field_url` Field handler to provide a simple renderer that turns a URL into a clickable link.

## Sort Handlers

- `views_handler_sort` Base sort handler that has no options and performs a simple sort.
- `views_handler_sort_broken` Special handler to take the place of missing or broken handlers.
- `views_handler_sort_date` Basic sort handler for dates.
- `views_handler_sort_formula` Base sort handler that has no options and performs a simple sort.
- `views_handler_sort_menu_hierarchy` Handler that sorts items in menu hierarchy order.

## Filter Handlers

- `views_handler_filter` Base class for filters.
- `views_handler_filter_broken` Special handler to take the place of missing or broken handlers.

## Handlers for Arguments

- `views_handler_argument` Base class for arguments.
- `views_handler_argument_broken` Special handler to take the place of missing or broken handlers.
- `views_handler_argument_date` Abstract argument handler for dates.
- `views_handler_argument_formula` Abstract argument handler for simple formulae.
- `views_handler_argument_many_to_one` Argument handler for use in fields that have a many-to-one relationship with the table(s) to the left.
- `views_handler_argument_numeric` Basic argument handler for arguments that are numeric.
- `views_handler_argument_string` Basic argument handler to implement string arguments that may have length limits.

### Relationship Handlers

- `views_handler_relationship` Simple relationship handler that allows a new version of the primary table to be linked in.
- `views_handler_relationship_broken` Special handler to take the place of missing or broken handlers.

# Views Plugins

Plugins are used to format and display the contents of a view. They are grouped according to display, style, and row.

## Display Plugins

- `views_plugin_display` Default display plugin handler.
- `views_plugin_display_attachment` Plugin that handles an attachment display.
- `views_plugin_display_block` Plugin that handles a block.
- `views_plugin_display_default` Plugin that handles defaults on a view.
- `views_plugin_display_feed` Plugin that handles a feed, such as an RSS or atom feed.
- `views_plugin_display_page` Plugin that handles a full page.

## Style Plugins

- `views_plugin_style` Base class to define a style plugin handler.
- `views_plugin_style_default` Default style plugin to render rows one after another with no decorations.
- `views_plugin_style_grid` Style plugin to render each item in a grid cell.
- `views_plugin_style_jump_menu` Style plugin to render each item as a row in a table.
- `views_plugin_style_list` Style plugin to render each item in an ordered or unordered list.
- `views_plugin_style_rss` Default style plugin to render an RSS feed.
- `views_plugin_style_summary` Default style plugin for summaries.
- `views_plugin_style_summary_jump_menu` Default style plugin for summaries.
- `views_plugin_style_summary_unformatted` Default style plugin for summaries.
- `views_plugin_style_table` Style plugin to render each item as a row in a table.

## Row Plugins

- `views_plugin_row` Default plugin to view a single row of a table.
- `views_plugin_row_fields` Basic "fields" row plugin.

# Views Classes

All of the classes, structs, unions, and interfaces of Views are listed here, along with a brief description of each.

- `view` Object to contain all of the data to generate a view, plus the member functions to build the view query, execute the query, and render the output.
- `views_db_object` Base class for Views' database objects.
- `views_display` Display type in a view.
- `views_handler` Base handler from which all the other handlers are derived.
- `views_handler_argument` Base class for arguments.
- `views_handler_argument_aggregator_category_cid` Argument handler to accept an aggregator category ID.
- `views_handler_argument_aggregator_fid` Argument handler to accept an aggregator feed ID.
- `views_handler_argument_broken` Special handler to take the place of missing or broken handlers.
- `views_handler_argument_comment_user_uid` Argument handler to accept a user ID to check for nodes that a user posted or commented on.
- `views_handler_argument_date` Abstract argument handler for dates.
- `views_handler_argument_file_fid` Argument handler to accept a file ID.
- `views_handler_argument_formula` Abstract argument handler for simple formulae.
- `views_handler_argument_locale_group` Argument handler to accept a language.
- `views_handler_argument_locale_language` Argument handler to accept a language.
- `views_handler_argument_many_to_one` Argument handler for use in fields that have a many-to-one relationship with the table(s) to the left.
- `views_handler_argument_node_created_day` Argument handler for a day (DD).
- `views_handler_argument_node_created_fulldate` Argument handler for a full date (CCYYMMDD).
- `views_handler_argument_node_created_month` Argument handler for a month (MM).

- `views_handler_argument_node_created_week` Argument handler for a week.

- `views_handler_argument_node_created_year` Argument handler for a year (CCYY).

- `views_handler_argument_node_created_year_month` Argument handler for a year plus month (CCYYMM).

- `views_handler_argument_node_language` Argument handler to accept a language.

- `views_handler_argument_node_nid` Argument handler to accept a node ID.

- `views_handler_argument_node_tnid` Argument handler to accept a node translation ID.

- `views_handler_argument_node_type` Argument handler to accept a node type.

- `views_handler_argument_node_vid` Argument handler to accept a node revision ID.

- `views_handler_argument_null` Argument handler that ignores the argument.

- `views_handler_argument_numeric` Basic argument handler for arguments that are numeric.

- `views_handler_argument_string` Basic argument handler to implement string arguments that may have length limits.

- `views_handler_argument_taxonomy` Argument handler for basic taxonomy tid.

- `views_handler_argument_term_node_tid` Handler to allow taxonomy term ID(s) as argument.

- `views_handler_argument_term_node_tid_depth` Argument handler for taxonomy terms with depth.

- `views_handler_argument_term_node_tid_depth_modifier` Argument handler to modify depth for a previous term.

- `views_handler_argument_user_uid` Argument handler to accept a user ID.

- `views_handler_argument_users_roles_rid` Handler to allow role ID(s) as an argument.

- `views_handler_argument_vocabulary_vid` Argument handler to accept a vocabulary ID.

- `views_handler_field` Base field handler that has no options and renders an unformatted field.

- `views_handler_field_accesslog_path` Field handler to provide simple renderer that turns a URL into a clickable link.

- `views_handler_field_aggregator_category` Field handler to provide a simple renderer that allows linking to an aggregator category.

- `views_handler_field_aggregator_title_link` Field handler that turns an item's title into a clickable link to the original source article.
- `views_handler_field_boolean` Handler to provide proper displays for Boolean values.
- `views_handler_field_broken` Special handler to take the place of missing or broken handlers.
- `views_handler_field_comment` Field handler to allow linking to a comment.
- `views_handler_field_comment_depth` Field handler to display the depth of a comment.
- `views_handler_field_comment_link` Base field handler to present a link.
- `views_handler_field_comment_link_delete` Field handler to present a link to delete a node.
- `views_handler_field_comment_link_edit` Field handler to present a link node edit.
- `views_handler_field_comment_link_reply` Field handler to present a link to delete a node.
- `views_handler_field_comment_node_link` Handler for showing the comment module's node link.
- `views_handler_field_comment_username` Field handler to allow linking to a user account or home page.
- `views_handler_field_contact_link` Field that links to the user contact page, if access is permitted.
- `views_handler_field_counter` Field handler to count rows.
- `views_handler_field_custom` Handler to provide a field that is completely customized by the administrator.
- `views_handler_field_date` Handler to provide proper displays for dates.
- `views_handler_field_file` Field handler to provide a simple renderer that allows linking to a file.
- `views_handler_field_file_size` Handler to render a numeric value as a size.
- `views_handler_field_file_status` Field handler to translate a node type into its readable form.
- `views_handler_field_filter_format_name` Field handler to output the name of an input format.
- `views_handler_field_history_user_timestamp` Field handler to display the marker for new content.
- `views_handler_field_is_online` Handler to determine whether a user is online.
- `views_handler_field_locale_group` Field handler to translate a group into its readable form.

- `views_handler_field_locale_language` Field handler to translate a language into its readable form.
- `views_handler_field_locale_link_edit` Field handler to present a link to edit a translation.
- `views_handler_field_markup` Handler to run a field through `check_markup`, using a companion format field.
- `views_handler_field_ncs_last_comment_name` Field handler to present the name of the last comment poster.
- `views_handler_field_ncs_last_updated` Field handler to display the newer of the last comment or node updated.
- `views_handler_field_node` Field handler to provide a simple renderer that allows linking to a node.
- `views_handler_field_node_comment` Field handler to display the node comment status.
- `views_handler_field_node_language` Field handler to translate a language into its readable form.
- `views_handler_field_node_link` Field handler to present a link to the node.
- `views_handler_field_node_link_delete` Field handler to present a link to delete a node.
- `views_handler_field_node_link_edit` Field handler to present a link node edit.
- `views_handler_field_node_new_comments` Field handler to display the number of new comments.
- `views_handler_field_node_revision_link_delete` Field handler to present a link to delete a node revision.
- `views_handler_field_node_revision_link_revert` Field handler to present a link to revert a node to a revision.
- `views_handler_field_node_translation_link` Field handler to present a link to the node.
- `views_handler_field_node_type` Field handler to translate a node type into its readable form.
- `views_handler_field_numeric` Field handler to render a field as a numeric value.
- `views_handler_field_prerender_list` Field handler to provide a list of items.
- `views_handler_field_profile_date` Field handler to display a profile date.
- `views_handler_field_profile_list` Field handler to display a profile list item.
- `views_handler_field_search_score` Field handler to provide a simple renderer that allows linking to a node.

- `views_handler_field_taxonomy` Field handler to provide a simple renderer that allows linking to a taxonomy term.
- `views_handler_field_term_node_tid` Field handler for terms.
- `views_handler_field_upload_description` Field handler to provide a list of roles.
- `views_handler_field_upload_fid` Field handler to provide a list of roles.
- `views_handler_field_url` Field handler to provide a simple renderer that turns a URL into a clickable link.
- `views_handler_field_user` Field handler to provide a simple renderer that allows linking to a user.
- `views_handler_field_user_language` Field handler to render a user's language field.
- `views_handler_field_user_link` Field handler to present a link to the user.
- `views_handler_field_user_link_delete` Field handler to present a link to delete a user.
- `views_handler_field_user_link_edit` Field handler to present a link to edit a user.
- `views_handler_field_user_mail` Field handler to provide access control for the email field.
- `views_handler_field_user_name` Field handler to provide a simple renderer that allows using a themed user link.
- `views_handler_field_user_picture` Field handler to provide a simple renderer that allows using a themed user link.
- `views_handler_field_user_roles` Field handler to provide a list of roles.
- `views_handler_field_xss` Handler to run a field through simple XSS filtering.
- `views_handler_filter` Base class for filters.
- `views_handler_filter_aggregator_category_cid` Filter by aggregator category cid.
- `views_handler_filter_boolean_operator` Simple filter to handle matching of Boolean values.
- `views_handler_filter_boolean_operator_string` Simple filter to handle matching of Boolean values.
- `views_handler_filter_broken` Special handler to take the place of missing or broken handlers.
- `views_handler_filter_comment_user_uid` Filter handler to accept a user ID to check for nodes that the user posted or commented on.
- `views_handler_filter_date` Filter to handle dates stored as a timestamp.

- `views_handler_filter_equality` Simple filter to handle "equal to" and "not equal to" filters.
- `views_handler_filter_file_status` Filter by file status.
- `views_handler_filter_float` Simple filter to handle "greater than" and "less than" filters.
- `views_handler_filter_history_user_timestamp` Filter for new content.
- `views_handler_filter_in_operator` Simple filter to handle matching of multiple options selectable via check boxes.
- `views_handler_filter_locale_group` Filter by locale group.
- `views_handler_filter_locale_language` Filter by language.
- `views_handler_filter_locale_version` Filter by version.
- `views_handler_filter_many_to_one` Complex filter to handle filtering for many-to-one relationships, such as terms (many terms per node) or roles (many roles per user).
- `views_handler_filter_ncs_last_updated` Filter handler for the newer of the last comment or node updated.
- `views_handler_filter_node_access` Filter by node_access records.
- `views_handler_filter_node_comment` Filter based on comment node status.
- `views_handler_filter_node_language` Filter by language.
- `views_handler_filter_node_status` Filter by published status.
- `views_handler_filter_node_tnid` Filter by whether the node is the original translation.
- `views_handler_filter_node_tnid_child` Filter by whether the node is not the original translation.
- `views_handler_filter_node_type` Filter by node type.
- `views_handler_filter_numeric` Simple filter to handle "greater than" and "less than" filters.
- `views_handler_filter_profile_selection` Filter by a selection widget in the profile.
- `views_handler_filter_search` Field handler to provide a simple renderer that allows linking to a node.
- `views_handler_filter_string` Basic text field filter to handle string filtering commands including equality, like, not like, and so on.
- `views_handler_filter_term_node_tid` Filter by term ID.
- `views_handler_filter_term_node_tid_depth` Filter handler for taxonomy terms with depth.

- `views_handler_filter_upload_fid` Filter by whether a node has attached files from the Upload module.
- `views_handler_filter_user_current` Filter handler for the current user.
- `views_handler_filter_user_name` Filter handler for usernames.
- `views_handler_filter_user_roles` Filter handler for user roles.
- `views_handler_filter_vocabulary_vid` Filter by vocabulary ID.
- `views_handler_relationship` Simple relationship handler that allows a new version of the primary table to be linked in.
- `views_handler_relationship_broken` Special handler to take the place of missing or broken handlers.
- `views_handler_relationship_node_term_data` Relationship handler to relate terms to nodes (uses some tricky queries).
- `views_handler_relationship_translation` Handler of relationships for content translation sets that provides multiple options.
- `views_handler_sort` Base sort handler that has no options and performs a simple sort.
- `views_handler_sort_broken` Special handler to take the place of missing or broken handlers.
- `views_handler_sort_comment_thread` Sort handler for ordering by thread.
- `views_handler_sort_date` Basic sort handler for dates.
- `views_handler_sort_formula` Base sort handler that has no options and performs a simple sort.
- `views_handler_sort_menu_hierarchy` Sort in menu hierarchy order.
- `views_handler_sort_ncs_last_comment_name` Sort handler to sort by last comment name, which might be in two different fields.
- `views_handler_sort_ncs_last_updated` Sort handler for the newer of the last comment or node updated.
- `views_handler_sort_random` Handler for a random sort.
- `views_handler_sort_search_score` Field handler to provide a simple renderer that allows linking to a node.
- `views_join` A function class to represent a join and create the SQL necessary to implement the join.
- `views_many_to_one_helper` A many-to-one helper object that is used on both arguments and filters.
- `views_object` Basic definition for many Views objects.
- `views_plugin` Abstract base class to provide an interface common to all plugins.
- `views_plugin_access` Base plugin to handle access control.

- `views_plugin_access_none` Access plugin that provides no access control.
- `views_plugin_access_perm` Access plugin that provides permission-based access control.
- `views_plugin_access_role` Access plugin that provides role-based access control.
- `views_plugin_argument_default` The fixed argument default handler; also used as the base.
- `views_plugin_argument_default_current_user` Default argument plugin to extract the global $user.
- `views_plugin_argument_default_node` Default argument plugin to extract a node via `menu_get_object`.
- `views_plugin_argument_default_php` Default argument plugin to provide a PHP code block.
- `views_plugin_argument_default_user` Default argument plugin to extract a user via `menu_get_object`.
- `views_plugin_argument_validate` Base argument validator plugin to provide basic functionality.
- `views_plugin_argument_validate_node` Validate whether an argument is an acceptable node.
- `views_plugin_argument_validate_numeric` Validate whether an argument is numeric.
- `views_plugin_argument_validate_php` Provide PHP code to validate whether an argument is acceptable.
- `views_plugin_argument_validate_taxonomy_term` Validate whether an argument is an acceptable node.
- `views_plugin_argument_validate_user` Validate whether an argument is a valid user.
- `views_plugin_cache` Base plugin to handle caching.
- `views_plugin_cache_none` Caching plugin that provides no caching.
- `views_plugin_cache_time` Plugin that provides simple caching of query results for Views displays.
- `views_plugin_display` The default display plugin handler.
- `views_plugin_display_attachment` Plugin that handles an attachment display.
- `views_plugin_display_block` Plugin that handles a block.
- `views_plugin_display_default` Plugin that handles defaults on a view.
- `views_plugin_display_feed` Plugin that handles a feed, such as an RSS or atom feed.

- `views_plugin_display_page` Plugin that handles a full page.
- `views_plugin_row` Default plugin to view a single row of a table.
- `views_plugin_row_aggregator_rss` Plugin that loads an aggregator item and formats it as an RSS item.
- `views_plugin_row_comment_rss` Plugin that formats the comments as RSS items.
- `views_plugin_row_comment_view` Plugin that performs a `comment_view` on the resulting object.
- `views_plugin_row_fields` The basic "fields" row plugin.
- `views_plugin_row_node_rss` Plugin that performs a `node_view` on the resulting object and formats it as an RSS item.
- `views_plugin_row_node_view` Plugin that performs a `node_view` on the resulting object.
- `views_plugin_row_search_view` Plugin that performs a `node_view` on the resulting object.
- `views_plugin_style` Base class to define a style plugin handler.
- `views_plugin_style_default` Default style plugin to render rows one after another with no decorations.
- `views_plugin_style_grid` Style plugin to render each item in a grid cell.
- `views_plugin_style_jump_menu` Style plugin to render each item as a row in a table.
- `views_plugin_style_list` Style plugin to render each item in an ordered or unordered list.
- `views_plugin_style_rss` Default style plugin to render an RSS feed.
- `views_plugin_style_summary` Default style plugin for summaries.
- `views_plugin_style_summary_jump_menu` Default style plugin for summaries.
- `views_plugin_style_summary_unformatted` Default style plugin for summaries.
- `views_plugin_style_table` Style plugin to render each item as a row in a table.
- `views_query` Object used to create a SELECT query.
- `views_tab` An object to represent an individual tab within a tabset.
- `views_tabset` Object to contain a set of tabs as well as the ability to render them.

# Index

# F

# The Practical, Complete Guide to Customizing Drupal Sites

**Emma Jane Hogbin and
Konstantin Käfer**

ISBN: 978-0-13-713669-8

*Available in print and
eBook formats!*

*"For Drupal to succeed, we need books like this.
...Drupal faces a common problem on the Web—the
relative lack of new, high quality themes.* **Front End
Drupal** *tackles this problem directly and is designed
to help both experienced designers and rank novices
get an understanding of how Drupal theming works.
In fact, I'll be the first to admit I learned a lot from
this book."*

—Dries Buytaert, founder and project lead of Drupal,
   CTO of Acquia

In *Front End Drupal*, two expert Drupal developers cover
everything you need to know to create great visual designs
and state-of-the-art interactivity with Drupal's behaviors,
themes, and templates.

# Developer's Library

## ESSENTIAL REFERENCES FOR PROGRAMMING PROFESSIONALS

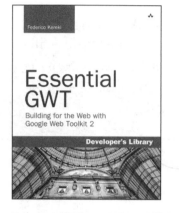

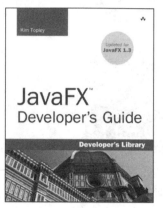

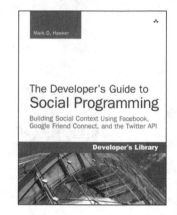

**Essential GWT**

Federico Kereki

ISBN-13: 978-0-321-70514-3

**JavaFX™ Developer's Guide**

Kim Topley

ISBN-13: 978-0-321-60165-0

**The Developer's Guide to Social Programming**

Mark D. Hawker

ISBN-13: 978-0-321-68077-8

## Other Developer's Library Titles

| TITLE | AUTHOR | ISBN-13 |
| --- | --- | --- |
| **Android™ Wireless Application Development, Second Edition** | Shane Conder / Lauren Darcey | 978-0-321-74301-5 |
| **The iPhone™ Developer's Cookbook, Second Edition** | Erica Sadun | 978-0-321-65957-6 |
| **Python Essential Reference, Fourth Edition** | David M. Beazley | 978-0-672-32978-4 |
| **PHP and MySQL® Web Development, Fourth Edition** | Luke Welling / Laura Thomson | 978-0-672-32916-6 |

Developer's Library books are available at most retail and online bookstores. For more information or to order direct, visit our online bookstore at **informit.com/devlibrary**.

Online editions of all Developer's Library titles are available by subscription from Safari Books Online at **safari.informit.com**.

Addison
Wesley

**Developer's Library**

informit.com/devlibrary

Addison
Wesley

# REGISTER

## THIS PRODUCT

informit.com/register

Register the Addison-Wesley, Exam Cram, Prentice Hall, Que, and Sams products you own to unlock great benefits.

To begin the registration process, simply go to **informit.com/register** to sign in or create an account. You will then be prompted to enter the 10- or 13-digit ISBN that appears on the back cover of your product.

Registering your products can unlock the following benefits:

- Access to supplemental content, including bonus chapters, source code, or project files.
- A coupon to be used on your next purchase.

Registration benefits vary by product. Benefits will be listed on your Account page under Registered Products.

## About InformIT — THE TRUSTED TECHNOLOGY LEARNING SOURCE

INFORMIT IS HOME TO THE LEADING TECHNOLOGY PUBLISHING IMPRINTS Addison-Wesley Professional, Cisco Press, Exam Cram, IBM Press, Prentice Hall Professional, Que, and Sams. Here you will gain access to quality and trusted content and resources from the authors, creators, innovators, and leaders of technology. Whether you're looking for a book on a new technology, a helpful article, timely newsletters, or access to the Safari Books Online digital library, InformIT has a solution for you.

## informIT.com

THE TRUSTED TECHNOLOGY LEARNING SOURCE

Addison-Wesley | Cisco Press | Exam Cram
IBM Press | Que | Prentice Hall | Sams
SAFARI BOOKS ONLINE

# informIT.com
## THE TRUSTED TECHNOLOGY LEARNING SOURCE

**PEARSON**

**InformIT** is a brand of Pearson and the online presence for the world's leading technology publishers. It's your source for reliable and qualified content and knowledge, providing access to the top brands, authors, and contributors from the tech community.

Addison-Wesley • Cisco Press • EXAM/CRAM • IBM Press. • QUE • PRENTICE HALL • SAMS | Safari

---

# LearnIT at InformIT

Looking for a book, eBook, or training video on a new technology? Seeking timely and relevant information and tutorials? Looking for expert opinions, advice, and tips? **InformIT has the solution.**

- Learn about new releases and special promotions by subscribing to a wide variety of newsletters.
  Visit **informit.com/newsletters**.

- Access FREE podcasts from experts at **informit.com/podcasts**.

- Read the latest author articles and sample chapters at **informit.com/articles**.

- Access thousands of books and videos in the Safari Books Online digital library at **safari.informit.com**.

- Get tips from expert blogs at **informit.com/blogs**.

Visit **informit.com/learn** to discover all the ways you can access the hottest technology content.

## Are You Part of the IT Crowd?

Connect with Pearson authors and editors via RSS feeds, Facebook, Twitter, YouTube, and more! Visit **informit.com/socialconnect**.